Counseling lesbian women and gay men

A LIFE-ISSUES APPROACH

A. Elfin Moses, DSW, is Associate Professor at the Graduate School of Social Work, University of Tennessee, Knoxville. She has received training at the Rational Behavior Therapy Institute of the University of Kentucky School of Medicine. She has been involved in therapy with gay clients in private practice and has given numerous workshops and invitational papers.

Robert O. Hawkins, Jr., is Associate Dean and Associate Professor at the School of Allied Health Professions, Health Sciences Center, State University of New York at Stony Brook. He is a board certified sexologist (American College of Sexologists) and a certified sex educator and counselor (American Association of Sex Educators, Counselors, and Therapists).

COUNSELING LESBIAN WOMEN AND GAY MEN

A LIFE-ISSUES APPROACH

A. Elfin Moses, DSW

Associate Professor, Graduate School of Social Work,
University of Tennessee, Knoxville, Tennessee

Robert O. Hawkins, Jr.

Associate Dean and Associate Professor,
School of Allied Health Professions,
Health Sciences Center,
State University of New York at Stony Brook,
Stony Brook, New York

The C. V. Mosby Company

ST. LOUIS • TORONTO • LONDON   1982

MOSBY

1906 **75** 1981
YEARS

A TRADITION OF PUBLISHING EXCELLENCE

Editor: Diane L. Bowen
Assistant editor: Susan Dust Schapper
Manuscript editor: Teri Merchant
Design: Susan Trail
Production: Jeanne Bush

The C.V. Mosby Company
11830 Westline Industrial Drive, St. Louis, Missouri 63141

Library of Congress Cataloging in Publication Data

Moses, A. Elfin, 1944-
    Counseling lesbian women and gay men.

    Bibliography: p.
    Includes index.
    1. Homosexuals—Counseling of.   I.   Hawkins,
Robert O. II.   Title.
HQ76.25.M67   362.8   81-11233
ISBN 0-8016-3563-2   AACR2

AC/VH/VH 9 8 7 6 5 4 3   03/C/338

Contributors

J.L. Bernard, JD, PhD, is a lawyer and a diplomate in clinical psychology. He is a member of the faculty of Memphis State University, a psychological consultant to several hospitals, and in private practice. His research interests include civil liberties, domestic violence, jury behavior, and forensic psychology.

Janet A. Buckner received her Master's Degree in Social Work from the University of Tennessee and is currently in practice at the University of Tennessee Center for the Health Sciences in Knoxville. She has worked with individuals and families in rural east Tennessee and North Carolina since 1970.

Holly Peters was Executive Director of the Tennessee affiliate of the American Civil Liberties Union from 1977 to 1980. She is currently a law student at the University of Tennessee.

For
Janet, Michele, Edmund,
and
Susan Elizabeth

Preface

Statement of need and general purpose

Lesbian women and gay men occasionally seek professional help for concerns or problems in their lives. There are many essays, articles, reports, and books written for, by, and about homoerotic people, but among them we could find no single source whose purpose was to educate those professionals to whom a lesbian woman or gay man might turn for help *and* that presented information from the standpoint that being gay, or homoerotic, is or can be a positive way of life. We have also found that many of our students, both graduate and undergraduate, gay and nongay, and some of our colleagues are unfamiliar with many aspects of being gay in this culture and therefore find themselves either frustrated in attempting to determine appropriate intervention techniques or acting in good faith on distorted beliefs and incorrect information. Consequently, this book has been written for those people who either are or are studying to become members of the helping professions, with two basic objectives: to educate and to suggest counseling approaches based on the premise that homoeroticism is as valid an orientation as heteroeroticism or ambieroticism.

For those professionals and students who do not support our premise, we hope that this book will help clarify the reasoning behind their disagreement and enable them to see the appropriateness of referring homoerotic clients to someone else. We are fully cognizant of the fact that some people firmly believe that exclusive heterosexuality is the only healthy way of living. This book is not written for them.

For those professionals and students who support our premise or who are uncertain, this book may be viewed as a beginning. Throughout the text we have suggested other sources that cover certain topics in more depth. These are generally meant to serve some of the reader's own special interests, and we trust that they will be as useful for the reader as they were and continue to be for us.

Organization of book and sources of information

We have divided the book into several parts: first, an examination of historical and current cultural attitudes toward gays; second, an examination of various general issues faced by gay people living in this culture; and third, some special counseling issues for gays, such as ethnicity, rural living, legality, aging, and parenthood. Within each of the chapters, we present information and suggest various counseling and therapy approaches as they relate to the issues under discussion. Since our basic objectives are education and counseling, we suggest several therapeutic approaches, but we do not present them in detail. There are several reasons for this decision: our definitional distinctions between education, counseling, and therapy; our determination of the approaches needed to address the majority of concerns of gay clients; and our very strong belief that once the similarities and differences between gay and nongay lifestyles are understood, the need for special therapeutic approaches for gays lessens.

Distinctions between education, counseling, and therapy. Making distinctions between these three terms is never simple, and books have been devoted to definitions of each of them. Many times the three processes overlap. However, we have developed some general guidelines that, though simplistic, were used in our decisions about whether to present more or less detail.

Education is providing information or explanation or helping the person recognize existing feelings or separate mythology from fact. *Counseling* is a process of exploring alternatives for thought and behavior during which the counselor suggests alternative ways of viewing a particular situation or discusses with the client possible ways of acting. *Therapy* is a more directive form of intervention in which the therapist essentially teaches the client new ways of thinking and acting in order to achieve the client's goals.

From education to counseling to therapy. Intervention with gay clients will usually follow a progression from education to counseling to therapy, with the majority needing primarily or only the first, some of those needing counseling, and even fewer needing therapy. What often happens is that the professional will first educate, then explore alternatives, and if the client chooses therapy, the professional will either provide that if qualified or refer the client to someone who is qualified. It is our belief that many clients can best be served by education and counseling, and we have focused primarily on those two aspects.

Lessening the need for special therapies. Throughout the book we discuss the similarities and differences between gay and nongay lifestyles. Once these are understood, many of the intervention approaches used to help nongay clients can be used with gay clients with little or no alteration. For example, training in assertiveness, communication, social skills, reality testing, problem solving, and sex therapy are some of the therapeutic needs

of both gay and nongay clients. The basic techniques used to provide these are essentially the same for both. The therapist, however, must be cognizant of the ways in which gay lifestyles differ from those of nongays.

Repetition. Our integration of counseling and therapy approaches into the discussion of the various issues associated with being gay results in some repetition. The process of living from day to day is not broken into discrete categories. A person's life is an intermingling of many aspects of that person, with each affecting the other in some way. Our somewhat arbitrary categorizations of life issues are artificial; therefore, information that is pertinent to one aspect of a person's life may also be pertinent to others. We have attempted to be less detailed in the repetitions, but we chose not to eliminate them. We also feel that some repetition is warranted as a reinforcer of basic ideas.

Sources of information. In presenting information and suggesting approaches, we have judiciously drawn from empirical data when they were available. We have also depended on our own and others' experiences, recognizing the pitfalls of such subjectivity. We have tried to make the reader cognizant of those pitfalls by using end notes liberally, and have provided references in our end notes, as well as a bibliography, which should be helpful for anyone who wishes to check on our criticisms and conclusions or learn more about the topics covered.

Cautions. While writing this book, we discovered some possible sources of reader discomfort. Readers who are exclusively heterosexual may be uncomfortable reading about so many positive aspects of being homoerotic. Although our own purpose is not to create discomfort, we have chosen not to tone down our positiveness. Instead, we suggest that the reader realize that viewing gayness as positive does not imply a negative impression of nongayness.

Another source of discomfort relates to content on sexual activity. We are fully aware that some readers will be uncomfortable reading the more explicit material on gay sexual behavior. However, we have chosen to include this material for two reasons. First, sexual activity is an integral part of the lives of most people. It is therefore an issue that can and should be raised in many counseling and therapy situations. To write a book attempting to inform helping professionals about gay lifestyles while omitting sexual activity would be a disservice to both professionals and clients. Second, it is the sexual activity of gay people that is so often a source of disapproval, misunderstanding, and ignorance. If we ignore the subject, or present it other than factually and forthrightly, as we have tried to do, we contribute to the myths, condone the disapproval, and help maintain a state of ignorance.

We have attempted to discuss the sexual activity of lesbian women and gay men in a nonjudgmental manner. Readers who are uncomfortable with sexual activity in general and gay sexual activity in particular may interpret our approach as proselytizing or as an attempt to titillate. It is neither. We do not believe that any helping professional has the right to dictate the sexual behavior of consenting adults. We do believe that counselors must be able to discuss any aspect of a person's life in a relaxed, nonpejorative, and forthright manner. In order to be able to do that in this culture, most people need some desensitization. We also hope that readers will be able to separate their personal values and preferences from those of their clients. Parts of the chapter on sexual activity provide the reader with an opportunity for evaluating his or her ability to do so.

Descriptors

There are really no completely satisfactory generic terms for describing people on the basis of sexual preference. We have chosen to use the word *gay* throughout the book as our primary generic descriptor. Although this term has the disadvantage of being used often to refer to men alone, it is nonetheless preferable to most other alternatives.

Gay also has a number of distinct advantages. It is a term preferred by many gay people themselves.[1] It does not share with other generic terms such as *homosexual* and *homoerotic* the myopic focus on sexual behavior characteristic of many

people's perceptions of gays, but rather refers to the lifestyle choice itself, regardless of sexual behavior. In distinction to the generic *homosexual,* it is indicative of conscious choice and is less likely to be used to describe other same-gender emotional or sexual relationships. Finally, it is appropriate in describing such things as gay lifestyles, gay culture, gay art, gay music, and so forth.

For the contrasting generic, we have followed Boswell in using the term *nongay*.[2] Like him, we find the term *straight* inappropriate as the opposite of gay, although it is a term widely used within the gay community. To some, the term *straight* suggests that its opposite must somehow be crooked, or deviant. They may view anything that is not straight as less desirable, healthy, acceptable, and so forth. Other nongays resent the term because it suggests a quality of being square, out of it, or conservative. Nongay people who are comfortable with gays and gay lifestyles may understandably resist being cordoned off in this way from people they see as being much like themselves. The word *nongay* is used as an alternative generic because gays are the major focus of the book and it seems appropriate to contrast all others with them.

We have also used the terms *homoerotic* and *heteroerotic* in some places as generics. Although these words focus attention on the sexual aspect of gay and nongay relationships, they seem to us to be less offensive than the words *homosexual* and *heterosexual*. This is because the root *-erotic* can be taken as an indication of attraction or arousal without necessarily implying sexual activity.

The term *homosexual* has been used on a very limited basis and only when the usage is consistent with the literal meaning of the word: of one sex. We would consider it appropriate, therefore, to refer to a sexual encounter between two women or two men as a ''homosexual encounter'' whether or not the two participants actually considered themselves gay. The term *homosexual* does not suggest, as the term *gay* does, that the individual referred to is self-labeling or is making a lifestyle choice.

Thus, an individual who is happily nongay in all facets of his or her life may enjoy homosexual fantasies. Many adolescent boys who grow up nongay have homosexual experiences. The contrasting term *heterosexual* is used in an equally limited way.

When distinguishing between men and women, we have used the terms *gay* and *lesbian,* or sometimes, *gay man* and *lesbian woman.* Although *gay* is the best available generic, it is also the preferred descriptor for men, so we have used it in both senses. We are aware that this perpetuates the use of the male referent to apply to both genders, but we could not arrive at another option that was acceptable. Although it may seem redundant to write *lesbian woman,* we have done this on occasion to stress that lesbians are and think of themselves as women, not (as some people believe) as pseudo or counterfeit men.

Shortcomings

No book is perfect, and ours is no exception. We view its major imperfection as one of omission. There are undoubtedly some studies that we have failed to include. There are certainly some topics that we have omitted, and some of the ones we included could have been more extensively covered. We leave the remedy of these omissions either to others or to a revised edition, knowing that some readers will take us to task for leaving out what they consider to be a crucial topic. We look forward to feedback and shall weigh it carefully.

Summary

We have attempted to present information that will be useful for anyone who is or will be working with gay people. We began writing this book because we saw a need for information that could be used by helping professionals who want to provide gay clients with positive, appropriate treatment. We recognize that this volume is only a beginning.

We hope, however, that, even though it is only a beginning, it will help accomplish two major tasks. First, we know that there are professionals and students who sincerely wish to learn about working with gay clients without condemning them for their sexual preference. We have tried to present some of the realities and consequences of being gay that will help counselors accomplish this. Second, we know that some homoerotic people are harmed more than helped when they seek counseling. We hope this book will in some way alter that situation. If only a few helping professionals learn something from this book, our efforts in writing it will have been worthwhile.

A. Elfin Moses
Robert O. Hawkins, Jr.

END NOTES

1. Jay, K. & Young, A. *The gay report.* New York: Summit Books, 1979, p. 766 report that 81% of their male respondents preferred *gay* (51%) or *gay man* (30%) to refer to themselves. Although most of their women respondents (63%) preferred the term *lesbians,* this obviously will not serve as a generic term. Thirty percent did prefer either *gay* (13%) or *gay woman* (17%). Approximately 80% of both the men and women said that the concept of ''gay community'' was important to them. We have taken this as at least minimal recognition by women as well as men that the word *gay* is meaningful and acceptable as a generic term.
2. Boswell, J. *Christianity, social tolerance, and homosexuality.* Chicago: University of Chicago Press, 1980, pp. 41-45 provides a provocative discussion of the problems encountered in identifying people on the basis of sexual preference.

Acknowledgments

That this book has come into being at all, whatever its shortcomings, is a testament to the encouragement, commitment, and hard work of a number of people besides the authors. We have chosen to express our appreciation in separate acknowledgments.

From A. Elfin Moses

I would like to extend special thanks to the following:

Those helping professionals, clients, and students, both gay and nongay, who are dissatisfied with the available information on counseling gay clients and have urged and supported the preparation of this book.

Diane Bowen, our editor, and her assistant Susan Schapper, for their patience, support, and help and, most of all, for their willingness to learn as well as teach.

Dr. Roger Nooe, who has been more than generous in providing institutional support for this endeavor.

Robin Ayers and Larry Davis, for their invaluable contributions.

Chris Bailey, who undertook much last-minute typing and duplication and who put up with my increasing disorganization as the manuscript due date drew closer.

Jane Harris, for her diligence in making many last-minute corrections and for being so marvelously organized.

One of the most rewarding consequences of writing this book has been the chance to become acquainted with two people who have become both respected colleagues and dear friends. That this book is being published now is a testament to the foresight and persistence of Susan E. Abrams, an extraordinary and gifted woman. Nor would the book have been completed without the herculean labors of my coauthor. I am indebted to him for his professional competence and dedication and for the conviction, sensitivity, and superb sense of humor he has brought to this endeavor.

Final and most special thanks go to Janet Buckner, who did much of the original library research, contributed extensively from her own professional knowledge and experience, and critically reviewed each chapter in each of its many revisions. Most remarkable of all, she kept patience with me through the long hours and has done more than her fair share to keep the home fires burning.

From Robert O. Hawkins, Jr.

Without the efforts of many researchers, this book would have been, at best, a very subjective undertaking. My first note of appreciation must, therefore, go to the people who have taken the interest and time to do the research that has been cited.

I also deeply appreciate the trust that some people placed in me by seeking my help when they had concerns. Without them, I would have little faith in suggesting that certain approaches mentioned in this book are helpful.

I owe a special note of appreciation to my students, from whom I always learn. They listened critically to my ideas, questioned, challenged, and suggested alternatives. They also were very helpful in criticizing some of the chapters.

Then there are those friends who read through early drafts of the various parts of the manuscript for which I had responsibility. To Ed McTernan, Michele McTernan, Blossom Silberman, Marge Sherwin, Rose Walton, Reggie Wells, and Rosemary Coates, I extend my appreciation.

To Diane Bowen, our editor, I wish to acknowledge my gratitude. She managed to ease the pressure and at the same time maintain my guilt level at each missed deadline. She also was an excellent sounding board for some of the more difficult portions of the book, and I even recall an occasional outburst of laughter, for which I am grateful.

Anyone who has ever written a book will certainly understand the appreciation I extend to those closest to me who understood my late hours, grouchiness, irritability, and general unavailability while trying to meet the deadlines. Somehow they managed to continue to feel my love.

Most of all, I want to thank my coauthor, who exhibited what must be the most extreme case of blind faith and trust that I have ever experienced when she asked me to join her in this enterprise. She has been a cajoler, editor, prodder, and friend, and no other person deserves more thanks and appreciation from me than does she. Without her, none of the other notes of appreciation would have existed.

From both of us

To Teri Merchant, our manuscript editor, a special note of gratitude and appreciation.

Contents

PART ONE

How the world views gay people

1 Attitudes toward gay people: a historical overview, 3

2 Current attitudes toward gay people, 15

3 The legal rights of gays, 21
   Holly Peters

PART TWO

The gay experience

4 Development of sexual identity and sexual preference, 27

5 Becoming gay, 42

6 The gay lifestyle, 54

7 Coming out, 80

8 Lesbian and gay male sexual activity, 99

9 Lesbians' and gay men's relationships, 123

PART THREE

Special issues in counseling gay clients

10 Third World lesbians and gay men, 169

11 The special problems of rural gay clients, 173
   A. Elfin Moses
   Janet A. Buckner

12 Confidentiality, 181
   J.L. Bernard

13 The rights of gay students on the college campus, 186
   J.L. Bernard

14 Aging, 190

15 Gay parents, 198

PART FOUR

Summation

16 Positive intervention with gay clients: a summation and conclusion, 215

Appendix

Toward a new model of treatment of homosexuality: a review, 221
Eli Coleman

Bibliography, 231

Counseling lesbian women and gay men
A LIFE-ISSUES APPROACH

PART ONE

How the world views gay people

1

Attitudes toward gay people: a historical overview

Gay people and those helping professionals who want to work effectively with them are forced to contend with an enormous amount of prejudice, myth, and misconception about gays and gay lifestyles. Religion, law, and social custom are, in most cases, still strongly opposed to the legitimation of gay behavior, and the social sciences are only slowly moving toward a more progressive point of view. The negative attitudes that exist now are directly traceable to attitudes and beliefs that have been extant for hundreds of years. During that time, gay people have often, but not always, been persecuted and oppressed by the heterosexual majority, at first on religious and more recently on allegedly "scientific" grounds.

It is an underlying assumption of this book, and our firm belief, that these negative attitudes are based on prejudice and myth, not fact. Gay people as a group are as well functioning as nongays, and gay lifestyles are viable, potentially productive, and fulfilling. The major factors in creating difficulties for gay people as a whole are the prevailing social, legal, and religious attitudes that identify gay people as sick, illegal, and sinful because of their emotional and sexual preferences.

Over the last 10 years, increasing numbers of researchers and writers have reached these same conclusions. The evidence pointing to gay pathology is at best questionable, and at worst, totally subjective and invalid.[1] Research findings are now beginning to accumulate evidence that gay people

in general function at least as well psychologically, emotionally, and sexually as nongays, and in some cases may function even better.[2]

In spite of new evidence and some changes in attitudes, however, the general public still views homosexuality and lesbianism negatively and is likely to continue to do so.[3] Although attitudes within the helping professions seem to be growing more enlightened, there is evidence that a large number of helping professionals still hold traditional beliefs about the pathology of gay people.[4] Such attitudes are far from benign in their effects on gay men and women. Marmor states:

Psychiatric labeling of homosexuality as a mental disorder lends authoritative weight to those who would discriminate against homosexuals in employment, discharge them from military service without honor, deprive them of various legal rights, and indeed sometimes confine them involuntarily in mental institutions. There is no doubt that such a psychiatric judgment . . . can have catastrophic consequences for countless homosexuals, both male and female.[5]

The attitudes and beliefs of social scientists and mental health professionals directly affect the ways gay men and lesbian women are studied and treated by members of these professions. The attitudes of religious leaders, educators, and those in the legal professions obviously affect the treatment of gays by the church, the educational system, and the courts. All these attitudes feed into the lay

3

4

community and, combined with other influences, affect the ways the average individual thinks about, talks about, and acts toward gay people. And, of course, since gay people grow up in the same environments that nongays do, these attitudes affect the ways gay people think about themselves.

In this chapter, we shall present a brief overview of historical attitudes toward gay people in Western countries, especially as reflected by the church and the disciplines of sociology and psychology.

Those who believe that lesbianism and male homosexuality are natural and desirable lifestyles, as well as those who believe they are perverse and decadent, often rely on historical arguments to augment their point of view. Those who believe that a gay lifestyle is viable sometimes point to the sanctioned occurrence of homoerotic behavior in other cultures, other times, or to the homosexuality of famous people such as Socrates and Plato, Sappho, Alexander the Great, or Virginia Woolf, as though this automatically proved their point. Those who believe that gays are sick or sinful insist that rampant homosexuality was responsible for the decline and fall of Rome, or they point out the continued persecution of lesbians and homosexuals in other times or societies, as though these were telling indictments that justify contemporary intolerance.

As far as we are concerned, history neither justifies nor impugns homosexuality and lesbianism. The fact is that, at present, somewhere between 5% and 15% of the population of the United States is estimated to be gay. Gay people are an integral part of this society, as they have been of every other, and decisions about how to treat gays and lesbians demand a perspective that is immediately relevant, not based on historical precedent. Current opinions and practices regarding gay people must be evaluated on their own merit in the light of current knowledge. An understanding of how these opinions and practices developed may give some insight into the reasons people believe and act toward gay people as they do. We hope that these insights will result in a more positive and, we believe, enlightened approach toward gay people and gay lifestyles than is currently the case.

HISTORICAL OVERVIEW

Attitudes toward gay people have varied considerably throughout the history of Western culture from the ancient civilizations of Greece and Rome, where homoeroticism was considered quite unremarkable, to the intolerance and persecution characteristic of both the Middle Ages and the twentieth century.[6] Regardless of opposition or tolerance, some group of people in every age turns out to be gay, and the greatest difference between periods is not in the proportion of the population that is gay, but in the way sexual preference is expressed.[7]

In those periods of time, such as the classical period of Greece, when homoerotic attachments, especially among men, were considered commonplace, gay individuals married and had children. The current kinds of concerns over gay role playing and, in the men's community, effeminacy did not exist.[7] In fact, gay relationships were often viewed during these times as superior to nongay relationships.

> Many Greeks represented gay love as the only form of eroticism which could be lasting, pure, and truly spiritual. The origin of the concept of "Platonic Love" (which postdates Plato by several centuries) was not Plato's belief that sex should be absent from gay affairs but his conviction that only love between persons of the same gender could transcend sex. The Attic lawgiver Solon considered homosexual eroticism too lofty for slaves and prohibited it to them. In the idealistic world of the Hellenistic romances, gay people figured prominently as star-crossed lovers whose passions were no less enduring or spiritual than those of their nongay friends. In Rome, Hadrian's undying devotion to his dead lover Antinous was one of the most familiar artistic expressions of erotic fidelity. . . . Even among primitive peoples some connection is often assumed between spirituality or mysticism and homosexuality. Only in comparatively recent times have homosexual feelings come to be associated with moral looseness.[8]

Position of the church

Religious institutions are certainly not the only representatives of social doctrine that have taken a position on homoeroticism, but we have chosen the church as representative of historical attitudes because "through most of Western history, the church was the chief reflection and instrument of sociosexual values, and it was not necessarily out of harmony with widespread values and other institutions."[9]

In the dominant religions of this society, sexual activity is supported primarily for procreative purposes, men are placed in the most powerful positions, and women are expected to serve their husbands and bear and raise children. There are clear, distinctly different roles for men and women, both within and outside the church, and heterosexuality is the only condoned form of sexual behavior.

Wysor believes that "the church bears heavy responsibility for our present attitude toward sex deviates and their problems, and for the severe penalties with which the law has requited them for their offenses."[10] Boswell, on the other hand, refutes the idea that religious beliefs have *caused* intolerance.[7] He believes that, instead, they have served to justify oppression of disliked groups, including gays, by those who hold personal animosity or prejudice.

In the particular case at issue, the belief that the hostility of the Christian Scriptures to homosexuality caused Western society to turn against it should not require any elaborate refutation. The very same books which are thought to condemn homosexual acts condemn hypocrisy in the most strident terms, and on greater authority; and yet Western society did not create any social taboos against hypocrisy, did not claim that hypocrites were "unnatural," did not segregate them into an oppressed minority, did not enact laws punishing their sin with castration or death. No Christian state, in fact, has passed laws against hypocrisy per se, despite its continual and explicit condemnation by Jesus and the church. In the very same list which has been claimed to exclude from the kingdom of heaven those guilty of homosexual practices, the greedy are also excluded. And yet no medieval states burned the greedy at the stake.[8]

The position of both the Jewish and Christian religions as carried by religious teachings has been essentially the same for hundreds of years. The actual interpretation of the ancient Jewish and Christian doctrines on homosexuality and lesbianism as reported in early Hebraic writings and in the Old Testament of the Bible has been the subject of extensive debate.[11] In this connection, Boswell notes that, with regard to the Bible as the source of Christian attitudes toward homosexuality, "it is . . . quite clear that nothing in the Bible would have categorically precluded homosexual relations among early Christians." He further states that the word *homosexual* does not appear in the Bible in any of its original texts and that, in fact, "none of these languages [Hebrew, Greek, Syriac, or Aramaic] ever contained a word corresponding to the English 'homosexual,' nor did any languages have such a term before the late nineteenth century."[12]

Although the word *homosexual* is not mentioned in the Bible, there are several passages that have been latterly interpreted as condemning homosexual acts, such as those regarding the destruction of Sodom. These have also been called into serious question as referring to homosexual behavior. The more contemporary view is that the crime of the Sodomites was not one of homosexuality, but of inhospitality to strangers.[13] It is not within the scope of this volume to review the extensive literature and arguments on the interpretation of scriptures. The interested reader is referred to Boswell and Wysor for further discussion and references.

What is of importance is that the scriptures have been and are being used by contemporary Christians to justify vilification and harrassment of gays with very questionable support from theology. Wysor says that her research revealed

exactly seven references in the entire Bible to what is interpreted by some as activity involving homosexuality. Six of these seem to refer to such activity among men, and one appears to refer to women.

However, these have been quite sufficient to help generate over two thousand years of condemnation and judgment against persons who express their emotional and sexual natures man to man or woman to woman.[14]

It is also interesting that the relationships in the Bible that most closely resemble homoerotic relationships are not so viewed by religious heterosexuals. The descriptions of the relationships of David and Jonathan, Ruth and Naomi, and Jesus and John comprise some of the most moving, noble, and intensely loving sentiments in the Bible. Although there is nothing to indicate that these beautifully described love relationships involved physical intimacy, there is no reason to believe that relationships between two men or two women that include a sexual dimension need be any less beautiful, noble, or moving.[15]

Historically, as well as in contemporary society, male homosexual behavior has received much stronger proscriptions than lesbianism. As noted above, male-male sex acts are mentioned more often in the Bible. Furthermore, within ancient Judaic interpretation, a wife who engages in sexual activity with another woman is not subject to mandatory divorce, because the activity doesn't involve any sperm and therefore is not considered an abomination. Sexual activity between men is considered an abomination, however, and is specifically condemned.[16] This lack of concern over lesbianism is consistent with devaluation of women and women's roles by both Judaic and Christian religions.

Nongays in many countries have historically used the teachings of the church to justify persecution of gays, including everything from verbal harassment to castration and execution.[17] Homosexuality and lesbianism are still considered by many to be sinful and perverse, and the "will of God" (as interpreted by humans) is still cited by many who are opposed to equal rights, or any rights at all, for gay people.[18]

DEVELOPMENT OF ATTITUDES WITHIN THE SOCIAL SCIENCES

The transition from the religious view of homoerotic behavior as sinful, heretical, and immoral to the more historically recent view that it is indicative of mental illness began in the midnineteenth century. The major researchers and theorists at the time were criminologists who were concerned with determining the causes of criminal behavior in order to control it. Criminologists and members of the medical profession were the first to begin studying homosexuality, along with other "perversions of nature," in what was considered a "scientific" fashion. Since then, both psychology and sociology have developed as independent disciplines and have undertaken the study and, in the case of psychology, the diagnosis and prescription of treatments for male homoeroticism and lesbianism.

Scientific approach

The so-called scientific approach to the treatment of gayness actually grew out of earlier theological conceptions about homoerotic behavior.[19] This new perspective was supported by the growth of social Darwinism in the late 1800s when it was believed that

> Victorian sexual and social morality represented Nature's best judgment. The poor man, the criminal, the deviant, the prostitute, were hereditary adaptive failures sliding backward to destruction amid the ranks of a progressing species. The idea that such "failures" owed their problem to degeneration of their genes gave rise to the term "degenerate." . . . Science had replaced religion as a justification of traditional mores.[20]

This transaction from a moral to a scientific basis for studying and evaluating gay people was adopted by the professions of medicine and criminology.

During this period, members of the medical community, like the church fathers before them, became concerned with all nonprocreative sex, including "excessive" heterosexual intercourse and masturbation as well as gayness. It was finally decided that nonprocreative sex was a contagious disease that could result in all kinds of symptoms and disorders.[21]

Even though all sexual activity was considered potentially dangerous, the major concern was with those individuals whose sexual activity was exclusively nonprocreative, namely, gay men and women. Since nonprocreative sexual activity was considered to be either an illness or the forerunner of an illness, and since homosexual behavior is exclusively nonprocreative, it was easy for the medical profession to reach the conclusion that gays were themselves pathological beings.

Causes of "degeneracy." Criminologists during this period were pursuing a concurrent and parallel path with a somewhat different focus. The major emphasis of criminological research and writing during the nineteenth century was on social control and the protection of society from "social failures." In order to provide this protection, it was necessary to ascertain the causes of various types of degeneracy in order to figure out if they were curable, and if they were, how to cure them.

Most of the early students of sexual behavior believed that homoerotic behavior and other "perversions of nature" were biological in origin, stemming from such things as degeneration of genes, abnormal or incomplete embryonic development, incomplete social evolution, and disorders of the brain or sex glands or both. In order to determine what had gone wrong with these people and to be able to identify possible degenerates, there were a number of attempts to isolate their distinctive features.

So gay men and lesbians as well as other "perverts" had their skulls measured, the amount and pattern of their body hair noted, tests made of their ability to whistle, and so forth. These and other characteristics and abilities were all at one time or another considered potential indicators of gayness.[22] Although this approach may now seem naive and laughable, we shall find it repeated with scarcely more sophistication by more contemporary social scientists. Unfortunately, some people are apt to take these later researchers more seriously than they would their forerunners.

Nature versus nurture. A second area of concern to criminologists of the 1800s was whether homoerotic behavior was innate or the result of environmental conditions, another theme we shall find repeated. If it were innate, then the unfortunate pervert could not be blamed, but neither could she or he be cured. If, on the other hand, environmental conditions could be found that caused homoeroticism, it might be possible to prevent this perversion. Karlen reports that

> by the turn of the century, a major scientific view had emerged and began to filter down to laymen. Homosexuality was congenital, caused by hereditary damage that appeared as neuropathy, and exacerbated by masturbation. . . . Since it was congenital, it was incurable.[23]

The work of these early criminologists and psychologists (Charcot, Westphal, Jenet, Lombroso, Krafft-Ebing, and others) helped set a tone for research and writing that varied little between the late 1800s and early 1970s. The definition of gayness as deviant and pathological and the consequent focus on characterization, etiology, diagnosis, and cure have persisted to the present with changes appearing only in the last few years.

Indeed, in many respects, the role of helping professionals as agents of social control augmenting those of the church and courts has become more sophisticated and perhaps more effective.[24] With the proliferation of mental health agencies and the professionals that staff them, the increased use of drugs and therapy, and the dissemination of mental health concepts throughout a growing percentage of the public, helping professionals are in an increasingly better position to exercise control over individuals classed as deviant or mentally ill. To the extent that gays are so identified, they are still potentially under the social control of the mental health industry.

Psychology, psychiatry, and psychotherapy

The history of the psychological approach to sexuality in general and to homosexuality and les-

8

bianism in particular can be said to have started with Kurt Westphal in 1869 and Krafft-Ebing's *Psychopathia Sexualis* in 1887. It was certainly supplemented by Havelock Ellis' monumental work, *Studies on the Psychology of Sex*. However, none of these individuals left a legacy as visible, far reaching, or as frequently abused as that of Sigmund Freud.

Freud's impact. Freud believed that homoeroticism was a stage to be passed through on the way to heterosexuality, and in that sense certainly espoused the view that homoeroticism was symptomatic of incomplete development of the person. But his writings cannot be said to have advocated the view that gayness is inherently pathological or indicative of severe dysfunction, as many psychoanalysts currently believe. In his often quoted "Letter to a Grateful Mother," he states that

> homosexuality is assuredly no advantage, but it is nothing to be ashamed of, no vice, no degradation, it cannot be classified as an illness; we consider it to be a variation of the sexual function produced by certain arrest of sexual development.[25]

Freud's belief that gayness was indicative of arrested development and that heteroerotic behavior is the only fully functional mode of adult expression was ultimately taken by many psychoanalysts as grounds for labeling gays as sick. Since a large proportion of the psychologically related thinking, research, and writing on gays until the 1970s was done by individuals who espoused a psychoanalytic point of view, the typical therapeutic position was that lesbians and gay men were suffering from some form of sickness and needed to be "cured."

Societal pressures on psychiatry and psychology. The pressure on psychologists and psychiatrists to diagnose and cure gays has not come exclusively from their theoretical predispositions. Silverstein has pointed out that early practitioners were under pressure to cure many social ills.[26] He suggests that as reliance on religion declined, psychiatry came to be seen as a panacea for the correction of so-called social problems. Because of this, professionals in medicine and psychiatry came to serve conflicting functions as both guardians of health and agents of social control. This dual role has persisted until the present.

Gayness as pathology. A brief summary of some of the literature of the first 50 years of this century shows some of the paths down which the pathological viewpoint of gayness has led researchers. The attitudes toward gay people reflected in this literature are almost without exception negative and demeaning.

Until the 1960s, homoerotic behavior is described in the literature as, among other things, a neurotic structure,[27] a mental disease,[28] a behavior symptom of deep-seated and unresolved neurosis and a personality disorder,[29] a symptom of underlying psychological pathology and an expression of faulty interpsychic and intrapsychic processes,[30] and as a neurotic disease that stems from the gay person's striving for defeat, humiliation, and rejection.[31] Gays have been characterized as egocentric, satirical, lonely, unhappy, tormented, alienated, sadistic, masochistic, empty, bored, repressed, and neurotic.

The apparent fear of and antipathy toward gays have elicited some extreme characterizations, to be sure. An example of one such may be taken from Socarides, who writes that gayness

> is a masquerade of life in which certain psychic energies are neutralized and held in a somewhat quiescent state. However, the unconscious manifestations of hate, destructiveness, incest, and fear are always threatening to break through. Instead of union, cooperation, solace, stimulation, enrichment, healthy challenge and fulfillment, *there are only destruction, mutual defeat, exploitation of the partner, and the self, oral-sadistic incorporation, aggressive onslaughts, attempts to alleviate anxiety and a pseudosolution to the aggressive and libidinal urges which dominate and torment the individual* [italics added].[32]

Further examples of such violently negative characterizations can be found in a number of other sources.[33]

Attempts to find causes of pathology. Convinced of the pathology of lesbianism and male gayness, psychologists and psychiatrists have gone to great lengths to elucidate the causes of this pathology, to develop means of diagnosis, and to differentiate gay people from both "normals" and other "sick" people. The focus of much of this research has differed little from the studies undertaken in the 1800s by Lombroso and other criminologists of that era. The focus on pathology and presumably extensive and consistent differences between gays and nongays is still exactly the same.

The greatest number of these studies were done in the 1950s and 1960s, and the subjects were frequently gay men who were either in therapy or incarcerated. A number of reviews of such studies have been done elsewhere that demonstrate both their often questionable validity and underlying prejudices against gays.[34] Some examples of the kinds of research undertaken may help demonstrate our point.

Studies have been done to find distinguishing signs of homosexuality on Rorschach,[35] the Minnesota Multiphasic Personality Inventory,[36] and the Blacky test.[37] Studies have compared gays with a variety of other groups of individuals such as hysterics and alcoholics,[38] "normals" and general criminals,[39] epileptics,[40] neurotics and "normals,"[41] and sociopaths without sexual deviation.[42] Researchers have also looked for signs of latent homosexuality among alcoholics,[43] early schizophrenics,[44] male paranoid schizophrenics,[45] and mothers of schizophrenic women.[46] A number of studies have been undertaken to compare lesbian and nongay women in terms of personality variables[47] and supposedly etiological factors.[48]

The only bright spots in much of the research and writing on gays during this period were the writings of Kinsey and Hooker, two researchers who did not share the almost universal attitude that being gay was a sickness.[49] Although there were others who believed as they did, it was largely the work of Kinsey and Hooker that gained publicity for a nonpathological perspective on homosexuality and lesbianism.

An increasing number of authors have questioned the validity of the assumption that gayness is an indication of mental illness or pathology.[50]

Some have pointed out the negative consequences of using the medical model as a paradigm for attempting to understand and intervene in problems of living that are not demonstrably the result of physiological dysfunction.[51] The medical approach, it is argued, leads to the equation of behavior that is considered socially undesirable by the majority (or at least by those in power) with physical illness. This in turn leads people to believe that the behavior ought to have a cure, in the manner of physical illness. Parsons has pointed out that once an individual has been defined as ill, it is then considered incumbent upon that person to get well as quickly as possible. The "sick" individual and his or her family are expected to see that all available resources are used to bring the sick person back to health.[52] This kind of assumption provides justification for the use of force in getting gay people into treatment and of extreme methods for "curing" them of their illness. These methods include incarceration, electroshock and other forms of aversion therapy, as well as the more time-consuming attempts at conversion through "talk" therapy.

Szasz, who takes what many consider a radical view, says that in order to

support their ideology and to justify their powers and privileges, institutional psychiatrists combine the notions of mental illness and criminality and resist efforts to separate them. They do this by claiming that mental illness and crime are one and the same thing and that mentally ill persons are dangerous in ways that mentally healthy persons are not. . . . Instead of saying that "criminals are evil" the authorities say that they are "sick"; in either case, however, the suspects continue to be seen as dangerous to society and hence fit subjects for its sanctions.[53]

He quotes Lindner on this subject as saying further that

nonconformity and mental disease have become synonymous. . . . Declaring the homosexual mentally ill, therefore, brings him within the compass of this re-

10

gressive view and the range of all the "therapies" devised to ensure his conformity. It may masquerade as a boon to the invert and a humanitarian modification of historic prejudice and hate; it is, in fact, but another way to obtain the conformance—this time in the area of sex behavior—our dangerously petrifying institutions demand.[54]

In summary, it can be seen that the attitudes of mental health professionals as reflected by research and writing up until the 1970s were typically negative in regard to gay men and women. The view of gayness as a sin was essentially translated into the belief that it was symptomatic of mental disease or dysfunction. We have suggested that this change in labeling was caused by a shift in social attention from the church to the mental health professions as arbiters of social acceptability and that this represented little more than a shift in the locus of social labeling and control.

SOCIOLOGICAL PERSPECTIVE

Although sociologists have had much to say about a number of groups and behaviors traditionally classed as deviant, until recently the study of sexual behavior has been left to psychologists, psychiatrists, physicians, and the like.

> Theologians had written of sex for many centuries. . . . Men of letters . . . had illuminated this area of darkness of the human condition. Criminologists of the 18th and 19th centuries—Tarde, Lombroso, Beccaria—were deeply concerned with the sexual offender. But a literature of the sociology of sex could hardly be said to exist.[55]

Sagarin suggests that one reason this may have been so is that the first major writers in the area of sexuality—Krafft-Ebing, Havelock Ellis, and Freud—essentially claimed the field for psychology.[55] Freud's influence and his conviction that many human ills had their roots in infantile sexuality and that these ills were the purview of psychoanalysis made it difficult for sociologists to get in on the act. It was not until the 1930s and 1940s that sociologists began moving into the study of sexual

behavior when Kingsley Davis began to study illegitimacy, prostitution, and the like. In 1948, Kinsey's study appeared and, according to Sagarin, this study may well have legitimized human sexuality as an area of sociological research.[55]

Lesbianism and homosexuality have been studied by sociologists primarily as forms of social deviance, a fact that is perhaps not surprising. Most of the studies that have involved gays have been done since the 1960s. Like psychology, sociology was long concerned with criminals and crime, and gays did not appear as objects of study before this period.[56]

Appreciative approach to deviance

It was not until the 1930s that a new approach toward deviance began to develop among sociologists. This new way of looking at deviance was what Matza has called *appreciative*.[57] Rather than having the traditionally negative view of deviance, appreciative sociologists are more apt to try to empathize with the groups they are studying and to attempt to understand the ways in which these groups fit into society. A concurrent change took place in sociological thinking and theorizing regarding the functions of social deviance. Instead of being outside the boundaries of society, deviance began to be viewed as a natural part of social life, the inevitable concomitant of codes and laws attempting to legislate conformity.[58]

Labeling theory. Labeling theory was the major theory to develop out of this new appreciation of deviance. It is a theory that has great relevance to working with clients who are considered by society to be deviants, because of its focus on the effects of being labeled (for example, as a lesbian, alcoholic, welfare recipient, or unwed mother) on the individual who is labeled.

The labeling approach stresses the role of social definition in the creation and maintenance of deviance, as opposed to earlier notions that deviance was something inherent in a given act.[59] In this view, gayness is considered deviant not because there is something inherently wrong or bad or immoral or socially destructive about it. Rather, it is because society has decided that gayness is undesirable and because people label certain acts and those who perform them (and sometimes those who are only suspected of performing or even of only wanting to or thinking about performing them) as "lesbian" or "homosexual" and then react negatively to them on the basis of the label. These theorists argue that it is the labeling that creates the deviance and not the other way around.[60]

Primary and secondary deviance. According to labeling theory, there are two types or stages of deviance, depending on whether the deviance has or has not been labeled. Primary deviance refers to the original unlabeled act.[61] A woman who goes to bed with a woman friend on the spur of the moment or under the influence of alcohol, or a man who allows another man to fellate him could be said to be commiting acts of primary deviance. These are acts that society would label as deviant, but the individual engaging in them does not label them as conforming to a deviant definition. The woman does not think of herself as a lesbian perhaps because she was drunk and so "not really herself" or "just didn't know what she was doing." The man may be able to convince himself that he is not gay because he is in prison and has no other sexual outlet or because he is only the passive recipient of a sexual act and did not *really* do what homosexuals do.

If the woman were to fall in love with her friend and to continue to have other sexual encounters with her, or perhaps only to fantasize sex with a woman, or if she told a therapist about this occurrence and the therapist told her she was lesbian, she would then be entering the realm of secondary deviance. Her behavior would have become labeled either by herself, by another, or by both. At this point, her behavior may begin to change in accordance with the label.

Secondary deviance occurs when others stigmatize and punish the individual or when the individual perceives that others could do this on the basis of her or his behavior.[62] An important feature of this labeling process is that it does not have to be undertaken directly by societal agents. As social beings capable of symbolic representation, humans can symbolically either apply or anticipate the application of social labels and their consequences to themselves.[63] So the woman need only be aware that the kind of behavior she is engaging in is considered socially deviant, that it has a label, and that people like herself are vulnerable to social sanctions. Without the direct intervention of society, she could then be said to be a secondary deviant. She has now changed her self-identity to incorporate the label "lesbian" and make it a part of her self-concept. Furthermore, her behavior may now change to accommodate the label. She may start calling herself a lesbian, may "come out" to others, may begin to go to gay bars, subscribe to gay magazines, march in Gay Pride Day parades, and so forth.

Labeling theory has provided a major thrust within the social sciences toward viewing socially disapproved behavior as neutral behavior with a negative social label, rather than as something inherently wrong with the individual. This does not mean that all social codes should be discarded or disregarded or that there are not sound reasons for many societal reactions. It does mean that, perhaps especially in the case of "victimless crimes," such as consenting homosexual acts, society often punishes people simply for nonconformity, not for behavior that can be demonstrated to be socially harmful.

Selection of "deviants" for study. A major criticism of the sociology of deviance by some sociologists is that those who study deviance have picked the wrong objects for scrutiny. These critics have seriously questioned the predisposition of sociologists to accept societal definitions and to study labeled groups rather than either the society that has labeled them or potentially more harmful groups, for example, industrial polluters, or those whose business is the waging of war.

As early as 1943, C. Wright Mills criticized his colleagues for on one hand saying they wanted to reform society and on the other assuming society's norms "and often tacitly sanction[ing] them."[64]

12

Furthermore, he states that "there are few attempts to explain deviations from norms in terms of the norms themselves—and no rigorous facing of the implications of the fact that social transformations would involve shifts in them."[65]

Others have argued that the use of the term *deviant* itself may have negative consequences for the person so labeled. Szasz argues for discontinuing use of the term. He notes first that the appellation *deviant* is used to describe "addicts and homosexuals . . . but never Olympic champions or Nobel Prize winners," thus refuting those who say it simply refers to "difference" without any negative connotation.[66] This lopsided usage, he argues, inevitably results in those who are labeled as deviant being assigned the negative characteristics that have accrued to the term. He also rejects its usage because

> it does not make sufficiently explicit—as the terms "scapegoat" or "victim" do—that majorities usually categorize persons or groups as "deviant" in order to set them apart as inferior beings and to justify their social control, oppression, persecution, or even complete destruction.[66]

Liazos also urges that sociologists both abandon the term *deviance* and turn their attention to groups besides those typically studied.

> Even when we do study the popular forms of "deviance," we do not avoid blaming the victim for his fate; the continued use of the term "deviant" is one clue to the blame. Nor have we succeeded in normalizing him; the focus on the "deviant" himself, on his identity and sub-culture has tended to confirm the popular prejudice that he is different.[67]

Although these criticisms are valid and should be taken seriously, it is also true that the growth of the appreciative approach in general and labeling theory in particular has done much to sensitize social scientists to the effects of social labels and to the responsibility of society in creating groups of people called deviants against whom sanctions are then applied. The work of many sociologists who have studied gay men and women has provided an increasing fund of knowledge about attitudes toward gays, gay lifestyles, and the consequences of being gay.

SUMMARY

Historically, attitudes toward homoerotic people have fluctuated along a positive-negative continuum and, at any one time, have been inconsistent across cultures. An examination of the genesis of the present prevailing social, legal, and religious approaches to the topic indicates that religion and the disciplines of sociology and psychology have been influential in shaping the current attitudes. It was not until sociologists began to seriously question the "scientific" approach by examining "deviance" with an appreciative rather than a negative approach that the academic community began to look upon homoerotic people as potentially healthy human beings and research began to look at the problems associated with the norm that was being espoused.

END NOTES

1. Excellent reviews and discussion of possible methodological problems are presented in Mannion, K. "Female homosexuality: A comprehensive review of theory and research." JSAS *Catalog of Selected Documents in Psychology,* 1976, *6*(22), 44. (Ms. No. 1247); Morin, S.F. "An annotated bibliography of research on lesbianism and male homosexuality (1967-1974)." JSAS *Catalog of Selected Documents in Psychology,* 1976, *6,* 15. (Ms. No. 1191); Morin, S.F. "Heterosexual bias in psychological research on lesbianism and male homosexuality." *American Psychologist,* 1977, *32*(8), 629-637; Morin, S.F. "Psychology and the gay community: An overview." *Journal of Social Issues,* 1978, *34*(3), 1-6; and Sang, B. "Lesbian research: A critical evaluation." In G. Vida (Ed.), *Our right to love: A lesbian resource book.* Englewood Cliffs, N.J.: Prentice-Hall, 1978.
2. Bell, A., & Weinberg, M. *Homosexualities: A study of diversity among men and women.* New York: Simon & Schuster, 1978; Masters, W., & Johnson, V. *Homosexuality in perspective.* Boston: Little, Brown, 1979; and Freedman, M. *Homosexuality and psychological functioning.* Belmont, Calif.: Brooks/Cole, 1971.
3. Nyberg, K., & Alston, J. "Analysis of public attitudes toward homosexual behavior." *Journal of Homosexuality,* 1976/1977, *2*(2), 99-107.

4. See Chapter 2 of this book for discussion of these attitudes.
5. Marmor, J. "Epilogue: Homosexuality and the issue of mental illness." In J. Marmor (Ed.), *Homosexual behavior: A modern reappraisal*. New York: Basic Books, 1980, p. 392.
6. For in-depth treatments see Bullough, V.L. *Sexual variance in society and history*. Chicago: University of Chicago Press, 1976; and Boswell, J. *Christianity, social tolerance, and homosexuality*. Chicago: The University of Chicago Press, 1980.
7. Boswell, 1980.
8. Boswell, 1980, p. 27.
9. Karlen, A. "Homosexuality in history." In J. Marmor (Ed.), 1980.
10. Wysor, B. *The lesbian myth*. New York: Random House, 1974, p. 65.
11. See Wysor, 1974, pp. 22-63 for a summary of the debate. Also see Boswell, 1980, pp. 91-166 for a remarkable treatment of scriptural tradition, early Christian opinion, and early theological objections to homosexuality.
12. Boswell, 1980, p. 92.
13. Boswell, 1980, pp. 93-98; and Wysor, 1974, pp. 23-25.
14. Wysor, 1974, pp. 22-23.
15. Wysor, 1974, p. 49.
16. Schwartz, B. "Homosexuality: A Jewish perspective." *United Synagogue Review*, Summer 1977, pp. 4-5; 23-27; and see also Orbach, W. "Homosexuality in Jewish law: Part IV, lesbianism." *GALA Review*, 1980, *3*(5), 15-21.
17. Karlen, A. *Sexuality and homosexuality: A new view*. New York: W.W. Norton, 1971; also Boswell, 1980.
18. Wysor, 1974.
19. See Bullough, 1976, pp. 461-503; Bullough, V. "Homosexuality and the medical model." *Journal of Homosexuality*, 1974, *1*(1), 99-110; Karlen, 1971; Klaich, D. *Woman plus woman*. New York: Simon & Schuster, 1974; and Szasz, T.S. *The manufacture of madness*. New York: Harper & Row, 1970, especially pp. 242-259.
20. Karlen, 1971, p. 184.
21. Bullough, 1974.
22. Karlen, 1971.
23. Karlen, 1971, pp. 195-196.
24. Szasz, 1970.
25. Quoted in Wysor, 1974, p. 186.
26. Silverstein, C. "Even psychiatry can profit from its past mistakes." *Journal of Homosexuality*, 1976/1977, *2*(2), 153-158.
27. Barahal, H. "Female transvestism and homosexuality." *Psychiatric Quarterly*, 1953, *27*(3), 390-438.
28. Bergler, E. "Lesbianism, facts and fiction." *Marriage Hygiene*, 1948, *1*(4), 197-202.
29. Caprio, F. "Female homosexuality." *Sexology*, 1955, *21*(8), 494-499.
30. Gershman, H. "Considerations of some aspects of homosexuality." *American Journal of Psychoanalysis*, 1953, *13*, 82-83.

31. Bergler, E. *Homosexuality: Disease or way of life?* New York: Hill & Wang, 1956.
32. Socarides, C. *The overt homosexual*. New York: Grune & Stratton, 1968.
33. Barahal, 1953; Bergler, 1948; Caprio, 1955; Gershman, 1953; Bergler, E. *Counterfeit sex: Homosexuality, impotence, frigidity* (2nd ed.). New York: Grune & Stratton, 1958; Cattell, R., & Morony, J.H. "The use of the 16 PF in distinguishing homosexuals, normals, and general criminals." *Journal of Consulting Psychology*, 1962, *26*(6), 531-540; Demaria, L.A. "Homosexual acting out." *International Journal of Psycho-Analysis*, 1968, *49*(2-3), 219-220; Gillespie, W. "Notes on the analysis of sexual perversions." *International Journal of Psycho-Analysis*, 1952, *33*(4), 397-402; Greenspan, H., & Campbell, J.D. "The homosexual as a personality type." *American Journal of Psychiatry*, 1945, *101*(5), 682-689; Harper, R.A. "Can homosexuals be changed?" In I. Rubin (Ed.), *The third sex*. New York: New Book Co., 1961; Saul, L., & Beck, A. "Psychodynamics of male homosexuality." *International Journal of Psycho-Analysis*, 1961, *42*(1-2), 43-48; Socarides, C. "Theoretical and clinical aspects of overt male homosexuality (panel report)." *Journal of the American Psychoanalytic Association*, 1960, *8*, 552-566; Socarides, C. "Theoretical and clinical aspects of overt female homosexuality." *Journal of the American Psychoanalytic Association*, 1962, *10*, 579-592.
34. Morin, 1978; Riess, B., Safer, J., & Yotive, W. "Psychological test data on female homosexuality: A review of the literature." *Journal of Homosexuality*, 1974, *1*(1), 71-85.
35. DeLuca, J. "The structure of homosexuality." *Journal of Projective Techniques and Personality Assessment*, 1966, *30*(2), 187-191.
36. Burton, A. "The use of the masculinity-femininity scale of the MMPI as an aid in the diagnosis of sexual inversion." *Journal of Psychology*, 1947, *24*, 161-164.
37. DeLuca, J. "Performance of overt male homosexuals and controls on the Blacky test." *Journal of Clinical Psychology*, 1967, *23*(4), 497.
38. Reitzell, J. "A comparative study of hysterics, homosexuals, and alcoholics using content analysis of Rorschach responses." *Rorschach Research Exchange and Journal of Projective Techniques*, 1949, *13*(2), 127-141.
39. Cattell & Morony, 1962.
40. David, H., & Rabinowitz, W. "Szondi patterns in epileptic and homosexual males." *Journal of Consulting Psychology*, 1952, *16*(4), 247-250.
41. Davids, A., Joelson, M., & McArthur, C. "Rorschach and TAT indices of homosexuality in overt homosexual, neurotics and normal males." *Journal of Abnormal and Social Psychology*, 1956, *53*(2), 161-172.

42. Hartman, B. "Comparison of selected experimental MMPI profiles of sexual deviants and sociopaths without sexual deviation." *Psychological Reports,* 1967, *20*(1), 234.

43. Botwinick, J., & Machover, S. "A psychometric examination of latent homosexuality in alcoholism." *Quarterly Journal of Studies on Alcohol,* 1951, *12*, 268-272.

44. Chapman, A., & Reese, D. "Homosexual signs in Rorschachs of early schizophrenics." *Journal of Clinical Psychology,* 1953, *9*(1), 30-32.

45. Klaf, F., & Davis, C. "Homosexuality and paranoid schizophrenia: A survey of 250 cases and controls." *American Journal of Psychiatry,* 1960, *116*(12), 1070-1075.

46. Lidz, R., & Lidz, T. "Homosexual tendencies in mothers of schizophrenic women." *Journal of Nervous and Mental Disease,* 1969, *149*(2), 229-235.

47. Armon, V. "Some personality variables in overt female homosexuality." *Journal of Projective Techniques,* 1960, *24,* 292-309; Hopkins, J. "The lesbian personality." *British Journal of Psychiatry,* 1969, *115,* 1433-1436.

48. Bene, E. "On the genesis of female homosexuality." *British Journal of Psychiatry,* 1965, *111,* 815-821; Gundlach, R., & Riess, B. "Birth order and sex of siblings in a sample of lesbians and non-lesbians." *Psychological Reports,* 1967, *1*(20), 61-62; Kaye, H., Berl, S., Clare, I., Eleston, M., Gershwin, B., Gershwin, P., Kogan, L., Torda, C., & Wilbur, C. "Homosexuality in women." *Archives of General Psychiatry,* 1967, *17*(5), 626-634; Kenyon, F. "Studies in female homosexuality. IV. Social and psychiatric aspects. V. Sexual development, attitudes, and experience." *British Journal of Psychiatry,* 1968, *114,* 1337-1350; Kremer, M., & Rifkin, A. "The early development of homosexuality: A study of adolescent lesbians." *American Journal of Psychiatry,* 1969, *126*(1), 91-96.

49. For example, Kinsey, A., Pomeroy, W., & Martin, C. *Sexual behavior in the human male.* Philadelphia: W.B. Saunders, 1948; Kinsey, A., Pomeroy, W., Martin, C., & Gebhard, P. *Sexual behavior in the human female.* Philadelphia: W.B. Saunders, 1953; Hooker, E. "Male homosexuals and their worlds." In J. Marmor (Ed.), *Sexual inversion: The multiple roots of homosexuality.* New York: Basic Books, 1965.

50. See, for example, Green, R. "Homosexuality as a mental illness." *International Journal of Psychiatry,* 1972, *10,* 77-128; Hoffman, M. *The gay world: Male homosexuality and the social creation of evil.* New York: Basic Books, 1962; Silverstein, 1976/1977; Szasz, 1970; Wysor, 1964.

51. For example, Begelman, D. "Homosexuality and the ethics of behavioral intervention." *Journal of Homosexuality,* 1977, *2*(3), 213-219; Davison, G. "Homosexuality: the ethical challenge." *Journal of Consulting and Clinical Psychology,* 1976, *44*(2), 157-162; Bell & Weinberg, 1978, pp. 229-231; Moses, A.E. *Identity management in lesbian women.* New York: Praeger, 1978, pp. xix-xx; Silverstein, 1976/1977.

52. Parsons, T. "Definitions of health and illness in the light of American values and social structure." In E. Jaco (Ed.), *Patients, physicians and illness* (2nd ed.). New York: Free Press, 1972.

53. Szasz, 1970, pp. 17-18.

54. Szasz, 1970, p. 257.

55. Sagarin, E., & MacNamara, D. (Eds.). *Problems of sex behavior.* New York: Thomas Crowell, 1968, p. 1.

56. For the history of sociological thought during this time as it relates to the later development of labeling theory, see Matza, D. *Becoming deviant.* Englewood Cliffs, N.J.: Prentice-Hall, 1969; and Taylor, I., Walton, P., & Young, J. *The new criminology.* London: Routledge & Kegan Paul, 1973.

57. Matza, 1969.

58. See, for example, Dinitz, S., Dynes, R., & Clark, A. "Deviance, norms and societal reactions." In S. Dinitz, R. Dynes, & A. Clark (Eds.), *Deviance: Studies in the process of stigmatization and societal reaction.* New York: Oxford University Press, 1969; Douglas, J.D. "Conceptions of deviant behavior: The old and the new." *Pacific Sociological Review,* 1966, *9,* 9-14; Kitsuse, J. "Societal reaction to deviant behavior." *Social Problems,* 1962, *9*(3), 247-256; Lemert, E. *Human deviance: Social problems and social control* (2nd ed.). Englewood Cliffs, N.J.: Prentice-Hall, 1972; Rubington, E., & Weinberg, M. (Eds.). *Deviance: The interactionist perspective.* London: Macmillan, 1968; Plummer, K. *Sexual stigma: An interactionist account.* London: Routledge & Kegan Paul, 1975; and Scott, R. "A proposed framework for analyzing deviance as a property of social order." In R. Scott & J.D. Douglas (Eds.), *Theoretical perspectives on deviance.* New York: Basic Books, 1972.

59. Lemert, 1972.

60. Scheff, T. "The societal reaction to deviance." *Social Problems,* 1964, *11,* 401-413.

61. Lemert, 1972, p. 62.

62. Lemert, 1972, p. 63.

63. Plummer, 1975.

64. Mills, C. "The professional ideology of social pathologists." *American Journal of Sociology,* 1943, *49*(2), 169.

65. Mills, 1943.

66. Szasz, 1970, pp. xxv-xxvi.

67. Liazos, A. "The poverty of the sociology of deviance: Nuts, sluts, and preverts." *Social Problems,* 1972, *19,* 103-120.

2

Current attitudes toward gay people

SOCIETAL ATTITUDES

In this chapter we will look at attitudes toward gay men and women that are held by most of the general population. Many of these extremely negative attitudes are based in myth and misconception, and it is difficult to be a member of our society and not have adopted the general attitude. Gays and nongays alike are affected, and it is especially important to helping professionals to understand these attitudes and be able to separate mythology from fact. We will talk later about the pain caused by misinformation and prejudice; here we will try to define the content of the prejudice.

Most Americans today have an extremely negative attitude toward gays that does not augur well for advancements in gay rights, at least in the near future.[1] In 1970, a nationwide probability sample of approximately 30,000 Americans demonstrated clearly that the majority of Americans hold negative attitudes and subscribe to incorrect, prejudiced beliefs about gay people.[2] This survey found that over three fourths of the people studied believed that sex acts with someone of the same gender are wrong if no love is involved, and 70% believed that they are wrong even if love is involved. Substantial majorities of these people believed that gays should not be allowed to hold positions of influence and authority such as those of court judge, schoolteacher, minister, medical doctor, or government official.[3]

Over half the people in this sample agreed, and many strongly agreed, with the following ideas: "Homosexuals are dangerous as teachers or youth leaders, because they try to get sexually involved with children." "Homosexuals try to play sexually with children if they cannot get an adult partner." "Homosexuality is a social corruption that can cause the downfall of a civilization."[3] Sixty-five percent of the sample believed homosexuality is very obscene and vulgar.[4] Between half and three quarters of the sample believed that homosexuals act like members of the opposite sex, have unusually strong sex drives, and are afraid of the opposite sex. Over one third believed that it is easy to identify homosexuals by their appearance,[5] and support for the rights of gays was predictably minimal.[6]

In 1974, a second nationwide probability sample was taken, and respondents were surveyed regarding their attitudes toward gay people. The findings of this second survey were essentially in agreement with those of the first study: "The overwhelming majority of white Americans do not approve of homosexual relations."[7] Furthermore, the researchers found that, compared with the 1970 study,

little or no change has occurred in the public's attitudes toward homosexuality despite increasing media exposure, public relations efforts of gay and other organizations, and alterations in the formal labels

16

applied by professional societies. Thus, unless these efforts alter the audience to which such remarks and actions are addressed, a more liberal public attitude toward homosexuality cannot be anticipated in the near future.[8]

Given these attitudes, it should hardly be surprising that gays are concerned about their rights, or that they engage in marches and protests, making every attempt to inform the public of the realities of gay lifestyles. Nor should it be surprising that so many gay people still have negative perceptions of themselves and of gays in general. In fact, it is amazing that gay people are as psychologically and emotionally healthy and positive about their sexual preference as they are.

CORRELATES OF ATTITUDES TOWARD GAYS

There are some consistent characteristics of those who hold negative attitudes toward gay people. They tend to be rural, white, raised in the rural Midwest or South, less well educated and more religious than those who hold positive attitudes.[9] They are also likely to hold more conservative attitudes toward sex. They typically hold unfavorable attitudes toward premarital and extramarital sex, sexual experimentation, and nongay sexual activities such as oral and anal sex.[10] They are more inclined to believe that sex should serve a reproductive function only and to feel guilty about their own sexuality.[11] Those who are antigay or heterosexist are also more likely to be sexist and racist.[12] Catholics and Protestants (particularly fundamentalist Protestants) are more likely to be heterosexist than Jews and those who do not espouse a particular religion.[13] There also appears to be a relationship between support of traditional gender roles and homophobia.[14]

Homophobia is a term that has been coined to describe those who have a fear or dread of homosexuals or homosexuality, and can apply to both gays and nongays.[15] Although the term suggests a phobic reaction, it has been used in a more global way to refer to anyone who generally does not like or is afraid of gay people or gayness.[16]

PROFESSIONAL RESPONSES

The term *homophobia* focuses attention on the irrational fears, attitudes, and resulting behaviors of those who react negatively to gays, rather than on gay people themselves. The negative attitude toward gays characteristic of Americans in this century is not justified, as we shall show in succeeding chapters. It is the product of factors having to do with this society and culture, not with anything inherent in gay people themselves.

The importance of the concept of homophobia and of understanding attitudes toward gays and their correlates is threefold. First, the professional who is going to work with gay clients must be aware that fear of gays and gayness is pervasive in this culture and that it is unfounded. Helping professionals are likely to experience it at one time or another, since all of us live in a homophobic culture. Gay clients grow up with it and can expect to live with it the rest of their lives. This means that helping professionals and their gay clients will have a constant, though not necessarily difficult, battle with homophobia in themselves and in society.

Second, those who live in a rural area or an area where traditional religion, especially fundamentalism, is a strong force are likely to find clients faced with extremely heterosexist, sexist, and racist attitudes. These professionals can anticipate more problems for their clients and themselves than they might in a more urban or less religiously oriented environment. Professionals can help clients cope with this by educating *them* about homophobia and the other attitudes and beliefs that often go along with it and by helping them realize that others have irrational beliefs about gay people and that these beliefs do not necessarily mean there is anything wrong with the gay person himself or herself. Mental health professionals can also expect that clients who fit into the homophobic stereotype themselves—that is, live in rural areas, hold fundamental religious beliefs, and are sexist and racist—are also going to be more afraid of their own gayness and of the gay community than those who do not have these characteristics.

Third, counselors should try to be aware of the ways that their own fear of gay people and gayness may be manifested. There is nothing to be ashamed of in such a response; but at the same time, it is not a response conducive to working effectively with gay clients. An awareness of homophobia and homophobic attitudes and what they mean may help the counselor learn new ways of thinking about gay people. Attitudes toward gays are certainly changeable by learning more about gay people. In fact, nongays who have had social contact with gays are more likely to have positive attitudes toward them than those who have not had such contacts.[17]

There are two groups of counselor attitudes that do not bode well for gays who want to receive unbiased treatment. First are counselors' attitudes toward gender and gender-role (often referred to as "sex-role") conformity as bases for judgments about mental health. Second are attitudes specifically related to homosexuality and lesbianism.

Very little research has been done to date on gay gender-role behavior. What has been done shows that gay women may be much more likely than nongay women to be masculine gender–typed, whereas gay men are more likely than nongay men to be androgynous.[18] Thus far, these characterizations refer only to the extent to which a person conforms on paper to societal descriptions of stereotypical male and female behavior. They do suggest however, that both gay men and lesbian women may be better off in terms of gender-role behavior and coping skills than some of their nongay counterparts. Obviously, more studies must be done in this area.

It is likely, however, that gay people pay socially if they cross over gender-role boundaries, and they are particularly likely to do so in a treatment context. There are indications that people in general, and helping professionals in particular, may respond negatively to individuals who display behavior considered appropriate to the opposite gender and especially toward individuals displaying stereotypically feminine behavior.[19] If this is the case, then gay people may be in a bind in therapy situations, especially if they are women or if they manifest stereotypically feminine behavior. Broverman et al. found clear evidence that the characteristics that are perceived as making up a

"healthy" woman are judged by helping professionals to differ substantially from the characteristics perceived as making up a healthy person, gender unspecified.[20] In fact, the characteristics perceived as making up a healthy woman are often *opposite* from the characteristics believed to typify a healthy person. Healthy person characteristics are the same as the characteristics perceived as making up a healthy man. There is at least one study that suggests that women's attitudes in the lay community are changing to perceive the ideal woman and man as having equal numbers of masculine characteristics. Men, however, continue to expect their ideal women to be significantly less masculine than the ideal man.[21]

Another problem gays may face is that those who act in ways not socially accepted for their gender may be viewed as more disturbed than those who enact stereotypical roles.[22] Thus, a woman who manifests certain so-called masculine traits, such as assertiveness or lack of self-disclosure, may be viewed as less healthy than one who acts "appropriately" feminine. On the other hand, a woman who acts stereotypically female may not be viewed as equally healthy in general. The opposite could be true of a man. If he demonstrates stereotypically feminine traits, he may be viewed as an unhealthy person both because of the feminine characteristics and because he has crossed gender role boundaries.

In working with gay clients, mental health professionals should keep in mind that gay men and women may manifest characteristics that are considered more appropriate to the opposite gender. If these behaviors are problematic for the client for some reason, then it is certainly worthwhile to discuss the reasons for the problem and what can be done about it. For example, some gay men who demonstrate mannerisms considered effeminate may be concerned about these, may believe they have no control over them, and may worry about others' reactions.

It is, of course, not true that the client has no control over his mannerisms, and he must be told

18

this. Second, he must be assured that so-called effeminate mannerisms are not an indication that something is wrong with him anymore than the way he eats or brushes his teeth. They are, however, much more likely than some other kinds of mannerisms to get him in trouble. He can be shown that he does have control over his mannerisms by practicing them and actually exaggerating them in the therapy situation. He may then determine where, when, and with whom he wishes to use them.[23]

The most important thing is that the counselor be aware of his or her own reaction to the client's behavior and be sure that the client's behavior is not a problem for him or her and that health or illness is not equated with either gender-role conformity or with a particular gender's behavior. It should be recalled that it is common for people to be most comfortable with those things that are familiar and to which they are accustomed. Cross-gender behavior, if it is unfamiliar, can blind a therapist to a client's essential health and strengths (and it takes a great deal of both to function as a gay person who demonstrates cross-gender behavior in this society), and it can also cause the counselor and client to be sidetracked into gender-role issues that may not be of importance to the client. With this, as with so many other things, the counselor's best bet is to start "where the client is," trite though that may sound.

THERAPIST'S ATTITUDES TOWARD GAYS

As of the mid-1970s, therapists' attitudes toward gayness were less repressive than those of the general public, but still not really accepting. Those studies that have explored therapists' attitudes have not employed probability sampling, so it is impossible to determine to what extent they are reflective of the attitudes of therapists as a whole, and their findings must be interpreted with caution.

Nonetheless, although therapists are generally willing to concede that homosexuality and lesbianism should not be considered illnesses, they are still viewed by many as indicative of pathology and of some kind of disturbance in the "normal" maturational process.[24] Some therapists are still willing to attempt to alter a client's sexual preference, even in some cases without the client's consent, and a great many believe that "conversion" to a nongay lifestyle is possible and presumably desirable.[25]

On the positive side, many therapists do appear to be moving toward more enlightened positions with regard to sexual preference, and a great many of those are behavior therapists.[26] Behaviorists have traditionally been viewed with great disfavor by gays because of their use of aversive measures to attempt to alter gay behavior.[27] It is therefore very encouraging to find that this group of therapists is beginning to question the ethics not only of aversive therapy with gays, but of any attempts at conversion.[28]

Therapists' attitudes can obviously greatly affect the mental health and well-being of members of the gay community. Therapists who believe that lesbianism and male gayness are symptoms or signs of incomplete development of the person or who see it as a disorder of any kind are going to reflect this both in their intervention and in their communications with colleagues and with the nongay community.

Homophobia within the helping professions

Helping professionals often express dismay, and sometimes insult, at suggestions that they, too, may be homophobic. Yet we are often asked for suggestions with regard to treating gay clients that confirm this belief. The most common are those that, either by tone or wording, reflect the professional's distaste or discomfort with something about a gay client. We are often asked, for example, what to do with male clients who insist on acting "feminine" or lesbian women who are obviously attracted to the (female) counselor. Frequently, these questions are asked because the counselor is afraid of or disgusted by the client. A counselor who thinks a gay client's behavior is disgusting, perverted, sick, or scary should refer the client elsewhere if possible.

Sometimes, though, the feeling is not one of disgust but of discomfort with someone who displays marked cross-gender behavior. If this kind of uneasiness is experienced, the counselor should try to determine its source. Some people are uncomfortable with cross-gender behavior at first because of its novelty and because they don't know what it means, how to act, or what to do about it. They may think they should ignore the behavior, although at the same time it is salient to them. If someone's behavior is noticeable to the therapist, it is probably noticeable to the rest of the world. It might be worthwhile for the counselor to mention it and see what kinds of experiences the person is having because of his or her behavior. If the client is experiencing no problems and likes behaving as he or she is, then there is probably no reason for intervention.

Therapists who find themselves uneasy with gay clients of the same gender, as is often the case, may be afraid that the client is going to approach them sexually. Although social sanctions make this less likely with gay than with nongay clients, the professional may feel more comfortable if she or he realizes that both gay and nongay sexual approaches are handled the same way. The therapist should simply consider what he or she would do if the approach were made by a nongay person of the opposite gender and do the same thing. The therapist should respond to the approach, not the person. Sexual approaches during professional contracted interactions are inappropriate from any of the interactants. If a client does not realize that he or she and the counselor have a professional relationship, then that must be clarified. The matter should be handled assertively and directly whenever possible.

Those who are uncomfortable with a person of the opposite gender may be responding to what they believe is a caricature of their own gender or may resent the fact that here is someone of the opposite gender who will not respond to them sexually. Both are common and understandable responses. The first response is probably more common among women, particularly feminist women, who see mannered gay men as representing all the features of oppressed womanhood that they themselves have been struggling against. Indeed, many lesbian women have negative reactions to men who wear drag. Professionals who feel this way can find it well worth their while to talk to such a client and find out what drag or effeminate mannerisms mean to him.

Resentment of a gay person for being sexually unavailable or unresponsive is a reaction that both men and women have, but it is probably more common among men in relation to lesbian women. Many people believe that a lesbian woman can be changed into a nongay woman by a sexually competent man, although not nearly as many believe the reverse.[29] In fact, some men seem to find lesbian women an irresistible challenge to their masculinity.[30] Even if a man does not wish to become sexually involved with a lesbian client, he may believe that it is in her best interest to look and act more "feminine," that is, more attractive to *him*.

Our suggestion is simply that counselors try to be aware of their own reactions to gay clients and to their client's gender-role behavior. Counselors who feel a great deal of discomfort or who feel compelled to get their clients to change their behavior are urged to examine the reasons for this and, if they involve attitudes that are not likely to change or are very negative, to consider referring the client. If the counselor is either afraid of a sexual approach by the client or distressed by the client's indifference to him or her as a possible sexual choice, awareness of this may help ease the situation. If not, again we strongly urge that the client be transferred to another counselor.

END NOTES

1. Brudnoy, D. "Homosexuality in America: At 200 years." *Homosexual Counseling Journal*, 1976, *3*(1), 10-22.
2. Levitt, E., & Klassen, A., Jr. "Public attitudes toward homosexuality: Part of a 1970 national survey by the Institute of Sex Research." *Journal of Homosexuality*, 1974, *1*(1), 29-43.
3. Levitt & Klassen, 1974, pp. 32; 34.
4. Levitt & Klassen, 1974, pp. 32; 34.

5. Levitt & Klassen, 1974, p. 34.

6. Levitt & Klassen, 1974, p. 35

7. Levitt & Klassen, 1974, pp. 35; 37.

8. Nyberg, K., & Alston, J. "Analysis of public attitudes toward homosexual behavior." *Journal of Homosexuality*, 1976/1977, *2*(2), 99-107.

9. Nyberg & Alston, 1976/1977, pp. 106-107.

10. Levitt & Klassen, 1974; Nyberg & Alston, 1976/1977; Irwin, P., & Thompson, N. "Acceptance of the rights of homosexuals: A profile." *Journal of Homosexuality*, 1977, *3*(2), 107-121.

11. Levitt & Klassen, 1974; Nyberg & Alston, 1976/1977; Irwin & Thompson, 1977; Dunbar, J., Brown, M., & Amoroso, D. "Some correlates of attitudes toward homosexuality." *Journal of Social Psychology*, 1973, *89*, 271-279.

12. Dunbar, Brown, & Amoroso, 1973.

13. Henley, N., & Pincus, F. "Interrelationship of sexist, racist and antihomosexual attitudes." *Psychological Reports*, 1978, *42*, 83-90.

14. See, for example, MacDonald, A., Jr. "Identification and measurement of multidimensional attitudes toward equality between the sexes." *Journal of Homosexuality*, 1974, *1*(2), 165-182; MacDonald, A. "Homophobia: Its roots and meanings." *Homosexual Counseling Journal*, 1976, *3*(1), 23-33; MacDonald, A., Jr., & Games, R. "Some characteristics of those who hold positive and negative attitudes toward homosexuals." *Journal of Homosexuality*, 1974, *1*(1), 9-27; Millham, J., San Miguel, C., Christopher, L., & Kellog, R. "A factor-analytic conceptualization of attitudes toward male and female homosexuals." *Journal of Homosexuality*, 1976, *2*(1), 3-10; San Miguel, C., & Millham, J. "The role of cognitive and situational variables in aggression toward homosexuals." *Journal of Homosexuality*, 1976, *2*(1), 11-27; and Weinberger, L., & Millham, J. "Attitudinal homophobia and support of traditional sex roles." *Journal of Homosexuality*, 1979, *4*(3), 237-246.

15. MacDonald, 1976; Marmor, J. "Overview: The multiple roots of homosexual behavior." In J. Marmor (Ed.), *Homosexual behavior: A modern reappraisal.* New York: Basic Books, 1980.

16. MacDonald, 1976.

17. Millham, San Miguel, Christopher, & Kellog, 1976.

18. Heilbrun, A., Jr., & Thompson, N. "Sex-role identity and male and female homosexuality." *Sex Roles*, 1977, *3*(1), 65-79; Thompson, N., Schwartz, D., McCandless, B., & Edwards, D. "Parent-child relationships and sexual identity in male and female homosexuals and heterosexuals." *Journal of Consulting and Clinical Psychology*, 1973, *41*, 120-127; Bernard, L., & Epstein, D. "Androgyny scores of matched homosexual and heterosexual males." *Journal of Homosexuality*, 1978, *4*(2), 169-178.

19. Aslin, A. "Feminist and community mental health center psychotherapists' expectations of mental health for women." *Sex Roles*, 1977, *3*(6), 537-544; Cowan, G. "Therapist judgments of clients' sex-role problems." *Psychology of Women Quarterly*, 1976, *1*(2), 115-123; Figliulo, M., Shively, M., & McEnroe, F. "The relationship of departure in social sex-roles to the abridgement of civil liberties." *Journal of Homosexuality*, 1978, *3*(3), 249-255; Israel, A., Raskin, P., & Pravder, M. "Gender and sex-role appropriateness: Bias in the judgment of disturbed behavior." *Sex Roles*, 1978, *4*(3), 399-413.

20. Broverman, I., Vogel, S., Broverman, D., Clarkson, F., & Rosenkrantz, P. "Sex-role stereotypes: A current appraisal." *Journal of Social Issues*, 1972, *28*(2), 54-78.

21. Gilbert, L., Deutsch, B., & Strahan, R. "Feminine and masculine dimensions of the typical, desirable, and ideal woman and man." *Sex Roles*, 1978, *4*(5), 767-778.

22. Cowan, 1976; Israel, Raskin & Pravder, 1978.

23. These issues are discussed more fully in Chapter 7, especially the section on cross-dressing.

24. Davison, G., & Wilson, G. "Attitudes of behavior therapists toward homosexuality." *Behavior Therapy*, 1973, *4*, 686-696; Fort, J., Steiner, C., & Conrad, F. "Attitudes of mental health professionals toward homosexuality and its treatment." *Psychological Reports*, 1971, *29*, 347-350; Gartrell, N., Kraemer, H., & Brodie, H. "Psychiatrists' attitudes toward female homosexuality." *Journal of Nervous and Mental Disease*, 1974, *159*, 141-144; Morris, P. "Doctors' attitudes to homosexuality." *British Journal of Psychiatry*, 1973, *122*, 435-436.

25. Davison & Wilson, 1973; Fort, Steiner, & Conrad, 1971; Morris, 1973.

26. Davison & Wilson, 1973; Gartrell, 1974.

27. Davison, G. "Homosexuality and the ethics of behavioral intervention." *Journal of Homosexuality*, 1977, *2*(3), 195-204.

28. Davison, 1977.

29. Levitt & Klassen, 1974.

30. There is no research evidence to substantiate this. However, there are many anecdotes within the lesbian community about men who believe that all a lesbian needs to change her behavior is a sexual experience with a man and that it is up to those specific men to prove it. See for example, Lewis, S. *Sunday's women: A report on lesbian life today.* Boston: Beacon Press, 1979, pp. 28-29.

3

The legal rights of gays[1]

HOLLY PETERS

The legal rights of gay people are developing slowly and intermittently throughout the nation. A major obstacle to the establishment of expansive legal rights for gays is the continual refusal of the Supreme Court to review cases dealing with sexual preference. This is part of a larger trend in Supreme Court decisions to dodge controversial issues whenever possible and return them to the legislative branch of government at the local, state, or federal level.

Some conservative justices, notably Rehnquist, have cited in several key decisions the "will of the majority," in settling thorny public policy matters. This position has been seen in opinions on abortion, zoning multifamily dwellings (communes) out of residential areas, and other issues. With this sentiment present, it is perhaps just as well that the Burger court has refused to hear gay rights cases.

AUTHORITY OF THE SUPREME COURT

In order to understand the significance of Supreme Court decisions, an explanation of the Court's authority is helpful. A Supreme Court decision creates binding precedent that affects the status of gays nationwide. Once a Supreme Court decision is made, it is binding on the entire country. Positive decisions by a state supreme court or a federal appeals court are binding only in the geographical area within the jurisdiction of that court. Such decisions are only persuasive precedent in other areas. That means a judge hearing a similar case in another area of the country can choose to ignore decisions from another lower court.

When a case is appealed to the Supreme Court, the Court has several options. It may deny the request for an appeal, remand (send the case back to a lower court for further study), or affirm (agree with lower court decision without hearing formal arguments). The Court may also choose to hear formal arguments on a case and issue a written opinion. This latter option confers the subsequent opinion with the strongest precedent.

KEY CASES

Following are recent key cases that the high court has been asked to review and their results.

Gaylord v. Tacoma School District.[2] In this case a Washington State public school teacher was dismissed after years of outstanding work because he acknowledged that he was gay when asked by school officials. The Supreme Court refused to hear this case, thus allowing the dismissal to stand. This case was a major setback for two reasons. First, it presented a perfect fact situation for litigation. There were no side issues concerning Gaylord's job performance. The only thing under debate was whether or not his sexual preference could be sufficient cause for dismissal. Second, Gaylord was dismissed solely for his status as a gay person, not because of any specific conduct.

22

He had not been active politically nor had he been arrested for solicitation or other illegal acts.

Singer v. U.S. Civil Service Commission.[3] The Supreme Court remanded this case to the U.S. Civil Service Commission for review under its liberalized guidelines on sexual preference. Singer was a clerk-typist for, ironically, the Equal Employment Opportunity Commission. He was fired because of his gay activism and the publicity concerning his attempts to obtain a marriage license so he could marry his male lover.

After the case was filed in federal court, the Civil Service Commission altered its guidelines to state that termination could not be solely on the basis of sexual preference. Singer was reinstated with back pay, but his case left no national precedent because it had been resolved administratively without the Supreme Court issuing an opinion.

Doe v. Commonwealth Attorney for Richmond.[4] This case challenged the state antisodomy law on the grounds that it chilled the exercise of freedom of association. The case lost in the lower courts. The Supreme Court denied a hearing and affirmed the district court decision, which stated that privacy rights extend only to that conduct that society approves.

In this case, the High Court clearly supported repressive laws against gays. Because the Court did not grant a hearing and issue its own opinion, the decision is not as damaging as it could have been. However, it is still a setback and has been cited in lower court opinions against gays.

PROTECTION AND DISCRIMINATION
Employment

Some gays are protected from discrimination in the work place. Whether they are protected depends on who their employer is and where that employer is located. There are no federal statutes prohibiting discrimination on the basis of sexual preference like those that prohibit discrimination on the basis of sex, race, and so forth. But there are protective statutes in some states, cities, and counties, a list of which can be obtained from the National Gay Task Force.

Another variable is whether the employer is a governmental body. The federal government has passed civil service guidelines that prohibit termination solely on the basis of sexual preference. These guidelines could be stronger than they are, but they do provide some measure of protection.

State and local service guidelines vary in their positions. In some areas, governors or mayors have issued executive orders prohibiting discrimination within their branch of government. If there is no other form of protection, government employees can usually challenge discriminatory treatment on constitutional grounds.

Private or nongovernmental employees have fewer options if they live in a geographical area where there is no statutory protection. A significant number of major corporations (such as IBM, NBC, Exxon, McDonald's, Bell System, and Eastern Airlines) have internal policies of nondiscrimination against gays.[5] That is presently the only source of hope in areas without protective statutes.

Obviously, many gay people are left with no coverage under any statute or policy. Efforts have been mounted over the last few years to amend Title VII of the 1964 Civil Rights Act to outlaw job discrimination based on sexual preference. This would dramatically improve the legal rights of gay employees by elevating gays to the same status women, Blacks, and other groups have in employment law. Until this amendment passes, gays will continue to be potential targets for legal discrimination on the job.

A major obstacle to using already existing law to support the rights of gays on the job is that the courts have generally not classified gays as a group coming under the equal protection clause of the U.S. Constitution. However, gays do fit the guidelines historically used to define protected classes: they have historically been subjected to unequal legal treatment, and they are victims of legislative prejudice who are politically powerless and whose class is based on traits that they are powerless to control.

The California Supreme Court, a leader in human rights law, recently (1980) held that gays do fall under the equal protection clause. *Gay Law Students Association v. Pacific Telephone and Telegraph*[6] is the first major case in which a court has supported that position. The court also held in the case that gays come under the California Labor Code section that prohibits discrimination on the basis of political action. The justices reasoned that being openly gay is a political act and therefore should come under the code. This was also a first, and helps expand the concept of gay rights in case law.[7]

Housing

Legal rights to discrimination-free housing do not exist nationwide. There is no federal protective statute. There is protective legislation in some cities, counties, and states. Some of the areas that offer protection are the state of Pennsylvania and the following cities: Champaign, Illinois; Columbus, Ohio; Los Angeles, California; Madison, Wisconsin; Minneapolis, Minnesota; Tucson, Arizona; and Washington, D.C.[8]

Military

Recent victories have improved the status of gays in the military. For the most part, gays can no longer be kicked out of the armed services solely on the basis of sexual preference. The government must show a nexus (reason linking status with performance). However, so far the courts have supported minor things such as disrupting fellow employees as a sufficient nexus.

The most comprehensive positive change has been in the area of less-than-honorable discharges on the basis of sexual preference. Regulations have been reformed so that anyone with a gay discharge can have it upgraded unless he or she was convicted of an offense involving force or conduct involving sex with a minor.

Problems still exist for those who are openly gay and wish to enter the military. However, case law is changing for gays in the armed forces, and those affected should carefully monitor new developments.

Immigration

Whether or not gays can be denied admittance to the United States because of their sexual preference has been in dispute over the last few years. Until recently, gays could be legally denied admittance to the United States once they had been certified by Public Health Service physicians as sexual deviants.

In late 1979, the Surgeon General ordered his staff to stop issuing such certificates. The immigration authorities asked the Justice Department to rule on whether they still had to exclude gays without certificates. The Justice Department issued an opinion that the law still had to be enforced because Congress intended the statute to exclude gays. Since the practical problem remained of how to enforce the law, the Justice Department continued to work on resolving the problem. In the fall of 1980, the Department announced that gays would be denied admission to the United States only if they inform the immigration officer of their sexual preference.

Student organizations[9]

Gay student organizations in public institutions must be recognized. Under the First Amendment, students at public schools and universities have the right to speech and assembly on any issue. The courts have consistently recognized this right, with few exceptions. Students in private schools do not have the same constitutional protections and generally are subject to the discretion of the school administration.

Sodomy laws

The following states have no restrictions on adult consensual sex acts: Alaska, California, Colorado, Connecticut, Delaware, Hawaii, Illinois, Indiana, Iowa, Maine, Massachusetts, Nebraska, New Hampshire, New Jersey, New Mexico, New York, North Dakota, Ohio, Oregon, Pennsylvania, South Dakota, Vermont, Washington, West Virginia, and Wyoming. In the remaining states, there are periodic challenges to existing sodomy laws.

24

Doe v. Commonwealth Attorney for Richmond, mentioned previously, was a major setback to attacks through the federal courts. A successful challenge of the New York state sodomy law was won in December 1980. Another successful state court challenge was in Pennsylvania, where the Pennsylvania Supreme Court declared the state's sodomy laws unconstitutional in early 1980.

Child custody

This is an especially difficult area of law to improve because of the great discretionary powers of juvenile and family courts. Across the nation there is practically a split record of wins and losses in gay parent custody cases. The outcome of each case depends on its individual circumstances. Resource materials for those involved in custody cases are available from several sources.[10]

Personal relationships and finances

Marriage between gays is not legally recognized in any state. Many challenges have been filed, but the Supreme Court has consistently refused to hear cases.

A challenge to IRS regulations by an Arizona man failed. The plaintiff claimed his lover as a dependent, and the IRS would not accept the deduction. The lawsuit was not appealed because courts have historically not allowed joint returns or the counting of dependents from nonmarried, nonblood relationships regardless of sexual preference.

Gay people have no right of inheritance when their partner dies unless there is a will. Even with a will, relatives may challenge it using the "undue influence" theory. To prevent a successful challenge by relatives, evidence should be built up that the will is the independent choice of the person writing it. This can be done by updating the will periodically, having assets reviewed with the attorney, and documenting that review. This will help establish that, if one's financial situation changes as the result of an inheritance or some other factor, the original will was clearly intended to stand.

SUMMARY

The legal rights of gays are going through a period of rapid change. There will be more cases advocating the rights of gay people in all areas of the law, and if current trends continue, gays will prevail and become full citizens under the law. As it stands now, however, gays still have minimal protection in employment, housing, the military, and personal relationships, particularly those involving child custody.

END NOTES

1. The information in this chapter is current as of December 1980. For updates on areas discussed, contact the National Gay Task Force, 80 Fifth Avenue, New York, N.Y. 10011; your local chapter of the American Civil Liberties Union; or a local gay rights organization. The ACLU is scheduled to publish a revised edition of *The Rights of Gay People* in 1981, which will be an excellent resource for helping professionals.
2. *Gaylord v. Tacoma School District,* 88 Wash. 2d 286, 559 P. 2d 1340 *certiorari denied* 434 U.S. 879 (1977).
3. *Singer v. U.S. Civil Service Commission,* 530 F. 2d 247 (9th Cir. 1976) *certiorari granted* 429 U.S. 1034 (1977).
4. *Doe v. Commonwealth Attorney for Richmond,* 403 F. Supp. 1199 (E.D. Va. 1957), summarily affirmed without opinion, 425 U.S. 901 (1976).
5. "How gay is gay?" *Time,* 23 April 1979, pp. 72-73.
6. *Gay Law Students Association v. Pacific Telephone and Telegraph,* California Supreme Court, No. S.F. 23625 (1979).
7. Case law consists of court decisions that interpret existing laws.
8. "It's time." *National Gay Task Force Newsletter,* July-August 1980, p. 4.
9. For further discussion of this see Chapter 13, Bernard, J.L. "The rights of gay students on the college campus," in this book.
10. The National Gay Task Force (address given in note 1) is a good source. Also see Stevens, M. "Lesbian mothers in transition." In G. Vida (Ed.), *Our right to love: A lesbian resource book.* Englewood Cliffs, N.J.: Prentice-Hall, 1978, pp. 207-211. She also suggests Lesbian Mothers National Defense Fund, 2446 Lorentz Place North, Seattle, Wash. 98109.

PART TWO

The gay experience

4

Development of sexual identity and sexual preference

The concepts of sexual identity and sexual preference refer to a person's perception of self as a sexual being. The development of sexual identity is strongly influenced by the culture and has little meaning outside a cultural context. Understanding the way sexual identity develops requires an understanding of the components of psychosexual development in general. It is our belief that the most appropriate model of psychosexual development is one that incorporates biological, sociological, and psychological factors and the interrelationships among these. We will present one such model in this chapter, and then present specific information on sexual identity within the framework of that model.

SEXUALITY

Theories of psychosexual development attempt to explain the factors involved in the formation of an individual's sexuality and to elucidate the ways in which these act and interact within an individual. Sexuality, in this sense, encompasses much more than genital functioning or methods by which orgasmic release is attained. It includes recognition of maleness and femaleness and the ways a particular person expresses these. Sexuality also includes attitudes toward relationships with people of both the same and opposite gender, toward touching and being touched, and toward general physical closeness. It includes attitudes about and participation in various forms of explicit sexual activity, such as masturbation, cunnilingus, fellatio, and intercourse. The scope of the term is exemplified by the definition developed by a colloquium of international sex educators in Uppsala, Sweden, and subsequently accepted by the SIECUS[1] board of directors.

> The concept of sexuality refers to the totality of being a person. It includes all of those aspects of the human being that relate specifically to being boy or girl, woman or man, and is an entity subject to life-long dynamic change. Sexuality reflects our human character, not solely our genital nature. As a function of the total personality it is concerned with the biological, psychological, sociological, spiritual, and cultural variables of life which, by their effects on personality development and interpersonal relations, can in turn affect social structure.[2]

The method by which sexuality develops and the factors involved in that development have been addressed by a number of theorists, among them Freud, Erikson, Maslow, and Fromm.[3] Although each of these has made a significant contribution to our understanding of human behavior in general and sexuality in particular, there is another approach that we find particularly useful: the biosociopsychological model.[4]

28

BIOSOCIOPSYCHOLOGICAL MODEL OF PSYCHOSEXUAL DEVELOPMENT

The biosociopsychological model, as the name implies, provides a framework for examining the effects of and interrelationships among biological, sociological, and psychological variables in psychosexual development. It helps clarify the similarities and differences among various groups of people who express their sexual preferences differently, such as heterosexuals, ambisexuals, and homosexuals, as well as other groups of people who have been identified according to some aspect of their sexuality. It also allows for an investigation of ways in which the development of sexuality occurs in different individuals.

After the model is presented, Table 1 is provided to aid in clarification. Table 1 includes not only the three major factors and their components but also categorical headings often used in the literature, such as orientation labels of heterosexual, ambisexual (often referred to as bisexual), and homosexual, and other sexually related labels of transsexual, fetishist, transvestite, and so on. Alongside each categorical heading, the individual components of the biological, sociological, and psychological factors appropriate for that category can then be identified to enable comparisons of categories. For example, it enables the reader to compare the individual components of biology, sociology, and psychology as these relate to the categories of homosexual, ambisexual, and heterosexual.

Biological factor

The biological factor, although extremely complex, is the simplest of the three. It is initially responsible for the development of gender, that is, whether one is genetically male or female. It is the somatotype, composed of chromosomes, hormones, internal and external genitalia, and gonads. Each of these five components plays an important role in determining biological maleness or femaleness, and together they lead to the designation of gender.

As far as we know, most people are chromosomally either 46,XX (female) or 46,XY (male)[5]; have either predominantly estrogen or androgen for hormones; possess internal and external genitalia and reproductive systems that are identified as female or male; and have either ovaries or testicles. However, each of these aspects is subject to variation.

Biological variations—chromosomes. A person may have triple chromosomes (a trisomy), such as XXX, XXY, or XYY, or a single chromosome (a monosomy) identified as XO. There is no YO chromosomal pattern. The triple chromosome pattern XXX and the single pattern XO (Turner's syndrome) will develop into a female body. The XXX female will usually develop with diminished fertility, and the Turner's syndrome female usually will not have functional ovaries and will be shorter than average.[6] The triple patterns XXY (Klinefelter's syndrome) and XYY develop male bodies. In Klinefelter's syndrome, the onset of puberty may be delayed and fertility diminished, whereas the XYY male is usually characterized as being taller than average and poor in behavior control.[7]

Biological variations—hormones. The sex hormones are active before birth during embryonic and fetal development and are then dormant until puberty. Sometime around the sixth week of gestation, if there is a Y chromosome present, signaling the development of a male body, two substances are produced. One is called the müllerian-inhibiting substance, which halts any further development of the tissue that would have been the uterus and fallopian tubes. The other substance is androgen, which escalates the development of the penis, scrotum, and testicles from the tissue that would have been the clitoris, labia, and ovaries.[8]

Should any part of the complicated hormonal system be altered, either through external or internal forces, variances in internal and external reproductive organs could and do occur. For example, if a developing female fetus is subjected to androgens, as might happen when the pregnant woman takes pills containing androgen, the result could be an extended clitoris. If a developing male fetus does not receive sufficient androgen, the scrotal sac might not develop fully, leaving an opening that might be mistaken for labia.

There is also some evidence that fetal hormones have a relationship to the behavior of infants and children, such as occurs when young females are very active and energetic, leading to the label of tomboy.[9] However, this hormonal relationship to behavior is open to question. For example, there is no evidence to indicate that all tomboys have developed as such because of fetal hormones, and much of the research on hormonal influence on behavior has been carried out on animals, with questionable validity in interpreting human behavior.

Biological variations—other factors. When there is consistency between the chromosomes and the hormones, other factors may alter the development of the internal and external genitalia, reproductive tracts, and gonads. For example, in the case of the androgen insensitivity syndrome, the XY (male) chromosome present is responsible for the physiologically normal production of androgen, which usually causes the development of the penis, scrotum, and testicles. However, because of a gene dysfunction, the fetal tissue is not responsive to androgen, and male genitalia do not develop. The müllerian-inhibiting substance is still produced and carries out its function of halting the development of the uterus and fallopian tubes. However, the external genitalia of the newborn are female, usually with an incomplete vagina. The somatotype of the child is mixed, neither male nor female. It is assigned female gender at birth because of its external genitalia.[10]

Summary. Assuming no variation occurs, the biological factor results in a single, fully developed gender, either as male or female. A biologically normal female has XX chromosomes, with estrogen as the predominant hormone, appropriate internal and external genitalia, and ovaries. A biologically normal male has XY chromosomes, with androgen as the predominant hormone, appropriate internal and external genitalia, and testicles.

Sociological factor

With all these possibilities for variance, one cannot help marveling at the apparent consistency with which the biological components agree. When a baby is finally born, only the external genitalia are examined to determine whether "it's a girl" or "it's a boy." It is astounding that we can so accurately predict four of the five components of gender by observing only one.

The fact that a newborn is identified as a girl or a boy, rather than as a male or female, is significant. The labels *boy* and *girl* are social labels, not just identifications of gender. Once the infant is born and gender identification is made, the sociological factor begins to exert an influence on the individual with the development of gender identity and gender role behavior.

Gender identity. Gender identity refers to a person's concept of self as either female or male. This awareness begins to develop almost immediately after birth as the infant receives constant messages informing it of its gender, from the color of its baby clothes and blanket to the constant flow of verbal and nonverbal messages. Even with infants, adults use "gender-appropriate" language. "He" is good-looking, strong, and is going to be a football player. "She" is pretty, precious, dainty, and sweet. To appreciate the pervasiveness of these messages, simply watch adults and children interact with an infant, and note the gender appropriateness of the interactions. Or try to participate in such an interaction yourself without making any references to the child's gender. It is almost impossible.[11]

By about 3 years of age, children not only know that both boys and girls exist but are also aware of their own gender identity and have begun to differentiate gender role behavior in others. By age 5, they can use both biological and psychological cues in that differentiation.[12]

Once the child has an awareness of the existence of two genders and knows to which group he or she belongs, the child begins to learn how to validate that identity by expressing "boyness" or "girlness" to the society. In other words, the child begins learning the socially acceptable behavior for its gender, or its *gender role behavior*.[13]

Gender role behavior. The most complicated aspect of the socialization process is the acquisition of gender role behavior: learning how to behave as a girl or boy, man or woman. It begins at the point of gender identity acquisition and may change during one's life span.[14] The social structure that exists within many Western societies dictates that males and females will acquire their gender roles differently.

Women are generally the primary caretakers of young boys and girls. The movement of men as teachers into the primary grades is a somewhat recent phenomenon, and men are still very rare in kindergartens and day-care centers. This means that during the majority of their learning hours, infants and children have women as role models. The young female is therefore able to learn predominantly by direct modeling. "I am female, the people around me are female. Therefore, I must do what they do." For the young male, the learning process is different, with negation being predominant. "I am male, people around me are female; therefore, I must not do what they do." There is some direct modeling for males and some negating for females, but the social structure dictates a primary learning model for females that is different from that of males.[15]

The sex hormones are inactive while the young person is learning gender role behavior. This is not to imply that sexual activity is dormant. To the contrary, from infancy through prepuberty, children are sexual. However, their activity, including genital interest, appears to be primarily exploration and curiosity.[16] Many attitudes toward adult sexuality are learned during this time, including ways of expressing love toward and caring for another person.[17]

The present situation in the United States is one in which many people are questioning traditional, polarized, gender-specific behaviors. There is some confusion about definitions of femininity and masculinity. This questioning has come primarily from women who view the descriptors of feminine behavior as restrictive and smothering[18] and who want female gender role behavior redefined by expansion.[19] Although there has been resistance to this redefining,[20] socially acceptable behavior for women has changed somewhat. Although men are also beginning to view the traditional descriptors of masculine behavior as restrictive,[21] there appears to be less motivation for change among men than among women.[22]

Societal definitions of appropriate gender role behavior. At birth and during early childhood, the only true distinguishing characteristics between males and females are the differences in external genitalia. Those differences are the basis for the establishment of the child's gender identity and for society's determination of which behaviors are appropriate for the child to learn. The name society gives to that gender and the behaviors expected on the basis of the name are the components of the sociological factor of the model.

The initial development of gender role behavior is strongly influenced by the prevailing societal definition of what behaviors are gender appropriate. Because of the close link between gender-related behavior and gender identity, a child whose behavior does not fit the societal definition may experience gender identity confusion. This is particularly likely to be the case with boys. Those boys who show cross-gender ("sissy") behavior are much more likely to show gender confusion than girls who show cross-gender ("tomboy") behavior.[23]

This difference in occurrence of gender confusion between boys and girls may be related to the differential status and power of males and females in this culture. At a very early age, children learn that it is permissible for girls to play with boys' toys, but not for boys to play with girls' toys, and that it is more acceptable for a girl to act tomboyish than for a boy to be a sissy. In learning these rules of behavioral acceptability, children are also beginning to learn the dynamics of gender-based power. It is well known that it is acceptable for a submissive group to emulate a dominant group, but not for a dominant group to emulate a submissive one. The social message may be, therefore, that it is understandable that a girl could want to engage in boyish behavior and still be a girl. It is not understandable that a boy would want to engage in girlish behavior, unless he is not a "real" boy.

The general message, then, is that a person can be either masculine or feminine. For years, the assumption in psychological testing has been that these were opposite ends of a single continuum, and that as one became less masculine, one simultaneously became more feminine. Researchers have only recently begun to conceive of masculinity and femininity as two separate, independent continua. The concept of psychological androgyny has developed out of this reconceptualization.[24]

Psychological androgyny. Research on psychological androgyny and masculinity and femininity has shown that some people are high on either one dimension or the other (gender-typed); that is, high masculine and low feminine (masculine-typed), or high feminine and low masculine (feminine-typed). Some people are high on neither dimension (undifferentiated), and some are high on both (androgynous). There is increasing evidence that psychological androgyny, the ability to display both masculine and feminine gender behaviors, may be much more healthy and functional than conformity to a gender stereotype. This means that, if we were to come to accept androgynous behavior as a viable alternative to stereotyped masculine and feminine behavior, both men and women would have more socially acceptable behavioral options. Assertiveness, emotionality, warmth, aggression, activity, passivity, dominance, submission, gentleness, and harshness, to name only a few types of behavior, would be acceptable for any individual regardless of gender without raising questions of gender appropriateness or gender identity.[25]

Psychological androgyny is not yet culturally accepted as an alternative goal for child rearing. However, researchers have found that there are quite a few individuals who do manifest androgyny and are now attempting to determine some of the factors that can facilitate the development of a person who is psychologically androgynous.[26]

Psychological factor

Of the three factors, the psychological is the most complex; and in discussing this aspect of the model, we are left with two choices: omit it because it is too complex to discuss, or simplify it to an extent that may possibly introduce confusion. In order to present the model, we have chosen the latter option.

As one moves through puberty and into adolescence, the psychological factor appears to become dominant. Its simplified components are (1) with whom or what does a person engage in explicit sexual behavior *(object)*, (2) why does a person engage in explicit sexual behavior *(goal)*, and (3) what is the person's arousal stimulus *(arousal pattern)?* Examining each of these reveals the complexities of this factor.

Sexual object choice. This refers to the gender of the sexual activity partner. It is not, as some people believe, a determinant of whether a person is homoerotic, ambisexual, or heteroerotic. For example, if a woman (man) engages in sexual activity with another woman (man), the sexual *act* is homosexual. This fact carries no implication for either person's orientation, because orientation includes much more than sexual activity; its primary components are preference for gender of sexual activity partner and preference for gender of affectional relationship partner. A specific sex act (or two or seven or ten) might well have *no* relationship to preference. (A more detailed discussion of orientation is included later in this chapter.)

Development of sexual object choice. Research investigating the age at which a person becomes aware of sexual attraction to someone else, although scarce, indicates that it begins during puberty and adolescence, with clear preferences for partners developed around ages 15 to 17 for males and 18 to 20 for females.[27] Exactly how that attraction develops is unknown. The clues that exist indicate that it is not a result of the influence of the prebirth biological factor.[28] Instead, it appears that environmental influences are responsible. This development does not always occur as an either-or situation. It may begin with sexual activity with both genders, and either remain that way or develop into a preference for one gender.

Confounding variables relating to object choice. As we have mentioned, for most people, gender and gender identity match. However, there are some for whom this is not true. These are transsexuals, people whose gender identity is at odds with their gender. For example, a genetic female may have a male gender identity, or a genetic male may have a female gender identity. Discussing the gender of a person's sexual partner is a simple process when the gender and gender identity of the partner match. When they do not, as in the case of transsexuals, the discussion becomes much more complex.

Take, for example, two genetic males who are engaging in sexual activity. If one of them is a preoperative transsexual (that is, no operation has yet been performed to alter the appearance of the body), an outside observer would view the act as homosexual. However, to the transsexual, the act is heterosexual, because the transsexual's gender identity is female,[29] and the partner is of the opposite gender. If that person chose a female partner, the observer would identify the act as heterosexual, that is, a male and a female engaging in sexual activity. To the transsexual, it would be viewed as a homosexual act, because both participants consider themselves female.

In establishing an act as heterosexual or homosexual, one must, therefore, consider the gender *identity* of the participants as well as their genders. However, for purposes of presenting the model, the identification of the object choice will be by gender identity with the understanding that the designation assumes an agreement of gender and gender identity for the object choice.

Sexual goal. The second part of the psychological factor is the identification of the reasons for engaging in sexual behavior with a partner. These reasons are probably as varied as snow-flakes, with combinations for a particular person comprising a unique set. For some, the reason is simple: reproduction. For others, it is pleasure; and for others, it may be pleasure and reproduction.[30] Among the many reasons is also the goal of reaching orgasm. This is one of the more common, as is pleasure. In addition to these more commonly known reasons, there are other possible motivations for engaging in sexual behavior with a partner, such as validating gender identity and role; establishing or reaffirming a statement of control or power; obtaining a favor; wanting to please a partner; obtaining money; releasing tension; expressing anger, commitment, love, ownership; or any combinations of all of these. Trying to identify any one goal that would help distinguish one category from another is not simple.

Because many people engage in sexual activity for its pleasure-providing qualities, using pleasure as the goal for sexual activity will enable us to indicate an instance in which some other very specific motivation exists, such as might be true under the categorical heading of prostitute, where money would appear instead of pleasure. Although some prostitutes may report that pleasure is included in the activity, the term implies that the activity is pursued for monetary reasons. Pleasure would appear as the goal under the category homosexual, because gays engage in sexual activity for the same reasons that nongays do. However, if the categorical heading were homosexual prostitute, then the category would be distinguished from others by using the term *money* opposite the goal component.

Arousal pattern. The third part of the psychological factor, arousal pattern, refers to the means by which a person becomes sexually aroused or excited, or in common parlance, what "turns the person on." Although it is not certain when arousal patterns begin developing, the reports of beginning conscious masturbation and seeking sexual activity with a partner seem to indicate that they have begun to exist as a person moves through puberty.

There are multiple sources of arousal. They include fantasies, people with particular types of bodies, specific body parts, passages from stories, movies, scenery, animals, inanimate objects, textures, situations, odors, emotions, sensations, and combinations of these. Most individuals have a variety of arousal sources. For example, one person might be aroused by reading a sexually explicit passage from a book, seeing someone with a particular buttock or leg shape, lying in a sylvan glade with a waterfall, or being massaged in a candlelit room while the stereo plays some appropriate music.

Trying to identify any one source that would help analyze similarities and differences across a variety of categories is simple *only* when an individual has a limited or exclusive means of arousal. This might be the case with an exclusive fetishist who would be aroused only if the partner were wearing a specific blue and yellow scarf around the left ankle.

In searching for a common arousal source to use as a representation of the many variations, we chose manipulation of the genitals. This is with full recognition of the fact that genital manipulation will not always create sexual arousal. Anyone who has had a physical examination in which the genital area is touched is apt to be aware of the nonarousing quality of these manipulations. Also, the person who finds a particular sexual encounter filled with anxiety or concern might not respond to genital manipulation.[31] However, manipulation of the genitals is effective in establishing or maintaining arousal for most people, if the circumstances are considered appropriate. Where something other than ''genital manipulation'' appears in the chart, it is indicative that the identified arousal source is predominant and may be exclusive.

Interrelationship of factors

As we have indicated, the biological factor is most influential before birth. After that, the sex hormones become dormant and the sociological factor becomes strongest. The psychological factor is interrelated with the sociological factor during the development of gender identity and gender role behavior. However, before puberty, its influence primarily establishes a person's ability to integrate biology, sociology, and psychology at puberty when all three exert strong influences at the same time. Before that, the psychological factor is still developing and is reflected in the child's self-image, relationships with peers and adults, attitudes toward explicit sexual behaviors alone and with others, and attitudes toward appropriate (for self) role behavior.

During puberty, the biological factor again exerts influence as sex hormones are reactivated, causing changes in body structure and thereby affecting self-image. The sociological factor is also strong in that dating behavior usually begins during puberty and adolescence, and attempting to behave like a man or a woman appears to create some concern. In addition, it is during puberty and adolescence that most people appear to become aware of sexual arousal sources, especially the gender of a potential sex partner. The manner in which a person deals with each of the three factors and their interrelationships with each other during this period of puberty and early adolescence depends on his or her psychological development before this.

In some instances, there may have been a very strong negative predisposition established earlier, as in a case where some traumatic event centered around sexual expression, such as sometimes happens with masturbation. For example, after a classroom discussion of masturbation, a female college student confided to the instructors that she was very uncomfortable masturbating and could not enjoy it, even though she knew there was nothing physically harmful about it. After some questioning, she related that her mother had discovered her masturbating when she was about 7 years old. Her mother scolded her and chastised her by forcing her to repeat the action in front of her father, to show him ''what a terrible thing she was doing.'' This totally inappropriate parental reaction quite obviously had a psychological effect on that woman's attitude toward masturbation.

The negative predisposition could also be a result of consistent messages that the child receives about particular aspects of sexuality. For example, some children often hear negative information about people who are homoerotic. Believing that gays are sick, terrible, horrible people is not apt to make the awareness of one's own gayness a positive experience, and, in fact, might cause considerable trauma. Similarly, with arousal pattern, if someone develops an arousal pattern that is not in keeping with the society's model, it will perhaps cause concern, as with the male transvestite who is aroused by wearing women's clothes.

The sociological factor influences the psychological and biological factors. For example, Julia Heiman's study on sexual arousal sources in women indicated that some women had either not learned to recognize the biological signals that were present at arousal or else were taught to deny that they existed.[32] In sex therapy, the power of the social dictates for male gender role behavior has been illustrated in that erectile dysfunction has sometimes been caused by a man's inability to live up to the societal expectations for masculinity.[33] Each of these examples indicates that all three factors are interrelated to some extent.

Summary

The development of the model attempting to describe the possible interrelationship and importance of each of the dimensions—biological, sociological, and psychological—permits an analysis of the similarities and differences between and among various categorized individuals. The fact that variances can and do occur in each component of the three factors and that each of the components interrelates with the others in some way indicates that the total outcome of the process of psychosexual development can be different for each individual. We have discussed the factors and their components in a rather broad general sense. There are many more complexities to each one than can be presented here. Indeed, a discussion of each component is worthy of at least a book. How-

ever, we have attempted to present the model in a manner that will make the reader aware of some of the more important aspects of the development of the sexual adult, while at the same time indicating possible sources of concern to the child.

THE TABLE AND ITS INTERPRETATION

Table 1 is an attempt to present the model visually and to show the way in which it can be used to analyze the similarities and differences in various categories of people. To simplify the chart, the *gender* designation as F or M represents the label given as a result of external genitals. *Gender identity* is presented as F or M, either corresponding to or contrasting with gender. *Gender role* is identified as F or M, recognizing that within either of those identifications, androgyny could be assumed if it is an acceptable social behavior for either or both genders. That is, if appropriate behavior for a genetic female is androgynous behavior, then the interpretation of the F identified as gender role would include androgyny. If androgyny is not acceptable, as appears to be the case in some cultures, then a separate identification of androgyny must be included. It might also be appropriate for a categorical heading modifier, such as androgynous heterosexual or androgynous homosexual.

As one reads through the few categories given as examples, certain facts should become evident. An examination of the first three categories—heterosexual, ambisexual, and homosexual—shows that the only difference evident among the three appears in the psychological factor next to the object component. Although many people believe otherwise, object choice is really the only major difference between the three groups; yet this one difference has led to a social stigmatization of gays that is bound to have some effect on psychosexual development.

However, whether that effect is positive or negative varies. For example, the lack of a socially acceptable role model may inhibit some people and may allow others to express their creativity. The existence of a very negative role model may mean that some people will adopt the model whereas others will view it as not being applicable to them.

Table 1 □ Chart for biosociopsychological model of psychosexual development

	Biological		Sociological		Psychological		
	Somatotype*	Gender	Gender identity	Gender role	Object choice	Goal	Arousal pattern
Heterosexual	XX	F	F	F	M	Pleasure	Genital manipulation
	XY	M	M	M	F	Pleasure	Genital manipulation
Ambisexual	XX	F	F	F	M or F	Pleasure	Genital manipulation
	XY	M	M	M	M or F	Pleasure	Genital manipulation
Homosexual	XX	F	F	F	F	Pleasure	Genital manipulation
	XY	M	M	M	M	Pleasure	Genital manipulation
Male heterosexual transvestite	XY	M	M	M	F	Pleasure	Cross-dressing
Heterosexual transsexual	XX	F	M	M	F	Pleasure	Genital manipulation
	XY	M	F	F	M	Pleasure	Genital manipulation
Homosexual transsexual	XX	F	M	M	M	Pleasure	Genital manipulation
	XY	M	F	F	F	Pleasure	Genital manipulation
Heterosexual masochist	XX	F	F	F	M	Pleasure	Receive pain
	XY	M	M	M	F	Pleasure	Receive pain
Heterosexual fetishist	XX	F	F	F	M	Pleasure	Inanimate object
	XY	M	M	M	F	Pleasure	Inanimate object
Androgynous heterosexual	XX	F	F	F & M	M	Pleasure	Genital manipulation
	XY	M	M	M & F	F	Pleasure	Genital manipulation

*Chromosomes, hormones, internal and external genitalia, gonads.

36

Gays, as a group, are just as varied individually as nongays are. Just as some heterosexuals are socially well adjusted, so are some homosexuals. Just as some heterosexuals are pedophiles, so are some homosexuals. The only real differentiating characteristic that exists is the gender of the person who is preferred for sexual activity and affectional relationships.

There are some biases evident in the chart. Note, for example, the two categories for transsexual: heterosexual transsexual and homosexual transsexual. The definition of transsexual is satisfied by the fact that gender does not match gender identity. The orientation aspect is indicated at the object component. This is obviously a bias that indicates that gender *identity* is more important than gender in identifying orientation when the two do not match. Although there may be some disagreement with that bias, it is based on the fact that treatment for transsexuals has primarily followed a procedure in which the actual appearance of the body is altered as much as possible to coincide with the gender identity.

Although neither the chart nor the presentation of the model answer all the questions associated with psychosexual development, they at least establish a beginning. When all the components of the factors and the ways in which individuals differ within those components are considered; it is no wonder that Havelock Ellis, in his *Studies on the Psychology of Sex* in the early twentieth century, wrote, "So far from the facts of normal sex development, sex emotions, and sex needs being uniform and constant . . . the range of variation within fairly normal limits is immense, and it is impossible to meet with two individuals whose records are nearly identical."[34] Or as Edward Brecher paraphrased, "Everybody is not like you or your friends and neighbors. . . . Even your friends and neighbors may not be as much like you as you suppose."[35] In a more recent publication, John Gagnon wrote, "No individual's sexual script or actual pattern of sexual activity is an exact replica of the sexual script that is offered or preferred by the culture."[36]

Each of them is indicating that sexuality is very individualistic or idiosyncratic. Table 1 groups people according to category, but one must realize that individuals are not easily categorized. The components included in each of the three factors are extremely complex, and that complexity must not be overlooked when one is dealing with another individual.

SEXUAL IDENTITY

A person's sexual identity is defined as a combination of his or her gender identity, gender role behavior, and sexual orientation.[37] Since we have already discussed the first two components in the section on the biosociopsychological model, we will limit discussion in this section to the third component, orientation.

Sexual orientation/sexual preference

Sexual orientation refers to the *object* component of the psychological factor of the biosociopsychological model. It is an attempt to identify the gender of the person's sexual and primary relationship partner. Simply stated, sexual orientation is usually defined by two factors: (1) the physical, which includes gender preference for sexual partners and sexual relationships,[38] and (2) the affectional, which includes gender preference for primary emotional relationships.[39]

This orientation has traditionally been labeled homosexual, bisexual or ambisexual,[40] and heterosexual, and has sometimes been presented as existing on a continuum with homosexual at one end and heterosexual at the other.[41] However, most research literature is inconsistent in establishing criteria for identifying orientation of subjects, with the majority of studies dichotomizing into heterosexual and homosexual, often based on physical activity alone.[42] Although certainly simplifying matters for the researchers, this dichotomy has done much to further complicate the acquisition of knowledge through research by ignoring the multiple components of orientation. From this dichotomy arise such statements as, "Well, you have to be either homosexual or heterosexual,'' or ''If I engage in sexual activity with someone of the same sex, then I must be a homosexual.'' Neither statement is necessarily true.

Although the definition of orientation involving only the two previously mentioned factors may be sufficient for simplicity, it is not sufficient for full understanding. In addition to the preference for sexual and affectional partners, a historical perspective should be included, along with an exploration of partners in sexual fantasy. Thus, rather than a simple two-factor phenomenon, sexual orientation is composed of six parts: past and present partner preference for sexual activity, primary affectional relationships, and fantasy; with each of the six parts existing on a continuum from exclusively homoerotic to exclusively heteroerotic. This means that it is possible to develop a six-part orientation profile for an individual.

Components to be considered in exploring orientation

Partner preference for:
1. Sexual activity and relationships
   a. Historically
   b. Presently
2. Affectional relationships
   a. Historically
   b. Presently
3. Fantasy
   a. Historically
   b. Presently

Within each of the six parts, a continuum exists from exclusively homoerotic to exclusively heteroerotic. Various points along the continuum may be identified as follows:

exclusive homoerotic—preference for same-gender partners only

predominant homoerotic—preference primarily for same-gender partners; occasional preference for opposite-gender partners

ambisexual homoerotic—usually preference not based on gender; occasional preference for same-gender partners

ambisexual bisexual—preference not based on gender

ambisexual heteroerotic—usually preference not based on gender; occasional preference for opposite-gender partners

predominant heteroerotic—preference primarily opposite-gender partners; occasional preference for same-gender partners

exclusive heteroerotic—preference for opposite-gender partners only

The fact that these points have been identified does not make them discrete categories. On any one of the six parts of orientation, a person might be somewhere between any two points. It is important to remember that this is a continuum, not a set of discrete points.

Identifying orientation is not too difficult when all the components match. If someone prefers to engage in sexual activity with, to establish sexual relationships with, to form primary relationships with, and to fantasize about someone of the same gender and accomplishes all of these, then the orientation is clear. That person has a homoerotic orientation. However, one is less likely to find this person seeking help to identify or clarify orientation than someone for whom the components do not agree. Therefore, it is important to explore each of the components with the understanding that it is possible for the physical and affectional aspects of orientation to differ. One person might have a physical heteroerotic orientation and an affectional homoerotic orientation, or one might have an ambisexual orientation for both aspects.

Preference. The issue of preference is critical in understanding orientation. For some people there is no gender preference. For others it may be only in one or two of the three aspects: physical, affectional, or fantasy. For some people, preference is realized, and for others it is not, because conditions may exist that preclude that realization. This does not negate the orientation.

For example, a woman might prefer to establish sexual relationships with another woman, but the social pressures against such relationships cause her to limit her sexual activity to a man. At the physical level of orientation, she would be homo-erotic, because her preference is for same-gender partners, even though she is not acting on this preference. Another woman might have no prefer-ence; she might enjoy sexual activity with either gender but find herself in a prison with no oppor-tunity to engage in sexual relationships with men. The fact that she might establish a satisfying sexual and emotional relationship with another woman does not alter her ambisexual orientation at the physical activity preference level. If this same woman also has no gender preference for affec-tional relationships, then her physical and affec-tional orientation components are ambisexual.

If a man prefers sexual relationships with an-other man and prefers affectional relationships with a woman, then his physical orientation would be homoerotic and his affectional orientation would be heteroerotic. The if's could obviously continue. The important fact is that there are people who fit each of these and their orientations are not always easily categorized by a single word.

History. Orientation may have a historical component that is different from the present. This means that orientation may change over a person's life span. Someone may have a clear preference for gender of physical and affectional partners at present that is different from that of the past. This is exemplified primarily in the literature on ambi-sexuality.

Ambisexuality or bisexuality. In his attempt at defining bisexuality, Fred Klein emphasizes the importance of time by identifying four types of bisexuals: transitional, historical, sequential, and ones without a modifier.[43] Transitional bisexuality is a stage from a heteroerotic to a homoerotic orientation (or the reverse). Historical bisexuals presently have a clear preference for gender of partners but have bisexual preferences in their past. Sequential bisexuals have a heteroerotic ori-entation at one time during their lives and then later have a homoerotic orientation, then a hetero-

erotic, and so on. As Klein described it, "In se-quential bisexuality a person's sexual relationships are with only one gender at any given time. The frequency of gender change, of course, varies ac-cording to person and circumstance."[43] There are also bisexuals—people who physically and emo-tionally establish relationships with both genders. There are two major points in the discussion of time: (1) it is possible for a person's preferences to alter over a lifetime, which means that orientation can be dynamic; and (2) identifying orientation should include an added dimension of time, which means that there should be a historical orientation as well as a current orientation.

Fantasy. The role of sexual fantasy in orienta-tion is not clear. It is possible that sexual fantasy, especially masturbatory fantasy, is the ultimate in-dictor of one's orientation.[44] However, it may also be true that sexual fantasy is a totally separate phenomenon, having no necessary relationship to reality.[45]

Shively and DeCecco suggest that behavior and fantasy should be included in a complete iden-tification of orientation, realizing that there may be a difference between the two.[46] This appears to be the most practical approach, since studies of sexual fantasy and its relationship to reality indicate that often little, if any, relationship exists between the two. For example, in her study of women's sexual fantasies, Barbara Hariton found that the primary function of sexual fantasies for the women in her study was to enhance sexual pleasure,[47] and that the content of the fantasies had little or no relation-ship to the reality of their lives. However, there appeared to be an indication that the more self-confident women were able to enjoy their fantasies more. Hariton suggests that these women are able to separate fantasy content from reality with an understanding that the two have nothing in com-mon. As Hariton states, "[The self-confident woman] permits herself inexplicable images and ideas without feeling any threat to her integrity or sanity."[48] Exploring fantasy orientation is valid; however, inferring reality from that exploration of fantasy is questionable.

Summary

Our six-part approach to sexual orientation begins to identify some of the complications that arise in working with individuals. With this model, there is a physical orientation, an affectional orientation, and a fantasy orientation, with each of those three further divided into a past (historical) component and a present component. A person's behavior may be totally at variance with all aspects of orientation, and the various parts of orientation might not all agree. Thus, the gender of the sexual partners might be of little help in determining sexual orienation, and it might be impossible to identify a single orientation for some people.

Two case histories may help explain the orientation categories. Janice currently identifies herself as a lesbian. Her self-identity is based on her perception of both her historical and current preferences. Janice is in her late thirties, and her current legal status is "divorced."

Her sexual partner history includes both women and men, but her preference has always been toward women. She enjoys occasional sexual activity with men, but considers that to be, as she states, "fun and games," and she does not view that activity as relevant to her orientation. However, she does indicate that in the past about once a year, for a very brief period of about one day, she has had a desire for a male sex partner. The last time this occurred was about 3 years ago. Her primary emotional relationships have always been with women, including the duration of her marriage. She reports that her sexual fantasies are about 90% heteroerotic, a fact that she views as irrelevant to her orientation.

Thus, at the physical level, her orientation is (1) historically—predominant homoerotic; (2) presently—exclusive homoerotic. At the affectional level, the orientation is (1) historically—exclusive homoerotic; (2) presently—exclusive homoerotic. At the fantasy level, orientation is (1) historically—predominant heteroerotic; (2) presently—predominant heteroerotic. Note that these labels generally ignore her sexual activity with her husband, because that activity was not her preference at that time.

Although all this information is important for any research on orientation that would include Janice as a subject, she considers herself to be lesbian, viewing her fantasies and her activity with her husband as of no consequence in her orientation.

Geoff currently accepts no general orientation label for himself. His statement about his orientation is, "I know what I'm not, but I'm not sure that any single label would apply to me." He is in his early forties, and his current legal status is "single." His sexual partner history includes both women and men, although until his midthirties his partners were exclusively men. His sexual partner preference followed that same pattern, that is, exclusively men until his midthirties and then both men and women. Presently, his preference includes both genders; however, frequency of preference is higher for men than for women. His primary emotional relationships were with men until his early thirties, when he began a primary relationship with a man and a woman. That relationship is still in existence at present. His sexual fantasies are predominantly homoerotic, with occasional heteroerotic fantasies, and on rare occasions his fantasies include both genders in a bisexual context.

Thus, at the sexual activity level, his orientation is (1) historically—predominant homoerotic; (2) presently—somewhere between predominant homoerotic and ambisexual homoerotic. His affectional orientation is (1) historically—exclusive homoerotic originally, then moving to ambisexual bisexual; (2) presently, ambisexual bisexual. At the fantasy level, orientation is (1) historically—exclusive homoerotic, moving to predominant homoerotic; (2) presently—predominant homoerotic. He mentioned that some of his friends identify him as gay, but he feels that the label negates an emotional and sexual component of his life that he considers very important.

Using this model in a counseling situation

means that the client will be encouraged to explore the many aspects of his or her life that constitute sexual orientation. It may be necessary for the counselor to reinforce the fact that orientation is not a simple, single concept and that it is not necessary for the various components to agree in order for the person to be considered healthy. A client seeking help in sorting out sexual orientation will usually be looking for a single label. This is not always possible, nor is it always necessary. It is important to explain that there are various aspects to orientation and to help the client explore the meaning of each of those aspects in her or his life.

END NOTES

1. Sex Information and Education Council of the U.S., Inc. (herein after referred to as SIECUS), 84 Fifth Avenue, New York, N.Y. 10011.
2. SIECUS. "The SIECUS/Uppsala principles basic to education for sexuality." *SIECUS Report,* 1980, *8*(3), 8.
3. Hyde, J. *Understanding human sexuality.* New York: McGraw-Hill, 1979, pp. 5-10.
4. DeLora, J., & Warren, C. *Understanding sexual interaction.* Boston: Houghton Mifflin, 1977, p. 21.
5. Snively, W., & Beshear, D. *Textbook of pathophysiology.* Philadelphia: Lippincott, 1972, pp. 16-17.
6. Money, J., & Ehrhardt, A. *Man and woman, boy and girl.* Baltimore: Johns Hopkins University Press, 1972, pp. 32-33.
7. Money, J. "Human behavior cytogenetics: Review of psychopathology in three syndromes—47,XXY; 47,XYY; and 45,X." *Journal of Sex Research,* 1975, *11*(3), 181-200.
8. Money & Ehrhardt, 1972, p. 7.
9. Money & Ehrhardt, 1972, pp. 95-114.
10. Lewis, V. "Androgen insensitivity syndrome: Erotic component of gender identity in nine women." In R. Gemme & C. Wheeler (Eds.), *Progress in sexology.* New York: Plenum, 1977, pp. 61-62; Luria, Z., & Rose, M. *Psychology of human sexuality.* New York: Wiley & Sons, 1979, pp. 139-142.
11. For an excellent example of the pressures, see Gould, L. "Stories for free children: X—A fabulous child's story." *Ms.,* December 1972, pp. 74-76; 105-106; and Gould, L. *X—A fabulous child's story.* Houston: Daughters Publishing, 1978.
12. Brown, D. "Sex-role development in a changing culture." *Psychological Bulletin,* 1956, *55*(4), 232.
13. Money & Ehrhardt, 1972, p. 4.
14. SIECUS principles. Principle 3, p. 8.
15. Chodorow, N. "Being and doing: A cross-cultural examination of the socialization of males and females." In V. Gornick & B. Moran (Eds.), *Woman in sexist society.* New York: Basic Books, 1971, pp. 259-291; see especially pp. 270-286.
16. Katchadourian, H., & Lunde, D. *Fundamentals of human sexuality* (2nd ed.). New York: Holt, Rinehart and Winston, 1975, pp. 214-221.
17. SIECUS/Uppsala Principles, pp. 8-9.
18. Friedan, B. *The feminine mystique.* New York: W.W. Norton, 1963; Hite, S. *The Hite report,* New York, Macmillan, 1976.
19. Hite, 1976, p. 365.
20. Morgan, M. *The total woman.* Old Tappan, N.J.: Fleming H. Revell, 1973.
21. Zilbergeld, B. *Male sexuality.* Boston: Little, Brown, 1978.
22. Farrell, W. *The liberated man,* New York: Bantam Books, 1975, p. 4.
23. Green, R. "'Sissies' and 'tomboys.'" *SIECUS Reports,* 1979, *7*(3), 1-2; 15.
24. Bem, S. "Sex role adaptability: One consequence of psychological androgyny." *Journal of Personality and Social Psychology,* 1975, *31*(4), 634-643.
25. Bem, S., Martyna, W., & Watson, C. "Sex typing and androgyny: Further explorations of the expressive domain." *Journal of Personality and Social Psychology,* 1976, *34*(5), 1016-1023.
26. Kelly, J., & Worell, J. "Parent behaviors related to masculine, feminine, and androgynous sex role orientations." *Journal of Consulting and Clinical Psychology,* 1976, *44*, 843-851; Kelly, J., & Worell, J. "New formulations of sex roles and androgyny: A critical review." *Journal of Consulting and Clinical Psychology,* 1977, *45*(6), 1101-1115; Spence, J., & Helmreich, R. *Masculinity & femininity: Their psychological dimensions, correlates, and antecedents.* Austin: University of Texas Press, 1979, esp. pp. 130-228.
27. See section on development of awareness in Chapter 5 of this book.
28. Masters W., & Johnson, V. *Homosexuality in perspective,* Boston: Little, Brown, 1979, pp. 409-411.
29. Money, J., & Tucker, P. *Sexual signatures: On being a man or a woman.* Boston: Little, Brown, 1975, pp. 31-35.
30. SIECUS/Uppsala Principles, Principle 6, p. 8.
31. Masters & Johnson, 1979, p. 225.
32. Heiman, J. "Women's sexual arousal." *Psychology Today,* April 1975, pp.93-94.
33. Gould, R. "Measuring masculinity by the size of a paycheck." In J. Pleck & J. Sawyer, *Men and masculinity.* Englewood Cliffs, N.J.: Prentice-Hall, 1974, pp.96-100. See also Zilbergeld, 1979, pp. 241-242.
34. Ellis, H. *Studies in the psychology of sex.* As cited in E.

Brecher, *The sex researchers*. Boston: Little, Brown, 1969, p. 39.

35. Brecher, 1969, p. 39.

36. Gagnon, J. *Human sexualities*. Glenview, Ill.: Scott, Foresman, 1979, p. 6.

37. Hawkins, R. "The Uppsala connection: The development of principles basic to education for sexuality." *SIECUS Report*, 1980, *8*(3), 13-14.

38. Hawkins, 1980, p. 14.

39. Shively, M., & DeCecco, J. "Components of sexual identity." *Journal of Homosexuality*, 1977, *3*(1), 45.

40. Coons, F. "Ambisexuality as an alternative adaption." *Journal of the American College Health Association*, 1972, *21*(2), 142-144.

41. The most commonly used continuum has been the one suggested by Alfred Kinsey and associates in Kinsey, A., Pomeroy, W., & Martin, C. *Sexual behavior in the human male*. Philadelphia: W.B. Saunders, 1948, p. 638.

42. For examples of differing definitions, see Masters & Johnson, 1979, pp. 9-12; and Bell, A., & Weinberg, M. *Homosexualities: A study of diversity among men and women*. New York: Simon & Schuster, 1978, pp. 29-34; 49-52.

43. Klein, F. *The bisexual option: A concept of one-hundred percent intimacy*. New York: Arbor House, 1978, p. 17.

44. See, for example, Klein, 1978, p. 16; and Shively & DeCecco, 1977, p. 46.

45. Goleman, D., & Bush, S. "The liberation of sexual fantasy." *Psychology Today*, October 1977, pp. 48-53; 104-107.

46. Shively & DeCecco, 1977, p. 46.

47. Hariton, B. "The sexual fantasies of women." *Psychology Today*, March 1973, pp. 39-44.

48. Hariton, 1973, p. 44.

5

Becoming gay

ETIOLOGY VERSUS ANTECEDENTS

We have pointed out at various places in this book that, contrary to popular opinion, lesbianism and homosexuality cannot be said to have an etiology; sexual preference is not a condition for which there are specifiable "causes." Indeed, the very concept of looking for causation, particularly as used by the medical and psychoanalytic schools, suggests all too often that one needs to find the cause of homosexuality in order to effect a cure. It is our belief that gay people learn to gain satisfaction in relationships with members of the same gender in the same ways that nongays learn to gain satisfaction from relationships with members of the opposite gender. Since all voluntary (that is, nonreflexive) behavior is learned, we also assume that the learned behaviors making up sexual preference have some kinds of antecedents; something leads to a given individual learning one sexual preference over another. One must be careful to distinguish between etiological and antecedent conditions for several reasons.

First, as pointed out above, the concept of etiology implies that homosexuality and lesbianism have a specifiable cause. There is no evidence to indicate that this is the case any more than that heterosexuality has a single specifiable cause. We shall discuss research findings relating specifically to this issue in succeeding chapters.

Second, the notion of etiology is often associated in people's minds with illness. We want to be sure that we remove the concepts of lesbianism and homosexuality from any connection with the concept of illness and that we make it clear that where there is no illness, there can and need be no cure.

Third, we want to identify any variables that may be related to lesbianism and homosexuality during stages of the life cycle, especially as these may affect the counseling process. The difference here is essentially one of implication; for, although etiology implies causation, antecedents do not. Thus, for example, an individual growing up in England learns to drive on the left side of the road, whereas someone from the United States learns to drive on the right. There are a number of antecedents to these kinds of behaviors, some of them directly causal, some of them not. An antecedent to learning how to drive on the left hand side of the road would be residence in England, but residence in England does not cause one to drive on the left. Furthermore, there could be a number of antecedents to driving on the left, among them, residence in any country in which residents drive on the left side of the road. Knowing that someone drives on the left doesn't automatically tell us where she or he comes from. Similarly, there are undoubtedly antecedents to being gay, and some of them may even occur frequently and show a high degree of association with same-gender sexual preference. This does not make them causes of homosexuality or lesbianism, or even necessarily good predictors of sexual preference.

Because being gay involves a complex set of behaviors, thoughts, and feelings, it is virtually impossible to pinpoint any specific antecedents to becoming gay that may not in a number of instances also be antecedents to becoming heteroerotic. Like being nongay, being gay includes sexual, social, psychological, and emotional experiences. Gay people, like nongay people, come from all racial, ethnic, and socioeconomic walks of life; from one- and two-parent homes, happy homes, broken homes, mediocre homes; from families in which the father is dominant, in which the mother is dominant, and in which father and mother are equally dominant. Given the great diversity of gay childhood, adolescent, and adult experiences, it is not only almost impossible, but virtually meaningless to try to pinpoint one, two, or even a multiplicity of factors that inevitably will lead to an individual's being gay.

In this section we will discuss some of the common features of gay male and lesbian experiences in various stages of the life cycle, particularly as the gay person goes about the difficult task of developing her or his sexual identity. There are indeed some commonly occurring variables in the lives of most gay people, and it is important that helping professionals understand the possible effects of these variables on gay clients.

SEXUAL IDENTITY

An understanding of the components of sexual identity and the way sexual identity develops is essential to any discussion of homosexuality and lesbianism. Sexual identity is composed of three components: gender identity, gender role behavior, and sexual orientation. In our preceding chapter on the biosociopsychological model of psychosexual development, we discussed each in detail. However, because researchers and others often confuse them, we would like to briefly summarize the explanations of gender and the sexual identity components here.

Gender is the core morphology. It is the biological aspect of the human that differentiates male and female. As we pointed out, for most of us it appears that all the aspects of core morphology match; those with XX chromosomes are born with all the components of a female body, and those

with XY chromosomes are born with all the components of a male body.

Gender identity is personal identification of gender. Again, most of us who are born with male or female bodies develop an internalized knowledge of ourselves that corresponds to our gender. Most of us who are born male develop a male gender identity, and most of us who are born female develop a female gender identity. As far as can be determined, the most common situation in which internalization does not match gender is in the case of transsexualism. Gay men and lesbians develop gender identities consistent with their genders.

Gender role behavior, called sex role behavior in much of the literature, is the behavior that is exhibited by the individual. Most gender role behavior is culturally determined, and will, therefore, vary culturally. Also, because it is learned behavior, it will vary individually. It is on this aspect that much of the research on lesbians and gay men is carried out, primarily because the gay stereotypes indicate opposite-gender role behavior; that is, the research supposes that lesbians act like men and gay men act like women. Although gender role behavior may be of concern to the lesbian or gay man in that some may be concerned about their feminity or masculinity, respectively, it is most often of concern to others. *"masculine" or "feminine" according to social stereotypes*

The last component of sexual identity, sexual orientation, is the indicator of the gender of the person's sexual and affectional partners. Does the person prefer someone of the same gender or opposite gender for sexual activity and primary relationships, or is gender not an issue? There are several components to orientation: sexual attraction, sexual activity, affectional attraction, and fantasy, with each of these having a historical and a present component. For most gay men and lesbian women, all the components match.

In addition, there is the self-concept aspect: how does the individual identify himself or herself? In counseling, this is probably one of the most important aspects of sexual identity. If a woman has only one or two of the orientation components consistent with a lesbian orientation, yet self-identifies as such, then it is the self-identity that is most important.

For example, a woman may have historically exhibited a preference for male sex partners, but presently prefers females. She may have a historical and present fantasy orientation that is heterosexual, with a historical affectional preference that included both men and women, and a present affectional preference for women only. If her present self-identity is lesbian, then that is her orientation. She may seek counseling because of concern about the discrepancy between her historical orientation and her present fantasy orientation. It is important to explore each of those components in a way that will support her self-identification.

Again, we have simply summarized the three components of sexual identity here. Each of them has many complexities, some of which we discussed in Chapter 4, and the counselor must be aware of those complexities if he or she is to be of help to homoerotic individuals.

DEVELOPING A HOMOEROTIC ORIENTATION
Childhood and adolescent correlates of adult homosexuality and lesbianism

Family background. It is difficult to draw any useful conclusions from available studies that have attempted to determine what "causes" an individual to become a lesbian or a gay man. Those that have been done to date suffer from a variety of problems in both methodology and interpretation. All have the major drawback of relying on the respondents' recall of childhood and adolescent experiences, a procedure that, at best, really tells us more about the relationship of sexual preference to subject recall than to actual historical events.

It is impossible to know to what extent a gay person's current relationships with family members, knowledge of accepted beliefs about the "causes" of lesbianism or homosexuality, experi-

ences with therapists, or other variables may have affected either his or her recall or recounting of childhood events. Anyone who has ever asked a parent and child to describe the same current event (much less an event 10, 20, or 30 years past) is aware of the differences in perception. We can certainly expect such differences in perception to be exacerbated by differential life experiences, particularly when they are likely to be as different as those of a nongay and gay person. We can also expect, of course, heterosexual subjects' recollections of past events to be altered by their life experiences.

Family backgrounds of lesbian women. Mannion,[1] in her excellent review of theory and research on lesbianism, points out several other problems in interpreting data, along with that of recall. Two studies of the family backgrounds of lesbian women[2,3] used projective tests, devices that are inevitably of questionable validity. Kaye et al.[4] used a questionnaire completed by the respondent's analyst, a procedure that moves the data even farther from validity, as well as providing a very biased sample. Swanson et al.[5] had similar problems in that they used case records of lesbians and nongay women in an out-patient clinic. Mannion also notes that, in a number of these studies, "the number of variables compared . . . seemed unlimited. For those in which massive and elaborate questionnaires, individually comparing as many as 400 items, were used, *chance factors alone are likely to produce some significant differences* [emphasis added]."[6]

A final problem that seems to us of major importance, also mentioned by Mannion,[6] is the use of statistical significance by some researchers to suggest practical significance. For example, Kenyon reports that 21.1% of the lesbian women and 0.8% of the nongay women in his study rated their relationship with their mother as a poor one.[7] This is highly statistically significant ($p < .001$), but is of questionable meaningfulness, since both percentages are so low.. If we reverse the percentages and say that 78.9% of the lesbian women and 99.2% of the nongay women had average or better relationships with their mother, it is clear that the great majority of both groups reported good relationships, not poor ones. If we also consider that Kenyon's nongay subjects were married and that gays very often encounter strained relationships with parents because of their sexual preference, it seems possible that the current relationships that these two groups have with their parents may be coloring their perceptions of the qualities of those relationships in the past. In any event, such findings are far from conclusive and can at best be considered suggestive.

Family pathology and lesbianism. There is no clear evidence to substantiate the psychoanalytic belief that lesbianism is the result of family pathology. The conclusions of those studies that indicate pathology[8] are thrown into serious doubt by the kinds of weaknesses discussed previously.

Studies that have fewer methodological weaknesses are less likely to suggest pathology. Swanson et al.[9] Siegelman,[10] and Gundlach and Riess[11] all have done studies that support the notion that serious family problems may mean problems for the adult child that are unrelated to sexual preference. Gundlach and Reiss[11] and Hogan, Fox, and Kirchner[12] collected data that show that *nonclinical* samples of lesbians do not report the kinds of family problems that both nongay and lesbian client samples report. Hogan, Fox, and Kirchner say of their nonclinical samples of 205 lesbian women that "basically these women stemmed [sic] from intact homes, from parents who were not perceived as showing favoritism, and from parents whose marriage was rated at the midpoint in a happiness-unhappiness dimension."[13] Mannion summarizes the findings of the studies she reviewed as follows:

> There is no obvious conclusion to be drawn from the data available about the parental factors that may contribute to lesbian development without the issue being clouded with the related variables of the lesbian's psychological health.[14]

Family backgrounds of gay men. Conclusions based on studies of gay males who are psychiatric patients[15] or institutionalized[16] or on studies of single case histories[17] often suggest that the family

dynamics during the gay male's childhood were responsible for his sexual orientation. For example, Allen, basing his conclusions on his psychoanalytic treatment of homosexuals, published seven articles identifying the following *causal* factors: either excessive affection for or hostility toward the mother; hostility toward the father or affection for a father who is perceived as less masculine than other males; or a divorce or death that resulted in the absence of the father from the home.[18] Greenblatt, studying gay males who were not psychiatric patients or institutionalized, reported that they perceived their fathers as good, generous, pleasant, dominant, and underprotective; and their mothers as good, generous, pleasant, not dominant or subordinate, and not overprotective or underprotective.[19] Wood, in his study of 127 noninstitutionalized homosexuals found that over half reported happy, stable family structure during childhood.[20] Saghir and Robins' study of 89 homosexuals indicated that 40% perceived their fathers as dominant in the household, whereas 71% of the heterosexuals perceived their fathers as such.[21] In her summary of research on the family backgrounds of gay men, Evelyn Hooker indicates that the studies do "not support the assumption that pathological parent-child relationships are either necessary or sufficient antecedents or determinants of adult homosexuality."[22] In his discussion of research on childhood family relationships of homosexuals, Marmor refutes the notion that family dynamics are causal[23] and agrees with Siegelman, who shows that exclusive homosexuals who do not exhibit stereotypical feminine behavior and who are socially and psychologically adjusted come from families that are not described as being pathological.[24]

Family background data—implications. The relevance of these data to intervention with lesbian women and gay men seems to be twofold. First, homoerotic individuals who have serious psychological and emotional problems as adults may have had problematic childhood experiences, but there is no reason to assume that these experiences are related to their sexual orientation. In fact, such an assumption would probably be irrelevant, if not counterproductive, to successful intervention. Second, treatment of lesbian women and gay men who do not have serious emotional and psychological problems but seek professional help can be usefully focused on here-and-now problems of living rather than on some presumed family background problem. In no event is a clinician justified in assuming either individual or family pathology on the basis of a client's sexual preference.

Early sexual behavior

Early sexual behavior of lesbians. Gundlach and Riess and Saghir and Robins both found a number of significant differences in the recalled sexual experiences of heterosexual and lesbian samples, but many of the differences are based on unimpressive percentage differences like those discussed earlier. For example, 31% of the lesbian women and 18% of the heterosexual women in Saghir and Robins' study recalled dating boys before age 16. Although this difference is highly significant statistically, it leaves 69% of the lesbian and 82% of the nongay women recalling that they began dating after 16.[25]

It is not clear what can be inferred from these kinds of data that will be of help in intervention with lesbian clients at any age; and unfortunately, a great many of the significant findings either are based on similar percentages of the two groups or are difficult to interpret or apply for present purposes. In general, the early sexual behavior of lesbians and heterosexual women seems to be comparable, based on the recall of these two groups. The major differences in sexual behavior begin to appear when the women are older and more sexually active.

A number of studies have found that the majority of nonclinical samples of lesbian women report having dated and having had sexual experiences with men.[26] The difference between lesbian and nongay women with regard to these experiences

may well be in their reaction to them. In her review, Mannion notes that contrary to the analytic expectation, most lesbian women report neither aversion to nor fear of heterosexual experiences, but rather indifference and lack of arousal.[27] Hogan, Fox, and Kirchner report that 202 of their sample of 205 lesbian women had experienced sex with a male partner, but 28% had never reached orgasm and another 56% had reached orgasm only one to five times. With heterosexual women, however, 64% had reached orgasm one to five times, and another 22% had reached orgasm six to ten times.[28] Whatever the reason for the differential rate of orgasm, this finding certainly suggests a difference in frequency, interest, arousal, or quality of the sexual experiences that these women had with men.

Early sexual behavior of gay men

Masturbation: Self- and mutual. Self-masturbation is the first genital sexual activity of most males, and Saghir and Robins found that this was true for the majority of their heterosexual and homosexual male subjects, although the frequency was significantly higher for the gay men.[29] They further reported that 60% of their gay male sample experienced mutual homosexual masturbation during preadolescence, and an additional 25% did so between the ages of 14 and 19. In their heterosexual sample, 23% had experienced mutual homosexual masturbation, all before the age of 15.[30] Jay and Young found that the majority of their gay men had their first male-male sexual experience during puberty or adolescence, but they do not specify the activity. Their examples reveal mutual masturbation, oral-genital stimulation, and anal intercourse; but it is not possible to clarify frequency for each activity.[31]

Gender of first partner. Neither Saghir and Robins nor Jay and Young investigated the gender of the first sexual partner, but Whitam found that 84% of the exclusive homosexual and 67% of the predominant homosexual men experienced first sexual contact with a male, whereas 82% of the exclusive and 70% of the predominant heterosexual men experienced first sexual contact with a female.[32]

Heterosexual intercourse. Saghir and Robins found that 49% of the gay men and 50% of the heterosexual men started heterosexual intercourse during adolescence.[33] Jay and Young report that 66% of their gay male sample had engaged in heterosexual intercourse at least once, but there is no indication of ages of first heterosexual intercourse.[34]

Dating. Dating behavior for both heterosexual and homosexual males in the Saghir and Robins study was equivalent in frequency during ages 16 to 23. However, the gay men were more likely to date for shorter periods of time than were the heterosexual men.[35] As with the lesbian studies, the gay men generally report neither aversion nor fear of heterosexual activity, but rather emotional and sexual indifference[36] or pleasure that they found to be less satisfying than sexual activity with a man.[37]

Age of awareness of sexual orientation

Awareness of sexual orientation in lesbian women. The majority of lesbian women say that they became aware of their lesbianism (or at least of being sexually "different") and had a sexual experience with another woman before the age of 20. A fairly large number (percentages differ from study to study) knew and/or had such experiences before the age of 15.[38]

Anecdotal evidence suggests that there is a lot of variability regarding the childhood and adolescent experiences and awareness of lesbian women. It seems that many lesbian women may be aware early of crushes on or attractions to female teachers, girlfriends, or other women, of sexual indifference to boys, or both. This may be experienced as exciting and pleasant, as frightening, or as an indication that something is "wrong" with the individual. Some women report that they were comfortable with their behavior until it somehow became labeled. Some report having always been uncomfortable, even though they may not have known why. Some few women seem never to have had any doubts about their sexuality, nor any negative feelings about it.

The quotes below give some examples of lesbian women's recollections of their childhood experiences. The interested reader is referred to the original sources for further examples and information.

☐ My feelings were directed toward girls instead of boys like everyone said they should be. I had no name for my feelings so I decided I was a freak of some kind. During the next couple of years those feelings increased and on a few occasions I made mild advances toward other girls but it seemed as though they thought I was only trying to act silly. I thought I was the only person in the world who possessed these feelings, and it confirmed my belief that I was a freak. I knew absolutely no adult or peer that I could talk to about this. My relationships with everyone became strained, my schoolwork failed badly, and I often considered suicide as an escape from my miserable life.[39]

☐ [Childhood] was a terribly lonely period: I was an only child and I didn't have a hell of a lot to do. I was always looking for friends, for people. I was terrified of boys. They chased you and beat you up. I wasn't really attracted to girls either. Loneliness was my whole battle. Maybe gays feel different very early on? I don't know. I just knew somehow that I was terribly different, an outcast.[40]

☐ I always had a token boyfriend—you had to have that—somebody to escort you to the proms and to homecoming dances. I wasn't particularly thrilled about any of them, but I figured that's the way it was—you have to have one of them around. . . . I've always known that when I really needed to relate to someone that I always could with a woman—its always been a woman.
Did you have any gay feelings at that point?
I didn't have *any* feelings at that point, I was like a robot. We weren't physical at all. I didn't even consider it with girls and when I was physical with boys, it was nothing. God! I thought it was the worst. I literally never thought about gayness. My biggest feeling in high school was that here I was doing everything that I could possibly think of to make it, and I was miserable.[41]

☐ I can . . . remember having a crush on a schoolmate in grade six. . . . We were never overly close friends, as I was aware of my feelings and afraid of them. My next strong feelings didn't come until grade nine. They all seemed to come at once. I was in love with so many people, but again was frightened of my feelings and never attempted anything. I was more afraid of what my parents would think if they ever found out and also I was thinking that it was just a passing phase (a rather long one at that) and that I'd eventually be interested in men. My only interest in boys was whether they were good tree climbers, baseball players, or snake catchers. I was a "tomboy" in every respect.[42]

☐ I remember my first awareness of sexual feelings when I was 11 years old. The source of these feelings was another girl my same age at Campfire Girls. . . . I could hardly keep my hands off her. I thought she was magic. I was that naive and we were incredibly happy. . . . It was not until she had moved away and I had gone on to junior high that the full realization of what those feelings meant to other people came crashing down on me. It was at that time I heard the words "queer" and "homo" for the first time, and I felt very ashamed and guilty.[43]

It's worth noting that a number of incidents, for example, some of those in the Jay and Young book, involve relationships between two or more children or adolescents, one of whom frequently grows up to become heterosexual.

☐ My best friend [from ages 9 to 12] and I used to play with each other quite often though she insists today that she's straight and tells me *I'm* sick. Oh, Lord. . . . At the time, though, we knew it was something to hide.[44]

It is interesting to speculate how these kinds of childhood incidents would be recalled, or if indeed they would even be remembered, by heterosexual adults.

Whatever else we may deduce, it's clear that a sizable number of lesbian women recall having felt different, having known "there was something wrong with them," and often having had sexual experiences with other girls in late childhood or during adolescence.

Awareness of sexual orientation in gay men. Whitam found that feelings of homosexual orientation emerge generally at the same time as feelings of heterosexual orientation. By age 17, all the heterosexual men in his study had experienced sexual attraction to females, and 91% of the homosexual men had experienced sexual attraction to males. He also notes that a few did not become aware of their homosexual orientation until late twenties or thirties, and about one third reported first awareness before the age of 10, but the majority were first aware of sexual attraction to men during puberty and adolescence.[45] The majority (60%) of Jay and Young's gay male respondents first realized their gay orientation during the ages 9 to 15, with an additional 16% from ages 16 to 19. There were a few before age 9 and after age 19.[46] Whitam indicates that awareness of a homosexual orientation sometimes occurs before a person becomes aware that other homosexuals exist or when the only knowledge about gay people is a very negative stereotype that does not seem appropriate for the individual.[47]

In discussing his reaction to gym class in the seventh grade, one man states:

☐ [I was convinced] . . . without knowing any of the labels which might be put to it, that I was somehow different from most of [the other males]. If I had not been very different, they all would have been openly staring and admiring each other; if they *were* doing so, it wasn't evident to me.[48]

In addition, self-awareness, which may begin as acceptable for the individual, may turn into feelings of shame because of reactions of others.

☐ When I first became aware that I had gay feelings, I did not right off realize that this was a "no-no." Somehow I had stumbled across the word "homosexual" and realized that it applied to me. When I was about 12, I told my older brother that I thought I was a homosexual, and proceeded to tell him of the various boys and men I was attracted to. His reaction was the predictable horror and revulsion, and that was the first time I heard the words "fag" and "queer." Needless to say, I was mortified by his reaction, and from then on I realized that I had to be ashamed of my gay feelings, and repress them at all costs.[49]

Cross-gender behavior

Cross-gender behavior in lesbians. Cross-gender (tomboy) behavior, interest in doing so-called masculine things, and possibly even the desire to be a boy or man rather than a girl seem to be much more often recalled by lesbian than heterosexual women. Gundlach and Riess found that 78% of their lesbian sample and 48% of their heterosexual sample reported having been tomboys.[50] Saghir and Robins similarly report that 75% of their lesbian sample and only 16% of their nongay sample said they had been tomboys. They further report that tomboy behavior continued into adolescence and adulthood in about half the lesbian sample who reported tomboy behavior, whereas this continuation was not reported by heterosexual women.[51]

Green reports a study underway that will attempt to link childhood and adult behavior patterns in two groups of girls: one group identified as "tomboys," and the other not so identified.[52] In an earlier paper, Green notes that girls who show cross-gender behavior are not confused about their gender identity:

> While many girls of seven to twelve may prefer participating in the more adventurous and autonomous activities of same-aged boys, they see themselves as female. They have adopted a masculine gender-role preference but maintain a basic female sexual identity. With adolescence, social circumstances change such that advantages accrue from being a girl, particularly if one is physically attractive. Thus, gender-role behavior becomes modified accordingly and tomboyishness typically disappears.[53]

Brown[54,55] and Mussen[56] also found in their research that little girls very often play with boys' toys and want to be boys up to the age of 9 or 10.

The finding that a high percentage of lesbian women recall having been tomboys does not mean that any child or teenager who manifests cross-gender behavior will be a lesbian. Nor does it mean that those lesbian children or adolescents who display cross-gender behavior have any gender confusion or are manifesting a pathology.

Because adolescence is a time when deviant behavior is strongly punished by peers, nonconformity to traditional gender roles may result in social ostracism.[57] The adolescent who chooses not to conform can expect some kind of negative social response from peers. She may, however, also experience some positive consequences. Bem's work[58,59] indicates that a high level of gender role stereotyping does not go along with intellectual achievement in adults. Other sources indicate that a positive evaluation is placed on masculine traits and that this evaluation is independent of gender in at least some situations.[60,61] Therefore, it is quite possible that the adolescent who continues to manifest cross-gender behavior may get conflicting messages about herself. She may be reinforced by adults for instrumentality, competence, assertiveness, intelligence, and athletic ability on one hand and punished socially by peers on the other.

The adolescent who does not want to be stereotypically female is faced with several options. She can reject her peers and continue to be a tomboy. She can reject her tomboyishness and fit into the adolescent heterosexual world. She can play both sides of the fence: act "female" around boys and continue to do the things she likes when and where she won't be ostracized for it. If the adolescent, along with differences in her gender role behavior also finds that she is different in her sexual and affectional interests, this may be the time when she begins to put two and two together and develop a sense of identity as a lesbian.[62] Obviously, some women become lesbian without ever being tomboys. These women presumably discover their sexual preference on the basis of sexual and affectional involvement alone.

Cross-gender behavior in gay men. Boys who exhibit an interest in toys that are labeled "feminine" and who behave in ways that are described as "feminine" are often labeled "sissy." These boys are sometimes described as "feminine boys," and, as noted earlier, they are subjected to social alienation for their cross-gender behavior, whereas most girls who exhibit cross-gender behavior are not.[63]

Green, in his summary of research comparing cross-gender behavior of gay males, transvestites, and transsexuals indicates that "there is a considerable body of data suggesting that a significantly higher proportion of adults with same-sex partner preference recall childhood behaviors considered more typical of other-sex children."[64] It is important to note that, although Green's statement is accurate, it might be misleading.

First of all, his conclusion follows citations of studies of not only gay males but also transsexuals and transvestites. Although it is certainly possible to state that transsexuals prefer "same-sex" partners, implying that they are necessarily homosexual would not be accurate. Transvestites, as Green indicates, are usually heterosexuals, so their preference is opposite-gender.

Although some studies of gay and heterosexual men do support Green's statement, many studies of gay men indicate that the *majority* of subjects did not recall cross-gender behavior and were not identified as sissy during their childhood. For example, the study by Bieber, in which the subjects were psychiatric patients, found that only one third recalled cross-gender behavior, leaving 67% who did not.[65] Whitam found that 71% of his sample were not labeled sissy during childhood.[66] However, Saghir and Robins indicate that the majority (67%) of their sample did recall being labeled sissy.[67] Whitam also investigated doll play and cross-dressing, with the majority of the gay men indicating that they did neither.[68] Thus it is certainly true to say that the comparative studies of gay males and heterosexual males indicate that significantly higher proportions of gay males engaged in cross-gender behavior than did heterosexual males. However, concluding from that statement that gay males, even the majority of them, engaged in cross-gender behavior as children is inappropriate and not substantiated by research.

In his discussion of tomboys and sissies, Green also indicates that the feminine male child is more apt to experience feelings of cross-gender identity than is the masculine female child; that is, the sissy boy more often reports feeling like a girl than the tomboy girl reports feeling like a boy. This may be a result of the messages that the child receives that indicate that certain behaviors can be exhibited only by the other gender. For example, "Boys don't cry, girls cry," or "Girls play with dolls, boys play with trucks and trains." Since both boys and girls receive these messages, why should they affect boys more than girls? Perhaps they are given more often and with more emphasis to the boys. It is certain that boys and girls very quickly develop the notion that it is all right for girls to do "boys' things" but definitely not all right for boys to do "girls' things."

There is an attempt today to ease this dichotomy by supporting boys who wish to engage in some cross-gender behaviors. Marlo Thomas' "Free to be You and Me" is an example of that attempt, but it seems that the boys are still receiving the "boys don't cry" messages. We agree with Green that the boy who exhibits cross-gender behavior today "is treated in as cruel a manner as his counterpart of a generation or two ago," and may therefore be a candidate for some type of intervention.[63]

It appears that boys who exhibit varying degrees of cross-gender behavior may grow up to be adults anywhere on the homoerotic-heteroerotic continuum, and may or may not be transsexual or transvestite. Working with these boys and their parents will require some ethical considerations. It is very likely that the child may be, as Green describes it, prehomosexual, pretranssexual, pretransvestite, or preheterosexual.[69] He may also be preambisexual. Each of these will present varying degrees of difficulty in adulthood, and there is no way at present of knowing which situation exists. There appears to be some indication that the boy who consistently cross-dresses *and* identifies himself as a girl may be experiencing pretranssexualism, but this is not clear, nor are both conditions seen in the history of all genetic male transsexuals.

Once the need for intervention has been established, there are some alternatives that need to be explored. Green considers it important for the boy to find peer groups of other males who enjoy the activities that he enjoys in order for him to receive support for maintaining his appropriate gender identity.[63] It is also important to help the child understand the reasons for his being teased as a sissy and to help him cope with the teasing either by ignoring it or altering behavior or situations in a way to lessen the frequency of incidents in which he might be teased. The parents or parent figures must have a chance to explore their feelings about the child and his life as an adult, including a discussion of their beliefs and expectations about his happiness. It may also be necessary to explore the parents' feelings about the responsibilities of parenthood and about reactions of others toward them. It is not unusual to discover that parents who think their son may be gay are concerned about the reactions of relatives and neighbors toward them as parents, sharing a notion that they have in some way failed.

Intervention implications

How does any of the information on antecedents assist in intervention with a lesbian or gay male? Essentially, it doesn't! There has been no evidence to show that any specific family dynamics are necessarily responsible for any adult problems, although there have certainly been attempts at providing evidence of that relationship. As we indicated, many of those attempts have been made with the basic premise that having a homoerotic orientation is not only deviant but also undesirable and detrimental for the society. That premise has been pervasive throughout the culture.

This means that lesbians and gay men have also received that message, and some of them believe it. They might also believe that whatever problems they face as an adult are directly related to their early childhood family dynamics. It is the responsibility of the counselor to explore those beliefs with an understanding that they may have no basis in fact. If a lesbian or gay man is uncomfortable with her or his orientation, it serves little purpose to suggest that the orientation is a result of their particular childhood family situation.

No one knows why some people spend their adult lives as exclusive heterosexuals. It is not simply a matter of the very strong cultural messages that heterosexuality is the only model, nor is it that exclusive heterosexuals all were raised in very stable families in which exactly the right amount of parent-parent and child-parent interactions occurred. Children from troubled homes do not necessarily end up as unhappy or strained adults, nor do children from stable, happy homes necessarily end up as well-adjusted adults.[70] Skolnick, in her review of research on parental influence over child development, indicates that "increasing evidence suggests that parents simply do not have that much control over their children's development; too many other factors are influencing it."[71] Although many of us are led to believe differently, the influence of the parents and of the family dynamics appears to be minimal in determining most adult behavior.

If the client believes that his or her parents were to blame for any problems that he or she experiences as an adult, then that belief should be explored in light of current knowledge. It may indeed be true that one or both parents were responsible for some traumatic event or a series of such events that are at the base of some present problems. If so, then perhaps the client needs support for disliking the parents or help in understanding the parents' situation, but there is no clear evidence that, for the majority of people, early family life is solely or primarily responsible for either maladaptive behavior or successful adjustment as an adult.

If the counselor is working with parents who are concerned about the future orientation of the child, or with an adolescent who is concerned about her or his orientation, attempting to alter the family dynamics may do little in the way of easing either of those concerns. Perhaps the parents need to explore their concerns and expectations about a son or daughter who is homoerotic. There is an excellent chance that they will have some stereotypical notions of the life of a lesbian or gay man that should be discussed. They will also need to

52

explore their own feelings about their role in the development of their child's orientation.

If the adolescent is concerned about her or his sexual orientation, it will be necessary to explore his or her ideas about the lifestyle and to dispel the ignorance that will almost certainly exist. It will also be necessary to explore the person's concepts of the role of the family in forming her or his orientation.

There are not many role models available to the adolescent lesbian or gay man; and often, especially if she or he is seeking help for concern about the orientation, stereotypical ideas about the lifestyle may exist. The counselor will have to spend time suggesting alternatives to the myths, in order to help the person realize that being lesbian or homosexual has advantages and disadvantages, just as being heterosexual or ambisexual has. It is also essential that the counselor allow the person to explore all options, that is, indicate that a person may have an orientation anywhere along the continuum, rather than only at one end.

SUMMARY

We have presented data on the family background and early sexual behavior of lesbians and gay men primarily to show that there is no single pattern that exists. It appears that homoerotic and heteroerotic individuals become aware of their orientations at about the same range of ages, with the majority aware of an orientation by ages 17 to 20. How those orientations come to be is anyone's guess. We have some clues that suggest that there is no single phenomenon, situation, activity, or physiological or anatomical structure that is invariably responsible. However, there are still many people who view homosexuality and lesbianism as being abhorrent, including some gay men and lesbians. People will, therefore, continue to search for causes. The helping professional must be able to accept homosexuality and lesbianism as viable orientations within this culture if he or she is to be of any significant help to a lesbian or a gay man.

END NOTES

1. Mannion, K. "Female homosexuality: A comprehensive review of theory and research." JSAS *Catalog of Selected Documents in Psychology,* 1976 6(2), 44. (Ms. No. 1247).
2. Bene, E. "On the genesis of female homosexuality." *British Journal of Psychiatry,* 1965, *111,* 815-821.
3. Loney, J. "Family dynamics in homosexual women." *Archives of Sexual Behavior,* 1973, *2*(4), 343-350.
4. Kaye, H., Berl, S., Clare, J., Eleston, M., Gershwin, B., Gershwin, P., Kogan, L., Torda, C., & Wilbur, C. "Homosexuality in women." *Archives of General Psychiatry,* 1967, *17*(5), 626-634.
5. Swanson, D., Loomis, S., Lukesh, R., Cronin, R., & Smith, J. "Clinical features of the female homosexual patient: A comparison with the heterosexual patient." *Journal of Nervous and Mental Disease,* 1972, *155,* 119-124.
6. Mannion, 1976, p. 60.
7. Kenyon, F. "Studies in female homosexuality. IV. Social and psychiatric aspects. V. Sexual development, attitudes, and experience." *British Journal of Psychiatry,* 1968b, *114,* 1339.
8. Bene, 1965; Kenyon, 1968b; Kenyon, F. "Studies in female homosexuality. VI. The exclusive homosexual group." *Acta Psychiatrica Scandinavica,* 1968c, *44*(3), 224-236; Loney, 1973; and Kaye, et al., 1967.
9. Swanson, et al., 1972.
10. Siegelman, M. "Adjustment of male homosexuals and heterosexuals." *Archives of Sexual Behavior,* 1972b, *2*(1), 9-25.
11. Gundlach, R., & Riess, B. "Self and sexual identity in the female: A study of female homosexuals." In B. Riess (Ed.), *New directions in mental health.* New York: Grune & Stratton, 1968.
12. Hogan, R., Fox, A., & Kirchner, J. "Attitudes, opinions, and sexual development of 205 homosexual women." *Journal of Homosexuality,* 1977, *3*(2), 123-136.
13. Hogan, Fox, & Kirchner, 1977, p. 126.
14. Mannion, 1976, p. 54.
15. Allen, C. *Homosexuality: Its nature, causation, and treatment.* London: Staples Press, 1958; Bieber, I., Dain, H., Dince, P., Drellich, M., Grand, H., Gundlach, R., Kremer, M., Rifkin, A., Wilbur, C., & Bieber, T. *Homosexuality: A psychoanalytic study,* New York: Basic Books, 1962.
16. West, D. "Parental figures in the genesis of male homosexuality." *International Journal of Social Psychiatry,* 1959, *5*(2), 85-97; Nash, J., & Hayes, F. "The parental relationships of male homosexuals: Some theoretical issues and a pilot study." *Australian Journal of Psychology,* 1965, *17*(1), 35-43.
17. Socarides, C. "A provisional theory of aetiology in male homosexuality: A case of preoedipal origin." *International Journal of Psycho-Analysis,* 1968, *49*(1), 23-37; Regardie, F. "Analysis of a homosexual." *Psychiatric Quarterly,* 1949, *23*(3), 548-566; Monchy, R. "A clinical

type of male homosexuality." *International Journal of Psycho-Analysis,* 1965, *46*(2), 218-225.

18. See Weinberg, M., & Bell, A. *Homosexuality: An annotated bibliography.* New York: Harper & Row, 1972, annotations 88-94, pp. 45-46.

19. Greenblatt, D. "Semantic differential analysis of the 'triangular system' hypothesis in 'adjusted' overt male homosexuals." Unpublished doctoral dissertation, University of California, 1966.

20. Wood, R. "New report on homosexuality." 1961. Reprinted in Rubin, I. (Ed.). *The third sex.* New York: New Book, 1961.

21. Saghir, M., & Robins, E. *Male and female homosexuality: A comprehensive investigation.* Baltimore: Williams & Wilkins, 1973, 144.

22. Hooker, E. "Homosexuality." In *International Encyclopedia of the Social Sciences* (Vol. 14). New York: Macmillan, 1968, 224. See also Hooker, E. "Parental relations and male homosexuality in patient and non-patient samples," *Journal of Consulting and Clinical Psychology,* 1969, *33*(2), 140-142.

23. Marmor, J. "Overview: The multiple roots of homosexual behavior." In J. Marmor (Ed.), *Homosexual behavior: A modern reappraisal.* New York: Basic Books, 1980, 11.

24. Siegelman, M. "Parental background of male homosexuals and heterosexuals." *Archives of Sexual Behavior,* 1974b, *3*(1), 3-18.

25. Saghir & Robins, 1973, p. 243.

26. For example, see Gundlach & Reiss, 1968; Saghir & Robins, 1973; Hogan, Fox, & Kirchner, 1977; Hedblom, J. "Dimensions of lesbian sexual experience." *Archives of Sexual Behavior,* 1973, *2*(4), 329-341; Jay, K., & Young, A. *The gay report.* New York: Summit Books, 1979.

27. Mannion, 1976, p. 58.

28. Hogan, Fox, and Kirchner, 1977, p. 127-128.

29. Saghir & Robins, 1973, pp. 47-48.

30. Saghir & Robins, 1973, p. 50.

31. Jay & Young, 1979, p. 107.

32. Whitam, F. "The homosexual role: A reconsideration." *The Journal of Sex Research,* 1977b, *13*(1), 7.

33. Saghir & Robins, 1973, p. 88.

34. Jay & Young, 1979, pp. 123-124.

35. Saghir & Robins, 1973, p. 85.

36. Saghir & Robins, 1973, p. 92.

37. Saghir & Robins, 1973, p. 93; Bell, A., & Weinberg, M. *Homosexualities: A study of diversity among men and women.* New York: Simon & Schuster, 1978, p. 288; Jay & Young, 1979, p. 124.

38. See Belote, D., & Joesting, J. "Demographic and self-report characteristics of lesbians." *Psychological Reports,* 1976, *39,* 621-622; Hedblom, 1973; Gundlach & Riess, 1969; Jay & Young, 1979.

39. Jay & Young, 1979, p. 49.

40. Adair, N., & Adair, C. *Word is out: Stories of some of our lives.* New York: Dell, 1978, p. 55.

41. Adair & Adair, 1978, pp. 123-124.

42. Jay & Young, 1979, p. 45.

43. Jay & Young, 1979, pp. 46-47.

44. Jay & Young, 1979, p. 43.

45. Whitam, 1977b, p. 4.

46. Jay & Young, 1979, p. 105.

47. Whitam, 1977b, p. 5.

48. Jay & Young, 1979, p. 106.

49. Jay & Young, 1979, p. 114.

50. Gundlach & Reiss, 1969.

51. Saghir & Robins, 1973.

52. Green, R. "Patterns of sexual identity in childhood: Relationship to subsequent sexual partner preference." In J. Marmor (Ed.), *Homosexual behavior: A modern reappraisal.* New York: Basic Books, 1980.

53. Green, R. *Sexual identity conflict in children and adults.* New York: Basic Books, 1974, p. 281.

54. Brown, D. "Masculinity/femininity development in children." *Journal of Consulting Psychology,* 1957, *21*(3), 197-202.

55. Brown, D. "Inversion and homosexuality." *American Journal of Orthopsychiatry,* 1958, *28,* 424-429.

56. Mussen, P. "Early sex-role development." In D. Goslin (Ed.), *Handbook of socialization theory and research.* Chicago: Rand McNally, 1969.

57. Pleck, J. "Masculinity—femininity: Current alternative paradigms." *Sex Roles,* 1975, *1*(2), 161-178.

58. Bem, S. "Psychology looks at sex-roles: Where have all the androgynous people gone?" Paper presented at the University of California, Los Angeles, Symposium on Women, Los Angeles, May, 1972.

59. Bem, S. "The measurement of psychological androgyny." *Journal of Consulting and Clinical Psychology,* 1974, *42,* 155-162.

60. Israel, A., Raskin, P., Libow, J., & Pravder, M. "Gender and sex-role appropriateness: Bias in the judgment of disturbed behavior." *Sex Roles,* 1978, *4*(3), 399-413.

61. Shapiro, J. "Socialization of sex roles in the counseling setting: Differential counselor behavioral and attitudinal responses to typical and atypical female sex roles." *Sex Roles,* 1977, *3*(2), 173-184.

62. Lewis, S. *Sunday's women: A report on lesbian life today.* Boston: Beacon Press, 1979.

63. Green, 1980, p. 264.

64. Green, 1980, p. 257.

65. Bieber, et al., 1962.

66. Whitam, F. "Childhood indicators of male homosexuality." *Archives of Sexual Behavior,* 1977a, *6*(2), p. 92.

67. Saghir & Robins, 1973, p. 140.

68. Whitam, 1977a, p. 93.

69. Green, 1980, p. 263.

70. Skolnick, A. "The myth of the vulnerable child." *Psychology Today,* February 1978, pp. 56-65.

71. Skolnick, 1978, p. 56.

6

The gay lifestyle

WHAT IT MEANS TO BE GAY

It is almost inevitable that being a gay person in this country has consequences different from being nongay. Some of these consequences are positive, and some negative. Some are the same for both gay men and gay women, some differ. In any event, choosing, or believing one is compelled to live a lifestyle that is not condoned by most Americans makes the gay individual vulnerable to a multitude of complex harrassments and heir to a host of adjustments, negotiations, compromises, and pains. The effects can be felt across the entire spectrum of an individual's life, including his or her feelings about self, relationships with lovers, family, and friends, and interactions with others. The effects of discrimination against gay people and the negative societal attitudes that underlie this discrimination are pervasive and frequently (though by no means always) subtle. This negative side to the gay lifestyle is the one most often presented. It is important that helping professionals be aware of the difficulties inherent in a gay lifestyle, but it is equally important that they be aware of the positive consequences.

Being gay is an experience that is viewed positively by many gay women and men.[1] Gay people may be tolerant and supportive of a wider range of behaviors for both men and women than are nongay people. There may be a sense of freedom from traditional gender role constraints, a feeling of unity and support from other gay people, and in general, a sense of enjoyment of one's lifestyle.[2] Indeed, the fact that gay people as a group are at least as healthy and well-functioning as heterosexuals suggests that there are some very positive aspects to being gay.[3]

The experience of being gay

The experience of being gay differs depending on age, sex, location, race, social status, involvement in the gay lifestyle, and so on. Being a (gay) white, middle-class man is different from being a (gay) Asian-American man; being a (gay) woman in San Francisco is different from being a (gay) woman in Thunder Bay, Montana. Being a (lesbian) mother on welfare in Alabama involves different life experiences than being an upper-class (lesbian) mother in Beverly Hills, California; and being a (gay) businessperson involves different experiences than being a (gay) Army officer, blue collar worker, or prison inmate. Nevertheless, there are some facts of life that are present for all gays and not present in the same way for nongays.

Social recognition. The gay lifestyle is almost never recognized by nongay society as an acceptable alternative to heterosexuality. Gay men and women do not find their sexual and affectional preference continually reinforced the way nongay people do. In fact, heterosexuality and its affirmation are so pervasive that nongays are probably unaware of their societal monopoly.

Gay people are surrounded and bombarded with the trappings and fanfare of the nongay lifestyle. There is almost no place outside the gay community where gays can find an affirmation of their way of life. There are no advertisements that depict gay men or women. Questionnaires and forms usually allow space for no orientation but heterosexuality, so gay couples who have lived and loved together for 15 years must identify themselves as "single." The overwhelming majority of books, movies, plays and other media fare do not deal with gayness at all. Those that do are often pornographic, involve gross misrepresentation or stereotyping, or represent lesbians and male gays as bizarre, unusual, or sick. Television programs that deal with the subject generally carry a network announcement warning parents that the subject matter may be "too mature" for children, even though there is neither explicit sexual activity nor violence. Family, friends, acquaintances, teachers, doctors, employers, ministers, insurance salespeople, and neighbors assume a person is not gay, sometimes even in the face of strong evidence to the contrary, and gay people know that they disabuse nongays of their comfortable assumption only at a high personal risk.

Role models. The absence of gay role models is a big problem for all gays, and is especially serious for gay teenagers. Teenagers usually select people who are highly visible as role models: actresses and actors, professional athletes, and fictional characters from books or television, as well as respected figures they know personally. Fortunately for nongay teenagers, there are usually role models who are close at hand, easily observable, and who offer more realistic behaviors and goals for them to model than do most media heroines and heroes.

Nongay adults can also learn from a variety of models who are supposedly average on television, in books and magazines, and everyday life. Even so, it is often difficult for nongays to strike a balance between the ideal self and the real self, between the unattainable dream and the attainable reality.

For gays, the balance may be much more difficult. The tendency for most gays to keep their sexual preference hidden makes it hard for gays to find realistic role models. Those models available are typically either famous or notorious; few are

contemporary. Many, such as Oscar Wilde, Virginia Woolf, or Gertrude Stein, are either impossibly romantic or deeply tragic. Such people are difficult legends to live up to not only because of the kinds of people they were, but because their sexual and affectional preference is almost always seen as secondary to their genius. For the average lesbian or gay man, genius in unattainable, and the world is liable to see the gayness as primary in importance. Those more or less average people among us who could serve as gay role models are usually reluctant to be identified as gay, and for good reason. Those who do identify themselves publicly are more than likely to pay a heavy price.[4]

This means that anyone who grows up or becomes gay is unlikely to know how to go about being gay in the same way that a nongay person knows how to go about being heterosexual. That is, a person who has decided that he or she is a gay person may not know what this means. A gay man may believe that in order to be gay, he must wear drag; or a lesbian may believe that all lesbians are either "butch" or "femme" and not want to be either. There are nongay models for the roles of wife, mother, husband, lover, and father, and for nongay male and female behavior vis-à-vis people of the same and opposite gender. There are no comparable models for gay people to follow. Therefore, most gays follow the nongay model in public situations (with perhaps a few variations) and develop a second identity or set of behaviors for those situations when they are around other gays.

Gay history. The lack of role models for gays is closely associated with another problem: a lack of gay history. Until the early 1970s written gay history was virtually nonexistent, and many gay people knew little about it. Families of origin are not a source of gay history, pride, or culture, and gay culture that might have developed earlier has been lost because gay men and women have created and taught in the prevailing heterosexual mode. So writers such as Virginia Woolf, George

Sand, Marcel Proust, or Christopher Isherwood have traditionally hidden their sexuality when practicing their art. Gay dancers dance to nongay themes that are sometimes written by gay composers. Gay teachers teach nongay history that either excludes gay figures or ignores their sexual and affectional preference.

It has only been recently that a history and culture of gay people has begun to develop and be written down, and it has grown rapidly over the past few years.[5] Although the majority of gay people are still not public about their sexual preference, publications, music, theater, movies, and even television shows by, for, and about gays are beginning to appear.[6] These are important steps in helping gay and nongay people have a sense of the place of gays both historically and currently in the making of culture.

Even though times are changing, the culture is still overpoweringly nongay in focus and tolerance. Gays who do not live in areas that are accepting of diverse lifestyles are not likely to be exposed to developing gay culture. Many gay people still grow up and live without support; many still feel outcast and alone; all are surrounded by a nongay culture that allows them little in the way of representation, affirmation, or support.

Helping professionals can aid gay clients who are suffering from "culture shock" by referring them to material on gay history and by making them aware of the current material by and for gays. This is particularly important with gay teenagers, gays who are just coming out, and gays who live in rural areas where they are not exposed to these materials and are least likely to know of their existence. In the case of teenage clients, it is not advisable for the counselor to actually supply these to the client, except in the rare event that the parents are supportive of such exposure. The counselor can, however, tell the gay adolescent that such materials exist and that they are often available in university or public libraries. Even though the adolescent gay client may not be able to get to

some of these materials, it may at least be a comfort to know that they exist.

Effects of gayness on personal functioning

Being gay and living in a predominantly nongay world has surprisingly little effect on personal functioning as measured by personality tests and the like. It can create problems of living and adjustment, however, particularly when it comes to coping with nongay social situations.

Psychological health and adjustment. Being gay can certainly create personal difficulties, but it is not the automatic sentence to anguish, alcoholism, loneliness, and neurosis that it must sometimes appear. Because the prevailing view of gayness has been that it is an illness, there have been many studies done in an attempt to discover its etiology and to find out whether and in what ways gay men and women are less well adjusted than nongay men and women.

We have already discussed the literature on etiology and have shown that this concept is meaningless in relation to gayness. The results of the research on psychological adjustment have been largely equivocal, and many have been questioned on methodological grounds.[7]

Although differences have been found between gay and nongay samples, these differences vary from study to study. Furthermore, noncomparability of samples, methodology, and instrumentation makes reported differences difficult to interpret.[8] Data are also questionable in many instances because of researcher bias that is almost always in the direction of the expectation that gays are sick or more neurotic than nongays. The studies most likely to show pathology are those utilizing projective devices such as the Rorschach, Bender Gestalt, and Draw-a-Person. Riess et al. critically reviewed these findings regarding lesbian women and concluded that "[t]here is little from the projective literature to suggest that female homosexuality is a specifiable clinical entity."[9]

Mannion notes that Riess et al. failed to discuss the very questionable validity of the projective tests themselves, in particular the Rorschach.[10] Not only are such devices highly susceptible to researcher bias, but there is little evidence that they have any appreciable construct validity. Mannion quotes Dana in a 1970 review of the studies attempting to demonstrate construct validity of the Rorschach as saying "'The lack of replication, systematic or otherwise, or of consensus in definition of variables, and the capricious dilettantism of some investigators, renders such scrutiny empty and mechanical.'"[10]

Nonprojective tests of male homosexuals have usually shown either inconsistent differences or no differences at all between gay and nongay men, whereas in a number of studies, lesbian women have appeared healthier than their heterosexual counterparts.[11] Mannion summarizes these findings regarding lesbians:

> There emerges a picture of the lesbian as a woman who is more dominant, autonomous, assertive, self-actualizing, and inner-directed than her heterosexual counterpart. In some ways, she has been described as being more healthy than the heterosexual controls, both in terms of freedom from neurosis and productivity in the professional world. This picture does not support the psychoanalytic position that the lesbian is a malfunctioning neurotic.[12]

In a more recent study, Bell and Weinberg did find differences between gay and nongay men and women, and they relate these differences to differences within subcategories among homosexual (but for some reason not among heterosexual) individuals.[13] They found that among both men and women, two "types" of gays, which they call *dysfunctionals* and *asexuals,* are the individuals who "appeared to be less well off psychologically than those in the heterosexual groups."[14] With regard to the other types of gay men and women (close-coupleds, open-coupleds, and functionals), they report that "it would appear that homosexual adults who have come to terms with their homosexuality, who do not regret their sexual orientation, and who can function effectively sexually and socially, are no more distressed psychologically than are heterosexual men and women."[14]

Homosexuality and lesbianism as clinical entities. Bell and Weinberg, Morin, and Marmor all stress that neither male homosexuality nor lesbianism can be considered discrete clinical entities.[15] Morin points out that the words *homosexual* and *lesbian* refer only to sexual preference and tell nothing about individual patterns of behavior. Although they have typically been understood and researched as clinical entities, they are not; they are purely descriptive terms for choice of sexual partner.[16]

Looking at all this information, we can conclude that gayness is not a clinical entity and is neither indicative of nor a causal factor in psychological disturbance or social malfunctioning. Individuals who are homosexual or lesbian have every chance of leading lives as productive, fulfilling, and mentally healthy as their nongay counterparts.

This is not to say, however, that there are not costs to the gay lifestyle. There are costs and, like the costs of a nongay lifestyle, they may lead members of the gay community to seek professional help. It is important to remember that gay people who seek help are not doing so because of something innately dysfunctional about being gay. They may be seeking help for reasons unrelated to their lifestyle, for problems exacerbated by membership in a population at risk, or for problems arising directly from their sexual preference. Professional helpers should be as careful in assessing the specific problems with gay clients as with nongay clients and should not assume with gays any more than with nongays that sexual orientation is a problem.

Gender role behaviors in the gay community

Society typically focuses on the sexuality of gay people, and in so doing, overlooks the vast majority of gay experience. One part of this experience has to do with gender role behavior. This is an area that may be especially salient for gay men and women because the boundaries of acceptable gender role behavior are very often different within the gay community than outside it.

Gender role behaviors are those typically considered appropriate for or indicative of belonging to one gender, and inappropriate for someone of the other gender. In this culture, women have more freedom to cross gender role boundaries than men do, a difference in social permissiveness that starts early and is probably connected to the relative social valuation of males and females and their roles.[17]

What this means is that boys whom society is willing to consider "normal" are essentially never allowed to engage in behaviors that are considered feminine. Girls are allowed to engage in so-called masculine behaviors until they reach puberty and are then expected to either give them up or at least drastically reduce and temper them with a proper show of "feminine" behavior.

Included with the overt behaviors that are assigned and reinforced on the basis of gender are other behaviors relating to the experience and display of emotion and feeling. Girls are expected to be more expressive of feelings, more sensitive, and "weaker"; that is, they are not expected to be able to control their emotions. Boys, on the other hand, are expected not to show and preferably not to have feelings, except anger. They are not supposed to show happiness, tenderness, fear, anxiety, softness, and the like. For both genders, the spectrum of available behaviors and feelings is shortened to include only those that our society considers to be gender-appropriate.

Gender role behavior is not and should not be considered prognostic of sexual preference either in children or adults. Most gay men and women demonstrate what society considers appropriate gender role behavior a good part of the time. Nonetheless, cross-gender behavior is one of the few things that seems to show up more consistently in children who later become gay than in those who do not, as we discussed in Chapter 5. The consequences of so-called cross-gender behavior may be different for boys and girls.

Research on women who achieve and are successful in a wide range of endeavor demonstrates that most of them were tomboys. They were more independent, risk taking, adventurous, strong, achievement-oriented than their passive, conforming, dependent sisters. We're beginning to find out that muscle development and coordination go hand-in-hand with learning.[18]

Cross-gender behavior in male children may be of more concern simply because society reacts so negatively to boys who act effeminate and because advantages in this society are generally considered to accrue to those who are more masculine. Yet it may be the very differences in expectations of male and female children that make cross-gender behavior attractive to some male children:

☐ I was a sissy right from the start. On a farm the male and female roles were very clearly defined. Outside, it was hot and you had to work like a bastard. . . . I didn't want that, you know. The alternative was to make busy work in the house and to relate to your mother—cool, comfortable, nothing to do, no sweat, you could read books. So I opted for that. Unconsciously, my behavior became what would, back then, have been construed as feminine, effeminate, sissy. It still is to this day, in a way, but I love it. I'm really not into physical hard work. . . . You're supposed to *like* to go out and do that stuff. Well, I didn't. It was easier, it seemed to make me happier, to do the things that, back then, looked like I was assuming a female role.[19]

We have noted earlier that there are indications, not yet well established empirically, that gay men are more androgynous and gay women more masculine-typed in their behavior than nongay men and women.[20] Our observations of the gay community would certainly bear this out on a subjective level at least. This should not, however, be taken to mean that all gay men and women show a lot of cross-gender behavior or that they cannot or do not engage in societally approved gender role behavior. Nor should it be taken to mean that children who show cross-gender behavior are going to grow up gay. Neither is true, any more than it is true that all nongay men and women show only traditional gender role behaviors or that all children who engage in so-called appropriate gender role behavior are going to grow up to be nongay.

It does mean, however, that both men and women may find support for aspects of themselves within the gay community that are not traditionally approved by the nongay community. So, for example, gay men may find it more acceptable and more necessary to cook, care for children, and be emotionally expressive; gay women may find it more acceptable and necessary to use tools, lift heavy objects, and be independent. Gay men and women both have to learn how to function in relationships without the benefit of gender differences to determine who will perform what relationship tasks.

Even so, remember that gay men and women have both been raised and socialized as members of their respective genders. Because of this, gay men are typically like nongay men and gay women are like nongay women in most facets of their lives. The similarities between gay and nongay members of each gender are often overlooked by observers. They are more likely to notice ways in which gay men and women differ from their nongay counterparts, especially with regard to deviation from traditional gender role behaviors, and to label these deviations as evidence of pathology.

In point of fact, deviations from rigid adherence to gender roles are probably healthy. As we have discussed elsewhere in this volume, people who demonstrate androgynous behavior are psychologically healthier than people who demonstrate rigidly gender-typed behavior. To the extent that the gay community can foster and support individuals whose behavior is closer to androgynous, it is decidedly productive of health.

Cross-dressing. In this culture at least, cross-dressing applies more to men than women. It is considered acceptable for women to wear men's clothes or styles that are similar to those worn by men, but not for men to wear women's clothes. Before it became commonplace for women to wear unisex styles, there may have been more actual cross-dressing than there is now, with women wearing men's clothes when it was considered socially inappropriate for them to do so. This was undoubtedly more prevalent during the period of time when lesbian couples were more prone to adopt roles that mimicked traditional nongay roles.[21]

Cross-dressing among gay men is unusual, in spite of the stereotypes to the contrary. According to Jay and Young, 96% of their sample of gay men never wear women's clothing, and 88% never wear makeup. Over three quarters of the sample said their sexual partners never wear women's clothing, and 72% said their partners never wear makeup.[22]

In general, men in this study reported very negative feelings about other gay men who wear women's clothing.[23]

☐ Once a guy came back in the room dressed as a woman. I ran away.[24]

☐ Transvestism is something I can't understand and frankly am tempted to term a "sickness" just as straights so often term gayness a sickness. I wish I could get away from this categorizing, but there it is.[25]

☐ One time, I put an end to sex because this guy was playing mind games with me and wanted me to wear his wife's panties.[24]

In a gay men's consciousness-raising group conducted by one of the authors, the men discussed the negative feelings that seem to exist in the majority of homoerotic men toward "drag queens," other gay men who wear women's clothes. The men finally realized that they disliked drag queens because they exhibit behaviors that fit the stereotype that nongays often have of gay men and that they were trying to overcome within themselves. They had been faced with the social message that gay men really want to be women and were not masculine. Although they knew that was not true, they were still struggling with the masculinity issue, especially those who had been labeled as "sissies" during childhood. The men in the group perceived drag queens and effeminate homosexuals as typifying the social stereotype and therefore considered them as "bad." Rejecting drag queens and effeminate homosexuals was a means of reinforcing their own sense of masculinity.

In order to help a drag queen who seeks intervention, the counselor must understand what it means to be a drag queen. Many people believe that men who wear women's clothes have a gender identity dysfunction, but this is not the case. There is a difference between gender identity (whether one thinks of oneself as a male or female) and gender role behavior (the extent to which one acts in ways considered appropriate to one gender or the other). Some people believe that gender identity and gender role behavior are always correlated and that gender role behavior is therefore an indication of a person's gender identity. Freund et al., for example, measured gender identity by a questionnaire that contained items such as, "Between the ages of 6 and 12, did you like to do jobs or chores which are usually done by women?"[26] Identifying this as a measure of gender identity may be inappropriate. It is certainly possible for a male to enjoy doing such jobs or chores without believing he is female, although admittedly, some boys are led to believe this is not possible. This blurring of the definition of gender identity with gender role behavior may very well lead to the belief that transsexuals, transvestites, and homosexuals have gender identity confusion (or dysfunction).

A drag queen or transvestite may choose to dress in women's clothes and behave in a manner considered appropriate only for females or think of himself as female. It may mean that he is aware in himself of feminine aspects, but that is not the same thing as being confused about one's gender.

☐ Who am I? I'm Tallulah Bankhead; I'm May West; I'm Gloria Swanson; I'm my mother; I'm Jean Harlow. I'm a lot of the archetypical female images from that particular era. But I'm also me, you know. I'm male and I love it. It's really fine.[27]

☐ Femininity to me seems to say passivity and a real idea of where a man wants a woman to be—like a male identification of what a woman is. A lot of early

drag feelings I had, and I think a lot of boys have, were around those passive female roles. . . . My wanting to wear women's clothes is representing something spiritual about me—that I'm female and male at the same time.[28]

Unfortunately, behavior that society considers gender inappropriate is usually very strongly punished, most particularly when it is a man who is enacting feminine role behaviors. Drag queens and very effeminate men usually are severely discriminated against both outside and inside the gay community. To the extent that a man adopts the feminine role, he may also internalize some of the negative conceptions about women. This, combined with being gay and being rejected by the gay community, puts drag queens and effeminate men in a difficult position. One gay man describes what it was like for him:

☐ I got stuff thrown at me and people yelling "Faggot." I lived in the ghetto. Just walking down the street . . . people would take out all their frustrations on me. . . . When I started passing more and more as a woman, they would treat me like a woman, so I was still treated like shit, but I felt more comfortable that way. I felt like at least I was having the freedom to live out some of my fantasy.[29]

Another man, a transvestite, says:

☐ Being a transvestite, I've experienced a lot of isolation and confusion in my life. I knew I was a TV before I knew I was gay. . . . Most people, gay and straight, think TV's are . . . crazy, sick people. . . . I refuse to remove all my body hair and was told I couldn't do drag [that is, wear women's clothes] with hairy legs.[30]

In working with a client who is a drag queen or is very effeminate but is not gender confused, you can obviously anticipate that the client is under a lot of stress. His friends may all be drag queens, and he may have a very poor self-image. He may also believe he has no choice about the kind of behavior he engages in. This is not true. You may want to point out that, although it is unfortunate and unpleasant for him that others respond as they do, you and he cannot change others' behavior. He certainly has every right to dress and behave as he chooses if he doesn't mind the consequences or prefers the consequences to the thought of changing his behavior. If he is very unhappy, however, he may want to consider modifying his behavior at least around nongays. He may also want to consider the possibility that he can enact those more feminine aspects of himself without engaging in stereotypical feminine behavior, as so many women are now attempting to learn to do.

If the client does want to modify his behavior, the counselor can help by teaching him some ways of changing those things that are particularly effeminate in appearance. He may for example, want to learn to walk, talk, smoke, or use his hands somewhat differently, at least under some circumstances. This does not mean that he has to learn to act "macho." On the other hand, many women are perfectly feminine without demonstrating "effeminate" behavior. The client may want to define for himself and attempt to learn a more androgynous approach that incorporates those parts of himself that he considers masculine as well as those he considers feminine.

Remember to stress that the demonstration of these behaviors, or any behaviors, for that matter, are optimally effective in self-expression if they are under the individual's control—if he can choose when to act in certain ways and when not to. To choose to act in a certain way in a given situation does not mean that he is "selling out" or being untrue to himself, any more than an actor or actress is being untrue when he or she portrays different characters. It simply means that he chooses to express himself in different ways at different times, to use his full potential in a variety of ways. The counselor may want to point out that almost all people modify their behavior from place to place and time to time. People do not act with business associates as with lovers, or with children as with adults, and so forth. Ideally, people change behavior to meet the particular demands of a given situation. Indeed, the ability to react situationally rather than stereotypically on the basis of perceived gender roles is apparently characteristic of healthier, more flexible individuals.[31] Nowhere is

it written that rigid adherence to a limited behavioral repertoire is a virtue or a sign of mental health. It is more likely to be an indication that the individual is constrained by preconceptions rather than spontaneously reacting to the situation at hand.[32]

If the client does not want to modify his behavior with regard to gender-appropriate actions, then he may be willing to modify other behaviors along with the way he thinks about himself vis-à-vis others in the gay and nongay communities. If, along with stereotypically effeminate behavior, he also thinks of himself primarily in feminine terms, he may have learned the kind of negative self-image sometimes typical of women. He may therefore benefit from the kind of consciousness raising one would do with a woman, as well as from assertiveness training. Ultimately, as with other kinds of problems, the client must be willing to take responsibility for his own behavior and recognize that, even if the consequences of that behavior are demonstrably unjust and uncalled for, the only thing he can immediately effect is his own behavior, and what he experiences is a direct result of his decisions about how to act.

Remember, too, that the fact that someone is a drag queen does not mean that he is necessarily unhappy. Although most such men will face difficult situations, particularly if they don't live in or near a supportive gay community, some certainly are able to create a positive lifestyle that they enjoy and are comfortable with.

☐ I can't help but feel drag is great. I mean, if male and female "roles" are just that, then drag is just as legitimate as me dressing up as a lumberjack to go to [a gay bar]—it's all the same. People threatened by it (superbutch gay men, some lesbians, etc.) are the problem.[24]

☐ The reason I exhibit—by choice—the behavioral characteristics which could be called a "screaming queen" is because—God!—we've got hands; we've got a voice that can cover two octaves. It's so damn foolish not to use them.[33]

Gender role changes within the gay community. The support of a broad spectrum of behaviors for gay men and women within the gay community is an important concept. Traditionally, gay men and women have both been characterized as conforming to either "butch" or "femme" roles, with butch individuals supposedly enacting highly stereotyped masculine, and femme (or in the men's community, "nelly") individuals supposedly enacting highly stereotyped feminine roles as these roles are defined by the nongay world.

Until perhaps 10 or 15 years ago, there was undoubtedly a lot of accuracy to this stereotype, and gay men and women frequently found themselves trapped in ill-fitting roles that imitated the gender roles of the nongay world. Indeed, some gay men and women still do this. During the last 15 years or so, however, changes have taken place in both the gay and nongay worlds that have radically changed the way gender roles are enacted within the gay community.

The old butch/femme dichotomy in relationships has all but disappeared in most gay communities. In the lesbian community particularly, gay women, encouraged and supported by the women's movement as a whole, are now more likely to engage in a variety of behaviors without being trapped into traditional gender role stereotypes for either men or women. Men are also beginning to explore new areas of gender role behavior. Because gay men have had to negotiate the difference between socially acceptable behavior in partner choice and their own needs in that respect, they often have a sensitivity to the repressive aspects of the traditional male gender role. Because of this, many gay men are apt to develop more of a feminist consciousness and stance as well as an awareness of the repressiveness of traditional women's roles.

Because of such changes, being gay is a more positive experience now than it has ever been. The lesbian community has always been supportive of strong, assertive, nontraditional women. Historically, however, such women in the gay community might have been expected to assume the trappings of the traditional male role. Now, gay women are finding that they do not have to be masculine, but can instead be more fully human and can express themselves in a variety of ways. The gay men's community has typically provided a place for nontraditional men, but has also frequently oppressed men who have dressed and behaved in a feminine manner.[34] This now appears to be changing as gay men find that they don't have to be either butch or nelly but can combine behaviors and feelings that have traditionally been acceptable for one gender or the other.

Effects of gayness on social functioning

The necessity for interfacing with nongay society is potentially one of the most difficult aspects of gay lifestyles.[35] Because the gay community exists in the midst of the wider nongay culture, it is virtually impossible for gay people to avoid contact with the nongay world, even if they want to. As with other things, the problems encountered may differ depending on where an individual lives, on race, sex, age, personal style, and so forth. Some individuals live their lives almost totally within the gay community, some almost totally outside of it. Wherever an individual spends most of her or his time, however, contact with nongays is inevitable sometime, so there is always the potential for conflict.

Managing deviant identities. To say that difficulties are encountered in dealing with nongays does not necessarily mean that social functioning is a problem for gays. It does mean that gays pay more attention to social interactions with nongays than they do to interactions with each other. This is particularly true if the gay person does not want others to know that he or she is gay. Nongays, too, frequently have trouble in social interactions because of attempts to hide or minimize certain features of their private lives. People who are having affairs with each other in a work setting, those with medical problems such as diabetes or epilepsy, women who are suffering from menstrual cramps or who enjoy weightlifting, men who like to knit or are going bald, and couples with marital problems are all examples of people who could be hetero-erotic. They are also examples of people who at various times and under various circumstances might want to hide these personal facts from others.

Most of the time, the things that people try to keep secret or disguise are things of which they believe others will disapprove or that will cause others to treat them differentially in ways they won't like. Such things are not necessarily seen as undesirable or bad to the person involved, although of course they may be. For example, two co-workers who are having an affair may be quite happy about it but not want others at work to know for fear of losing their jobs or suffering social sanctions. People who are diabetic or epileptic or who have colostomies, mastectomies, and the like certainly wish they didn't, but may not feel that these conditions make them sick or deserving of special treatment. It is not unusual, though, for others to react with discomfort or inappropriate concern to such conditions, so people who have them will usually try to keep them hidden.

Those who engage in behaviors that are not considered appropriate because of the performer's age, sex, class, status, or some other variable may feel that they have to hide these parts of themselves. So, women who enjoy weightlifting or bodybuilding or who know a lot about contact sports may choose to feign ignorance, or at least not to advertise their interests and knowledge. Men who enjoy activities such as ballet, knitting, and cooking or who enjoy and are willing to engage in child care and household duties may not tell others about it.

It is the same with gay people. Although a lesbian woman or a gay man may find her or his choice of lifestyle healthy, appropriate, and enjoyable, she or he may still choose to go to extreme lengths to prevent nongays from finding out about it. Obviously, the societal reaction to gayness is typically much more extreme than to baldness, diabetes, an office affair, or atypical choice of hobbies. This is what makes identity management more difficult for gay than nongay people in many cases.

Social relationships. In general, the social relationships gays have with other gays are easier than those they have with nongays. It is easier for gays to form relationships with nongays who know about their sexual preference than with those who do not know.[35] This is because it is not necessary to pretend to be nongay around those who know, but pretense is believed necessary around those who do not know.

Among nongays who do not know, gays experience more strain around those who are important to them or who have the power to hurt them emotionally or economically, such as friends, family, or co-workers.[36] Brief, task-oriented encounters with nongays who don't know are also not as difficult as extended, potentially intimate, or revealing interactions.

Relationships with people who do not know. Dealing with people who don't know that an individual is gay and to whom the gay person does not wish to reveal her or his sexual preference probably accounts for the major part of any difficulty that gay people have with nongay people. These types of interactions are most likely to occur at work, with family, and with close personal friends.

Job-related interactions are undoubtedly some of the most uncomfortable, because most gays are employed in positions that require them to spend a large proportion of their working life around nongay people. It is usual for people who work together to learn something about each others' lives away from work: about spouses, children, roommates, dates, hobbies, vacations, and the like. Gay people who wish to remain undiscovered may find that the social expectations of co-workers are problematic because their lives don't fit the norm for single men and women.

Single people, especially if they are young, are expected to be looking for a mate of the opposite gender. This means that individuals who are committed to and spend the majority of their time with someone of the same gender may have difficulty discussing evenings, weekends, and vacations. A single woman, for example, may feel awkward when telling co-workers that she did not date over a weekend or when she continually mentions activities enjoyed in the company of another woman.

There are several alternatives, short of identifying oneself as gay, none of which is completely satisfactory for everyone. Some individuals invent dates, mates, opposite-gender partners and the like. Some merely change the gender of the person with whom they do things. So, for example, a man might say "she" instead of "he" in describing his partner. Another alternative is to admit the gender of one's companion, but to pretend to be disappointed and act as though one were actively seeking someone of the opposite gender. This can create difficulties in that there are often members of the opposite gender available who must then be discouraged or rejected. A third alternative is to pretend to live and spend one's time alone. This again leaves one open to the invitations of people who would like to fill one's time. Perhaps the least satisfactory alternative of all is that of avoiding personal contact with nongay people in work situations. Gay people do this and find that they feel very isolated. They may also find their self-protectiveness and fear branded as coldness, aloofness, snobbishness, and disinterest. Gay people who are not or think they cannot be open about their sexual preference may find themselves doing one or all of the above in order to avoid being identified as gay by employers and co-workers.

Single status is often a problem at work. Frequently gay men and women are considered "eligible" by their nongay co-workers. Nongays typically find it inexcusable that a single person is not dating and will go to great lengths to "fix up" someone they consider available. This means that gays have to cope with well-intentioned but intrusive efforts on the part of nongays to get them dated and mated with someone of the opposite gender. It can be exasperating to the gay person and confusing to nongays when these attempts at matchmaking are not greeted with enthusiasm. Because they are afraid of offending or of being discovered, gays may be afraid to be assertive and simply tell nongays that they are not interested.

After-hours social interactions can also be difficult. Many jobs require that employees attend social functions such as office parties or meetings and conferences that require some amount of socializing or that typically require that one bring a spouse or date. Again, many gay couples prefer to do things together and would like to be able to attend office parties and out-of-town conferences in each others' company as many nongay couples do. Gays who choose not to do this must either appear alone at such functions or must take a "date." Some gay people have standing arrangements in which a gay man will serve as an "escort" for a lesbian woman, and vice versa, thus providing each other with acceptable public images.

Relationships with family members. A second major area of difficulty is interactions with family members. Gays who are open with other important nongay people in their lives may be reluctant to be open with their families. Not being open can put the gay person under considerable pressure.

Parents typically expect their children to marry and provide them with grandchildren. Men are expected to provide an heir to carry on the family name. So there are pressures on gays to provide their parents with a continuation of the family, with weddings and grandchildren and family celebrations at Christmas, Hanukkah, and the like. A gay individual may be subjected to continual questioning, jokes, and urgings aimed at getting her or him to marry and settle down. When visiting at home, gay people are liable to get endless questions about dates, marriage prospects, future plans, and so forth. This kind of family pressure may continue for years until family and friends are either placated by the marriage of another child or give up.

Into this familial anticipation of his or her marital future, the gay person must attempt to fit the realities of a gay lifestyle. Trying to lead a life that is totally concealed from parents over a period of years can be an awesome task. Anecdotes abound in the gay community of the convoluted attempts and complex subterfuges people have undertaken to avoid being found out by their parents.

Those individuals who have long-term involvements may be nervous about the fact that a "roommate" moves about with her or him from apartment to apartment, or from city to city. It is hard to explain joint ownership of home, property, and the like. Family gatherings and holidays present one of the classic difficulties of gay closet life. Like nongays, gay couples often want to spend holiday times together. Married couples, especially those with children, can legitimately spend holidays in their own home, rather than traveling to parents' homes every year. If a gay person wants to spend a holiday with a lover, the explanation is much more difficult. Taking a lover along is also a poor solution in many cases. If a nongay person goes home, he or she is often encouraged to bring a steady date or of course, a spouse. A young person may be able to get away with bringing home a same-gender "friend," but it gets more difficult to legitimize when one is in one's thirties and the "friend" has been the same for the last 6 years.

Continual contact with family members and visits from them can cause problems. Some gay people do not wish their parents to know that they are living with someone of the same gender. This is particularly true if they are maintaining the fiction that they are dating, engaged, or even married. This means that some couples have two phones with separate numbers. Each person answers only his or her phone so that parents don't know that the two people are living together. When parents visit, it can be awkward for the gay son or daughter to account for the living arrangements that exist. Since many gay couples sleep together in a single bedroom, it becomes necessary either to pretend that sleeping arrangements have been altered to accommodate the parents or to have two bedrooms with separate beds and to sleep separately while parents are around. Many gay people have literature on their bookshelves and gay magazines or newspapers that must be hidden while company is present. If the individual is pretending to be dating, a date must usually be produced. This means enlisting the help of a gay person of the opposite gender. As should be evident, the entire procedure can be a nuisance and certainly does not make for close relationships among family members.

Perhaps most important, gay people may feel guilty and unhappy because they are hiding important parts of their lives from people they care about. It is a sad situation for a gay man or woman to be very much in love and unable to share this love with family members. It also means that when a gay couple is around family or friends who do not know that they are gay, they may have to alter their style of interaction in order to disguise their relationship. This means that they will probably not feel free to show affection, particularly physical affection, or to act as people normally do who are in love with each other.[36] This type of restriction can create friction and put a strain both on the gay couple and on relationships with parents.

Interactions with friends. Problems encountered with friends who don't know an individual is gay are similar to those that occur with parents and family. The same types of pressures and difficulties arise. If they are friends of long standing, then the nongay person may have known the gay person before she or he became gay. This means that the nongay person, like the family, may have a lot of expectations about how the friend is going to behave in various circumstances. The change of lifestyle that may go along with becoming gay can be difficult to explain. With both new and old friends, intimacy is always likely to be a problem. The prospect of intimacy can be threatening to the gay person because there is so much that cannot be revealed without giving away the fact of sexual preference. For this reason, people often restrict their close relationships to gay friends and nongays who know they are gay.

No matter who the nongays are or what their relationship to the gay person is, the possible consequences are the same. To the extent that they are involved in the nongay world, gay people may feel isolated and lonely because they are cut off from a lifestyle that is compatible with their feelings and are immersed in a lifestyle that is different and nonsupportive. Gays may also feel guilty because they are afraid to share themselves with family, friends, and co-workers. These people, in turn, may be confused, frustrated, and irritated by the gay person's behavior. Because of society's attitudes about gay people, very few gays are able to relate to nongays as easily as nongays can relate to each other about areas that are central to most people's lives.

People who do know. Social interactions with people who know that an individual is gay are likely to be easier and more open than those with individuals who do not know. There is no necessity for the gay person to maintain a facade or make up stories about his or her lifestyle. A nongay person's attitude toward gay people can be inferred from her or his behavior so there is less need for the gay person to be concerned about how the other feels. Naturally, there are times when a nongay person will say that she or he is comfortable with gayness but will communicate discomfort in other ways. Even though this makes social interaction difficult, it is still preferable to having no idea how a person will react.

Although it might be expected that gay people would feel totally comfortable with nongays who know about their sexual preference this is often not the case. Many nongays are able to cope with the knowledge that a friend or family member is gay, but they are often unable to handle physical evidence and may act uncomfortable with any behavior on the part of the gay person that brings the fact of gayness into the forefront. Sometimes this awkwardness is simply because of ignorance about what to expect from a gay person or about what is socially "appropriate" as a response. Thus, for example, some nongays believe all gay couples mimic nongay couples and that one person plays the male role and one the female. They may expend quite a bit of energy trying to figure out whether a given person is "butch" or "femme" and how to treat the person on that basis.

Sometimes nongays are made uncomfortable by the expression of affection between any two people, gay or nongay. Sometimes it is threatening because it is new and unusual. Most people have not been trained to respond comfortably to the sight of two men or two women dancing, kissing, holding hands, and the like. Such behavior may thus be embarrassing to them, and as a result they may find it offensive, awkward, or inappropriate. In many cases, friends or family members may indicate in subtle ways that they are aware of an individual's sexual preference but do not wish to be openly confronted with it.

There are many instances of families, friends, and co-workers treating a gay couple as a couple: inviting them for dinners, parties, holidays, and the like, but at the same denying the type of relationship they have and expecting the couple to do the same. This may go on for years without the subject of sexual preference ever being raised directly but with the clear message, usually nonverbal, that the couple is not to behave as though they are more than friends. Berzon describes this as an "unspoken contract" reading:

> Party of the first part agrees not to identify reality: "I'm gay. _____ is my lover."
> Parties of the second part agree not to withold social invitations/job advancements/respect/admiration/acceptance/love/etc.
> Parties of the second part are allowed the luxury of never having to deal directly with the *awful* reality of homosexuality in their midst.
> Party of the first part is allowed to remain in their midst.[37]

In order not to "break" the contract, gay couples are most likely not to show physical affection for each other, not to talk about themselves as a couple, and to avoid the kinds of behaviors typical of lovers.[35] Berzon urges gays to come out to others as part of developing a positive gay identity and to "break this deadly contract, to negotiate a new one that enables love and trust rather than fear and embarrassment to determine the limits of relationships with those we care about."[37]

The perceived necessity for restricting behavior in these ways is experienced as a problem by many, but not all, gay people. However, as gay people become more and more militant about their rights, they are increasingly likely to resent and refuse to adhere to the traditionally closeted role expected of gays. Some gays already segregate themselves as much as possible from the nongay community. Others who are reluctant to give up nongay friends or who do not want to be pushed into segregated "ghettos," are becoming more and more assertive, hoping in this way to influence the nongay community.

Intervention implications. Working with members of any oppressed group necessitates striking a balance between recognizing and validating the person's experience of being oppressed and helping the client move out of the role of victim. Staying in the role of victim essentially abdicates responsibility to the oppressor. The total victim is helpless and hopeless, depressed rather than angry, always blaming society for his or her problems in living.

> Forever, it seems, gay people have been giving their power away to others: define me, explain me, structure my behavior, decide for me what I can and cannot hope to achieve in my life, make rules for my participation in society, let me know the limits of tolerability if I happen to go beyond the boundaries set for me.
>
> It takes uncommon courage to reclaim power once it has been given away. It is uncommon courage that is called for in developing a positive gay identity in any antigay society.[38]

Mental health professionals cannot provide clients with courage itself, but they can provide clients with information and skills necessary to develop courage, to exercise it, to make it manifest. Courage is essentially the ability to act in a way that is difficult or threatening now because of the belief that, in the long run, to act is better than not to act. So a gay woman may have the courage to come out to people at work because she knows that the risk today will be less than the cost of having to continue to lie about her lifestyle. A gay man may have the courage to speak out against someone

who is espousing the oppression of gays because, even though it frightens him to do so, he knows he will feel better about himself later.

But courage is a relative thing, something that is often forgotten by people who advocate that all gays come out of the closet immediately. The courage of those individuals who come out to the press and who become nationally known as gay is formidable indeed. But it is duplicated daily by men and women who make decisions to do things that frighten them: to speak up assertively about gay rights, wear a gay pride button for the first time, go to a consciousness-raising group and admit to being gay, admit to oneself that one has gay feelings, decide for the first time to have a sexual experience with someone of the same gender. All these actions are courageous for those who take them in fear and anxiety. So, although it is true that being gay, like being Black and being a woman, is inevitably to be "at risk" in this society, remember that not all individuals experience or react to that risk in the same way. Each client's needs, problems, and potential must be individually assessed.

Gay clients who come in with debilitating anxiety are undoubtedly a minority of gay people. Most gay people do not believe they have been discriminated against in employment; most do not believe they are "instantly visible" as gay people.[39] The overwhelming majority feel good about gay people of their own gender.[40] The vast majority of lesbians and about half of the gay men in Bell and Weinberg's study reported no regrets whatsoever about their sexual preference.[41] But there are still those gays who do experience regrets and who do suffer from anxiety. In fact, those people are probably particularly underrepresented in both the Jay and Young and the Bell and Weinberg studies because both studies required that the respondent volunteer to participate, something that a highly anxious gay person might be unlikely to do.

The problems of those clients who do experience anxiety or other difficulties discussed in this chapter can be addressed by giving clients relevant information and teaching them good coping skills. The fact that gay people live in a society that is intolerant of their way of life means that many, though certainly not all, gay people learn a variety of self-protective behaviors when they are around nongays. For some, these behaviors may be highly dysfunctional.

Jeff, a 23-year-old college student came into counseling because he was afraid to speak up in class and never left his room in the dormitory except to go to meals. He was afraid that if he called attention to himself, people would immediately realize he was gay. Terry, a graduate student, also came into counseling because his anxiety over being identified as gay was affecting his schoolwork. Marsha, a 27-year-old secretary, was afraid to go to lunch with the other women in the secretarial pool. She could not join in their lunchtime conversations about dates, available men, clothing, and upcoming marriages, so she stayed away. She soon became known as a snob. Sally was afraid to speak up during important staff meetings, even though she knew her ideas were good ones. She had learned to be so frightened of being identified that the thought of calling attention to herself by speaking out brought on a paralyzing anxiety attack.[42]

Attempts to keep others from identifying them as gay are common among gay people. If the individual is really afraid, the anxiety combined with an unwillingness to reveal facts about one's private life can cause the gay person to avoid all but the most superficial interactions with nongays. Here is where it is important to provide the client with information, anxiety management, and skill training.

There are already excellent intervention methods available for the relief of anxiety.[43] Many of these rely on cognitive techniques as well as relaxation procedures.[44] Cognitive restructuring is important with gay clients who experience social anxiety, because the anxiety is often triggered by irrational thoughts. These thoughts often relate to the client's visibility, vulnerability, and the awful consequences of being discovered to be gay. Frequently, the client is neither as visible nor as vulnerable as he or she believes, and the consequences of being found out would probably not be as ghastly as the client imagines. Rather than trying to convince the client that she or he is not terribly visible, you may want to have the client attempt to identify other gay people in crowds, to observe himself or herself on videotape, or to point out kinds of behaviors that she or he does that nongay people also do.

If there are, in fact, behaviors that the person has that are particularly mannered, you may choose to point these out and give the person the option of trying to change them. Another possibility is to have the client identify other people who do things that are considered atypical for their gender and see if the client can tell whether or not these people are gay.

It is often the case that gay clients are so anxious about being discovered that they neglect to look about them and observe others, or their observations may be "edited" to such an extent that they incorrectly or inappropriately interpret others' actions as reactions to them and their sexual preference. Sally, the young woman discussed earlier, told her counselors one day that she had reached the point that, whenever one of her co-workers left the coffee room when she was present, she worried that it was because she was gay. Later in the session, one of her counselors got up abruptly and left the room. Upon returning, he asked her why she thought he had left. She said she didn't know. Her counselors then pointed she also had no idea why people at work left the coffee room, and that there was no more reason there than in the counseling situation to believe that it was because of her sexual preference. She was told to spend the next week observing people at work to see how much of their behavior could realistically and rationally be attributed to her behavior. Of course, she found that almost none of it could be.

Gays sometimes become so concerned over their

visibility that they attribute to nongays a far greater interest in others' actions, histories, and sexual predilections than is usually the case. It can be calming for them to realize that nongay people, like gay people, are generally so engrossed in their own concerns that they are not likely to pay much attention to others' sexual preference unless the individual is particularly blatant or intrusive. A gay person who is comfortable with her or his sexual preference, who neither hides nor advertises it, will often be able to get along quite comfortably. This is not always the case, however, and the counselor must be careful in assessing with the client any possible dangers the client may really be facing because of her or his sexual preference. There are nongays who are sufficiently homophobic that they do worry about gay people and could be a definite threat. It is scarcely preferable, however, to have a gay person in constant fear and trembling over the possibility of something happening than to have the person facing the actual threat. The client must decide whether to begin taking more risks. We have consistently taken the position throughout this book that it is up to clients, not helping professionals, to determine how they wish to live their lives. We believe it is up to us to help clients reach their goals, not ours.

Working out relationships with nongays. Conflicts can arise for gays in attempting to work out relationships with nongay people, especially co-workers, family, and friends. Gays may have many of the same difficulties in these areas as nongays, such as lack of assertiveness, insufficient job skills, and poor social skills.

Along with a basic assessment of the problem itself, it may be necessary for the helping professional to take into account the effect of the client's sexual preference on his or her solutions to such problems. A very common problem faced by gay people, for example, is difficulty in distinguishing between those behaviors that will and those that will not enable nongay people to identify them as gay. This confusion may result in an attenuation of all behaviors. This, combined with others' responses to the gay person's withdrawal, may cause the gay person to feel guilty, inadequate, and so

forth. With family and friends, gay people may end up either cutting off communication entirely to avoid conflict and possible discovery or they may get "overused" by parents out of guilt and a sense of failure for which they continually try to make amends.

When this is the case, teach the client to discriminate between those behaviors, such as direct revelation, that are immediately relevant to her or his sexual preference and others, such as single status or animosity toward Anita Bryant, that are not. A gay person who does not want to be hassled about being gay has to learn for example, that she or he doesn't automatically have to put up with the kinds of heterosexist remarks that nongays are likely to make. There is no necessary connection between one's personal beliefs and attitudes and one's experience or characteristics: one does not have to be a woman to support the ERA, a Black person to oppose the Klan, or a gay person to support gay rights.

Summary

Being gay means living in a culture that does not recognize your lifestyle as legitimate, one in which gays are largely invisible. Until recently, there has been little written gay history or culture. This state of affairs is finally beginning to change.

Surprisingly, the pressures of being gay appear to have little negative effect on gay people's psychological and emotional health. Gays in general certainly are not any less healthy than their nongay counterparts, and may even be healthier. There is some indication that gay people, particularly men, may be more likely to be androgynous than nongays. This may be because there is sometimes a relationship between gender behavior and sexual preference, because in same-gender relationships both parties need to move out of rigid gender roles, or because the gay community allows and supports cross-gender behavior. The fact that cross-gender behavior occurs, even when the gay person demonstrates behaviors mostly considered appropriate for the opposite gender, does not mean that gay people are confused about their gender identity. It may mean that a person feels more comfortable with the behaviors of the opposite gender or that he or she wants to express both male and female characteristics. In any event, to the extent that gay people are able to express both masculine and feminine characteristics as the situation demands, they may be healthier than nongays who remain in rigid gender roles.

Being gay can cause individuals trouble as they attempt to relate to the nongay worlds of work, family, and friends. Although most gay people do not feel discriminated against or have any regrets about their sexual preference, some gay people experience extreme anxiety. This anxiety frequently stems from *irrational* worry over being discovered to be gay. Although there are certainly situations when it is quite rational and functional to be concerned about being identified, people who suffer from severe, debilitating anxiety have usually carried their fears to an extreme. The helping professional is cautioned to be sure the fear is not reality based before proceeding to help the client deal with it.

Anxiety about one's sexual preference can be dealt with just as one would deal with other types of anxiety. It is helpful, however, to be aware of some of the kinds of fears that are typically experienced by gay people. Suggestions for helping gay clients with these fears are based largely on helping gay clients view the world more objectively. The objective is not to remove all concern, but to help clients learn to distinguish situations that should be realistically fear producing from those that should not.

THE GAY COMMUNITY

The concept of the gay community is very important to a large number of gay men and women.[45] In most urban areas, the gay community is not a community of residence but of connection, consisting of bars, coffee houses, baths, restaurants, social and educational groups, churches, and those gay individuals who form an interconnected network.[46] In several larger areas, such as Los Angeles, San Francisco, and New York, there are geographical concentrations of gays and gay-related services and businesses that are considered by some to be classifiable as "ghettos."[47] These relate more to gay men than to lesbian women.

Although the gay community can be considered to encompass all gay people, is probably both more accurate and more informative to describe the gay men's and lesbian women's communities as separate entities, since that is the way they function in most cases. The two communities may join together for rallies, marches, community-wide meetings, and in gay organizations such as the National Gay Task Force. Men and women occasionally share the same bars, often the same restaurants, sometimes the same social circles. But for the most part gay society, like nongay society, is homosocial. Jay and Young found, for example, that both gay men and lesbians spent more time socializing with gays of the same gender than in mixed groups of gay men and women. Both men and women also reported feeling more positive about gays of their own gender than of the opposite gender. Interestingly enough, lesbians were much more likely to spend time in the company of both gay and nongay women than gay men were to spend time in mixed male company. This is presumably because of the overlap between lesbian and nongay feminist interests and because the women's movement may have led to greater acceptance of each other on the part of gay and nongay women.

Jay and Young also found that lesbians viewed lesbian culture and community as more important than gay culture and community, although both men and women view the concept of gay community as having about the same importance to them.[48] Jay and Young suggest that the stronger involvement of lesbians in lesbian culture and community may occur because their concurrent struggles as women cause them to view lesbianism as a "multilayered concept."[48] Gay men, who can usually fit more easily into the nongay male power structure, often do not have the same kind of investment in or need to develop a separate community structure except in relation to sexual needs. This is reflected in Jay and Young's further finding that lesbian women are much more likely than gay men to see gayness as "something other than a sexual orientation."[48]

The gay social scene

The organization of the gay social scene in a given location depends on the size of the gay community and the consequent availability of services. In large urban areas such as New York City, San Francisco, and West Los Angeles where there are bars, restaurants, discos, boutiques, and other businesses that serve clientele either exclusively or predominantly gay, the social activities of the gay community will differ radically from those in a small midwestern town with one bar serving both gays and nongays. Wherever there is a gay community, however, social activities will center to varying degrees on gay bars, parties, and organizations, with gays also participating in nongay activities as well.

The gay bar

Aside from local gay groups and services with which helping professionals should be familiar (such as gay or lesbian coffee houses, rap groups, and crisis or health hotlines), the major social institution in the gay community is the gay bar. A number of authors have talked about the centrality of the gay bar in the social network of the gay community and why it is a place of such importance.[49] Bell and Weinberg describe the functions of the gay bar:

> As they are for heterosexuals, bars are a place for homosexuals to eat and drink, get together with friends, be entertained, sit alone, dance—to feel a sense of community. In addition . . . gay bars are a setting in which to find new sexual partners. Beyond these ends, the gay bar has a more central place in the homosexual community than does a bar for heterosexuals. The gay bar is one place where homosexuals can relax and enjoy themselves without having to hide their sexual orientation (as many do, at least in some

contexts, all day). The bar is also a clearinghouse for information, where people find out what has become of old friends, what activities are coming up, when homophile organization meetings take place, and generally, the news in the gay community.[50]

In urban settings, gay bars are numerous[51] and cater to different gay clientele. A large metropolitan area such as San Francisco or New York, for example, will have bars that serve either gay men or lesbians exclusively. There are bars that cater to different groups on the basis of socioeconomic status, and among the men's bars, there are differences on the basis of the kinds of clothes, sexual interests, and fantasies of those served. Some bars, for example, attract men who wear and are sexually aroused by leather; others are primarily for men who are interested in S & M (sadism and masochism) or B & D (bondage and discipline); some have a western or cowboy motif; and still others have a military theme. Lest the reader gets the notion, as some do, that these kinds of sexual interests are unique to the gay men's community, a perusal of some nongay pornographic literature will show that sexual fantasies involving inflicting and receiving punishment or pain, bondage, and various kinds of costuming are ubiquitous within at least Western cultures among both gay and nongay men and women, although much more common among men.[52]

Although gay bars serve an important function for both gay men and women, they are probably not as central in the lives of most gays as the literature would lead one to believe. Their predominance is probably due more to the uniqueness of their social function and their visibility than to the importance they actually play in the lives of the average gay man or lesbian woman. Bell and Weinberg[53] and Jay and Young[54] both found that about 45% to 50% of their male and slightly fewer than one third of their female respondents went to gay bars very frequently.

Both of these samples are highly weighted toward large metropolitan areas, with all of Bell and

Weinberg's and about 50% of Jay and Young's sample coming from either major metropolitan areas or large cities. This may be a factor in the frequency of bar attendance for both men and women. Geographical areas with large numbers of gay people also support large numbers of gay services. In areas with fewer gay people, gays may have to travel farther to reach a gay bar, and there are many fewer bars available. Those that exist often cater to both gays and nongays; anonymity and therefore security are lessened, and there may be more harrassment from nongays.

Nonetheless, it is worthwhile for helping professionals to be aware of the existence of gay bars in their area, of the kinds of clientele, and the probability that a gay person would be subject to harrassment. For men especially, a gay bar is a reasonable place for a counselor to send a client to meet other gay people and to make both social and sexual contacts. In a small town, the helping professional would be well advised to talk with a client about the possibility of visiting a gay bar out of town, preferably in a larger urban center.

Bars are less likely to be good sources of contacts for lesbian women. They are used less frequently by women than men and are far down the list of lesbian women's preferred ways of meeting others.[55] The clinician would be wise to find out other contact sources for lesbians unless he or she lives in an area where there are bars that cater primarily to lesbians.

Gay bars and gay alcoholism. Alcohol abuse is considered a serious problem by many in the gay community. Because so many social contacts take place either in gay bars or in settings where alcohol and often other drugs are available, it is easy for some gay people to fall into a pattern of substance abuse. The ready availability of alcohol in social situations combined with the pressures of a gay lifestyle may be sufficient to create a substance abuse problem in people who would not otherwise have one.

Clinicians who are helping gay clients become involved in the gay community should be aware of the extent to which alcohol is a part of much gay social life, particularly in gay bars. If the client is already having substance abuse problems or if he or she is homophobic, highly anxious about being gay or about getting to know other gay people, or under other stress, the counselor may want to recommend an avenue other than the bar scene to provide community involvement.

Gays who come in for treatment as alcoholics may have tried Alcoholics Anonymous and found it unsatisfactory because of the predominance of nongays. Many areas now have lesbian and gay men's AA groups that have split away from the main AA organization. Groups specifically for gays are much more likely to attract gay alcoholics than are nongay AA groups because so many of the problems gay alcoholics face are related to their sexual and affectional preference in one way or another. Trying to stay in the closet and deal with one's alcoholism in a group is almost impossible, yet the thought of having to come out to other nongay AA members may be sufficiently threatening to keep a gay person away.

THE LESBIAN COMMUNITY

The meaning of the term *lesbian community* that is most common and therefore most relevant to us is that group of women in an individual's immediate geographical area who share the characteristic of being lesbian and who are accessible to the individual. In referring to the lesbian community in this sense one might say, ''the lesbian community in this town is really active,'' or ''most of the women in the lesbian community are still pretty much in the closet.''

The term may also be used to refer to all lesbian women in the United States or perhaps even the world. In both the narrow and the broad usage, the term refers not only to shared sexual and affectional preference, but to shared experiences as women and lesbians. The frequent use of the terms *sister(s)* and *sisterhood* by lesbian women to refer to other lesbian women and to the lesbian community attests to the perceived strength and importance of these bonds.

The concept of lesbian community may also incorporate women's bars, coffee houses, restaurants, and the homes of those women who entertain other lesbians. Also part of the concept for some women may be political organizations such as NOW, lesbian women's groups, religious affiliations, such as the Metropolitan Community Church, and other organizations such as AA.

Impact of the lesbian community on lesbian women

The community to which a lesbian woman belongs can have a powerful effect on her. For many women, the gay community is a source of strength and a positive influence.[56] Belonging to the gay women's community means knowing others who share one's lifestyle with whom one can relax; it means having a shared culture that is not based on the heterosexist model. It can mean having positive role models, allies, a strong support system, and a place of refuge. But the lesbian community is based not only on shared positive experiences but on shared negative experiences: the experience of being oppressed, of living in a heterosexist society, of having one's behavior viewed as sick, perverse, immoral, and illegal. Because of the sense of oppression, there is a strong element of being united, of being comrades in arms, so to speak, of sharing sisterhood, that many lesbian women experience and express toward other lesbian women. Thus, many women feel committed to their gay sisters (and often their gay brothers) in a political and moral sense.

The lesbian community can also have a negative impact on an individual. If the part of the community with which a client identifies is heavily into substance abuse, for example, that may make intervention difficult. If a woman belongs to a lesbian community that is in the closet and she wants to come out, she may encounter hostility and fear. In a very small lesbian community, women with differing interests may not find others with whom they feel compatible and thus may feel doubly isolated: from both the lesbian and the straight communities.

Identifying with the lesbian community. One

of the major reasons why the lesbian community can have so much impact on a lesbian woman is because the community plays a major role in the identity of many lesbians. Unlike the nongay community, in which membership is automatically assumed, the lesbian community must be "joined" by identifying oneself as lesbian, a step that has profound implications for many women.

The process of identifying with the lesbian community means different things to different women. For some, the lesbian community is their entire life: social, political, cultural, religious, emotional, intellectual. Some women read only women's books, listen only to women's music, and relate only to women. At the other extreme are women who rarely see or socialize with other lesbian women, who may in fact feel that their only link with the lesbian community is through an occasional book or news story, who may feel isolated and alone, and yet who choose to continue in that type of lifestyle. Between these two extremes are all possible varieties of commitment to and identification with other lesbian women.

Cindy, for example, is a well-known professional living in a large urban area. She has a wide circle of gay friends, visits gay bars on occasion, and socializes often with other gay people. Although she isn't open about her sexual preference, she lives with her lover and is not uncomfortable about being identified with gay projects or about being seen in the gay community. Although her social life is organized largely around the gay community, this is not the major part of her life. Her major identification is with her work.

Jean lives with her lover Maggie in an isolated rural area where she was born. She and Maggie socialize almost exclusively with straight friends and live a very closeted existence. For Jean, the lesbian community is a source of identification for her in that she knows there are other women "out there" somewhere who share her sexual preference and to whom she belongs in a vague way. She is anxious to make contact with other women and yet afraid to spoil the balance of her life so tenuously achieved.

Gail lives in a small urban area, and her entire life outside of work is committed to the lesbian community. She belongs to women's groups of various kinds, organizes within the local lesbian community, attends rallies and marches, openly identifies herself as lesbian, works actively with the Metropolitan Community Church, and lives in a gay commune. If she could support herself by working only within the gay community, she would do so. As it is, she has chosen to work part-time and earn the bare minimum that she needs in order to devote more time to women's issues.

These examples are given to provide the reader with a concrete notion of the wide variety of commitments to the lesbian community. What all these women do have in common is that all identify themselves as lesbian women, in some sense see their good as tied up with the good of other lesbian women, and seek to varying degrees to establish a sense of belonging to a wider community of women like themselves.

The lesbian community as extended family

One of the strengths of the lesbian community is the ability and willingness of women within it to function as extended family members for each other. On many of the occasions when heterosexuals typically turn to their own families for support, the lesbian woman has no family to turn to and so she turns to her gay sisters. And indeed, the concept of a sisterhood is important. The lesbian woman finds with her gay sisters many of the things she would not find in her family of origin: a sense of continuity, of shared experiences, common history, an acceptance and approval of her lifestyle, and the close-knit bonds of sharing and love that are part of the proverbial American family scene. For the lesbian woman in therapy, it is this family as well as, or more likely instead of, her family of origin that can be looked to as a source of both environment support and hindrance.

The lesbian extended family is in some respects similar in function to a nuclear family, but in most respects it is very different. The extended family is very likely to join together whenever possible to celebrate holidays and special occasions. It is a strong support group, and members of the extended family keep in close touch with each other. In the sense that the extended family provides a home base, it may be said to be similar to the concept of the nuclear family.

But there, for the most part, the similarity ends. The lesbian extended family community is an essentially egalitarian, all-woman group with a membership that changes over time. Observation of a number of lesbian communities suggests that members of such a group are likely to be similar in age, education, socioeconomic status, and race, although this is not necessarily the case. The unit is likely to be composed of a small number of couples and perhaps some women who are unattached, who spend a large part of their social lives in each other's company. Such groups of women frequently gather to celebrate holidays and special occasions and in this way provide positive support for each other by creating good times. These groups are also sources of support during bad times, whether there may be death, loss of a job, illness, or some other problem that a couple or individual may face.

Both of these functions are extremely important. Many lesbian women have no place else to turn for support for the kinds of things that are important to them. A lesbian woman can celebrate holidays with her nuclear family, but it is the rare case in which a lover or close friend is welcome with the knowledge that she is gay. Even in those rare situations where the family is accepting of their daughter's gayness and of her gay friends or lover, the predominant theme is still almost inevitably (and quite understandably) one in which heterosexuality is the norm. The gay woman either alone or with her lover may be expected to fit (and may indeed want desperately to do so) into a setting of married siblings, with parents anticipating or doting on grandchildren, of other relatives asking embarrassing questions or acting disapprovingly or, perhaps worse, being pointedly tolerant. This kind of setting is hardly one to evoke joy or merrymaking. Even if the feelings are positive, there is still liable to be something missing: the freedom to be oneself, to be openly, positively lesbian. It is this freedom that the lesbian extended family makes possible, along with the kinds of festivities that are supposed to make family gatherings so pleasant: good food and good company on holidays, presents and celebration on birthdays, congratulations for promotions, schooling completed, houses purchased or remodeled, and the like.

The extended family community may also play a substantial role in helping a woman or a couple overcome difficult circumstances. Not only do such groups provide emotional and financial support during periods of crisis, they may also provide long-term support for a woman or couple with some kind of life problem. Such things as emotional problems, alcoholism, drug abuse, and even occasional physical violence may be a "family matter" and the person involved may be accepted in a way that she might not be in a group of people who did not know her. This acceptance is not always beneficial and, in the case of intervention with such an individual, may not be in the client's best interest. One author has observed a number of situations in which the extended family network has, usually unwittingly, made change difficult for an individual by allowing behavior that was dysfunctional and disruptive.

In the case of Martha, for example, a group of women who had known each other for 20 years spent much of their social life together and frequently went on long weekend outings together. Most, but not all, of the women lived singly although they enjoyed occasional involvements with other women. Martha belonged to one of the few couples in the group. A woman in her late 30s, she had joined the group through her involvement with Georgia, an involvement that had eventually ended, although both women remained in the group. During her early 20s, Martha had been institutionalized for severe depression and was still inclined to get depressed. She was also a very heavy drinker. When her drinking and depression coincided, she would become either violent or suicidal, and was given to waving guns, knives, and axes with some abandon, threatening mayhem. These outbursts almost always occurred during the extended weekend parties that took place every 2 to 3 months. The response of the family group was extremely permissive and supportive of Martha's problem. Indeed, in some respects Martha fulfilled a role she was expected to play, providing everyone with someone to take care of and worry about, as well as creating lots of stories.

Anyone attempting to intervene in this situation would have had to take into account the kind of reinforcement Martha received from her extended family both for drinking and for her violent behavior. Indeed, she received more attention at these times than any others, and following her outbursts, people were usually particularly solicitous and supportive both of her and her partner. Even on those rare occasions when the group members became angry, the anger took the form of increased attention. The group members would then exhaust themselves over Martha, and when her depression subsided and she began to act "normal," attention would lag again. Although this cycle may not have been the cause of her behavior, it certainly did nothing to help her change her behavior had she wanted to.

There are many circumstances of this kind in which gay women in an attempt to be supportive to their sisters will condone and even reinforce severely dysfunctional behavior on the grounds that gay sisters should receive unconditional love and positive attention. This impulse is easy to understand. In a subculture in which the outside world is consistently perceived as punitive and in which the messages received from the heterosexual community are consistently negative, there is a strong desire to be cohesive, "positive," and supportive within the community no matter what the behavior and no matter what the cost. It becomes a matter of survival: if we do not support each other, where then can we turn for support? And indeed, all too often there is no place to turn for the kind of support that acknowledges the legitimacy of the lesbian lifestyle; there are too few helping professionals knowledgeable enough, even though they may be willing to provide the kind of intervention that many lesbian women need. So extended family members turn to one another.

Extended family networks

The groups of women who serve as extended family to each other are often joined by friendships and old love relationships to groups within the same geographical area as well as to groups across the country. This network makes it possible for women to travel across country and move from one geographical area to another without losing contact with a lesbian support group. Women frequently have friends in other cities and states who function in the role of extended family and on whom they can rely for temporary housing, food, and social support. Not only do such networks facilitate travel, they are also part of survival within the lesbian culture because they make it possible for lesbian women to move around without being totally isolated within the nongay community.[57]

Lesbian culture

A new and vital lesbian feminist culture has been growing rapidly during the last 10 years all over the United States. There are magazines and newsletters appealing to many parts of the lesbian community and two national women's musical festivals that are largely lesbian; lesbian women have been a strong power in women's politics; literature and poetry are beginning to develop seriously, as are art and most especially music. There are currently several recording companies run by women who produce women's music, much of it written by and for lesbian women. The best known of the women's recording artists made national tours in 1980. There is a market within the lesbian community big enough to support these new enterprises, at least in their inception.

This new, strong sense of culture is tied equally to concepts of lesbianism and feminism, because the two go hand in hand. The music and literature being written by gay women reflects the desires of lesbian women to be strong, brave, gentle, loving, passionate. Women appear as primary figures, as mothers, sisters, lovers of other women, as warriors, queens, mystics, witches. Reading some of this literature and listening to the music is one of the best consciousness-raising and enlightening experiences a nongay person can have about what it means to be a lesbian woman.

THE GAY MALE COMMUNITY

Jay and Young indicate that a sense of the existence of a community beyond the focus on sexual orientation is stronger among lesbians than among gay men. The general tenor of the responses from the men in their study indicates less need for a supportive community than exists for lesbians. Although the majority of men felt that the concept of a gay community and culture was important, they were not as strong in viewing their gayness as more than sexual orientation.[58]

Weinberg and Williams found that association with other homoerotic men tended to aid a gay man in that he found social support for a wide variety of sexual practices. The "perverted" label associated with many of his sex acts was removed. He also had the opportunity to meet other men who had successfully developed their gay identities and who could provide him with positive role models, thereby enabling him to develop his own identity in a positive, supportive manner.[59] They indicate that "social, sexual, and psychological rewards accrue from social involvement with other homosexuals."[60]

Humphries and Miller noted that the homosexual community consists of not only the social contact associated with casual sexual encounters but also consciousness-raising groups, a variety of social, recreational, and sports groups, and religious and political groups. They identify several gay subcultures that exist for the financial, professional, religious, and personal growth of gay men. They do note, however, that the vast majority of these exist in the larger urban areas.[61] They additionally point out the very positive influence of the emerging gay culture on gay male identity, allowing the man to meet, socialize with, and share a variety of interests with other gay men, permitting him to feel less of the general cultural stigma and more of the support of others like himself.[62]

Thus it appears that there are several different types of communities within the gay male culture. However, they are at present not as strong or as organized as those in the lesbian culture. The gay male culture provides the gay man with opportunities for exposure to a wide variety of role models, both positive and negative. Primarily, it provides him with an atmosphere in which he can develop a positive self-concept. The growing number of groups that are concerned with political issues, with self-awareness and improvement, with religious needs, and with recreation activities that are not sexually focused indicates that gay men are becoming more conscious of the need for a sense of community.

INTERVENTION IMPLICATIONS

It is important for helping professionals to realize that the gay community exists because it is a place where gay people can usually find strong support. The helping professional should have contact people within the community and should know, for example, some of the bars and if there are any gay hotlines, medical or counseling services, women's or men's rap groups, and the like. Even though these resources may not provide an immediate solution to a specific client problem, it is good to be able to refer the client to such places.

Realize also that the gay communities of both gay men and lesbian women are composed of individuals of great diversity whose only common characteristics are their sexual preference and their experiences because of their sexual preference. The advantage to the diversity is that, in a large enough city, almost any gay person can find a support group of people who are like him or her in some respects. The disadvantage is that people often assume that because others belong to the gay community they ought to have more in common than they do.

The growth and development of the gay community is positive for lesbians and gay men. Particularly in the women's community, the explosion of woman-identified, woman-centered art and music is providing lesbian women with new, positive ideas, ideals, models, and goals. It is turning the negative image gays have held for so long into a positive, strong, and very exciting one. This is a marvelous thing to know, to watch, and to become involved in for anyone with concerns about gay people. The existence of women's friendship and extended family networks is also useful because it provides support for women who need help. If you are going to work with a gay client, especially a lesbian, it is a good idea to find out if she belongs to such a network, because intervention may involve other members of her extended family.

END NOTES

1. See Jay, K., & Young, A. *The gay report*. New York: Summit Books, 1979; Moses, A. *Identity management in lesbian women*. New York: Praeger, 1978; and Vida, G. (Ed.). *Our right to love*. Englewood Cliffs, N.J.: Prentice-Hall, 1978b, for discussions of some of the positive experiences gay people have.

2. Albro, J., & Tully, C. "A study of lesbian lifestyles in the homosexual micro-culture and the heterosexual macro-culture." *Journal of Homosexuality*, 1979; *4*(4), 341-354; Jay & Young, 1979; Moses, 1978.

3. Bell, A., & Weinberg, M. *Homosexualities: A study of diversity among men and women*. New York: Simon and Schuster, 1978.

4. Lee, J. "Going public: A study in the sociology of homosexual liberation." *Journal of Homosexuality*, 1977, *3*(1), 49-78.

5. Foster, J. *Sex variant women in literature: A historical and quantitative analysis*. Oakland, Calif.: Diana Press, 1975; Katz, J. *Gay American history*. New York: Thomas Crowell, 1976.

6. There are a number of publications by and for the gay community. A list of some of these, with a strong emphasis on lesbian women's publications, appears in Vida, 1978b, pp. 286-288. The great majority of openly gay music, art, and literature appears to be coming out of the lesbian community at this time. For discussions of these areas, see: Nixon, J., & Berson, G. "Women's music." in Vida, 1978b, pp. 286-288; Harris, B. "Lesbian literature: An introduction." In Vida, 1978b, pp. 257-259; and Ham-

mond, H., & Damon, B. "Lesbian artists." In Vida, 1978b, pp. 261-263.

7. Mannion, K. "Female homosexuality: A comprehensive review of theory and research." JSAS *Catalog of Selected Documents in Psychology,* 1976, *6*(2), 44. (Ms. No. 1247); Morin, S. "Heterosexual bias in psychological research on lesbianism and male homosexuality." *American Psychologist,* 1977, *32*(8), 629-637; Morin, S. "Psychology and the gay community: An overview." *Journal of Social Issues,* 1978, *34*(3), 1-6; Morin, S. "An annotated bibliography of research on lesbianism and male homosexuality (1967-1974)." JSAS *Catalog of Selected Documents in Psychology,* 1976, *6,* 15. (Ms. No. 1191); Sang, B. "Lesbian research: A critical evaluation." In Vida, 1978b, pp. 80-86; Riess, B., Safer, J., & Yotive, W. "Psychological test data on female homosexuality: A review of the literature." *Journal of Homosexuality,* 1974, *1*(1), 71-85.

8. See especially Mannion, 1976; and Riess, Safer, & Yotive, 1974.

9. Riess, Safer, & Yotive, 1974.

10. Mannion, 1976.

11. Freedman, M. "Homosexuality among women and psychological adjustment." *Dissertation Abstracts International,* 1968, *28,* 4294B-4295B. (University Microfilms No. 86-3308); Freedman, M. "Far from illness: Homosexuals may be healthier than straights." *Psychology Today,* March 1975, *8,* pp. 28-32; Siegelman, M. "Adjustment of homosexual and heterosexual women." *British Journal of Psychiatry,* 1972a, *120,* 477-481; Siegelman, M. "Adjustment of male homosexuals and heterosexuals." *Archives of Sexual Behavior,* 1972b, *2*(1), 9-25; Thompson, N., Jr., McCandless, B., & Strickland, B. "Personal adjustment of male and female homosexuals and heterosexuals." *Journal of Abnormal Psychology,* 1971, *78*(2), 237-240; Wilson, M., & Green, R. "Personality characteristics of female homosexuals." *Psychological Reports,* 1971, *28,* 407-412.

12. Mannion, 1976, p. 37.

13. Bell & Weinberg, 1978.

14. Bell & Weinberg, 1978, p. 216.

15. Bell & Weinberg, 1978; Morin, 1977; Marmor, J. "Overview: The multiple roots of homosexual behavior." In J. Marmor (Ed.), *Homosexual behavior: A modern reappraisal.* New York: Basic Books, 1980, pp. 3-22.

16. Morin, 1977.

17. Shively, M., Rudolph, J., & DeCecco, J. "The identification of the social sex-role stereotypes." *Journal of Homosexuality,* 1978, *3*(3), 225-234. Shively, Rudolph, and DeCecco found in their research that stereotypes are dimorphous (that is, occur in two distinct forms based on gender) for personality, interests, appearance, mannerisms, speech, and habits. They also found that masculinity is the "reference point" for identifying each gender role stereotype and feminity is often defined as the *absence* of masculine characteristics.

18. Clarenbach, K. as quoted in Edgar, J., Sweet, E., & Thom, M. *The decade of women: A Ms. history of the Seventies in words and pictures.* New York: Paragon Books, 1979, p. 67.

19. Adair, N., & Adair, C. *Word is out: Stories of some of our lives.* New York: Dell, 1978, p. 217.

20. Bernard, L., & Epstein, D. "Androgyny scores of matched homosexual and heterosexual males." *Journal of Homosexuality,* 1978, *4*(2), 169-178; Heilbrun, A., Jr., & Thompson, N., Jr. "Sex-role identity and male and female homosexuality." *Sex Roles,* 1977, *3*(1), 65-79; McDonald, G., & Moore, R. "Sex-role self-concepts of homosexual men and their attitudes toward both women and male homosexuality." *Journal of Homosexuality,* 1978, *4*(1), 3-15; Shavelson, E., Biaggio, M., Cross, H., & Lehman, R. "Lesbian women's perceptions of their parent-child relationships." *Journal of Homosexuality,* 1980, *5*(3), 205-216; Thompson, McCandless, & Strickland, 1971.

21. For descriptions of this, see Adair & Adair, 1978, pp. 43-53; 55-65; and Martin, D., & Lyon, P. *Lesbian/woman.* New York: Bantam Books, 1972.

22. Jay & Young, 1979, pp. 490; 519.

23. Jay & Young, 1979, pp. 575-576.

24. Jay & Young, 1979, p. 579

25. Jay & Young, 1979, p. 578.

26. Freund, K., Langevin, R., Satterberg, J., & Steiner, B. "Extension of the gender identity scale for males." *Archives of Sexual Behavior,* 1977, *6*(6), 515.

27. Adair & Adair, 1978, p. 218.

28. Adair & Adair, 1978, p. 87.

29. Adair & Adair, 1978, p. 89.

30. Jay & Young, 1979, p. 529.

31. See, for example, Bem, S. "The measurement of psychological androgyny." *Journal of Consulting and Clinical Psychology,* 1974, *42,* 155-162; Bem, S. "Sex role adaptability: One consequence of psychological androgyny." *Journal of Personality and Social Psychology,* 1975, *31*(4), 634-643; Heilbrun, A., Jr. "Measurement of masculine and feminine sex role identities as independent dimensions." *Journal of Consulting and Clinical Psychology,* 1976, *44*(2), 183-190; and for a much longer discussion of the concept of androgyny, see Heilbrun, C. *Toward a recognition of androgyny.* New York: Alfred Knopf, 1973.

32. Bem, 1975.

33. Adair & Adair, 1978, p. 219.

34. Adair & Adair, 1978, pp. 81-93.

35. Moses, 1978.

36. Weinberg, M., & Williams, C. *Male homosexuals: Their problems and adaptations.* New York: Penguin Books, 1975, p. 258.

37. Berzon, B. "Developing a positive gay identity." In B. Berzon & R. Leighton (Eds.), *Positively gay*. Millbrae, Calif.: Celestial Arts, 1979, pp. 10-11.

38. Berzon, 1979, pp. 1-2.

39. Jay & Young, 1979, pp. 139; 188.

40. Jay & Young, 1979, pp. 220; 234.

41. Bell & Weinberg, 1978, pp. 122-127.

42. Also see Bell & Weinberg, 1978, pp. 144-147; Jay & Young, 1979, pp. 707-715 for brief examples.

43. See Gambrill, E. *Behavior modification: Handbook of assessment, intervention and evaluation*. San Francisco: Jossey-Bass, 1977, pp. 438-491 for an excellent review of the literature as well as suggestions for intervention.

44. See, for example, Burns, D., & Beck, A. "Cognitive behavior modification of mood disorders." In J. Foreyt and D. Rathjen (Eds.), *Cognitive behavior therapy: Research and application*. New York: Plenum Press, 1978, pp. 109-134; also see Gambrill, 1977, esp. pp. 440-444; 447-448.

45. Jay & Young, 1979, pp. 763-764.

46. For an in-depth description of the San Francisco Bay Area lesbian community, see Wolf, D. *The lesbian community*. Berkeley: University of California Press, 1979, esp. pp. 71-105; also see DeCrescenzo, T., & Fifield, L. "The changing lesbian social scene." In Berzon & Leighton, 1979, pp. 15-23. Regarding the gay men's community, see Hooker, E. "The homosexual community." In J. Gagnon & W. Simon (Eds.), *Sexual deviance*. New York: Harper & Row, 1967a, 167-184; Levine, M. "Gay ghetto." *Journal of Homosexuality,* 1979, *4*(4), 363-378; and Warren, C. *Identity and community in the gay world*. New York: Wiley & Sons, 1974.

47. Levine, 1979.

48. Jay & Young, 1979, p. 763.

49. Bell & Weinberg, 1978, pp. 250-259; Achilles, N. "The development of the homosexual bar as an institution." In Gagnon & Simon, 1967a, pp. 228-244; Lewis, S. *Sunday's women: A report on lesbian life today*. Boston: Beacon Press, 1979.

50. Bell & Weinberg, 1978, p. 250.

51. Bell & Weinberg, 1978, found over 80 bars catering to gay clients in the Bay Area, 15 of which cater mostly to lesbians.

52. For some examples, see Young, W. "Prostitution." In Gagnon & Simon, 1967a, pp. 116-119. Also see Gagnon and Simon's chapter on pornography in J. Gagnon & W. Simon, *Sexual conduct: The social sources of human sexuality*. Chicago: Aldine, 1973a, pp. 260-282.

53. Bell & Weinberg, 1978, pp. 182; 184; 412.

54. Jay & Young, 1979, pp. 215-216; 239-243.

55. Jay & Young, 1979, pp. 214-220.

56. Jay & Young, 1979; Moses, 1978.

57. Lewis, 1979; and Wolf, 1979.

58. Jay & Young, 1979, pp. 763-764.

59. Weinberg & Williams, 1975, pp. 281-284.

60. Weinberg & Williams, 1975, p. 284.

61. Humphries, L., & Miller, B. "Identities in the emerging gay culture." In Marmor, 1980, pp. 142-156.

62. Humphries & Miller, 1980, pp. 150-156.

7

Coming out

Coming out of the closet, that is, identifying or labeling oneself as gay, is one of the most difficult and potentially traumatic experiences a gay person undertakes. For many gays, it is a long process from the first awareness of being different to self-labeling, and from there to letting others know of one's sexual orientation.[1] A lot of gay people's energy goes into deciding where, when, how, and whom to tell about being gay and in worrying about the possible consequences of being "out" to significant others. Any gay client a helping professional sees has almost certainly labored long and hard at one time or another over the matter of coming out to self or to others. If a counselor is not gay, or if a client does not know the counselor's sexual preference, it is likely that he or she has worried about whether or not to tell the counselor and what the counselor's reaction would be. "Will my counselor (or therapist) think I'm sick if I tell her?" "Will it make a difference in the kind of treatment I receive if my social worker knows I'm gay?" "What if my guidance counselor finds out? Will I get kicked out of school?"

Unless they live and work primarily around other gay people, almost all gays have continual concerns about being found out, and a good many gay men and women have trouble dealing with their sexual preference themselves. In this chapter, we will present the various stages of coming out, some of the problems that occur at each stage, possible effects of coming out, and the relevance of these to intervention with gay clients. We separate coming out into four stages: coming out to oneself (signification), identifying oneself to others who are gay, identifying oneself to someone nongay, and going public.[2]

STAGES OF THE COMING-OUT PROCESS
Coming out to oneself: the process of signification

The first stage of coming out is coming out to oneself, thinking of oneself as gay or lesbian for the first time. Lee[3] suggests, and we have adopted, Matza's[4] term *signification* for this process. We call it a *process* because in most cases, signification takes time. There is usually a more or less extended period during which the individual puts together feelings, thoughts, and sometimes sexual experiences with a learned definition of what a gay man or lesbian woman is. The end result may be a sudden "aha" of recognition, or it may be a slower occurrence as the individual accumulates "evidence" about her or his sexual preference. The actual act of self-labeling is technically the act of signification. One person may be relieved to have a name to give to the feeling of being different, another may be devastated by the thought of being "queer" or "sick," a third person may be confused about what it means.

Signification of self as gay does not mean that a person will automatically come out to others or change her or his behavior, but it often does have wide-ranging effects. Because of prevailing negative attitudes, signification is likely to mean individuals will have concerns about their psychological health, femininity or masculinity, ways of relating to others as gay people, role expectations, visibility, and so forth. There is likely to be a period of identity shifting, of trying the label on to see how it fits, and of making adjustments in oneself or in one's preconceptions about the label. There is also a period, more often extended than brief, of trying to fit an identity as a gay person into a society that considers gay people to be set a bit askew. Sometimes the process is made easier by a social environment at least somewhat tolerant of diverse lifestyles. But often signification means taking a step into a hostile and isolating world. This is probably most frequently the case with gay adolescents.

Coming out to oneself in adolescence. In Chapter 6, we talked about the fact that most gay people studied become aware of their sexual preference (or at least of a difference between themselves and their peers) before the age of 20, and many before the age of 15. Jay and Young[5] found that the actual labeling of that difference seems to take a year or two. But even though adolescents may not know quite what it means, they are usually wise enough to know that they should not talk about it to others. This wisdom is certainly self-protective and functional, but it is also isolating. In a society where all sexual feelings and acts are taboo topics, it is unlikely that gay adolescents will be able to find either information or support. Most adolescents do not have access to either positive gay role models or information that presents gays in a positive light. This makes it likely that a young gay man or woman is going to end up with a distorted and negative image of gay people and of self.

Some gay adolescents head for the library to find out if there are others like them and what it means to be as they are. For many, this first attempt to find out about being gay is the first of a number of lessons that teach the gay adolescent that she or he is sick. Galana and Covina[6] report an interview with a woman who had this kind of experience.

G: You said sometime when you were in high school, you realized [that your attraction for girls] was lesbianism?

F: Yeah . . .

G: How did you think of it? Did you think something was wrong with you?

F: Yeah. Well, I don't know if I thought that myself. I thought . . . something was different at first. And then, when I found the books about homosexuality in psychology—then I thought something was wrong with me.

Another woman they interviewed reported a similar experience[7]:

G: When you first realized you were attracted to girls and felt different about that, what kind of a crisis did you go through?

B: The whole time I was growing up, my knowledge about nearly everything came from books, so I went running to the library and picked up things in book stores and that was how I caught on. I was about in the tenth grade. I took the psychology approach to the whole thing.

G: Can you remember any of the books you found?

B: Oh sure. One of them was by Frank Caprio called *Female Homosexuality*—that was my textbook for awhile.

G: How did that make you feel when you read those things?

B: My consciousness was on such a low level, I just believed it all and just thought well, okay, so I'm sick.

But libraries and reading are either not options or are not culturally accepted for a great many adolescents. Those who live in areas that do not have libraries or where libraries either do not carry books dealing with male homoeroticism and lesbianism or carry only books with a negative point of view, those who speak English as a second language, and those who cannot or do not like to read must rely for information on television (if it is available), magazines, and the collective wisdom of society at large and of their parents, religious leaders, teachers, peers, and heroines or heroes. An adolescent lesbian in rural Appalachia, a gay boy in Iowa, a Black adolescent in Watts, a gay Asian-American in San Francisco, a Chicana in New Mexico can all find the going rough.

It should be easy to see why the process of coming out to oneself can be especially traumatic for an adolescent. It is likely to mean that the young gay man or woman will learn to think of herself or himself as sick or bad and will come to feel isolated and trapped. (For a frightening account of such an adolescent experience, see Whitey's story in Adair and Adair.[8])

Because of either an intense desire to be "normal" or the lack of information that would provide a label for their feelings, some adolescents who are attracted to members of the same gender and even some who have sexual experiences do not identify themselves as gay or lesbian until they reach adulthood:

☐ My first experience with another girl was at 15. I didn't realize I was a lesbian until I was 20. It took a while—intellectually coming out was very hard and traumatic. I used to look at myself in a mirror and cry. I couldn't believe what I was. How could a young girl like me be something as wicked as a lesbian?[9]

Other adolescents may engage in nongay sex to "prove" to themselves that they really are not gay after all.[10]

In general, a large part of the problem that adolescents face in coming out can be attributed to their status as minors. They have no mobility, poor access to information, no rights in the matter of sexual preference; and they are legally and economically dependent on their parents. They are also surrounded by peers who are struggling with their own sexuality and enmeshed in the superconformist and highly antigay world of adolescence. Being minors, they cannot be actively helped by adult gays, which means that one of the major sources of support for gays is not available to them.

Although the process is difficult for many, some gay adolescents appear to have relatively few conflicts about their sexual preference. For a marvelous description of one such adolescent, the reader is encouraged to see Rita Mae Brown's fictionalized autobiography, *Rubyfruit Jungle*.[11]

Intervention with adolescents. Many of the things a helping professional might suggest to an adult are not possible with adolescents because of their status as minors. This limits the intervention process to some extent. Even so, the counselor can help gay adolescents develop a realistic approach to functioning in a nongay world. This means, of course, that the helping professional must remain reality oriented, helping the adolescent focus on current problems and potential solutions to these. If possible, the counselor should direct the adolescent to information sources that will help provide a positive, healthy, nonstereotypical picture of gay men and women and of what it is like to be gay in this society.[12]

The counselor should not be mislead into believing that adolescents do not *really* know what they feel or that gay feelings are "just a stage." It is not wise to attempt to dissuade an adolescent from thinking of himself or herself as gay or lesbian. It is helpful to explore with the client the reasons for thinking of self as gay, and what the client thinks it will mean to be a gay person both as an adolescent and as an adult. An attempt to discourage a young gay person from signification of self as gay not only invalidates the client's feelings, but also makes it clear that the counselor is sufficiently opposed to a gay sexual preference to try to talk someone out of or get them to deny gay feelings. Most counselors would not do the same thing to an adolescent with concerns about heteroerotic emotions.

It is possible that an adolescent with a clearly nongay sexual preference may be afraid of being gay because of being labeled by others or because of close friendships, sexual experiences, or strong emotions shared with someone of the same gender. Again, it is not desirable to try to dissuade the person from self-labeling. It is more beneficial to help such a client explore her or his fantasies, thoughts, and feelings and to educate the person about the differences among homoerotic, ambierotic, and heteroerotic preferences. It is appropriate to point out that sexual preference is complex and is not determined by a few isolated sexual or emotional experiences, thoughts, or feelings. The adolescent should be reassured that sexual preference whatever it may be is not something to be afraid of.

If the client is worried about his or her sexual preference because of lack of successful encounters with members of the opposite gender (as opposed to positive interactions with the same gender), it may be appropriate to assess the client's social and relationship skills. The counselor can help the client distinguish lack of skills from sexual preference.

If the client is worried about strong emotions for someone of the same gender, he or she can be reassured that strong positive feelings for other people are good, regardless of sexual preference, and that sexual preference need not dictate the direction of one's affections.

Finally, if the client demonstrates cross-gender behavior, this may be perceived by the client or others as an indication that the person is "queer" (probably a more likely occurrence with adolescent boys than adolescent girls). The client, whether gay or nongay, can be educated about the value of being able to do all kinds of things, not just the things that society says are acceptable for men or women. Counselors can reassure their clients that breaking away from gender role stereotypes is often a sign of mental health and is usually something to feel good about. Both gay and nongay people deviate from gender role stereotypes, and failure to conform to these does not tell anything about sexual preference, nor should sexual preference dictate the kinds of gender role behaviors one engages in.

If an adolescent client is showing cross-gender behavior (that is, if a boy is showing predominantly feminine-typed behavior or a girl is showing predominantly masculine-typed behavior), the counselor may want to talk with the client about broadening his or her range of behaviors, *if the adolescent perceives this to be a problem*. Particular attention should be given to a high proportion of feminine-typed behavior if there is a concurrent lack of self-esteem and self-confidence, whether the client is male or female. There appears to be a relationship between these variables, as noted elsewhere, and it would be worthwhile to talk with such a client about broadening her or his behavioral repertoire as well as helping provide a more positive self-image. We believe it is most impor-

tant that clients be encouraged to *increase* rather than decrease their behavioral options. Thus, an adolescent male who is demonstrating a high proportion of feminine-typed gender role behaviors and a low proportion of masculine-typed behaviors might seek counseling because he is finding this a problem. We would encourage counselors to help such a client learn to increase more masculine-typed behaviors such as assertiveness and independence, rather than decreasing feminine-typed behaviors. This helps the client move toward a more androgynous set of personal behaviors rather than attempting to switch him from a feminine to a masculine set of gender-typed behaviors.

Assertiveness training and social skills training may turn out to be exceptionally useful techniques, particularly with individuals such as effeminate males and gays who experience high anxiety around nongays. Although there are currently only two studies extant that document the use of assertiveness training with gay clients,[13] this promises to be a fruitful area for further research. We would urge clinicians who work with young gay men and women, particularly males who manifest a lot of cross-gender behavior and have concurrent problems and those males and females who show high anxiety, to explore the use of assertiveness and social skills training with these clients.

Coming out to oneself as an adult. Gay adults undergo many of the strains experienced by adolescents when they first admit their own gayness. This is because adults, too, often know only the prevailing societal attitudes toward gays as sick people and are afraid of the consequences of being gay. The counselor should not be surprised to encounter clients who want help in making a decision about whether to be gay or nongay or who want a professional opinion about their mental health (or lack of it) on the basis of their sexual preference.

Many gays struggle for years against physical and emotional attraction to people of the same gender before finally deciding to label themselves as gay or lesbian. Some take the route of marrying and having children in what, in retrospect, they come to see as an attempt to convince themselves and others of their heterosexuality. Some people live, become sexually involved with, and orient their lives around others of the same gender while continuing to avoid self-labeling. Some spend their time with other gays but avoid any sexual contacts in order not to feel compelled to self-label or to be labeled by others. Some have a single homoerotic experience, label themselves as gay or lesbian, heave a sigh of relief, and plunge headlong into the gay lifestyle. Some label themselves without ever having a sexual or emotional involvement; and some never find their sexual preference difficult to admit and experience no trauma about the fact of their gayness.

When coming out is not difficult. Those who have little or no difficulty are probably fairly rare and are, of course, unlikely to seek counseling for this particular issue. It is instructive, nonetheless, to realize that signification is not always painful and ghastly and to see if something can be learned from these people's experiences that can be helpful to others.

There seem to be two major situations in which signification is not traumatic. The first is when the individual isn't aware of popular opinions about gayness, doesn't care, or is able to combat these in one way or another. The second takes place when the original emotional or sexual experience of gayness is so delightful and positive that negative implications don't carry much weight. Ann's story from *Word is Out* typifies both of these.

A: When I look back, for some reason, I had a very positive feeling about gayness and homosexuality. I thought it was so unreal that people would be classified in a mental institution that way. I didn't think it was particularly sick to be homosexual. Maybe because I'd led such an isolated life. I hadn't had a lot of influence to make me have negative feelings toward gay people. . . .
N: *How did you feel after your first sexual relationship with a woman?*

A: Well, it was a wonderful feeling. Aside from being so much in love, it was definitely a different life for me. It was a whole . . . just like opening a new door into a new life.[14]

When coming out is difficult. Helping professionals are inevitably going to see individuals who are worried about being gay. People who have difficulty identifying themselves as gay do so because they have learned and accepted the negative social view of gayness and apply it to themselves and others who are gay. Those who are struggling with self-definition are almost always struggling with their perception of what it means to be gay, in terms either of mental health or of how they think they will have to live and act.

This is a time when it is easy to confuse who one is and what one does with society's expectations about who gay people are and what they do. A woman who began to discover her sexual preference while in college says of that period:

☐ It was about this time that I began to become aware of an attraction to women, which I kept trying to suppress. Women struck me as being warmer and more open than men. I was fascinated by the idea of loving a woman but was totally turned off by what I thought lesbians were supposed to be like. I didn't want to be a man nor look like one. Since I was out of my element socially, I always came on as tough and aggressive to cover up, and people started accusing me of being a dyke. At the time, I was terrified that my fantasies were showing in some way, and I began dating to cover up, to show that I wasn't "like that."[15]

A gay man describes his experience:

☐ While in the closet, I was certainly not one of them "faggoty queers over in the dark slimy corners of society." Hell, no. So I became as macho as I could to retain some integrity, fantasized about men—naked, muscular, wrestling, working, sweaty, fucking women, men, or me. Lived in dorms, barracks, etc., for ten years from age 14-24. Hid this and suppressed it and spent lots of energy denying it.

Marry and it will go away. Well, I married, and I was still full of those feelings. Fifteen years later, changes began; I was 42 years old and the kids were 11 and 13. . . . I cried at night for fear I would die without being loved by a man.[16]

A counselor can be instrumental in helping a client distinguish between the social conception of gay people and self as an individual. A woman may think that if she admits to her own lesbianism, for example, she will suddenly become like the nongay stereotype of a lesbian. She may believe that to identify herself as lesbian will suddenly make her behavior change, will make her masculine or sick or any of the other things that society says lesbians are.

One woman who decided she was lesbian in her early twenties spent a year in fear and apprehension, believing that because lesbians are "sex crazed," she might at any moment begin to run amok, attacking women on the street. A man, suffering from the same kind of confusion, entered therapy terrified that he would suddenly become very effeminate and feel a compulsion to dress as a woman. They were understandably relieved to find out that they would not be overcome by urges of these kinds just because they were gay.

Because of this confusion between the label and the actual behavior that people who are labeled engage in, a person may admit to and act upon emotional and sexual feelings for others of the same gender and yet be panic stricken by the thought of self-identification. Such people seem to believe that it is the label itself that is crucial, not the behaviors, thoughts, and feelings.

☐ I thought that I could have what people would call a gay relationship with my friend and not have to get into gay women's liberation or see myself as a lesbian. I had the choice not to do that. I knew by calling myself a lesbian I was asking for disapproval, distance, and perhaps violence from most people. . . . So for a long time I did not identify.[17]

Signification and the helping process. Professionals must use discretion and sensitivity in helping clients choose and define the meaning of the label they believe best fits them; because, like it or not, clients want their sexual preference labeled one way or the other. We want to stress that concern about the possibility of being gay or thoughts or fantasies about members of the same gender do not necessarily mean that it is appropriate for a person to think of herself or himself as gay.

There are probably lots of people who live nongay lifestyles and define themselves as heterosexual and yet are physically and emotionally attracted to people of the same gender. Certainly there are many nongays who have sexual fantasies about relationships with others of the same gender. When these kinds of experiences are not problematic, when the person is content with her or his sexual preference and shows primary interest in relationships with members of the opposite gender, we see no need to infer "repressed" or "latent" homosexuality or lesbianism.

The time for concern is when an individual is unhappy in a nongay lifestyle and is experiencing attraction to members of the same gender that she or he wants to act on, but is not, or when the conflict over either the desire or the fear of being labeled is causing pain or dysfunction. In such an event, the main issue is, of course, to help the client fully express her or his sexuality.

Positive effects of signification. Some people feel much better when they finally label themselves as gay or lesbian. Even though a person may have struggled with the label for months or years, the final process of deciding "this is what I am" may suddenly legitimize thoughts, feelings, and actions that the person has been uncomfortable with for a long time. It may help the person give himself or herself permission to do things that have not been previously acceptable, and it sometimes really seems to open doors and help an individual make positive life changes.

Francine came into counseling because she thought she might be lesbian and she was not sure what to do about it. She was in her early 30s, married, and in graduate school. She had always enjoyed women more than men, but had married because it never really occurred to her that there was any other option; it was expected and so she did it.

When she first came into counseling sessions, she appeared nervous and tense. She was intelligent and had a good sense of humor that she appeared to hide behind heavy glasses. Her whole being radiated a rigid control. She had no idea what it would mean to adopt a gay lifestyle but said that she at least wanted to find out about it. Her counselor agreed to provide her with information, resource materials, and people she could contact.

In counseling sessions, they talked about her various options, what she really wanted to do that she was not doing, what changes she might be able to make within her marriage in order to make that better, and what the probable consequences would be if she chose each of the courses open to her. Her counselor stressed that living a gay lifestyle had both advantages and drawbacks, that it was neither a prison nor a panacea, and that calling herself a lesbian would neither solve nor create problems. It would be what she did on the basis of her decision to be either lesbian or nonlesbian that would have consequences for her. The counselor's objective was to help the client see that, no matter what she chose to call herself, it was up to her to make positive changes in her life.

At about the fourth session, Francine came in looking quite pleased with herself and announced that she was going to separate from her husband and get a divorce. She had begun spending a lot of time with a woman she had been friends with for several months and was considering beginning a sexual relationship with her. She had also begun to visit the local women's coffee house, to read literature by and about lesbians, and to spend time with lesbian women. All of these were things she had wanted to do for a long time but had been forbidden to do by her husband. She appeared much happier and relaxed than on previous occasions and reported that several members of her family had, independently, commented that she seemed happier and more spontaneous than they had ever seen her.

Obviously, the changes in Francine's behavior were not caused by the label *lesbian,* but by what it meant to her to think of herself that way. It was as though thinking of herself as lesbian allowed her to

experience and express her positive feelings about other women and about herself and helped her give herself permission to get out of her marriage and do some of the things she had been wanting to do for a long time.

It is helpful to adults, as to adolescents, to explore the reasons for believing they are gay and what being gay means. Clients may enter counseling thinking they are gay because of a sexual relationship with or fantasy about someone of the same gender. Sometimes counselors themselves make unwarranted assumptions about their clients' sexual preference on the basis of such things. We do not believe that a man (woman) who has a sexual relationship with another man (woman) is necessarily gay. Being gay is a lifestyle choice, not simply a sexual act. A great many men, for example, engage in quick anonymous sex with other men while leading otherwise heterosexually oriented lives.[18] We are in agreement with Lee[19] that it is meaningless to talk about "latent homosexuality." A man who lives his whole life and defines himself as a heterosexual *is* a heterosexual, even though he may fantasize about and even enjoy sex with men on occasion.

It seems quite clear that all humans are innately capable of sexual and emotional relationships with other humans of either the same or opposite gender, although many people learn to relate sexually and emotionally to only one gender. For obvious social reasons, people concern themselves primarily with labeling their own and others' same-gender relationships, and a client may come into counseling concerned that a sexual experience, a fantasy, or an emotional relationship with someone of the same gender means that he or she is gay. Clients are often reassured to understand that having a close, loving, even sexual relationship with someone of the same gender is not necessarily indicative of homosexuality or lesbianism; nor, for that matter, is such a relationship with someone of the opposite gender necessarily indicative of heterosexuality. Although many gay people (and many nongays) are aware of their sexual preference very early without being able to put a name to it, some people become gay without having any early awareness. Some people who think they could enjoy being gay choose not to live that kind of lifestyle. It is important to help clients realize that, even though for some people there does not seem to be clear choice about whether they are aroused sexually and emotionally primarily by men or by women, there *is* choice about how to act on one's feelings.

If a client is frightened about the possibility of being homosexual or lesbian, then the helping professional would do well to talk over with the client the reasons for the fear. Often people are afraid of being gay because of misconceptions they have about the mental health of gays or myths about what gay people are like. It is up to the professional to provide the client with accurate information about gay people and help the client understand that a gay lifestyle can be enjoyable, healthy, and productive. Put the client in contact with some gay people, provide resource materials, or tell the client where he or she can find some accurate information. Help the client evaluate the pros and cons of living a gay versus a nongay lifestyle so that she or he can make a reasonably informed decision about what to do.

Some clients who prefer a nongay lifestyle are needlessly, irrationally concerned about feelings or thoughts they have. In such cases it may be sufficient to teach the client that not only do heterosexuals have fantasies about gay sexual experiences, but gay people have fantasies about sexual experiences with nongays. It is also a good idea to let clients (both gay and nongay) know that love and affection are positive emotions, whether felt for someone of the same or someone of the opposite gender.

Coming out to others

Once an individual has decided on an identity as a gay man or lesbian woman, the next step is usually to begin identifying oneself as gay to others. Because this process is necessarily very different for adolescents than for adults, we will discuss them separately. We have also chosen to discuss the issue of coming out to children in Chapter 15, "Gay Parents."

Coming out to others as an adolescent. Adolescents are definitely a population at risk when it comes to revealing their sexual preference. There are numerous terrible stories in the gay community and a number that have been published about the consequences to gay adolescents when others learn of their sexual preference.[20] In the best of circumstances, a gay adolescent would be able to tell parents, teachers, siblings, and friends and get their support. There are certainly some rare cases when this happens, but they are few and far between. More common are those cases in which an adult finds out that a child is gay or lesbian and either punishes the child severely or tries to have her or him "cured." Simpson points out in her excellent book that the family may become the gay person's first "closet," one that alienates him or her from others, and that adolescents who choose to be open about their sexual preference may not get a very favorable response.[21]

Jay and Young found that, among respondents who had told one or both parents of their lesbianism, over half of the mothers (58%) and over a third of the fathers (40%) had a negative response.[5] Among the men, 34% of the mothers told and 35% of the fathers told had a negative response. Although the average age at which respondents said they first told their parents was 23, the high proportion of negative responses to adult sexual preference does not bode well for parental responses to adolescent gayness.

Simpson says that

when a number of heterosexual women were asked how they would feel, and what they would do, should they learn that their daughters were lesbian, their responses were negative: "I would take her to a psychiatrist immediately and have her cured"; "I would rather she would get pregnant—at least that would be normal"; and a classic: "If her father ever found out, he'd kill me." Small wonder that homosexuals, by the time they reach maturity, are so used to hiding that it often becomes a way of life.[22]

She gives another example in which

> a father stood at the top of the stairs in his home and threw large, heavy construction nuts and bolts from his workshop at his daughter, screaming "Freak!" at her. He beat her several times, not telling her why. It was only later that the girl found out that a "well-meaning friend" had told her father that she was a lesbian.[23]

A social worker in a rural area in the Southeast reports an instance in which the mother of a young gay woman came into a regional mental health clinic complaining of her daughter's sexual preference. She said that she would rather see her daughter dead than a lesbian and was planning to shoot her. Although extreme, these examples are far from rare, and they are not examples of otherwise crazed individuals. There are many parents who feel equally extreme about the subject of gayness, and even more who, although they might not be moved to violence, would respond negatively.

Unless the gay adolescent is quite sure that his or her parents' response will not be a highly negative one, he or she is probably wise to wait to tell them until coming of age. Children who tell their parents are risking a sharp curtailment of rights and possibly some kind of direct action by the parents to get them "cured," "saved," or otherwise convinced to change their ways.

Adolescents must also be cautious with peers. Unlike gay adults, gay adolescents are usually not free to seek, and indeed may not know where to find, support from the adult gay community. They are trapped instead in a heterosexual peer group at a time when nonconformity is the kiss of death. To come out to peers during adolescence will almost inevitably result in ostracism of the most severe kind unless the adolescent lives in an area where there are enough gay adolescents to form a peer support group. This, of course, is unusual and unlikely.

Working with adolescents on the issue of coming out to others. This is a very difficult situation,

especially for gay helping professionals. As noted above, the counselor's intervention strategy should, in most cases, be to protect the adolescent by keeping his or her sexual preference confidential and to urge him or her to do the same. If the adolescent decides to stay "in the closet," the counselor's intervention will probably center around helping her or him function as well as possible while pretending to be heterosexual. If the client is already identified as gay or insists on so identifying, the counselor may then be in the position of acting as client advocate or as a buffer between the adolescent client and his or her parents or legal guardians.

In either event, the counselor's approach should have two basic components. First, intervention should be reality oriented. The adolescent will need help in figuring out what she or he can do to survive as well as possible until coming of age. Unless the counselor can somehow provide a support group, and this is unlikely, the gay adolescent will probably survive best by learning to live within a heterosexist society without feeling victimized. This means that options need to be maximized and the client helped to develop as much of a sense of control as possible. Above all, adolescents need to be continually reminded of the reality of their situation. It will be helpful to be supportive but not to be continually commiserating with the client about her or his plight.

The counselor also needs to be reality oriented with parents or legal guardians. This will often mean encouraging them to put the client's sexual preference itself (that is, the label) in the background and focus instead on any problems that are encountered as a result of sexual preference or that are being attributed to sexual preference.

The counselor's second major focus can be as an educator for both client and parents. In many instances, both the adolescent and his or her parents will have a distorted view of gays and lesbians and gay lifestyles. The helping professional can do a lot to alter this perspective. Even if there is no distortion of perspective, there is often simply a lack of information about gay people. The counselor who works with gay clients would be well advised to be familiar with writings by and about gays as well as possible contacts for adolescents and their parents.[24]

Coming out to others as an adult

Coming out to the gay community. Usually the first people to whom a gay adult self-identifies are other gay people. Because signification frequently takes place following or during a sexual relationship, the other person in the relationship may be the first person told. Within the gay community, however, coming out is often less a matter of telling people about one's sexual preference than it is of going to places that other gay people go and acting "appropriately," that is, by showing clear interest in members of the same gender. For men especially, the first steps may be in the form of sexual encounters.[19]

Appropriate behavior in the gay community must be learned like any other social behavior. Gay people who have just come out are sometimes at a loss about what to do and how to go about getting involved. One gay man, for example, came into therapy very depressed because he was so isolated. He had no idea about how to get to meet other gay men except through bars. He had been to one bar on a night when there had apparently been a drag show in progress. He immediately assumed that in order to belong to the gay community he would have to dress in drag, and he didn't want to do this because he didn't think he would look good in a dress. So he left the bar and never returned. Gay women may feel the same way if they happen to enter a bar or get to know a group of women who dress in a stereotypically masculine style. They may believe that this is necessary in order to identify themselves with the gay community and so may not be willing to take that step.

An effective helping professional is willing and able to help clients define their own style of being gay, as well as help them fit as well as possible into the gay community. Gay people do not have to go to bars, cruise, adopt particular modes of dress, or play particular roles in order to be part of the gay community. In some settings, especially rural or more conservative areas, the choice of kinds of people to associate with may be restricted. In this case, the client should be urged to try to find alternative support systems if she or he does not fit in with some part of the gay community. The main point to help clients understand is that, even if they cannot immediately find other gay people who are like them, that does not mean that such people do not exist. The person may have to make a choice between living in a particular locale and having lots of congenial friends.

There are definite advantages to identifying with the gay community. Being in contact with other gay people, or even just knowing that contacts are available, is a strong source of moral support. It is within the gay community that a person who has just come out can find support for an alternative lifestyle, access to gay community activities, information about regional and national gay events, and most important, a positive attitude about being gay.

Coming out to heterosexuals

☐ The process [of coming out] didn't end with my parents' discovery, and it will never end, for I live in a heterosexist world where the presumption is that I'm straight, so that every time I meet a new person (and that's quite often), I have to recommence that coming-out process. And still I decide whether it's worth telling someone. After all, I do discuss subjects other than sexuality, and often I have other things in common with straight people so that I try to find a balance between being a lesbian and a humanist. Thus we spend our lives coming out, and the reality is that none of us is completely "out" or "in."[25]

The reaction of nongays to the subject of gayness is often obvious and is carried in jokes, the media, and "off the cuff" comments. Most gay people have heard remarks about "faggots," "dykes," and "queers." Because gay people are not necessarily obvious, they may be expected to join in the general merriment when someone at the office tells about all the "faggots" at some bar he went into (by mistake, of course). They are expected to snicker along with the rest at a queer joke, or to manifest horror at those "dykey looking women.'' Having experienced a few of those situations can easily make one reticent to share one's sexual preference with nongays. This is particularly true with nongays who matter a great deal, such as a co-worker or boss. Even if a person does not expect severe negative sanctions, such as loss of a job, she or he may fear the loss of a good working relationship, family ties, or friendships.

Why do gay people come out?

☐ So when people ask why I speak publicly of being a lesbian and use my own name, I know the reason. God knows, it's not to answer the questions and listen to the slurs—sometimes more painful from the well-meaning liberals unaware of their own condescension than from forthright bigots. But coming out, since it is no less than recognizing who I am and letting that be seen by others, is a source of strength and exhilaration. I used enormous amounts of energy hiding: now I can use that energy to meet my needs. I can do my work and give to my daughter, my lover, and others with the creativity released in me by self-acceptance and self-assurance. And I hope, by taking the risk of self-exposure, to give courage to lesbians surviving with little or no support, and to invite all women, wherever they locate themselves on the continuum of sexuality, to respect their own and others' differences as equally valuable.[26]

☐ Being out at work erases all fear of ''being found out'' and some of the fear of being fired without redress. It brings to a halt the oppression of being treated as someone whom you are not (lesbians being asked when they will get married, etc.). For myself, being out at work means a new and very tangible freedom to deal seriously and competently with the people who come through my office each week, because I am not distracted by fears and intimidations. . . . Thus, from what had been an environment of intimidation and uncertainty, I now find my job to be a place where I feel pride and self-determination. If this is not a tangible increase in personal freedom, then I don't know what is.[27]

Being in the closet is depressing, exhausting, anxiety provoking, and time consuming. It necessitates continual efforts to dissemble, to persuade others that one is someone who one is not and produces anxiety over the prospect that one will be found out in spite of all that one can do. Gay people come out, as the above quotes show, to stop having to hide, to be closer to others, to validate their own sense of self-worth. They come out in anger, desperation, pride, joy, and sometimes simply because it's the easiest, most comfortable thing to do at the time.

Deciding whether to come out. Although it may seem a conservative stance to some readers, we take the position that the client should seriously and carefully consider the implications and possible consequences of coming out to others as well as the expected gains. This is because there are occasions when a gay person will see the act of coming out as the solution to many problems when it either has little to do with them or is not an adequate solution. This occurs because the struggle to conceal a gay identity not only demands energy but also leads to the development of an entire complex of self-protective measures that make it difficult to achieve and maintain satisfactory close relationships with nongays.

In the interest of keeping a gay lifestyle secret, a gay man or lesbian woman may be afraid to share many feelings and experiences with family and nongay friends. This may mean that others do not share their feelings with her or him. Gay people may also learn habits of communication and expressions that are difficult to change: for example, they may develop an ''aloof'' style of relating to nongays, experience anxiety around nongays when the conversation turns to personal subjects, and decrease all verbalizations to the point that communication with others (gay or nongay) becomes difficult. These and other difficulties take a long time to learn and in most instances are not remedied by the act of coming out. However, if any of these behaviors are either intentional or considered by the client to be caused by his or her gayness, the client may incorrectly believe that coming out is the only way to solve the difficulty.

During this part of the coming-out process, the client and practitioner will find it useful to decide which of the changes the client wants to make are directly related to sexual preference and which ones are related secondarily because of such things as decreasing social interaction, changes in communication styles, lack of appropriate skills, and anxiety. Some kinds of problems can be solved by changing the way the client relates to others whether they are told of the client's sexual preference or not. Some kinds of problems will only be solved by combining personal changes, such as new skills, with coming out. A few problems may be solved by coming out alone.

Coming out to parents. Somewhere between one third and one half of gay people studied are known by one or both parents to be gay, with the mother being the person most often told.[28] Comments from many gay people indicate that the decision about whether to tell parents, worry over parents' reactions, and efforts not to let parents know are frequently the most agonizing experiences that gay people go through around the problem of coming out to nongays. This is not surprising because of the intense and complex relationships that most people have with their parents and the power of both parents and children to hurt each other emotionally. As was indicated earlier, there is often cause for children to worry about their parents' response because a large number of those told do have negative reactions.

Deciding whether to tell parents. It is not always necessary or desirable for a gay person to tell parents that he or she is gay. If the relationship is satisfactory, there are not immediate problems, and it seems likely that the parents will have difficulty accepting their son's or daughter's sexual preference, it may not be wise to tell them. Some parents seem to be comfortable with their son's or daughter's lifestyle and lover, but would clearly be upset if their child's sexual preference were actually labeled. It is up to the client to determine in this instance whether it is worthwhile saying something.

Some clients are uncomfortable with the thought of telling parents about their sexuality but think they ought to do so because they feel guilty, because they think that doing so will improve family relationships, or for other less functional reasons.

In such cases, the professional's role is to help the client determine what would be gained from telling parents and how best to achieve this. If the major motivation is guilt, the professional would be wise to spend some time helping the client cope with those feelings before seriously considering whether to tell her or his parents. As with other situations, the practitioner should help the client realistically assess the impact of the revelation and the client's and parents' abilities to cope successfully with it.

If the motivation for telling parents is a desire for improved family relations, it is a good idea to help clients assess their own and their parents' existing skills, assets, and deficits, particularly regarding communication. It is often the case that clients (gay or nongay) may see one specific issue, such as the client's sexual preference, as the key to total harmony within the family. Obviously, if good communications and relationship skills do not exist or if the family is having other difficulties, it will not do much good for the client to reveal her or his sexual preference.

Parental reactions. Some parents have such negative reactions to finding out that their child is gay that the relationship with the child is permanently damaged or even ended. Other parents, however, either have a positive reaction initially or are able to achieve a positive relationship with their child over time. In a preliminary survey of members of Parents of Gays organizations, one of the authors asked respondents what advice they would give to gay children about how to discuss their sexual preference with their parents. In the first place, the majority of parents who responded believed that children should tell their parents as soon as possible. They also believed that children should expect parents to be shocked, hurt, and angry.

☐ I think sons and daughters should expect their parents to be shocked. Things may initially be said out of anger but the children must be patient. Even if they are turned away, they should be the ones to try to keep communication open after the initial shock has worn off. In other words, they may have to be the ones that act like adults while their parents act like children. They must remember their parents must have time to absorb what all is involved in this issue, and this may take a few months.

Another parent said, ''Tell them as calmly and lovingly as possible and then be calm while [your] parents explode!''

Many parents urged children to be patient, to ''keep the lines of communication open and remember [your parents] are having to change their concept of you and your life.'' And another parent said:

☐ Being frank with your parents will most likely result in a better relationship, but not immediately. Give them time, yet take the initiative in bringing the matter up several times. Realize most parents are victims of severe and archaic brainwashing and the most erroneous information.

The major point these parents made was that it would take time, but that if there were a good relationship between parents and child, eventually the parents would understand the situation.

The parents in the survey talked about the difficulty of coping with their negative feelings about themselves or their children and about their fear concerning the kind of life that a gay person may have to live.

☐ My first feelings were sadness that I had done this to him—a very lovable child and thoughtful son. My second emotion is fear—fear of how my husband and other children will react—and such heartache knowing what a minority group must face in this cruel world.

☐ [I feel] sad resignation—understanding how this would separate her from her father and from most of society. I feel like we've done our poor best—I don't feel guilt—do feel regret for lost grandchildren—fear for her state of mind when she has been out in the employment world long enough to understand the real force of people's prejudice and how it can affect her directly.

Some parents expressed regret for what their child had already suffered:

☐ Naturally this information came as quite a shock to me. My wife, in telling me, tried as best she could to cushion the shock. I was very saddened and I guess my deepest feelings were of sorrow for my son who had borne this burden alone for all these years.

☐ [I felt] terror for all that I imagined he would go through; guilt for my failing to raise a straight and true one; shame for having a child that was different; but most of all a different and stronger guilt for having hurt my child whom I love dearly.

☐ I was broken hearted because of my son's pain at all he had to go through, dreadfully upset because of my own reluctance to accept, due in turn to my own austere upbringing. You must remember that 80 years ago our views on sex (which at best was a dirty word) were very, very different from our acceptance of situations today. I had terrible feelings of guilt for what might have been my contribution to his homosexuality. In short, I was completely ignorant of the whole concept and at a loss as to how to cope.

☐ My first feeling—I said and meant, ''Oh, my darling, you have been through all this without me beside you.'' I felt at last I knew what had been troubling him all his life. He was gay from 13 on and led a double life all these long years until he came out at 35 and got a divorce and went to live with his lover.

Certainly, these parents are not representative of the parents of all gay children. The fact that they are connected with Parents of Gays at all suggests that they have come to grips with the issue in some way, and many of their comments show warmth, sensitivity, openness, and strength in dealing with what has clearly been a difficult experience. This is a unique group of parents. Yet the great similarity among their feelings, thoughts, and reactions suggests that there is a high degree of commonality of experience at least among those who achieve a degree of comfort with and understanding of a son's or daughter's gayness. For those who do not accept their child's sexual preference, we can infer an even more emotionally painful experience of anger, guilt, resentment, and pain without the ultimate relief of increased closeness between child and parent. And for their children, we can assume an equal burden of pain and resentment toward parents as well as toward self.

Implications for intervention. Clinicians are liable to be confronted with problems between gay adults and their parents under relatively few circumstances. Probably the most likely occurrence is that a gay client will come into counseling wanting to tell or having already told her or his parents that he or she is gay and being worried about the results.

Helping children tell parents. The parents interviewed in the study almost unanimously believed that gay children should tell their parents of their sexual preference, and we respect their point of view. However, as we have already said, this is unquestionably a select parent group. The experiences of gay people indicate that not all parents respond as positively even over time as these parents appear to have done.[28] Furthermore, both parents may not respond in the same way to their child's confidence.

Because of these different possibilities, we are inclined to urge a somewhat conservative approach. It is our belief that adult clients who want to come out to parents should be supported and encouraged in doing so. It is also our belief that clients should be urged to realistically assess the probable consequences of coming out to parents and should be clear about their reasons for wanting to come out.

We also believe that it is useful for clients to talk over with the counselor the way in which they are going to come out, the circumstances, and the best method of presenting what they want to say. The study of Parents of Gays indicated that children often "spring" their gayness on unprepared and unsuspecting parents. As we have seen, this information is apt to arouse strong emotions in all parties concerned. For this reason, it is best for children to plan how and when to bring up the subject and, ideally, to role play what they will say with the counselor. This kind of rehearsal, especially with appropriate prompting from the

counselor, can be extremely helpful in getting the client to visualize what his or her parents' actual responses are likely to be. This then gives the client a chance to practice remaining calm and rational in spite of volatile reactions by the parents.

A number of parents made excellent suggestions about ways they thought children could best tell their parents, and we want to share some of these suggestions with you. One parent recommended that gay children

☐ expect a strong emotional reaction. Tell [your parents] at a calm time; insist that they accept you anyway; be able to answer questions and reassure them; go back and continue talking about homosexuality after the first telling; show them the gay lifestyle slowly and surely; understand that they can be very unreasonable but will probably get over it; love [yourself] well enough so that [your] parents' fears won't rub off on [you].

Another parent describes how her son told her and her husband:

☐ I believe our son did it the right way—by telling us he had something that he thought it important for us to know and then simply telling us—how he came to know about it, what steps he took when he first became aware that he was a homosexual and what, if anything, he intended to do further about it. It is a shock but it is much better than having the parents learn about it from others or through innuendos and wisecracks, jokes, etc.

It is a good idea for the gay person to provide his or her parents with books or pamphlets about being gay. Three that parents have found particularly helpful are *Loving Someone Gay*,[29] *A Family Matter*,[30] and *Now That You Know*.[31] The gay person can also make contact with a local Parents of Gays organization if there is one or with the Metropolitan Community Church to find out if there are other parents of gays to whom his or her own parents can talk. Some parents find it comforting to talk with a minister, doctor, or other "authority" in order to get a professional opinion. Again, it is in the son's or daughter's as well as the parent's interest to find someone who has a positive view of gay and lesbian lifestyles. You may wish to offer to see the parents yourself with or without their son or daughter to provide them with information, resources, and the like.

In sum, these kinds of situations are best handled when the son or daughter is calm, rational, and prepared—ready to cope as understandingly as possible with parents' reactions and to provide them with information and support at a rate they can handle. This is not to say that children have no right to be angry, hurt, or anxious. They will certainly experience these emotions, and it is understandable and healthy for them to do so. It is our experience that rehearsal in a therapeutic setting allows the gay person not only to express her or his feelings but to deal with some of them appropriately before talking with parents. We particularly urge that clients be taught to take responsibility for their own feelings and reactions, and that they be taught and practice appropriate assertive behavior in the therapist's office before they attempt to talk with parents. The gay person will do much better if she or he has anticipated beforehand what is likely to happen, what her or his reactions may be, and how she or he chooses to handle various possible parental responses.

Helping parents cope. The second type of situation that a helping professional may encounter is one in which the parent(s) of a gay man or lesbian woman come to talk about their child. This is a perfectly normal and understandable action on the part of parents of a gay person. The helping professional's role, in our opinion, is to provide the parents with information, resources, and contacts with other parents of gays if possible. Furthermore, as a professional, your attitudes and opinions will carry the weight of your "authority," and it is appropriate to use that authority to give the parents accurate information.

The major concerns with parents of gays should be threefold: helping them gain accurate information about gay lifestyles, providing them with support through community sources if possible, and facilitating a positive, open relationship with their gay son or daughter. Parents of gays should not be encouraged to try to get their child to enter therapy in order to be "changed," nor should they be supported in believing myths about gay people. They should be told realistically the positive and negative consequences of a gay lifestyle, what they can expect, what their child can expect, and so forth. Their questions should be encouraged, no matter how foolish they may seem, and answers given forthrightly. Their attention should ultimately be directed toward the kinds of things they will want and need to do to make their life easier both in dealing with others and in dealing with their son or daughter.

After the initial shock, gay parents may have difficulty in coping with their child's sexual preference because they don't know what to say to friends, relatives, and neighbors about their child. As is often the case with gay people, the issue of sexual preference suddenly overshadows everything else. The parents, too, become caught in trying to hide what others may perceive as a stigma. Comments about "queers" hurt them. Questions from friends about what a son or daughter is doing may become awkward as the parents struggle with conflicting urges toward honesty and subterfuge. Like gay people themselves, parents must also come to terms with their own "closet." They must make decisions about whom to come out to and how to cope with others' assumptions about their abilities as parents and the like. And, as their gay children must, they must learn what situations warrant their concern and which do not, which people are worth telling and which are not. Information about gay lifestyles, myths, and parental roles in sexual preference as well as instruction in appropriate assertive behavior are all helpful. Most parents will simply have to take time and spend energy learning about gayness, about what to expect from their children, and about how being the parent of a gay child differs from being the parent of a nongay child.

If the respondents to our study are at all representative of people who are willing to come to terms with their child's sexual preference, the results are well worth the effort. Almost all respondents described positive experiences deriving from their son or daughter having shared their gayness. A number said that knowing had brought their family closer together, had opened their eyes, and had brought them closer to others. Almost all seemed to believe they had benefited from knowing more about gay people and getting to know their children's friends. Knowing that such positive experiences are possible may make it easier for gay parents and their children to get through difficult times.

Coming out to heterosexual friends. According to Moses, 56% of her sample had told their best heterosexual woman friend that they were lesbian, and 38% had told their best heterosexual male friend.[32] Nongay friends appear to present somewhat less of a problem than family members do. This is not surprising when one considers the societal expectations for children vis-à-vis their parents as compared with expectations about friends. Children are expected to love, honor, and respect their parents and ultimately to care for them in old age. Children arc also generally expected to provide parents with grandchildren. Friends may come and go, but parents are a continuing source of emotional energy for most people, whether positive or negative. Furthermore, friends have very different expectations of peers than parents have of children. All in all, it is often easier to tell friends because the risks are so much lower and the potential gains, in many cases, are higher and more immediate.

Even though coming out to nongay friends may be easier than coming out to one's parents, it is still very often difficult. The gay person who wants to come out to friends or acquaintances always takes the risk of being ostracized, a consequence over which she or he has no control and for which there is no recourse. It is impossible to be certain beforehand whether a heterosexual friend knows or suspects that a person is gay. It is also difficult to tell what her or his reaction will be when told. Some heterosexuals who make "queer" jokes and

whom one would expect to respond negatively do just the opposite, whereas some supposedly "liberal" and "open-minded" individuals turn out not to be.

In general, the same things apply to telling friends that apply to telling parents, but with somewhat less emotional strain anticipated. Coming out should ideally be a planned occurrence, although this is probably less important with friends than with family. Even though the time and place may not be planned, however, the client and friend will be well served if the gay person can be calm and relaxed and prepared to cope with possible negative reactions.

Deciding whether to tell friends. The issues involved in deciding whether to tell friends are similar to those involved in the decision with regard to parents. It will be helpful for the client to know why he or she wants to tell friends and what the anticipated consequences will be when and if he or she does so. Clients may also want to consider the consequences of *not* telling certain friends. Although not telling parents about one's sexual preference may necessitate subterfuge, not telling friends is liable to lead to a great deal more difficulty.

It is appropriate for clients to experience anxiety at the prospect of telling friends about their sexual preference. Gays who do so leave themselves wide open in the event that a friend has a negative response. It is important, however, that the client not confuse the possibility that others will respond negatively with the notion that there is something wrong with him or her. It is easy for clients to think they are at fault or are sick or immoral as they face the possible reactions others may have. Clients may also become very angry at the thought of others' negative responses. Both anxiety and anger are healthy responses, but if they continue so long or are so extreme that they are disruptive for the client, then it may be desirable to help the client work toward a different perspective before coming out.

The decision about whether to come out to friends may be affected by the milieu in which the client knows the individuals. If they are known in a work situation, it may be advisable to consider the implications for job and career if the nongay person responds very negatively. Sexual preference, once revealed, can be a stance that requires constant defending under certain circumstances. With people at work, the client really needs to think carefully about the reasons for letting others know about her or his sexual preference.

AFTER COMING OUT

The counselor may need to work with clients after they have come out to parents or friends, or both. If the reaction of others is negative, the professional may need to teach the client some ways of dealing with the response. Acknowledging one's gayness to someone who is nongay puts the client in a vulnerable position, and a negative reaction may be understandably difficult to deal with. If a client has any doubts at all about her or his own health as a gay person or feels any guilt about being gay, the heterosexual who responds negatively can trigger a self-directed negative response in the client. The client may think of self as a failure, a sick person, someone who is not worthwhile, and so forth. Any techniques that the counselor would normally use to work with such a client are appropriate here. (Some possible techniques are cognitive restructuring, assertiveness training, and the use of rational self-statements.)

The client may also respond to negative reactions with anger and resentment. This is to be encouraged as a preferable alternative to self-denigration. It is particularly helpful if the counselor can help the client differentiate anger at "the system" or at "society" from personal anger and pain over having been hurt by someone he or she cares about. It is true that the general societal response toward gay people is one that legitimately arouses anger in many instances. It is also true that the individuals who respond negatively toward the client are part of society. But they are also indi-

viduals with whom the client presumably wishes to continue a positive relationship, and as individuals, they are potentially educable. It may be helpful to the client to consider that, no matter how badly he or she feels hurt, the person who reacts negatively may also feel hurt. If the client wishes to maintain the relationship, she or he may have to be willing to undertake some education, to be tolerant, to continue to reach out, and to risk being hurt again.

Many gay people do not want to continue to make these kinds of efforts and often for good reason. It is frequently the case that the nongay who has difficulty coping with a gay friend or family member believes she or he is the one who has been hurt and expects the gay person to be repentent and contrite, to put up with emotional outbursts, and still to be "tolerant." Being gay and feeling good about oneself are generally sufficiently difficult without having to cope with this type of situation. In such circumstances, the counselor may be well advised to help the client terminate the relationship rather than stay in it to his or her detriment.

Another common occurrence with either friends or family is that the client may get a positive or at least neutral response and may not trust it. Allison was one such client. After deciding that she was, indeed, a lesbian, Allison wanted to tell a number of people who were important to her. Her mother and sisters responded positively, her father somewhat less so. She also told several nongay woman friends whose response was that they felt much closer to Allison and were delighted she had told them. One said that she had always thought that Allison might be gay and was pleased to see her so relaxed and comfortable with her decision. Allison was suspicious of their responses. Having struggled with her own negative feelings about lesbianism for many years, she convinced herself that, although they were saying positive things, they were actually thinking bad thoughts about her, were not really comfortable with her, and were only being nice to her because they felt sorry for her. Allison's social worker challenged her perceptions, and after some discussion, it became clear that Allison's friends were acting exactly as they said they were feeling. They were seeing her more often than they had been, were acting physically comfortable with her (that is, they were hugging her, sitting next to her, touching her), and they were expressing feelings to her and talking about things with her that had never been discussed before. Rather than feeling sorry for her, they were uniformly expressing admiration, support, and pleasure. All three friends as well as her mother and sisters had commented on how much more relaxed and happy Allison seemed and how much easier it was to talk to her and to be around her. Once she had closely observed their behavior and described it, Allison realized there really was no evidence to indicate that they were feeling anything different from what they said they were feeling.

This kind of reality testing is especially important with gay clients because of the inevitable and understandable expectation that others will react negatively to their sexual preference. Not only do gay people expect this type of reaction, they frequently experience it. Colleagues who generally act comfortable at work with a person they know is gay will suddenly become awkward or embarrassed when the subject of homosexuality comes up. A man who knows his co-workers are aware of his homosexuality may fail to get a promotion, a raise, or a transfer or may even lose his job. He may strongly believe and may in fact be certain that it is because he is known to be gay, but he will have no way of proving that this is the case. It is very easy for gay people to become paranoid under such circumstances, especially if they are unsure about whether others know or don't know of their gayness and of what their honest reactions are if they do know. The counselor must consequently strive to teach the client ways of realistically and objectively assessing other people's reactions on the basis of their actual behavior and of handling reactions the client considers negative or with which she or he is uncomfortable.

END NOTES

1. Cass, V. "Homosexual identity formation: A theoretical model." *Journal of Homosexuality*, 1979, *4*(3), 219-237, presents a six-stage model of identity formation that may be of interest to those concerned with a sociological model of the process of becoming gay.

2. We have essentially chosen to present coming out as a process that involves movement from private to public presentation of self as gay. In this, we generally follow the model set out by J.A. Lee ("Going public: A study in the sociology of homosexual liberation." *Journal of Homosexuality*, 1977, *3*[1], 49-78). He proposes three stages to the coming-out process with several steps in each stage: signification, coming out, and going public. He includes our stages 2 and 3 in coming out. He also points out that there has been quite a bit of confusion and overlapping of stages by observers of the gay community. Monteflores and Schultz and others have argued that a unidimensional model such as the one we use does not do justice to the coming-out process, and we agree. This particular model has served our purpose here since we are concerned primarily with giving the reader a simplified scheme within which to conceptualize the information we present, rather than with scholarly discourse. Those who are interested in the theoretical complexities of the coming-out process from the standpoint of psychology and sociology are referred to Monteflores, C. de, & Schultz, S. "Coming out: Similarities and differences for lesbians and gay men." *Journal of Social Issues*, 1978, *34*(3), 59-72 for discussions of these issues and further references.

3. Lee, 1977.

4. Matza, D. *Becoming deviant*. Englewood Cliffs, N.J.: Prentice-Hall, 1969.

5. Jay, K., & Young, A. *The gay report*. New York: Summit Books, 1979.

6. Galana, L., & Covina, G. *The new lesbians: Interviews with women across the U.S. and Canada*. Berkeley: Moon Books, 1977, p. 47.

7. Galana & Corvina, 1977, p. 23.

8. Adair, N., & Adair, C. *Word is out: Stories of some of our lives*. New York: Dell, 1978, pp. 3-13.

9. Jay & Young, 1979, p. 55.

10. See, for example, Galana & Covina, 1977, pp.157-165.

11. Brown, R. *Rubyfruit jungle*. Plainfield, Vt.: Daughters, 1973.

12. For example, Adair & Adair, 1978; Brown, 1973; Galana & Covina, 1977; Jay & Young, 1979; and Vida, G. (Ed.). *Our right to love: A lesbian resource book*. Englewood Cliffs, N.J.: Prentice-Hall, 1978b.

13. Duehn, W., & Mayadas, N. "The use of stimulus/modeling videotapes in assertive training for homosexuals." *Journal of Homosexuality*, 1976, *1*(4), 373-381; and McKinlay, T., Kelly, J., & Patterson, J. "Teaching assertive skills to a passive homosexual adolescent." *Journal of Homosexuality*, 1977, *3*(2), 163-170.

14. Adair & Adair, 1978, pp. 177-179.

15. The Boston Women's Health Book Collective. *Our bodies, ourselves* (2nd ed.). New York: Simon & Schuster, 1976.
16. Jay & Young, 1979, p. 120.
17. The Boston Women's Health Book Collective, 1976, p. 82.
18. Humphreys, L. *The tearoom trade: Impersonal sex in public places*. Chicago: Aldine, 1970.
19. Lee, 1977.
20. See, for example, Adair & Adair, 1978.
21. Simpson, R. *From the closets to the courts*. New York: Viking Press, 1976.
22. Simpson, 1976, p. 15.
23. Simpson, 1979, p. 30.
24. Many cities now have Parents of Gays organizations. A list of these organizations can be found in Vida, 1978b, pp. 276-279, or for a more current listing, contact the National Gay Task Force; 80 Fifth Avenue; New York, N.Y. 10011.
25. Jay, K. "Coming out as process." In G. Vida, 1978b, pp. 29-30.
26. Larkin, J. "Coming out." *Ms.,* March 1976, pp. 72-74; 84; 86.
27. Mager, D. "Out in the workplace." In K. Jay & A. Young (Eds.), *After you're out: Personal experiences of gay men and lesbian women*. New York: Links Books, 1975.
28. Jay & Young, 1979; Moses, A.E. *Identity management in lesbian women*. New York: Praeger, 1978.
29. Clark, D. *Loving someone gay*. Millbrae, Calif.: Celestial Arts, 1977.
30. Silverstein, C. *A family matter: A parents' guide to homosexuality*. New York: McGraw-Hill, 1977.
31. Fairchild, B., & Hayward, N. *Now that you know: What every parent should know about homosexuality*. New York: Harcourt Brace Jovanovich, 1979.
32. Moses, 1978.

8

Lesbian and gay male sexual activity

GENERAL ISSUES

Sexual activity is a source of both pleasure and concern for many people, including gays. In counseling, sexual issues are sometimes ignored for several reasons: the client may be too embarrassed to initiate a discussion or to admit concern, or the counselor may not be comfortable discussing sexual activity, may feel that he or she is ill prepared to offer alternatives, or may be reluctant or unable to suggest actions that are contrary to the counselor's value system. Whatever the reason, ignoring what might be an area of concern to the client is less than desirable counseling practice.

Several studies have shown that helping professionals who are sensitized to the possible sexual concerns of clients and who then seek information find that their clients express more sexually related concerns.[1] It appears that the clients have the concerns. Whether they are expressed may very well depend on the professional's willingness and ability to elicit them. This requires that the counselor be aware of the sexual activity of lesbians and gay men, be cognizant of possible areas of concern, and be able to aid the client in an exploration of alternatives relating to the concerns. It is also extremely important that the counselor maintain as neutral a perspective as possible, allowing the client to make decisions that are appropriate for his or her system of values, rather than those of the counselor. This chapter will attempt to address each of these issues.

Assumptions and realities about gay sexual activity

The subject of gay sexual activity has been the focus of a number of myths and misconceptions. Many of the negative beliefs that heterosexuals hold about gay men and lesbian women have to do with their sexual behavior, yet surprisingly little research had been published in this area until the late 1970s. Until publication of studies by Saghir and Robins,[2] Bell and Weinberg,[3] Masters and Johnson,[4] and Jay and Young,[5] there was little scientific evidence to indicate what kinds of sexual behaviors gay men and lesbians engage in, their patterns of sexual behavior, or the kinds of sexual problems they experience.

There are two sources of difficulty that gays encounter regarding their sexual behavior. The first is that there may be misinformation concerning what gay people actually do. For example, many people assume that gays are oversexed or that gay sex is "counterfeit," bizarre, or very different from heterosexual activity. The second difficulty is that when there are differences between gay and nongay sexual activity, people assume that this means there is something wrong with gay people or with gay sexual activity because of the difference.

In this section we will discuss both these sources of difficulty. We would like to alter misconceptions about gay sexuality that may be held by mental health professionals by presenting facts wherever possible. In those instances in which gay and nongay sexual activity differs in some way, we will challenge the assumption that the differences themselves are indicative of sickness and will present alternative ways of viewing them.

Levels of sexual interest. Nongay people often assume that gays are inordinately interested in sexual activity, that they spend a lot of time thinking about sex, and that their interests are often sex related. Bell and Weinberg report levels of sexual interest among the gay men and women they studied, and they summarize their findings as follows:

> Besides demonstrating the diversity of sexual interests among our respondents, these data fail to support the idea that homosexual men and women are sex-ridden people who think constantly of sexual matters or consider sex the most important part of their lives. It would appear that for most homosexuals, sex is not a particularly predominant concern. Regardless of race or gender, the largest numbers of those in our samples did only "some" thinking about sex and said that sex was only a "fairly" important aspect of their lives.[6]

They note further that their data tend to support a greater interest in sex among gay men than among lesbian women, a gender difference that would probably also appear among nongays.[7]

The interest of gay men in sexual activity is easily blown out of proportion for several reasons. First, gay people are like nongays in most aspects of their lives, so their nonsexual interests blend in with and are indistinguishable from those of heterosexuals, whereas their sexual interests, being different, stand out. Nongays and gays share the same types of employment, movies, banks, restaurants, insurance agencies, sporting events, and the like. What they do not share are places that involve either sexual activity or openly gay behavior, such as gay bars, theaters, and restaurants. These places exist in order to serve the sexual and social interests of gay people and to provide surroundings where gay people can be open about

their sexual preference and have it taken for granted.

In the area of sexual activity, especially for men, there are no heterosexual media sources that provide what gay men want and are interested in. Consequently, there are a number of publications that relate directly to the sexual interests and activities of gay men. There are undoubtedly as many, and probably a great many more, such publications that cater to the sexual interests and activities of nongay men. However, these are easily hidden among the rest of the publications and services that are presumably heterosexual in orientation but are not addressed to sexual activities per se. So, for example, a nongay banker in San Francisco may subscribe to a number of magazines on business and finance, as well as to *Playboy* and *Oui*. The latter two magazines are likely to be considered in the context of his other interests as indications of a well-rounded, appropriately masculine lifestyle. He may also belong to the Playboy Club, have a mistress, take his wife to some of the nightclubs that feature topless dancing, pick up a woman at a singles bar in Sausalito every once in a while, and make love with his wife three nights a week.

A gay banker, on the other hand, may subscribe to the same magazines on business and finance as well as *The Advocate, Christopher Street,* or *Ramrod*. He may pick up a trick at a gay bar or go to the baths one night a week, and make love with his lover three nights a week. In this case, because of his sexual preference, the subscriptions to gay magazines will not be considered in the context of his other interests, but will stand out as indicators of his sexual "obsession," along with his "frequent" one-night stands and visits to gay sexual scenes.

So it is possible that the sexual behavior of these two individuals who lead comparable lives might be judged very differently because the sexual activities of the nongay person are readily accepted in the context of his other interests, whereas those of the gay person are not. Unlike the nongay person, the gay person must move outside the boundaries of day-to-day (nongay) life to meet his or her sexual needs.

A second reason why gay people may be thought to be overly interested in sex is closely related to the first. Whereas nongays can and frequently do weave sexual or sex-related content into the fabric of their daily lives, this is difficult for most gay people unless they work in either a gay or a very accepting nongay environment. At work, for example, it is perfectly acceptable for a nongay man or woman to engage in sexual innuendo and repartee with a person of the opposite gender. Nongay men and women may both discuss sexual matters with each other in appropriately anecdotal fashion. They may discuss dates, lovers, spouses, and the like. For most gays, these avenues of sexual expression are not available.

A gay man is not likely to join with his nongay male co-workers in admiring a woman's figure, or if he does, he may be insincere if he implies that he is sexually attracted to her. He certainly cannot express his interest in an attractive man without attracting attention and opprobrium. A lesbian woman cannot, with impunity, share her excitement over the new lover or the neat woman she met at the women's coffee house the night before.

The consequence is that all sexual material in gay people's lives is very likely to be relegated to the period of time when they are not in nongay public. Of necessity, this increases the amount of time and energy spent on sexual matters within the gay community. Since the nongay world does not consider gay people except as they exist in gay settings (they are usually invisible otherwise), this may cause nongays to view gays as excessively interested in sexual matters. It would be an enlightening exercise for the nongay helping professional to observe the amount of time she or he (as well as colleagues) spends in sex-related communication, and to notice how little, if any, of this time it would be possible for a gay person to join in and not be ostracized.

Levels of sexual activity. Another assumption that nongay people make about gay men and lesbians is that their sexual activity level is either abnormally high or neurotically and abnormally low.[7] They believe gay men especially are not only constantly preoccupied with sex but also engage in sex

very frequently. Nongays may think lesbians are either hyperactive or abnormally inactive.

We speculate that nongays' perceptions of gay women's sexual activity may depend on the sexual attractiveness of the woman in question, according to heterosexual male standards. Our reason for believing this is that lesbian sexual behavior is a source of fantasy and sexual stimulation for nongay men and sometimes nongay women. In nongay pornography, sexual relations between two women may serve as a preliminary to sex with a man. These women generally meet heterosexual standards of attractiveness in terms of age, body build, and facial characteristics.

On the other hand, it may be difficult for nongays to envision a woman who does not conform to heterosexual standards for attractiveness in behavior and appearance as being sexually desirable and active. Such women may consequently be viewed as "old maids" who have settled for close, nonsexual friendships with other women because they could not "catch" a man. Or they may be depicted as sick, perverse "dykes" pursuing sweet and unsuspecting young things.

Bell and Weinberg also measured the levels of sexual activity of their sample. They say:

> Our data lead us to conclude that homosexual men and women cannot be sexually stereotyped as either hyperactive or inactive. Rather, the amount of sexual activity they reported varied among individuals, with black males reporting more than white males, men reporting more than women, and (with the exception of black males) younger people of either sex being more sexually active than their older counterparts.[8]

They comment on the difference between reported sexual activity of lesbians and gay men, noting that these differences may well be the result of either innate physiological or learned factors, or some combination of the two. The difference they found coincides with findings that show that, as we have noted elsewhere, lesbians and gay men are more similar to nongay women and men, respectively, than to each other, especially in the area of sexual behavior.

Sexual contacts. Available research indicates that gay people, and particularly gay men, have a higher number of different sexual partners and briefer relationships, on the average, than do non-gays.[9] This research also shows that, as might be expected, there are substantial differences between the sexual patterns of gay men and women as well as differences within both genders in number and importance of sexual contacts and average length of relationships.

Both Bell and Weinberg[3] and Jay and Young[5] found a wide range of sexual contact frequencies reported by their respective male samples, with some individuals reporting no sexual contacts during the preceding year and some reporting more than 50 partners during that time period. The range of sexual contacts for women was smaller than that for men, but still showed much individual difference, with some women reporting no sexual contacts and some reporting more than 11 different encounters during the preceding year. The issue of frequency of sexual contacts will be discussed further in the section on the sexual activity of adult gay men.

It is obvious from these studies that there are differences between gay men and women as well as among individuals within each gender. It is also accurate to say that, on the average, both gay women and men report more different sexual partners than do nongay women and men.[10] However, these data do not tell us anything about either the mental health of gay men and women in general or what sexual behavior to expect from a given gay man or woman. Nor do they tell us anything about how to help gay men and women who have sexual problems.

Comparison of gay and nongay sexual behavior. The only study that compares the sexual activity of gay and nongay couples was carried out by Masters and Johnson, who noted several important differences between these two groups. They found that genital manipulation took much longer and was much less demanding in the gay than in the nongay couples, teasing techniques were used more often by the gay couples, and during lovemaking, they communicated more about their personal preferences than nongay couples did.[11] They also noted a pattern of sexual behavior they labeled "my turn–your turn" in which partners took turns pleasuring each other, usually leading to orgasm.[11]

In both the lesbian and gay male couples, the initial activity involved the entire body, with some form of manual and/or oral stimulation of the nipples before stimulation of the genitals. In comparing this to the nongay couples' sexual interactions, Masters and Johnson noted that the gay couples "tended to adopt a slower, less demanding approach."[11] Furthermore, the gay couples became "more involved subjectively in the sexual interaction than married heterosexual couples."[12]

Masters and Johnson appeared to be particularly struck by the differences in subjective involvement in the sexual experience between gay and nongay committed couples. They attribute this to both intragender empathy and, more important, the far greater amount of verbal and nonverbal communication between gay couples as compared with nongay couples. They also assert that the higher levels of communication, and thus presumably higher levels of involvement in lovemaking, are because of the potential boredom inherent in gay sex, a conclusion that we find inexplicable. They believe that since gay couples are denied the mutual stimulation of coitus, they are sexually limited and these noncoital techniques "of necessity must be constantly varied and refined to the utmost to avoid the loss of stimulative effectiveness through long-continued familiarity."[13]

It is not at all clear why these authors believe that, in the long run, the stimulative techniques available to gays will be any more likely to lose their effectiveness than those available to nongays. Since the effects of genital stimulation are the same physiologically no matter how this stimulation is applied, there is certainly no evidence for some kind of physiologically based satiation to occur on a differential basis. The fact that gay couples took longer at lovemaking, were more sensitive to each other's needs, communicated more, and were more subjectively involved might suggest that gays would be less likely to become bored. It does not seem to us to suggest that gays developed these sexual patterns because they anticipated impending ennui.

In any event, the findings of Masters and Johnson do not suggest, nor do we, that gay lovemaking is somehow *inherently* better or more satisfactory than nongay lovemaking. Nor do we mean to ignore the absence in gay lovemaking of the potential satisfactions to be derived from coitus. We do believe it is important that helping professionals realize that the sexual experiences of gay couples are neither less enjoyable nor less effective than those of nongays and sometimes appear to be better among those gay couples who have good sexual techniques and communication.

This is an important issue because gay clients may come in who use heterosexual coitus as a standard against which to compare their own sexual experiences. They may believe that because they cannot engage in coitus with a loved one they are missing "the real thing" or that gay sex is somehow "counterfeit." Helping professionals can reassure such clients that they are capable of having sexual experiences every bit as satisfactory, fulfilling, and "real" as those that nongay couples have. The important features of lovemaking are not the genders of the participants but a slow, inventive approach to sex and good communication patterns while making love.

Sex therapy. The kinds of sexual activities gay men and women engage in and the kinds of sexual problems they encounter are obviously related to gender and are therefore different. In the next two sections, we will describe the sexual behavior of lesbians and gay men, the kinds of problems they are likely to have, and the kinds of basic interventions that may be necessary. We describe sexual activity itself in some detail. This is because we have found that nongays often do not know exactly how gay men and lesbian women make love and they may have incorrect ideas about what gay people do. It is our belief that mental health professionals function better when they are accurately informed. Furthermore, we anticipate that descriptions of gay and lesbian sexual activity may serve to desensitize nongays who are embarrassed or otherwise distressed by the idea of two men or two women making love.

We do not advocate that anyone without special training in sex therapy attempt to undertake such therapy with either gay or nongay clients. This chapter is not intended to provide that kind of expertise and is merely an overview. There are other volumes that address sex therapy in detail, and the interested practitioner is advised to consult these.[14] This chapter is intended to provide the professional with information that will be useful in those cases where issues arise related to sexual activity but not requiring sex therapy.

Unfortunately, gays are likely to encounter prejudice in seeking help for sexual problems just as they are in other areas of treatment. Masters and Johnson found that in their clinical population of sexually dysfunctional gays

> there was a widespread, well-founded fear that members of the health-care professions would be far from impartial in dealing with sexually distressed homosexual men and women. The available evidence certainly supports the homosexual population in their general contention that if they expected the worst from health-care professionals they would rarely be disappointed.[15]

Of the 84 men and women seen in treatment by Masters and Johnson, 40 had previously sought treatment elsewhere and 34 had been refused treatment (19 of these more than once). The couples who entered their program came from all over the United States and Canada, so these findings are not indicative of a local bias.

Clinicians who refer gay couples elsewhere for treatment of sexual dysfunction should obviously be careful about their referrals and should determine beforehand that the referred source actually does therapy with gay *couples*. It is also important to be sure that therapy done is directed toward increasing sexual functioning and satisfaction for the client as a gay person, rather than toward increasing conformity to imposed nongay standards.

LESBIAN SEXUAL ACTIVITY
Sexual behavior

Two women make love differently than a woman and a man do. In the first place, the primary goal of most nongay couples is to reach orgasm during coitus.[16] Coitus is not physically possible for lesbian couples, and lovemaking is not as likely to be "goal oriented" as it is for nongay couples.[16] In the second place, lesbian lovers share what Masters and Johnson refer to as *intragender empathy*, that is, the subjective, personal knowledge of how and what the other person feels during lovemaking.[17]

Lesbian women do not differ from nongay women in the physiology of their sexual response.[18] Those stimulative techniques that are arousing for nongay women are equally arousing for lesbian women. The difference between nongay and lesbian lovemaking with regard to the techniques used is that in nongay lovemaking, techniques such as cunnilingus and manual stimulation are often used by the man to prepare the woman for insertion and coitus. In lesbian lovemaking, these techniques are used to bring about orgasm and are thus endpoint, rather than preliminary, lovemaking behaviors.

The fact that lesbian couples cannot engage in coitus is seen by some as meaning that lesbian lovemaking is "missing something."[19] This is typically a nongay point of view. In point of fact, lesbian women perceive that sexual experiences with women are *more* satisfactory than sexual experiences with men.[20] The nongay counselor should not make the mistake of believing that lesbian sexual encounters are unsatisfactory simply because there is no penis involved and therefore coitus is not possible. This is simply not the case.[21]

Gender empathy. One of the greatest assets to

lesbian lovemaking is gender empathy. A woman making love to another woman knows what would feel good to her and tries those things with her partner. So lesbians are likely to be gentler and slower in lovemaking, more inventive during oral sex, and less oriented toward vaginal penetration than nongay men are inclined to be during nongay sexual activity.[22]

Unlike some men, women often like to stay close to a lover after lovemaking, to be held, stroked, and sometimes to fall asleep together.[23] This is more likely to happen with lesbian than with nongay couples. Lesbian lovers are also more likely to be sensitive to the stages of each other's menstrual cycles. Masters and Johnson noted that, among lesbian couples, it was common for the partners to anticipate and be sensitive to breast tenderness before menstruation, although this was not the case with nongay couples.[24]

In lesbian lovemaking, breast stimulation takes place for the pleasure of both partners, whereas Masters and Johnson indicated that in nongay lovemaking, breast play is often considered by the woman as something that pleases her partner and is often done by the man with little apparent awareness of his partner's reaction, which is frequently negative.[25] This difference in approach to breast stimulation is one possible reason for lesbian couples being so much more sensitive to the effect of the menstrual cycle on breast tenderness.

Stimulative techniques. Lesbian women use a variety of stimulative techniques including full body contact, kissing and caressing of the entire body, stimulation of breasts and genitals either manually or orally, body rubbing, and much less often, stimulation of the anal region either manually or orally.[26] Contrary to popular opinion, lesbians do not use dildos or penis substitutes very often.[27] Because the greatest areas of sensitivity for most women are outside the vagina, lesbian women concentrate their attention on the mons, labia, clitoris, and vaginal opening rather than within the vagina itself.[28] Masters and Johnson found that even with nongay couples, it is the man who most enjoys digital insertion into the vagina in the majority of cases, not the woman.[29] Most women do not require vaginal penetration to be orgasmic, and available evidence suggests that those women who do require vaginal penetration have learned to enjoy it, because it is not a physiological requisite of female orgasm.[30]

Stimulation to orgasm. There are three major techniques used in lesbian lovemaking: cunnilingus (oral stimulation of the partner's genital area), manual manipulation of the partner's genital area, and rhythmic pressure by some part of the body other than mouth or hand. Bell and Weinberg found that partner manipulation was the technique most frequently employed by the women in their sample, whereas cunnilingus was the technique most preferred.[31]

Cunnilingus. Cunnilingus, or oral sex, is probably the technique most often associated with lesbian lovemaking by nongays. Cunnilingus involves the stimulation of a woman's genital area by her partner's mouth until the woman reaches orgasm. Masters and Johnson found that both the partner receiving and the one performing cunnilingus reached high levels of arousal, and on occasion the partner performing cunnilingus reached orgasm during oral lovemaking.[32]

They also comment on the differences between cunnilingus as performed by lesbian women and by nongay men. They observed that

> there simply was no comparison between the skillfulness of men and women when cunnilingus was employed as a stimulative technique. Not only were committed lesbians more effective in satisfying their partners, they usually involved themselves without restraint in the cunnilingal activity far more than husbands approaching their wives. They demonstrated much more inventiveness in cunnilingal stimulative approaches and, above all, had the advantage of gender empathy. They inherently knew what pleased and used this knowledge to advantage.[32]

This difference in approach during oral sex may be related to differences in perception of both the purpose of cunnilingus and of women's genitalia. As we have discussed above, coitus is viewed as the endpoint activity in much nongay lovemaking. Consequently, all precoital stimulative techniques could be viewed as secondary in importance to the "goal" of intercourse and subsequent orgasm. The main purpose of cunnilingal activity would therefore be to get the woman ready for insertion and coitus, not to bring her to orgasm. If a man views coitus as the most important part of lovemaking and the true test of his sexual prowess, it is perhaps unlikely that he would feel compelled to be inventive in oral sex.

In lesbian couples, giving the other person pleasure sufficient to bring about orgasm is the whole point of lovemaking and ideally (and frequently) experienced as pleasurable by both partners. Without coitus as an exclusive end goal, lesbian partners are free to enjoy and take their time with those techniques that are pleasurable to both partners.

The second possible factor is an attitude difference between nongay men and lesbian women toward women's genitals, and their appearance, taste, texture, and odor. Lesbian women frequently "celebrate" the beauty of women's genitals, comparing them to flowers and rhapsodizing about their positive qualities.[33] This relatively new outlook has grown out of the feminist and lesbian-feminist movements, both of which are working to help women overcome their frequently negative body image. Lesbian women who view women's bodies positively, especially their genital areas, are certainly going to be more willing to engage in oral-genital sex than those men who view them as neutral or negative.

Use of hands (manipulation). This technique involves manual stimulation of the genital area, almost always with concentration on the clitoris, until orgasm is achieved. Masters and Johnson observed two major patterns of sexual behavior: an extended, "nondemanding" pattern, and a more intense type of sexual interaction. In the first type, the sexual activity they observed took on a teasing aspect as the responding partner was continually moved to high levels of arousal and then allowed to fall to lower levels before being restimulated to orgasm.[34] In the second pattern of interaction, one

106

partner stimulated the other with increasing intensity until orgasm occurred. In many instances, after a short pause, the responding partner indicated that she was satisfied. Masters and Johnson note that, although couples combined these two types of behavior, they typically prefer one or the other.[35]

In comparing lesbian and nongay couples, Masters and Johnson observed that lesbians tend to use more general stimulation of the genital area and slower, gentler stroking patterns than nongay men. The patterns of both men and women reflected their own masturbational patterns, which should account for these differences. They comment that "the lesbian's less forceful approach to masturbation and therefore to her partner's clitoris was generally the more acceptable or at least the less distracting."[36]

Body rubbing/body contact. This technique involves the use of body contact other than with the hands or mouth to bring about orgasms. As in other techniques, the usual focus of contact is the clitoris. Rhythmic friction of one woman's body against her lover's genital area can easily bring about orgasm in women who use this approach. According to Bell and Weinberg, this technique and mutual oral-genital stimulation were the second most preferred techniques among Black respondents, with 24% of the respondents preferring each.[37] Among white respondents, body contact was the fifth favorite technique with only 12% of the respondents preferring it.[37]

Frequency of sexual contact. Women have suffered over the last few generations from conceptions of their sexuality that may cause them to believe that they *should* have certain levels of sexual need on the basis of their gender. Until the last 15 years or so, women were not expected to want or need sex, but were supposed to put up with it for the sake of a husband. The only women who could conceivably be thought to enjoy sex were prostitutes (and maybe lesbians). More recently, women have been under pressure to express sexual free-

dom by being highly sexual. Lesbian women are under the extra pressure of being expected to be very highly sexual because they are lesbian, and lesbians are supposed to be sexually active and sexually expert.[38] Because of socialization, it is difficult to know what women's "natural" level of sexual responsiveness would be. Given the indistinguishability of lesbian and nongay women's physiological responses, it seems likely that whatever the parameters of "natural" sexual activity for women, they should be the same for both groups.

Summary. We have discussed only the more common forms of sexual activity that occur between women. Obviously, as with other sections of this book, the topic is worthy of much more discussion. For the interested reader, we suggest what is perhaps the most sex-positive, nonjudgmental, complete book on the subject: Pat Califia's *Sapphistry: The Book of Lesbian Sexuality.*[39]

Sexual problems of lesbians

The myth within the lesbian community that lesbians have or should have great sex all the time is a destructive one.[40] It undoubtedly means that some lesbians who would otherwise be quite satisfied with their sexual activity are not because sex is not always extraordinary, and some women who might otherwise seek help for sexual dysfunction do not do so because they are afraid of being considered inadequate. Lesbian women have sexual problems just as nongay women do, although the nature of the problems may differ somewhat because of the differences in lesbian and nongay lovemaking.

Sexual dysfunctions. As we have noted, it is not within the scope of this volume to treat adequately the subject of gay sexual dysfunction. For that reason, only cursory attention will be paid to sexual dysfunction in lesbian women.

Lesbian women are presumably prone to the same types of sexual dysfunction present in heterosexual women: orgasmic dysfunction, general sexual dysfunction, and vaginismus.[41] No data are currently available on the incidence of types of sexual dysfunctions among lesbians. Because of the differences in the sexual activity of gay and nongay couples, it would not be surprising if such data would show differences in rates of certain dysfunctions between gay and nongay women.

For example, in the case of situational anorgasmia (failure to reach orgasm), nongay women are defined as manifesting the dysfunction if they respond orgasmically to masturbation, cunnilingus, and partner manipulation, but not to coitus. Because lesbian women don't engage in coitus, they cannot be anorgasmic in relation to that form of stimulation within the context of a gay relationship.[42] So, gay and nongay women could both respond orgasmically to the same three stimuli, but not to coitus. The lesbian woman *would not be* considered sexually dysfunctional, the nongay woman *might be* so considered.

A second form of sexual dysfunction that is probably less frequent among lesbian women is vaginismus, the painful, spasmodic cramping of the vaginal muscles upon insertion of an outside stimulus.[40] This is less likely to be a complaint for lesbian women for two reasons. First, vaginal insertion is not a necessary part of lesbian lovemaking, whereas it is perceived as a necessary part of heterosexual lovemaking. As noted previously; in lesbian lovemaking, stimulation is focused mostly on the glans, labia, and clitoris, not on the relatively insensitive vaginal opening. Because of this, a lesbian might be unlikely to experience vaginismus during lovemaking and might not be aware of it as a problem. Second, even if a lesbian woman did experience vaginismus during lovemaking, it is quite possible that the couple would simply avoid types of stimulation that would bring about the spasms. This relatively simple solution might have the result that the vaginismus would be recognized but not labeled as problematic, and therefore would be ignored. This resolution would be most unlikely in a nongay couple because of the focus on insertion and coitus as the desired endpoint of lovemaking.

This is not to say that lesbian women never use or enjoy vaginal stimulation. They do. The difference is in the primacy of insertion as a desired technique in lesbian and nongay lovemaking. In lesbian couples, it is relatively un-

important and is therefore less likely to be viewed as a problem.

Other sexual problems. Lesbian couples can suffer from the same kinds of sex-related problems as nongay couples: lack of communication, miscommunication, differing or unrealistic expectations, and the like. Counseling for these kinds of problems is handled in the same ways regardless of the couple's sexual preference.[43] Among lesbian couples, however, counselors may want to watch for the following kinds of problems that are either unique or particularly problematic for lesbians.[44]

Carrying gender empathy too far. Lesbian couples can easily fall into the gender empathy version of the "if you loved me you'd know what to do/what I like/how I feel" fallacy. In this version, one or both partners may assume that because both are women, it is not necessary to communicate what does and does not feel good during lovemaking and that to do so is somehow a betrayal of trust. Although gender empathy means that many general sexual feelings and sensations are shared, each woman's specific responses and preferences are unique. Ignoring that uniqueness, or being afraid to communicate personal desires, can lead to sexual problems.

A corollary to this is the belief on the part of some women that because they are women, they should be exceptional in bed *all the time;* that sex should always be fantastic, romantic, meaningful, beautiful, and so forth. If a woman believes she *should* be good in bed because she is a lesbian, her subsequent anxiety is liable to get in the way. Lesbians have average and below average sexual experiences just like anybody else and must be given permission to do so.

Reluctance to engage in stimulative techniques. A lesbian woman may be uncomfortable performing one or more stimulative techniques. The technique that probably causes the most discomfort is cunnilingus, although there are no statistics to support this supposition. We are a culture obsessed with cleanliness and are taught to abhor the very suggestion of odor arising from the sexual and excretory organs, particularly female genitals. We are constantly bombarded with products to make ourselves and the products of our bodies smell like roses, pine forests, and the bodies of other animals (leather, musk, ambergris, and the like). As a culture, we are particularly distressed by women's body odors and functions. The message is clear. Genitals are nasty. They smell nasty, they excrete nasty substances, and they reside in awful proximity to even nastier, smellier, and more distasteful body parts. They are to be shunned.

In direct contradiction to these messages, women are also increasingly advised to "experience" their bodies; to touch, fondle, caress, pamper, celebrate, anoint, and generally get acquainted with themselves in the flesh. Television ads tell women to disguise or modify everything they can about themselves, while feminists say that if a woman hasn't tasted her own menstrual blood, she isn't really liberated. Lesbian women are not immune to these messages and may be particularly attuned to the more recent movement of women toward self-validation. This means that many women are caught between the ingrained aversion to the sight or smell of a woman's genitals and the concurrent desire to be liberated, to please a lover, or to be a "real" lesbian by engaging in oral sex. To do so may be distasteful; to avoid it may engender guilt.

The problem is most severe, of course, if one partner can only or most easily reach orgasm through oral-genital stimulation and the other partner is unwilling to perform. Above all, the helping professional should get the partners to distinguish enjoyment (or lack of it) of a particular sexual activity from love, normalcy, and instinctive reactions. Make it very clear that both the enjoyment of oral sex and the aversion to it are learned, not innate, responses, and they have nothing to do with being a "real" lesbian, liberated woman, sexual sophisticate, or good lover. One partner's reluctance to perform cunnilingus is not a com-

ment on how much in love she is but how well society is able to indoctrinate people. The professional should help the couple work out a temporary compromise that will allow both partners to relax and achieve mutual sexual satisfaction without using the technique in question. If the nonperforming partner wants to and the health professional is competent to perform desensitization to oral-genital contact (or any other problematic technique), that procedure may be undertaken. Otherwise, it would be desirable to refer the client to someone trained in sex therapy.

Some women are unwilling to touch their partners sexually at all. This, as well as reluctance to be touched, can be related to a woman's fear of being a lesbian.[40] She may believe that if she remains passive and does not actively make love to her partner, she is not *really* a lesbian because she is not actually doing anything.

The clue to this kind of problem would lie in the client's perception of herself as gay or nongay and her feelings about what it means to her to be one or the other, as well as the kinds of thoughts and feelings she has about herself and her partner during lovemaking. For example, a woman may refuse to make love to her partner because she "doesn't know how" and is afraid she won't do it "right." (Sometimes, of course, there are actual performance fears, but these are probably somewhat rare as presenting problems.) Upon exploration of these thoughts, you may find that she believes she does not know how because she is not "really" a lesbian, and only a "real" lesbian would know how to make love to another woman. In this case, intervention would be directed toward the woman's homophobia and her cognitions about herself, her sexual preference, and the connection between these and sexual activity.

Reluctance to allow stimulation by the partner. There are probably two major reasons for this. One is, again, the fear of being a lesbian. A woman may believe, for example, that if she makes love to another woman it does not mean she is a lesbian. If she allows herself to be made love to, enjoys it, and is able to reach orgasm, then, she believes, she would really be a lesbian. Or, if she has had or is having concurrent nongay sexual relations, she may fear that being made love to by a woman would make them unsatisfactory. Again, intervention would be directed at the underlying fear of being or becoming lesbian, rather than at sexual activity per se.

Differences in desired frequency of lovemaking. No two women are likely to want to make love with the same frequency. Sometimes differences in partners' sexual needs are seen by the couple as an indication that something is wrong with one partner or with the relationship. In making an assessment, be sure that there is not an underlying problem with the relationship itself, the partners' sexual compatability, or one or both partners' sexual functioning or sexual responsiveness. If any of these appear to be underlying causes, they must be dealt with first.

Problems sometimes arise because the couple lacks the skills for assertively communicating sexual interest or arousal. In this society, women are trained to subordinate their sexual needs to those of a man. They are not taught to consider their own sexual needs as primary, to be assertive in expressing and fulfilling these needs, or even to clearly recognize them. In nongay relationships, the responsibility for initiating lovemaking is traditionally the man's. In lesbian relationships, both women will ideally share the responsibility for initiating lovemaking. If the partners do not know how to do this, are afraid of being rejected, or think there is something wrong with openly expressing their desires, a situation can easily develop in which one or both partners are dissatisfied with the frequency of sexual activity.

As in so many other problem areas, one must first be certain the client(s) has the skills for expressing sexual need, either verbally or nonverbally. Next, be sure both partners are aware of each other's messages regarding desire and arousal. Third, help clients separate feelings of love and caring from frequency of sexual contact and ability or willingness to communicate about sexual needs. This is particularly important because women are taught to equate sexual desirability with love. If a woman is unable to initiate lovemaking, her part-

ner may assume that her lover does not find her sexually desirable and therefore does not love her. Fourth, help clients develop appropriate skills for assertively expressing their sexual needs, and finally, work with clients to develop appropriate cognitions about their own sexual needs.

Another major difficulty lies in actual partner differences in sexual needs. This is only problematic, of course, if one partner perceives her lover's needs as either excessive or inadequate. If there is no underlying difficulty causing one partner to be afraid of sexual activity, then it seems most appropriate to try to help partners reach some kind of compromise. Because lesbian lovemaking does not involve coitus, both partners are rarely satisfied at the same time. This means that, often, one partner will make love to the other, who will then reciprocate. If both partners believe that it is necessary for both to reach orgasm every time they make love, this may reduce the frequency of lovemaking. An alternative is for the partner who is more frequently aroused to be made love to without believing reciprocation is necessary for the experience to be satisfactory. Another alternative would be to explore masturbation alone or with the partner as an openly accepted option within the couple.

Summary. All in all, the biggest sexual problems specific to lesbian couples probably arise out of the fact that these are relationships between two women who are socialized within a nongay culture to function within male-female relationships. The uniqueness of problems involving communication difficulties, unwillingness to engage in or receive certain kinds of stimulation, and frequency of lovemaking all are based on learned fears of being lesbian, of one's own body, of being assertive, or of lack of skill. They are not indications of lesbian sexual pathology.

Once the underlying factors are understood and made clear to lesbian couples, intervention then involves education, skill training, desensitization, and problem solving. In almost every case, regardless of the presenting problem, it is important to help clients distinguish between the problem and feelings of love, individual competence, mental health, and relationship quality. Remember that lesbians, as women, have usually learned sexual response patterns that are functional for heterosexual, not homosexual, relationships. These patterns often include lack of sexual assertiveness, guilt over, denial of, or nonrecognition of sexual needs, and poor skills for communicating about sexual issues. A great many lesbian women learn to compensate for these patterns quite easily and, as we have said before, usually rate sex with women as more enjoyable than sex with men. If these patterns are brought into the counseling situation, they can be changed without assumptions of pathology or incomplete sexual development.

GAY MALE SEXUAL ACTIVITY
Sexual behavior

After viewing a film[45] showing two gay men involved in sexual activity that included anal intercourse, a female graduate student stated, "I'm so glad to see that they can have intercourse and kiss at the same time. I always thought that they could only do it in positions that didn't allow kissing, and I thought it was too bad because they were missing something special. Now I feel better about it." Other students often express their lack of knowledge about the sexual activity of gay men and after viewing films will sometimes respond with, "I often wondered what they did." Just as movies can show only the sexual activity of those particular subjects at that particular time, this section cannot possibly explain or even name all the possible variations in explicit sexual activity between two men. If more than two men are involved, the variations increase exponentially.

The best reference currently available for anyone who will be working with gay men in the area of explicit sexual activity is *The Joy of Gay Sex,* by Silverstein and White.[46] It provides a comprehensive description of the various activities and information on how to go about preparing for and engaging in some of them. Although there are some judgmental comments in the book, such as inferring that most people who engage in a particular behavior are on drugs of some kind,[47] it is a valuable resource for anyone working with gay male clients, and in some instances, might be helpful for someone working with nongay clients. For example, the section entitled "First Time"[48] discusses the steps to take in beginning anal intercourse in a manner that will decrease the probability of pain and increase the probability of pleasure.

Most frequent activities. There has been mild disagreement in the research literature in determining the most frequent activities of gay men. Saghir and Robins found that oral-genital activity and anal intercourse were by far the most frequent techniques in their sample, although respondents also engaged in mutual masturbation and frottage (rubbing against another person until reaching climax).[49] Jay and Young found oral-genital activity, mutual masturbation, anal intercourse, and frottage as the order of frequency for sexual activities, with oral-genital contacts the highest. A high number of respondents also reported "soul" kissing.[50] Bell and Weinberg found similarly that, of seven activities, the frequency, in decreasing order, was oral-genital activity (receiving, followed in frequency by giving), hand-genital activity (being masturbated, followed by masturbating the partner), anal intercourse (performing, followed by receiving), and frottage.[51] They also asked about feelings toward activities, and discovered that the order of favorite activities did not follow the order of frequency of engaging in them. For the white male homosexual group, the favorite activity was receiving oral-genital stimulation, and the next was performing anal intercourse, followed by mutual oral-genital stimulation (sometimes referred to as "69"). Among Black gay males, performing anal intercourse was the most preferred activity, receiving oral-genital stimulation was second, receiving anal intercourse was third, with mutual oral-genital stimulation fourth.[52]

Masters and Johnson were the only researchers who did not report anal intercourse as high on the list of preferences. They indicate that self-masturbation, partner manipulation, and fellatio are the most common forms of gay male sexual activity.[53]

Oral-genital sexual activity (fellatio). Fellatio is placing the penis in the partner's mouth. Oral-genital activity is stimulation of the genitals with the mouth, including but not limited to fellatio. Gay men report that this is one of their most pleasurable and frequent behaviors. An examination of the behavior indicates that much more than simple mouth on penis is involved. Oral-genital activity includes hand stimulation simultaneous with mouth stimulation of the penis, hand stimulation of the scrotum and anal sphincter while stimulating the penis, drawing the testicles into the mouth, licking the testicles, moving the mouth up and down the length of the penis, and licking the penis along its length, all being done while the recipient is either employing pelvic thrusting or being still. Simply referring to the activity as fellatio or even oral-genital activity is inaccurate in that it is more often hand-mouth-genital activity.

Anal intercourse. Anal intercourse is the insertion of the penis into the anus. It provides the gay man with stimulation that is similar to vaginal intercourse for the heterosexual man. There can be identical pelvic thrusting in many of the same positions employed by men engaged in vaginal intercourse, and it provides pleasure for both partners. Some men have reported orgasm while being the recipient of anal intercourse. It can be combined with hand manipulation of the penis and scrotum, and/or nipples, and can be accomplished lying down, standing up, or sitting, with partners facing or back to front. As suggested in *The Joy of Gay Sex,* it is also possible to combine anal intercourse with oral-genital activity,[54] and, as the student discovered from watching the film, it can also be combined with kissing, hugging, and general body contact.

For many men, some kind of lubrication is necessary. The most commonly used are saliva, several brands of sterile, water-soluble lubricants, Vaseline and vegetable shortening. Some men have reported that the more often they engage in this activity, the less lubrication is required, and sometimes there is sufficient natural lubrication so that no

additional is necessary. However, for most, some added lubrication is always necessary, with amount depending to some extent on the experience, level of arousal, and size of partner's penis.

Mutual masturbation. In mutual masturbation, each partner masturbates the other with his hand(s). The hand moves up and down and sometimes in a circular motion with varying amounts of pressure depending on the desires of the individual. Many men enjoy having the hand create friction on the coronal ridge as well as the shaft, with others enjoying only one or the other. Mutual masturbation may include additional stimulation of the nipples and/or the scrotum and/or the anus with the hand or mouth, and may also include lubrication.

Frottage. This activity is identical to the body rubbing described in the section on lesbian sexual activity. It is rhythmic friction of the penis against the partner's body. It may be against the abdominal area, the chest, the back, or between the thighs. According to Jay and Young[55] and Bell and Weinberg,[56] this is a pleasant activity for most gay men but is not often used as a source of achieving orgasm.

Place, time, and partner. Activity will sometimes vary according to place, time, and sexual partner. If the activity is occurring in a place that lends itself to quick, casual activity, such as a public toilet or a rest stop on a highway, the preferred activity might be different from one where more time is available, such as in a home or apartment. As one of Jay and Young's respondents reported:

☐ In quickie situations like a theater or toilet, I can respond with gusto to a blow job. In the comfort and privacy of my own bed, I prefer more body contact, caressing, etc.[57]

A difference in preference may also occur with different partners. For some men, receiving fellatio permits a wider range of partners than does giving or reciprocating. For example, a man might enjoy being the recipient of fellatio with an unseen stranger, but would reciprocate only if he knew what the other person looked like.

Options within the most frequent activities. Some gay men have very specific preferences, as was indicated by two respondents in the Jay and Young study.

☐ I enjoy having my tits rubbed more than having my cock rubbed, and only a combo of the two will bring me to orgasm.[58]

☐ Probably the most sensitive part of my body is my ears. These can, if treated properly, turn me on more than any other spot on my body.[58]

However, for most men, the sexual activity is varied. An individual may enjoy one or two activities at one time and entirely different ones the next time. He may include combinations of anal intercourse, oral-genital activity, masturbation, and frottage, or he may engage in variations of only one of those. Since each of the activities in its many forms can result in orgasm, there is vast potential for variety.

Less frequent activities. In addition to these more frequently occurring activities, there are others that Jay and Young describe as "erotic variations."[59] These include sadomasochism, urination (technically, urophilia; popularly, golden shower or water sports[60]), enemas (technically, klismaphilia; popularly, water sports), defecation (technically, coprophilia; popularly, scat), "fist fucking" (popularly, Crisco party), bestiality (technically, zoophilia), fetishisms, threesomes and orgies, toys, and pornography. Many of these activities are labeled "kinky," "weird," or "perverted" by some people, including some gay men and lesbian women.

For the counselor, it is crucial that an objective view be maintained. There are physical health concerns that need to be explored with some of the behaviors, but they carry the same import as discussing the physical health concerns of kissing. For example, fist fucking can be extremely dangerous if the insertor has sharp fingernails, because

the lack of sensory nerves in the intestines means that accidental perforations cannot be felt. When golden showers are discussed, it is important to point out that the urine might tend to toxicity and taste bitter if it is concentrated, so it is advisable to drink liquids before engaging in the activity to decrease the acid concentration and make the taste less bitter. Enemas will not usually be harmful; however, frequent use may cause a problem in that the defecation process usually depends on the peristaltic action of the bowels, and repeated enemas as the only stimulus to defecation will cause the action to cease, thereby making physiologically normal defecation difficult, if not impossible.

A comparison of the Jay and Young data on lesbians with the equivalent data on gay men shows that both sections include identical activities except that analingus (rimming), which is moving the tongue around and into the anus, is included in the section on lesbian activity entitled "The Specialized Tastes of a Few Lesbians," and is not in the equivalent section on gay male activity. For the men, it is included with the more frequently occurring activities mentioned previously.[61] This is because it is an activity that could be described as somewhat common in gay male activity and somewhat rare in lesbian activity. The counselor should be aware and should advise anyone engaging in this activity that it carries a high health risk because of the probability of ingestion of bacteria and viruses that may be disease producing. The use of soap and water in and around the anus before engaging in analingus may lessen these risks. Such measures will not, however, affect any harmful viruses higher in the intestinal tract.

Numbers of sexual partners. There is research evidence to suggest that gay men, as a group, have more different sexual partners over a life span than do lesbians or heterosexual men or women.[62] This by no means indicates that *all* gay men have very large numbers of sexual partners, but it does show that *some* gay men have hundreds or even thousands. In Bell and Weinberg's sample of 574 white gay men, 75% reported over 100 different partners, and of their 111 Black gay men, 59% reported over 100.[63] Saghir and Robins indicate that over 75% of their gay male sample had over 30 partners (they do not indicate how many over 30), whereas none of their heterosexual men reported over 30.[64] Since total number of partners is obviously age related, it is of interest to note that subjects in both gay samples averaged 35 to 37 years.[65]

Reasons for high number of contacts. There is speculation about the reasons for this phenomenon.[66] Some of those speculations refer to the socialization differences between men and women in general, indicating that men tend to be able to separate sexual activity from affection, whereas women tend to establish affectional relationships before any sexual activity.[67] Others refer to the different social settings for meeting people, indicating that nongay men are provided with many different types of socially approved meeting places; whereas for gay men, most of the meeting places not only lack social approval but also are oriented to sexual activity.[67] Bell and Weinberg also suggest that the homophobic nature of the society, wherein the gay man is subject to blackmail or unwanted exposure, reinforces a sexual activity pattern in which there is no commitment or little involvement.[67] If your sexual partner doesn't know your name or your job, he will have less chance of blackmailing you or of making your orientation known to others.

This behavior pattern has been viewed as the result of psychological problems, such as fears of intimacy, commitment to a relationship, or responsibility. There have also been suggestions of a strong neurotic component to the behavior, in that it is sometimes very compulsive.[68] These suggestions appear to view the behavior as being symptomatic.

Jay and Young provide a somewhat different picture. "For the gay male, sex is above all a source of fun, pleasure, recreation, and communication."[69] Silverstein and White suggest that "an endless round of one-night stands or short affairs can provide a gay man in a big city with constant novelty and excitement and introduce him to a wide variety of erotic delights. And these delights can be deeply rewarding."[70] In other words, some

gay men may have several or many different sexual partners because it is fun and exciting and pleasurable for them to do so.

Another factor is availability. There are several settings within the gay male community that exist primarily for casual sexual contacts. For example, gay steam baths, sometimes referred to as the "tubs," exist primarily to provide opportunities for recreational sex. The basic "bath" will have at least one private room, an open room where group sex can occur, toilet facilities, and a steam room. Depending on the location and the economic support, the bath may be very elaborate, with many private rooms, a pool, an exercise room, a lounge, and many other accoutrements that enhance a sexual atmosphere. Sexual activity may occur in pairs or groups, and may be private or not depending on the wishes of the participants. It is also possible to simply observe activity, if that is the desire of the individual. All this occurs without any monetary exchange except for the price of admission.

In addition to the existence of such places, there are several books available that list the gay meeting places throughout the United States and the world. This enables a gay man who is traveling to a strange city or town to have an idea of where to go to meet other men for social or sexual interactions.

Perhaps the reality is that all of the above are reasons why gay men report large numbers of sexual partners. For some gay men the behavior is symptomatic of a psychological problem; for others it is not. It may indeed be a reflection of the general differences between male and female socialization, for, as we have previously noted, gay men have male gender identities and lesbians have female gender identities, and they are generally socialized as men and women. It is also true that there are very few places where gay men can meet on a purely social basis. Although some gay bars are social places, there is still a sexual aura similar to that which one finds in many nongay singles bars. Some gay men engage in sexual activity with strangers because it is a readily available source of "fun, pleasure, recreation, and communication."[69]

As with other aspects of the lives of gay men, there is no single reason for the fact that some gay men have hundreds or thousands of different sexual partners, just as there is no single reason why some of them have one or two. However, the gay man who has many may be the one who seeks counseling in an attempt to alter his behavior. It will be incumbent on the counselor to ensure that the wide range of possible reasons for the behavior are explored, including the positive ones that are sometimes ignored. Also, the source of the client's discomfort needs to be examined. The pressure to limit one's sexual partners comes not only from the culture in general but also from some other gay men and lesbians. If indeed gay male sexual activity is as available and as much fun as Jay and Young or Silverstein and White suggest, then it is certainly possible that someone would engage in the behavior often and possibly even with willing strangers without this implying any kind of problem.

Sexual contacts and meaningful relationships. When numbers of sexual partners are discussed, there is another either-or situation that occasionally appears in the literature. It is perhaps best illustrated by a passage written by Marmor in his book *Homosexual Behavior*.

> Thus, despite the fact that homosexual contacts can be made with relative ease, it is clear that not all homosexuals pursue patterns of promiscuity or impersonal sex. Most of them, indeed, are searching for a meaningful human relationship.[71]

There appears to be an implication that those men who engage in "promiscuity or impersonal sex" do not have a "meaningful relationship." This implication is by no means unique to Marmor. In fact, he is one of the more knowledgeable writers and researchers and has consistently sought to point out the research biases and mythology in the literature on gay males. All the more reason to use his statement as an example. The reality is that a person may have both many sexual partners *and* a very deep, committed, meaningful, loving relationship with another man. It is not always an either-or situation.

For example, Carl and Drew are both in their middle to late forties, and have been identified as a couple for almost 14 years. Both love each other and have a very strong commitment to their relationship. They enjoy sexual activity with each other on an average of two to three times a week, and each of them has had approximately 20 to 25 different sexual partners during the last year, a pattern that has existed since the beginning of the relationship. They obviously do not measure their commitment to the relationship in terms of sexual exclusiveness.

Bell and Weinberg hint at this when they discuss the quality of gay relationships in their study, indicating that they involve commitment and affection similar to that expressed in heterosexual relationships.[72] Later in the book, they indicate that most of the couples in their study were ones in which sexual exclusivity was not part of the relationship contract.[73] Clearly, gay male couples have primary relationships that include love and commitment but do not necessarily include sexual exclusivity.

Sexual activity in couples. When one examines the sexual activity of gay male couples, two generalizations become apparent: (1) gay male couples are more likely than either lesbian[72] or nongay couples to accept sexual activity outside the pairbond; that is, they are less likely to be sexually exclusive (monandrous)[74] couples; and (2) they are more likely than nongay couples (but not lesbian couples) to spend time at and communicate about their sexual interactions with their partner.

Studies by Bell and Weinberg,[73] Saghir and Robins,[75] and McWhirter and Mattison[76] indicate that the great majority of gay male couples establish relationships in which sexual activity with someone other than the primary partner is acceptable to both partners. Saghir and Robins report that 75% of relationships that were established before the age of 20 were sexually exclusive throughout their duration, but only 25% of those established after age 20 were monandrous.[75] Jay and Young do not have data on the number of couples in their study who are sexually exclusive, but the excerpts in their section entitled "Fidelity, Monogamy, Jealousy" indicate that, although some couples are sexually exclusive, the majority are not.[77]

The only study that compares the sexual activity of gay male couples to that of lesbian and nongay couples was carried out by Masters and Johnson, who noted several differences between the gay male and nongay committed couples. One difference related to stimulation sites on the male partner. Almost 75% of the gay couples included nipple stimulation, whereas "no more than three or four in 100 married men were so stimulated by their wives."[78] Also, when nipple stimulation was included in the heterosexual couple, it did not last as long, nor did it stimulate erection, as it did with the gay males.[79]

Summary. The gay man's sexual activity is varied and complex, as are other parts of his life. He actually spends little of his time engaging in explicit sexual activity, yet this aspect of his life has often been the primary focus of interest in gayness of the culture, researchers, and the helping professionals, and in some cases, is the focus of the gay man himself. This focus is inappropriate. It is the cause of concern for some gay men. The danger for the counselor is that he or she may get caught up in that situation and also focus on the sexual activity. Gay men have many more aspects to their lives than their sexual behavior. They spend most of their time in nonsexual activities, just as nongays do, even though they may have many different sexual partners.

Counseling for sexual activity

Like nongays, gay men may seek counseling for concerns that focus specifically on sexual activity. These concerns usually fall into four categories: (1) thoughts about promiscuity, (2) sexual activity outside a relationship, (3) sexual dysfunction, and (4) inability to enjoy specific sex acts.

Concerns with numbers of sexual partners. We often operate under an assumption that it is

better to have one sexual partner than to have many. We assume that people should have only one or at most a few sexual partners over a lifetime and that those people who have large numbers of sexual partners are somehow mentally unstable or unhealthy. The words *few* and *large numbers* are subjective. Sometimes in the literature and in discussions such as this, you will hear the word *promiscuous*. It is a pejorative word, without a clear definition. Someone has defined a promiscuous individual as one who has more sexual partners than the person speaking. How many partners are "few"? How many are "large numbers"? There are gay men who have no sexual partners. There are others who have one or two during a lifetime, and still others who have one or two thousand,[63] and there are others who have over ten thousand.[80] Does this fact create a situation in which the one with 2000 sex partners is inherently unhappy or unstable, whereas the one with one partner is inherently happy and stable? No, it does not.[81] It may create a situation in which the counselor is envious of the one with 2000 partners, but the counselor must be able to recognize and understand his or her feelings as they relate to those of the client and not use them as a base for an assumption of psychological problems.

In counseling a gay male who expresses concern about his "promiscuity," the counselor should encourage the client to define what the term means to him. Then one should make certain that the client is not automatically judging himself to be "unhealthy." Enjoying sex with many different partners is not an automatic symptom of a psychological problem. A client *may* be searching for acceptance or attempting to disguise a sexual dysfunction,[82] or he may be engaging in sexual activity because it is fun and pleasurable and available. Helping a gay man sort out his motives for the behavior; being supportive of the possibility that it might be simply a fun, exciting, pleasurable activity; and keeping the counselor's personal biases (either for or against) and the culture's condemnation out of the exploration are all crucial.

When the client's pursuit of casual sex partners is symptomatic of a problem, such as fear of commitment, hiding a sexual dysfunction, maintaining homophobic attitudes, lack of self-esteem, or compulsiveness, the counselor should focus on the problem, not the symptom. However, identification of the problem, when one does exist, is not always easy.

David was a participant in a gay male discussion group. He expressed concern about the fact that he was 32, had never been in a primary relationship, and went into the city on weekends to engage in sexual activity with casual partners. When asked the reasons for his concerns, he replied, "Well, everyone knows you're supposed to be in a relationship and my friends keep telling me I should find someone and settle down." When asked if this was what he wanted to do, he replied, "No. I've been having too much fun, and I've never met anyone that I wanted to settle down with."

Although David didn't recognize it at the time, his answers implied a lack of self-confidence and homophobia. First, he enjoyed his weekends of socializing and sexual activity but was beginning to question his enjoyment because of pressures from other people. Second, he viewed a relationship as restrictive and saw it only from the narrow cultural perspective of marriage. In his mind the establishment of a primary relationship meant a curtailment of his variety of sexual partners. The group leader began to question David and discovered that the implications of the statements were correct. The group first dealt with his concerns, supporting the idea that his going into the city was a source of relaxation and recreation and was therefore positive. The group leader also assured him that his relationship history was in itself not necessarily indicative of some underlying psychological problem. Both of these actions eased his concern.

The next step was to explore his ideas about relationships. The individuals in the group were asked to develop an ideal contract for a fantasy relationship. They were given some hints about the topics to include, such as living arrangements, sexual exclusivity, visiting parents, deciding on where to spend holidays, and financial considerations. David completed the assignment, and when the group began discussing the contracts, David found that there were alternatives for relationship patterns that he had never considered.

David did have a problem. It was primarily one of homophobic attitudes, including lack of knowledge about viable alternatives for relationships. David needed support for his belief that his sexual activity was fun, and he needed to learn about viable alternatives for relationships. He also needed to become aware of his tendency to listen to his friends' advice on how to run his life, rather than take responsibility for himself.

Sexually transmitted diseases. The fact that gay men report higher numbers of partners than do lesbians or nongays is simply that—a fact. It carries no implication for judgment. It does, however, mean that they are at higher risk for sexually transmitted diseases (STD). In fact, if one looks at the three groups of partnered sex acts—male and female homosexual contacts and male and female heterosexual contacts—male homosexual contacts usually represent the highest incidence rate for each category of STD, except perhaps herpes. The fact that many homosexuals go to private physicians, rather than to clinics, lessens the chance of the incident being reported, providing additional evidence to suggest that gay men are more at risk for STD than any other group.

Homosexual contacts account for the highest percentage of early syphilis,[83] genital, rectal, and pharyngeal gonorrhea,[84] asymptomatic gonorrhea,[85] granuloma inguinale,[86] lymphogranuloma venereum,[87] hepatitis A[88] and B[89] and non-A non-B,[90] and shigellosis, amebiasis, and giardiasis.[91] One can only guess about venereal warts, chancroid, scabies, crabs, and nonspecific urethritis. In providing health care to a man who has engaged in homosexual activity, it is necessary to examine all sexually used orifices[92] and to determine how they are used. For example, oral-anal contact could lead to one of the gastrointestinal diseases, such as amebiasis or giardiasis,[93] or viral hepatitis A.[88] Hepatitis B has been isolated from saliva, semen, and urine,[88] which means that it is important to know if any of these are ingested.

As one can readily see, there are physiological disadvantages to having more than one sexual partner; however, there are also physiological disadvantages to kissing. If one finds kissing stimulating, then knowing the physical health risks is not likely to stop that individual from kissing. This issue should be discussed with any client who is sexually active with people other than his primary partner or whose partner is sexual with others. However, the counselor must be careful to explore this from a positive stance, with suggestions for frequency of examination, where to go for examination and for treatment should an infection occur, what sites should be examined, and how to go about informing contacts, if possible. In addition, the client's feelings about having an STD should be addressed. Contemporary Western culture still generally holds the view that getting an STD is bad, and the person who is infected is "dirty." If the client grew up in this culture, it is likely that he will also hold these views, and they must be explored with the goal of altering them.

In most instances, sexually transmitted diseases are curable, but some men are reluctant to seek treatment or are concerned about confidentiality of information that must be provided in obtaining treatment. Every counselor should be aware of the clinics in his or her area and should know which ones are nonjudgmental in treating gay clients. One way to do this is to get feedback from other gay men who have been to the clinic. A better, though sometimes threatening, way is for the counselor to go to the clinic for an examination. There is a very high probability that a gay man will have an STD at some time in his life. The counselor should ensure that the interests of the client are met.

Sexual activity outside a primary relationship. Gay men will sometimes seek counseling because one partner wants to have sexual activity outside the couple relationship, and the other one does not. This becomes a problem when one or both partners do not know how to go about incorporating this behavior into the relationship. It is sometimes easier for the counselor to guide the client in exploring advantages for maintaining sexual exclusivity, because that may be the only successful model known to the counselor.

Culturally, sexual exclusivity is often viewed as the sign of true love and commitment within the relationship, but this is not necessarily true. There are couples for whom sexual activity outside the pair has led to a strengthening of the relationship; conversely, of course, situations have occurred in which this activity has been the cause of separation.

Sexual exclusivity also lessens the need to deal with sexually transmitted diseases. However, there are some disadvantages that need to be explored, such as the possibility of monotony, the lack of opportunity to learn from sexual activity with others, or the inability for fulfillment of one person's desire to include variety in sexual partners, which may lead to feelings of resentment toward the existence of the relationship.

If the professional knows of no viable way to help two people continue to exist as a couple and yet openly share sexual activity outside that pair, the suggestions for alternatives for the client are likely to be very biased. Ways of overcoming the disadvantages of exclusivity exist; however, there are also alternatives to sexual exclusivity, or monandry. Some couples agree that sexual activity can occur outside the pair but also agree not to tell each other about it. Others find that hearing of the partner's sexual activity with someone else is sexually stimulating and pleasurable. Other couples agree that any outside partner will be shared, that is, that the activity would take place in a triad situation.

Still others profess sexual exclusivity to each other, yet have other partners in secret. And still others are monandrous.[94] We present a more detailed discussion of ways in which couples manage each of these alternatives in Chapter 9.

Sexual dysfunction. There is very little information on sexual dysfunction and gay men. There is little doubt that some gay men have sexual dysfunctions, but the extent of those is unknown, and no basis exists for making estimates. Because this book does not emphasize therapy, and dysfunctions are best treated therapeutically, we will simply describe the dysfunctions and discuss the implications for the counselor.

Sexual dysfunction essentially means that the sexual organs are not functioning as it is believed they should. The more common male dysfunctions have been identified as ejaculating too quickly (premature ejaculation or ejaculatory incontinence), not being able to ejaculate (retarded ejaculation or ejaculatory incompetence), not being very interested in sexual activity or not as frequently interested as the client thinks appropriate (lack of sexual desire), becoming nauseous or ill while attempting sexual activity (sexual aversion), and not being able to achieve an erection (erectile dysfunction or impotence).[95] The erectile dysfunction has been further divided into *primary,* in which the man has never had an erection; *secondary,* in which he once had erections but no longer does; and *situational,* in which he has erections only in some sexual situations and not in others.

In their book, *Homosexuality in Perspective,* Masters and Johnson indicated that erectile dysfunction was the most common gay male dysfunction presented at their clinic.[96] They also mentioned that they had to alter their definition of erectile dysfunction for gay men because their definition for heterosexual men depended on vaginal penetration. Thus they based their definition on those situations that they identified as "the most commonly used forms of homosexual interaction, . . . masturbation, partner manipulation, [and]

fellatio."[97] Although there are gay men who experience erectile dysfunction in anal intercourse, these were not included in their definition.

Kenneth George, in his therapy with 40 sexually dysfunctional gay men, indicated that lack of sexual desire was the most common dysfunction in his clients, with retarded ejaculation, premature ejaculation, and erectile dysfunction following in order of frequency. He also indicated that there were essentially two factors influencing the dysfunctions: homophobia and adherence to stereotypical gender role behavior. He identified homophobia as being responsible for the lack of desire and stereotypical gender role behavior as responsible for the other three. He commented that sexual dysfunction appeared when the man could not ask for what he wanted from his partner, when he had to maintain a competitive atmosphere, or when he felt he had to always win, to be constantly ready for sex, and to ejaculate every time.[98]

Masters and Johnson also noted that gay men are often able to hide their dysfunctions.[99] George suggested that this might be one of the reasons for some gay men having large numbers of sexual partners, in that they would not be "discovered" by casual partners as readily as by a primary partner.[98] This appears to be true for some gay men. Because of the reticence to seek sex therapy, it may be the counselor who discovers that a gay client is experiencing sexual difficulties. It may help for the counselor to explain that many of the treatment modes already shown to be successful with nongay men are appropriate for use with gay men.[100]

What may turn out to be the most difficult step in aiding a gay man with sexual dysfunction will be finding an appropriate therapist. The counselor can help by clarifying the situation for the client, by having at least one referral source, and by being supportive. If the counselor discovers that a gay man has been refused treatment or is receiving poor treatment, it then becomes a matter of being an advocate for him.

Inability to enjoy specific sex acts. The gay man might also express concern over his inability to enjoy very specific sex acts. This might be viewed as a minor dysfunction under the heading of sexual aversion, but it might not require the intensive therapy that is required when the aversion is general or when the feelings are ones of nausea rather than discomfort. This might be a man who feels uncomfortable during anal intercourse when his partner's penis is being inserted into his anus, or it might be a man who is uncomfortable swallowing semen or putting his mouth on another man's penis. For some of these concerns, exploring the reasons for the discomfort may indicate the need for education. For example, if the gay male indicates that a penis in his anus is painful, it is necessary to first discover if he is using a lubricant on himself and on his partner's penis. It is also important that he be able to relax the anal sphincter during anal intercourse, and he may need to discover some relaxation techniques, such as breathing through the mouth. There might also be a physical problem that requires a medical examination and treatment, but the counselor should first find out if the basics are being used—lubricant (in generous portions at first) and relaxation. The counselor should also explore his reasons for wanting to engage in anal intercourse. Anal intercourse is usually possible without pain and often with pleasure, but neither this activity nor any other is absolutely necessary, and motives should be explored, if only to help the man clarify them for himself. He may also be experiencing a sense of gender-inappropriate role behavior if he is the receiver of anal intercourse. In this instance, the counselor may want to discuss the client's feelings about role behavior in general, pointing out the possibility that sexual activity might have no implication for gender role.

If he is uncomfortable swallowing semen, explore his ideas about the cleanliness of ejaculate and urine. Many of us grow up believing that anything that comes out of the penis is dirty. That message is very strongly internalized by many of us. The reality is that ejaculate is sterile (assuming that there is no infection involved) and is not physiologically harmful to the body, nor will the man get pregnant by swallowing it. This may sound facetious, but some people acquire strange beliefs about sex as they grow up. Usually, taking

the man through a desensitization program in which he learns to touch, smell, and taste his own ejaculate will help him in overcoming this uncomfortableness. However, there is also the issue of the reasons behind his desire to swallow the semen. Although some people feel that it is symbolic of the relationship, and that spitting it out is a sign of dislike for the partner, this may or may not be true. The importance attached to the gesture is individual, or as someone once said, "Swallowing it is all a matter of taste."

Being uncomfortable with placing the mouth on the penis can also be worked through using a desensitizing program. This is a systematic program in which the partners shower together, wash and rinse each other's genitals, and then place the mouth as close to the penis as is comfortable. This process is repeated until the man is comfortable kissing his partner's penis, then putting his lips on the head of the penis, and then putting the penis in his mouth.

The discomfort usually arises from the misinformation that the genitals are dirty and from a fear that the partner will push his penis down the throat until it creates a choking sensation. The dirtiness myth can usually be overcome by stressing the use of soap and water to clean the penis. The distance the partner's penis travels down the throat can be controlled by using a hand as well as a mouth in the act of fellatio. This will not only add to the sensations but also give some control.

One other piece of information might be of help in exploring this with the gay man. In working with clients who have presented this concern, we have found that once the discomfort was dealt with, and the man reported that he was engaging in the activity, his primary pleasure during the activity was derived from knowing that he was giving his partner pleasure. However, the more he engaged in the behavior, the more he began to derive some pleasureable sensations for himself. In other words, practice seems to bring pleasure. This is important, because some people get concerned

120

when they do not really enjoy the activity for themselves. This transition might not always arrive, but it is apparent in some men.

Summary. Some gay men experience sexual dysfunctions or have concerns about explicit sexual activity. The counselor may find that education is necessary, along with suggestions for alternative viewpoints and behavior. Many of the sexual problems do not require extensive therapy for a solution, and a knowledgeable, nonjudgmental, supportive counselor can often be of help simply by educating and suggesting possible alternatives. However, it is extremely important that the counselor know of a competent, ethical, and supportive source to which she or he may refer clients who are in need of more expert therapeutic intervention.

END NOTES

1. Kurt, E., & Lief, H. "Why sex education for medical students?" In R. Green (Ed.), *Human sexuality: A health practitioner's text*. Baltimore: Williams & Wilkins, 1975, p. 2; Hawkins, R., & Friedman, E. "Human sexuality: A content area for continuing medical education." *The P.A. Journal*, 1978, *8*(4), 219.
2. Saghir, M., & Robins, E. "Homosexuality: Sexual behavior of the female homosexual." *Archives of General Psychiatry*, 1969, *20*(2), 192-201.
3. Bell, A., & Weinberg, M. *Homosexualities: A study of diversity among men and women*. New York: Simon & Schuster, 1978.
4. Masters, W., & Johnson, V. *Homosexuality in perspective*. Boston: Little, Brown, 1979.
5. Jay, K., & Young, A. *The gay report*. New York: Summit, 1979.
6. Bell & Weinberg, 1978, p. 115.
7. Bell & Weinberg, 1978, pp. 112-113.
8. Bell & Weinberg, 1978, p. 72.
9. Bell & Weinberg, 1978; Jay & Young, 1979; Saghir, M., & Robins, E. *Male and female homosexuality: A comprehensive investigation*. Baltimore: Williams & Wilkins, 1973; and Schofield, M. *The sexual behavior of young people*. Boston: Little, Brown, 1965a.
10. Saghir & Robins, 1973.
11. Masters & Johnson, 1979, pp. 212-214.
12. Masters & Johnson, 1979, p. 212.
13. Masters & Johnson, 1979, p. 214.
14. Excellent written material on providing sex therapy is provided in Kaplan, H. *The new sex therapy: Active treatment of sexual dysfunctions*. New York: Brunner/Mazel, 1974. A brief but worthwhile section on working with sexual problems in the context of marital therapy appears in Jacobson, N., & Margolin, S. *Marital therapy: Strategies based on social learning and behavior exchange principles*. New York: Brunner/Mazel, 1979; see especially pp. 290-300. Although their book is written from the perspective of counseling heterosexual clients, much of it is equally applicable to counseling gay couples.
15. Masters & Johnson, 1979, p. 247.
16. Masters & Johnson, 1979, pp. 64-91.
17. Masters & Johnson, 1979, pp. 212-213.
18. Masters & Johnson, 1979, p. 124.
19. Masters and Johnson, for example, unfavorably compare the "my turn–your turn" interactions of gay couples with the "our turn" interactions of nongay couples, and believe that the "our turn" approach is inherently more satisfactory. (Masters & Johnson, 1979, p. 214.)
20. Moses, A.E. *Identify management in lesbian women*. New York: Praeger, 1978; Schafer, S. "Sexual and social problems of lesbians." *The Journal of Sex Research*, 1976, *12*(1), 59.
21. For some beautifully vivid and moving passages describing lesbian lovemaking, see Millett, K. *Sita*. New York: Farrar, Straus, & Giroux, 1977. See also Sisley, E., & Harris, B. *The joy of lesbian sex*. New York: Crown, 1977; and Vida, G. (Ed.). *Our right to love: A lesbian resource book*. Englewood Cliffs, N.J.: Prentice-Hall, 1978, especially pp. 96-115.
22. Masters & Johnson, 1979, pp. 64-70
23. Masters & Johnson, 1979, p. 82.
24. Masters & Johnson, 1979, p. 68.
25. Masters & Johnson, 1979, pp. 67-69.
26. Masters & Johnson, 1979, pp. 66-70; Jay & Young, 1979, pp. 385-437; Bell & Weinberg, 1978, pp. 109-111; Califia, P. "Lesbian sexuality." *Journal of Homosexuality*, 1979, *4*(3), 255-266.
27. Jay & Young, 1979, pp. 543-547.
28. Masters & Johnson, 1979, pp. 68-70.
29. Masters & Johnson, 1979, p. 69.
30. Kaplan, 1974, pp. 27-29.
31. Bell & Weinberg, 1978, pp. 109-110.
32. Masters & Johnson, 1979, pp. 75-76.
33. See, for example, Brown, R. *Rubyfruit jungle*. Plainfield, Vt.: Daughters, 1973.
34. Masters & Johnson, 1979, pp. 68-69.
35. Masters & Johnson, 1979, pp. 69-70.
36. Masters & Johnson, 1979, p. 70.
37. Bell & Weinberg, 1978, pp. 109-110.
38. Toder, N. "Sexual problems of lesbians." In Vida, 1978, pp. 105-115.
39. Califia, P. *Sapphistry: The book of lesbian sexuality*. Tallahassee, Fla.: Naiad Press, 1980.
40. Toder, 1978.

41. Toder, 1978. Also see Kaplan, 1974, for description of and treatment for female sexual dysfunctions.

42. Masters & Johnson, 1979, p. 312.

43. See Jacobson & Margolin, 1979, on marital therapy, for example.

44. There are no data available on the kinds of sexual problems lesbians encounter other than sexual dysfunctions, and relatively little information on those. The material on lesbian sexual problems is compiled from the authors' personal experiences in providing counseling and therapy to lesbians, from conversations with colleagues, and by extension from what is known about lesbian sexual relationships and the problems that arise from these.

45. Cinematherapy, Inc. (Publisher). *Nick and Jon.* San Francisco: Multi-Media Resources. (Film)

46. Silverstein, C., & White, E. *The joy of gay sex,* New York: Crown, 1977.

47. Silverstein & White, 1977, p. 231.

48. Silverstein & White, 1977, p. 94.

49. Saghir & Robins, 1973, pp. 50-54.

50. Jay & Young, 1979, pp. 456-494.

51. Bell & Weinberg, 1978, pp. 108; 327-330.

52. Bell & Weinberg, 1978, p. 330.

53. Masters & Johnson, 1979, p. 237.

54. Silverstein & White, 1977, pp. 87-88.

55. Jay & Young, 1979, pp. 487-488.

56. Bell & Weinberg, 1978, p. 108.

57. Jay & Young, 1979, p. 445.

58. Jay & Young, 1979, p. 441.

59. Jay & Young, 1979, p. 553.

60. Although the term *water sports* does include sexual arousal from urination as well as from enemas, usually the two are differentiated by using *golden shower* for urinating and *water sports* for enemas.

61. Jay & Young, 1979, pp. 440; 490-493; 519-521.

62. Bell & Weinberg, 197, p. 101; Saghir & Robins, 1973, p. 59.

63. Bell & Weinberg, 1978, p. 308.

64. Saghir & Robins, 1973, p. 59.

65. Bell & Weinberg, 1978, p. 277; Saghir & Robins, 1973, p. 11.

66. For an excellent analysis of many of the positive reasons for casual sexual partners, see Tripp, C. *The homosexual matrix.* New York: New American Library, 1975, pp. 140-146.

67. Bell & Weinberg, 1978, p. 101.

68. Marmor, J. "Clinical aspects of male homosexuality." In J. Marmor (Ed.), *Homosexual behavior: A modern reappraisal.* New York: Basic Books, 1980, p. 220.

69. Jay & Young, 1979, p. 437.

70. Silverstein & White, 1977, p. 13.

71. Marmor, 1980, p. 269.

72. Bell & Weinberg, 1978, p. 102.

73. Bell & Weinberg, 1978, p. 138.

74. There are differing definitions of monogamy and fidelity in the literature. For example, Jay and Young equate monogamy and fidelity as being sexual only with one's partner (p. 359). Silverstein and White take a different stance, equating fidelity with sexual exclusiveness and indicating that monogamy can exist while including sexual partners outside the relationship. They apparently view monogamy as being faithful to the relationship (p. 93). Although this is an interesting distinction, most writers equate fidelity and monogamy. McWhirter, D., & Mattison, A. *Stages: A developmental study of homosexual male couples.* New York: St. Martins Press, in press, have suggested the term *monandry* to refer to sexual partner exclusiveness in a gay male couple.

75. Saghir & Robins, 1973, p. 57.

76. McWhirter & Mattison, in press.

77. Jay & Young, 1979, pp. 357-360.

78. Masters & Johnson, 1979, p. 72.

79. Masters & Johnson, 1979, p. 71.

80. Tripp, 1975, p. 143.

81. Silverstein & White, 1977, pp. 13-14.

82. George, K. "Etiology and treatment of sexual dysfunctions in gay male clients." Paper presented at Pre-Institute Workshop, "The Counseling Needs of Lesbians and Gay Men," American Association of Sex Educators, Counselors, and Therapists, Washington, D.C., April 1979.

83. Judson, F., Miller, K., & Schaffert, T. "Screening for gonorrhea and syphilis in the gay baths—Denver, Colorado." *American Journal of Public Health,* 1977, *67*(8), 741.

84. Wiesner, P. "Gonococcal pharyngeal infection." *Clinical Obstetrics and Gynecology,* 1975, *18*(1), 121.

85. Berger, R. "Report on a community-based venereal disease clinic for homosexual men." *The Journal of Sex Research,* 1977, *13*(1), 55.

86. McCormack, W. "Sexually transmitted conditions other than gonorrhea and syphilis." (USDHEW monograph, Public Health Service Publication No. 00-2765). Washington, D.C., U.S. Government Printing Office, 1974.

87. Luger, N. "Detection and management of other sexually transmitted diseases." *Bulletin of the New York Academy of Medicine,* 1976, *52*(8), 898.

88. Luger, 1976, p. 903.

89. Holmes, K. "Sexually transmitted diseases." (USDHEW Monograph, U.S. Public Health Service Publication No. 00-2908) Washington, D.C.: U.S. Government Printing Office, 1976. p. 23.

90. Romano, R. "Sexually transmitted diseases in the gay community." *The Suffolk County [N.Y.] Medical Society Bulletin,* 1979, *57*(1), pp. 20-21.

91. Luger, 1976, p. 904; Romano, 1979, p. 20.

92. Williams, D. "*Social aspects: Homosexuality and sexu-*

ally transmitted diseases.'' Paper presented at conference on Sexually Transmitted Diseases, Health Sciences Center, State University of New York at Stony Brook, 27 September 1978.

93. American Foundation for the Prevention of Venereal Diseases, Inc. *The new venereal disease prevention for everyone.* Pamphlet available from 335 Broadway, New York, N.Y., p. 7. See also Luger, 1976, p. 904.

94. Jay & Young, 1979, pp. 291-299.

95. Impotence is consistently used in the professional and popular literature to describe a man who is unable to achieve and maintain an erection. Impotence also means ''loss of power'' or ''sense of helplessness.'' Its genesis indicates that it is appropriate to use the term when one means ''loss of power.'' We can only protest its use in describing erectile dysfunction. It implies that an erection is the source of power for the male. It is this very implication that creates sexual problems for some men. We would like to see the word deleted from the professional literature when it is being used to describe erectile dysfunction.

96. Masters & Johnson, 1979, p. 274.

97. Masters & Johnson, 1979, p. 237.

98. George, K. ''Etiology and treatment of sexual dysfunctions in gay (homosexual) male patients.'' Paper presented at 5th World Congress of Sexology, Jerusalem, Israel, 25 June 1981.

99. Masters & Johnson, 1979, pp. 262-265.

100. Masters & Johnson, 1979, p. 255.

9

Lesbians' and gay men's relationships

Gay primary relationships take a variety of forms, and people in them have different relationship styles. All gay relationships do have two things in common, however, that differentiate them from nongay relationships and that affect gay couples similarly. First, gay dyads are partnerships between two people of the same gender, and because of this, they differ from relationships between a man and a woman in consistent ways. Second, gay relationships are enmeshed within a nongay culture. No matter how separated from this culture two people may try to be, or how involved they are in the gay culture, there are some inevitable points of overlap. Most gays do not attempt to separate from the nongay culture completely, so their relationships are often affected by pressures from that culture.

The consequences of these two factors—same gender of dyad partners and the necessity for existing in a homophobic, heterosexist culture—affect many facets of gay primary relationships. This chapter discusses issues that are of importance in understanding and working with gay couples, including relationship variables such as role differentiation, communication, and sexuality; stages of gay relationships; types of gay relationships; and ways gay couples cope with the nongay world.

Throughout the chapter, gay relationships are compared with nongay primary relationships so that the reader will become aware of differences

and similarities between them. Some of the differences create more and some result in fewer problems for gay than nongay couples. We discuss both the strengths and problems typical of gay primary relationships in general and relate these to intervention with gay individuals and couples.

CHARACTERISTICS OF RELATIONSHIPS

In our society, the traditional heterosexual marriage model is the only socially supported model for establishing and maintaining long-term sexual and affectional relationships. This model has never been really appropriate or functional for gay relationships. Although many gay couples still try to adapt the marriage model in one form or another, most now eschew relationships that completely conform to it in favor of relationships in which roles are not so rigidly formulated on the basis of gender role stereotypes.[1]

Naturally, this movement away from the marriage pattern, along with the realities of same-gender relationships, makes for differences between gay and nongay dyadic partnerships, as we discuss. There are also differences between the kinds of relationship characteristics typical of gay male and lesbian couples because of differences between genders and the ways men and women are socialized. These differences create different problems and raise different issues as we discuss in the separate sections on lesbians' and gay men's relationships. In spite of these differences, however, there are some general relationship issues that are common to both gay and nongay couples.

In his book, *The Family in Search of a Future,* Herbert Otto discusses several models for establishing successful relationships within a pluralistic society.[2] Although this book is helpful in suggesting alternatives, there is still an emphasis on marriage in one form or another as the standard. Sydney Jourard suggests that there are an infinite number of patterns for relationships and that the pluralistic nature of our society demands that these be available; however, he also raises the issue of social support in saying that the failure of society to legitimize experimentation on the part of individuals makes "life in our society unlivable for an increasing proportion of the population."[3]

This lack of support for experimentation means that the visible guidelines by which people attempt to set up relationships are primarily those of the traditional heterosexual marriage model. Those, like gay couples, who successfully develop alternative styles are seldom visible either because they are unwilling to risk exposure or because various media sources are unwilling to give them exposure as viable alternatives.

There are, however, some general characteristics of relationships that we may infer without regard to the style of the relationship itself:

1. A relationship is formed between two or more people.[4]
2. Each person in the relationship interacts in some manner with the other person (persons).[5]
3. Each person retains some degree of individuality within the relationship.
4. There are rules for the behavior of the participants.
5. The relationship exists to serve some function.

Although these characteristics exist in even the most casual relationships, our discussion focuses on relationships considered to be primary for the people involved. Because the most common primary love relationship is a dyad, the focus of our discussion is couples, although most of the considerations for couples are appropriate for other primary relationships as well.[6]

Formation of a relationship

Gay couples probably do not take as long as nongay couples to form committed relationships because there are no legal or religious bonds to ensure caution and there is no risk that sexual activity will result in pregnancy. A nongay man and woman who are dating will almost always have the issue of marriage somewhere in their minds, even if only as a "nonoption" for the relationship. This means that in many cases, particularly among older adults, a nongay relationship may continue for a long time without a move being made toward formal commitment either by actual marriage, agreement to marry, or formal engagement. Any of these actions signify an ultimate legal, economic, sexual, and often religious commitment. Although some couples do so without legal sanction, the legal commitment of matrimony usually means that a couple will take up a joint residence, share property in common, follow socially prescribed roles as husband and wife, bear and raise children together, and so forth.

In gay relationships, the absence of legal ceremony means that couples may move fairly rapidly into commitment and be considered by themselves and others in the gay community as a couple. They do so without any kind of legal protection or societal or religious mandates concerning their behavior, so the form of their interaction is at least theoretically open to innovation.

Couple interaction

The ways that gay couples interact are probably more varied than the ways that nongays interact precisely because of the lack of legal, religious, or societal directions regarding gay relationships and because the nongay marriage model often does not fit. For many gay couples, being committed means sharing a living space, but for others, separate housing is preferred. To gay couples, commitment may or may not mean that they are mutually sexually active, share money, clothes, work, ideas, or sexual partners. Some couples enact gender-typed roles; some do not. As is true of nongay relationships, there is no single pattern that can be identified to describe the interaction patterns of commited gay couples.

Problems in gay couples' interactions. The form of dyadic interaction is an important variable in gay relationships and one that can be a source of problems. Such problems usually arise because of differing interpretations by the partners of what constitutes appropriate or desirable interaction in a love relationship. Some of the most frequent problems we have encountered occur when one partner subscribes to the marriage model that specifies that two people who love each other "should" share the same living space, bed, checking account, interests, and so forth. This is essentially a derivative of the traditional marriage model in which the husband, as breadwinner, expects his wife to share his bed and interests because she is sharing his income. Although this model may be increasingly invalid for nongays as well, many of the beliefs that underlie it still persist.

In a gay male or lesbian relationship, there is not usually a situation of financial dependency of one partner on the other,[7] so there is no economic basis for one partner's subservience to the other. Because gays are single and cannot benefit financially from a partnership in the same way nongay married couples can, there is also less reason for gay couples to share living arrangements. Indeed, it appears that those couples who do share living space do so primarily because they love each other and want to be together, not for economic reasons.[8]

Jay and Young found that about half the commited couples in their sample (slightly greater for the men and slightly fewer for the women) lived together. Those who did not often cited a cause related to the need for more freedom or private time. A number of the men cited outside sexual interests.[8] Helping professionals who are used to the heterosexual model that generally includes cohabitation may have to revise some of their conceptions about "appropriate" couple behavior, and so may gay couples themselves. As gays try out new ways of interacting as couples, they may encounter difficulties, and helping professionals may be called upon to help partners work out nontraditional ways of interacting. Common areas of difficulty that we have found are those concerning shared interests, sleeping arrangements, time spent together versus private time, joint friendships, sexual exclusivity, and living arrangements. For example, one member of a dyad may believe that people who *really* love each other will want to live, sleep, and spend every possible waking moment together, whereas the other member wants increased freedom and private time. Some individuals have trouble coping with any separation of couple space, time, or interests, and others have trouble coping with too much togetherness. Some of the problems that appear to be more specific to either lesbian or gay male couples are addressed in the appropriate sections.

Maintaining individuality within a relationship

For a long time in this culture, a relationship was considered the melding of two people into one unit. In fact, the notion that "now we two are one" has been proposed as the true significance of the marriage ceremony.[9] Although this notion may have a great deal of attraction for people who are romantically inclined, the reality is that some individuality is necessary in any relationship. The amount of psychological independence and interdependence needed once a couple forms is specific to the individuals in the relationship, is liable to change over time, and is something that should be a matter of negotiation between the two people involved in the relationship.

There are two kinds of independent time needs that gay couples may experience and that may be more difficult to come by for gay than nongay couples. The first kind of time is independent leisure and social time in which an individual is free to do those things that are of special interest or importance that involve other people but do not involve the partner, such as taking a class, visiting with friends, work-related social events, and athletic pursuits. The second kind of time is "private time," time spent completely alone.[10] A person may want either, neither, or both of these kinds of time to be unaccounted for to the partner. Problems may arise in the negotiation of amount of independent time as well as over the issue of accountability.

Social and leisure time. Because of the way the gay community is organized and the way couples fit into it, some couples may have difficulty arranging independent social time in a way that does not threaten one or both partners. In nongay relationships, partners may spend time with others of the same gender in pursuits that are clearly both gender-typed and nonsexual, or they may spend time alone in such activities. For example, a husband may spend Saturdays at the golf course, the pool room, fishing, or talking with men friends at the hardware store while his wife goes shopping, plays tennis, or visits women friends. Because gay couples are of the same gender and usually spend time with other couples in the gay community, this kind of separation of the two partners on the basis of gender is not possible and requires more planning on the part of the partners. Other pressures also make it more difficult for couples who live together to spend leisure time alone.

In the first place, because they are rarely recognized as legitimate couples by the nongay world, gays may only feel comfortable interacting as a couple when around other gay people. This makes "couple time" in the gay community valuable. It is really the only time that their couple status is recognized—the only time they can really be themselves around others and interact with others present as people like to do who love each other, being physically close and affectionate, holding hands, and so forth.[11]

Second, the part of the gay community with which a given gay couple interacts regularly is probably relatively small, consisting of other individuals and couples whom both partners know. Very often, both partners are going to know and want to interact with the same members of the gay community so there may be little justification for them to see separate friends socially, or one member of the couple may become jealous of time spent with mutual friends by his or her partner. This is much more likely to be a problem in nonurban than in urban areas.[12]

Third, unlike nongays, gay friends of the same gender are potential sexual partners. This means that activities within the gay community undertaken without one's partner may be perceived by one or both partners as threatening because of their potential sexual meaning. This appears to be much more of a problem in the lesbian/feminist community where the issue of monogamy has been extensively debated and where the subject of monogamy apparently raises the issue of jealousy for many lesbian women.[13] The issue does not appear to be as significant in the men's community where "one gets the impression that monogamy is not much of an issue, i.e., few men, even long-term lovers, advocate adherence to an ethic of 'one spouse, faithful forever.' "[14] However, there are male couples who have dissolved their relationship because of this issue.

These differences between gay and nongay communities may mean that gay couples will encounter some difficulties in negotiating independent time. This may be particularly problematic for lesbians, especially those living in areas with small populations of gays where it may be necessary to intrude upon another relationship in order to find a partner.[15] It may also be difficult for those couples, whether gay men or lesbians, who do not have many friends, who do not trust their partners, or who have a dysfunctional conception of what a workable relationship entails in the way of mutual independence.

Private time. As well as social or leisure time spent apart, couples may benefit from having individual private time. If one partner in a dyad wants private time more than the other, there is likely to be a conflict. In a gay couple, the threat of independence, however expressed, may be heightened because of the lack of tangible, legal, socially sanctioned bonds. As long as a husband and wife are legally married, the wedding ring, marriage vows, joint property, and social pressures are clear, socially acknowledged reminders of the joint agreement of the partners to remain committed. Although such commitments obviously are not always permanent, they certainly provide a measure of security not found in gay relationships. Without these kinds of supports, a partner in a gay relationship who is at all threatened by her or his partner's need for private time may feel on shaky ground whenever the partner makes a move toward increased privacy. This sense of insecurity should not be considered an automatic indication of overdependence on the part of gay people. Many times it is an understandable consequence of the fact that gay relationships do not benefit from the security of legal and social sanction. Counselors working with gay clients may find their clients' reactions to private time issues more understandable if they keep this in mind.

Men's and women's reactions to these kinds of issues are more characteristic of their gender role socialization than of their sexual preference. We discuss these issues in greater depth in the sections on gay men's and lesbian women's relationships and make more specific suggestions there for intervention.

Contracting in gay relationships

All these issues indicate the desirability of contracting between partners before a couple is "formalized." The need for some kind of contract is just as great, and perhaps greater, for those who do not enter into a legally sanctioned relationship as for those who do. Whatever action is taken to formalize a gay relationship, it is preferable for the couple to discuss a contractual agreement beforehand. If a couple has not made such an agreement and comes into counseling, a contract can be made at any point during the relationship.[15a]

Some people balk at the notion of a contract, believing that it takes the romance out of the relationship or arguing that two people who *really* love

each other do not need a contractual agreement. If a counselor is involved in such a discussion, it is appropriate to point out that all relationships involve agreements and rules, but that difficulties often arise because these are not clearly spelled out or they are understood differently by the individuals involved. A contract, whether written or explicitly stated, provides a method by which both partners understand each other's assumptions about the relationship before it reaches a point where it is firmly established.

Some people actually draw up official contracts with a lawyer. Although this is certainly an option to consider, particularly where complicated finances are concerned, it is not usually necessary. A contract may simply be a discussion of issues that each partner considers important, along with clarification of some of the issues that often create problems for gay couples. Helping professionals may find that gay couples are afraid that writing up such a contract, or even formally discussing one, will uncover areas of conflict and prefer to take a "what we don't know won't hurt us" stance. The reality is that ignoring points of conflict is much more likely to damage a relationship than facing them openly. If there are irreconcilable differences, it is probably better for a couple to become aware of them before a formal commitment is made than afterward.

Contract content. To determine the general problem areas that a contract might address, one need only look at the material written about the causes of divorce. Usually the first stated cause is money.[16] Other important issues to discuss are sexual activity, sexual exclusiveness (or lack of it), children, expectations about work arrangements (for example, what to do if one partner receives a job offer that requires relocation), which set of parents to visit on what holidays, how to handle coming out, decisions about how to spend vacations, and what protection each partner will have in the event the relationship eventually ends either through dissolution or the death of one partner.

Individual couples will undoubtedly have their own unique areas of concern and negotiation.

The possibility of dissolution of a relationship is a very difficult one for a couple to discuss, particularly if they are just becoming involved. Very few people who are beginning a relationship want to consider the possibility that it will end, much less plan for that eventuality. In the gay community, however, this is an especially important possibility to consider for two reasons. First, the average relationship length for both gay male and lesbian couples is shorter than for nongay married couples, and is certainly not typically lifelong. Second, if a relationship is terminated by death, there are many legal threats to the surviving partner unless the couple's financial interdependence is carefully documented (see Chapter 3) and the deceased partner's will is strong enough to withstand challenges by relatives. Gay couples who balk at the idea of planning for the possible termination of their relationship may be more easily convinced if it is pointed out that such contracting is a form of insurance. Taking out insurance on a house, or on one's life, does not mean that one wants the house or one's life destroyed, or that there is anything unsound about either. It simply means that one realizes the possibility that something may happen and is prepared for such an eventuality. Discussing ways each partner can be protected in the event a relationship ends is nothing more than insurance for both partners and should be desired for the protection of both. It is not an announcement of expected dissolution, but an announcement of mutual caring and concern.

Finances. Using the traditional heterosexual marriage as a financial model for a gay partnership is often unwise. In traditional marriages, the husband and wife share incomes, bank accounts, and the like. This is based, of course, on the assumption that the "two are as one," as well as that the husband is the primary wage earner. In gay couples, both partners are likely to be financially

self-supporting, although there may certainly be an income differential.

Some couples may function well with a joint bank account and shared income. For other couples, this can become a source of friction. As in other areas of their relationships, gay couples must be helped to differentiate financial arrangements from emotional involvement. One partner may, for example, believe that "if you really loved me, you would want us to share everything, including our bank accounts." Or a couple, deeply in love and wanting to have some tangible evidence of their involvement, may start out with joint accounts and find that they disagree over the management of their joint finances.

One member may want to separate their money, and the other may consider this an indication that the relationship is declining, that he or she is not trusted, and so forth. Gay people, like nongays, must sometimes be taught that joint accounts, mutual friendships, and shared bedrooms do not necessarily make for either permanence or satisfaction in a relationship.

It may be helpful for the counselor to point out to a gay couple who are having these kinds of problems that their assumptions are based on a heterosexual marriage model that simply is not practical or realistic for gay couples to try to follow. Indeed, some of the things that make gay relationships positive and desirable to gay people are the very things that mitigate against the applicability of the traditional model. The role equivalence of both partners and their frequent desire and ability to achieve financial and personal independence are not provided for in the nongay marriage model and are factors that will become sources of problems in many cases.

Sexual activity. Sexuality and sexual activity are issues that probably should be and frequently are not discussed in gay relationships. There seems to be an expectation among most couples that once a primary relationship is established, the partners should be able to completely satisfy each other's needs so that all outside attractions are eliminated. This may be particularly true in lesbian relationships but may occur in gay men's relationships as well.

☐ [My partner and I] both have had outside sex. For me, when my lover takes another sex partner, I get very hurt because I consider it a preference thing. He swears to me it's just a sex thing and that he's not involved nor does he plan to get involved. He feels the same thing is okay for me if I want it. Usually if I do, it's out of spite to hurt him and myself. I would like it better if neither of us has outside sex.[17]

The reality is, of course, that whatever two people decide to do about sexual activity, sexual attraction to someone else is something that is likely to occur no matter how much in love two people are and no matter how satisfactory their sexual relationship. It is therefore important that partners distinguish between sexual attraction and sexual activity, and that they come to a decision about how to handle these two separate issues.

For many couples, it may also be important, as the above quote suggests, to help partners separate sexual activity from emotional involvement. Lesbians are much more likely than gay men to equate sexual activity and emotional involvement, consistent with the differential socialization of men and women in this regard. Lesbians are also much more likely to be emotionally involved when they have sex than are gay men.[18]

This may make it more difficult for lesbian women to separate sexual activity from emotional commitment, and will make sexual contacts outside the relationship more likely to be threatening. A problem is more likely to be encountered with a gay male couple if one partner does not equate emotional involvement with sex and the other does. If one partner believes that it is very important to him to have sexual contacts outside the committed relationship and is able to separate sex and emotional involvement, and his partner has difficulty doing so, some kind of compromise will have to be reached. This kind of issue is discussed much more fully in the section on gay men's relationships.

Renegotiating relationship contracts. Neither people nor relationships remain constant, so the

rules, demands, requirements, and needs that are addressed by a contract are likely to change over time. When this happens, the contract must be renegotiated. There should, ideally, be a renegotiation clause within the relationship contract, whether written or verbal, that specifies the time and manner of renegotiation. Some couples renegotiate every year, some do it informally as the need arises. Unless a couple has a predetermined time for renegotiation (and even then if something special comes up), partners need good communication and assertiveness skills in order to be able to raise, discuss, and solve problems or issues that require renegotiation of contract. For some couples who are comfortable with, and can afford, professional help or who have difficulty with this kind of negotiation, it might be wise for the helping professional to suggest that they seek short-term intervention when crisis issues arise to help them negotiate such issues more easily.

Relationship functions. Gay relationships have some, but not all, functions in common with nongay marriages. Gay relationships do not serve the functions that nongay marriages sometimes do of legitimizing sexual intercourse, providing a "proper match," or ensuring children. They do not, as marriages sometimes do, exist to provide one partner with financial security and the other partner with a caretaker, sexual partner, and child-bearer. They do share in common with nongay marriages the functions of providing emotional satisfaction and security, companionship, intellectual stimulation, sexual partnership, and frequently, mutual financial benefits.

The emotional, intellectual, sexual and even financial needs of a given individual are more likely to change over time than the desire for a caretaker, child-bearer, homemaker, or monetary provider. Without these latter desires to take into account, gay people may desire to change partners as their other needs change rather than attempting to make changes in a relationship itself.

130

The question of whether or not this is desirable depends on the ultimate satisfaction of the individual, the quality of the relationship(s) an individual enters, and his or her ability to form and maintain relationships. Whether or not nongay society thinks that changing relationships is a good idea, the fact is that gay couples are often minimally encumbered, legally or financially, in ways that prohibit changing relationships to meet changing personal needs. Nonetheless, gay couples, like nongay couples, can easily become invested in the "success" or "failure" of their current relationship, believing that a dissolution of the relationship implies that one or both partners have somehow failed as individuals.

This belief is sometimes reinforced by the gay culture itself, especially with couples who have been together for a number of years. For example, one lesbian couple had been together for 12 years. They were admired by their peers because they had what appeared to be a very stable relationship and they also allowed each other a great deal of personal freedom and showed little or no jealous behavior. During the twelfth year, their living and work situations changed, separating them by almost 3000 miles, and one of them began to experience life on her own for the first time. After being apart for several months, one decided she wanted to have the total freedom she felt she could have only if she were not in a relationship at all. They discussed the possibilities of altering their relationship contract and could not reach a mutually satisfactory agreement. In discussing the situation with one of the authors, one partner said, "the really sad thing is that we were so envied by everyone and now this has to happen. What will it do to other relationships? Where have I failed?" She was expressing a sense of failure not only within her own relationship, but in regard to the gay community as well.

The fear of failure may work to keep a couple together who are no longer happy or functioning well or who have moved in different life directions; it may cause unnecessary distress to partners who are breaking up. There is pressure in the gay community, as in the nongay community, for couples to stay together; friends take sides when a relationship dissolves, especially if one partner was unwilling for it to end. Even though gay couples may go through comparatively more relationships than heterosexuals, dissolution does not appear to get easier with practice. The partners must go through the same steps in termination each time, and a sense of failure is often involved in the process.

Counselors who work with gay clients would do well to understand some of the reasons why gay couples often do not last a lifetime. Do not assume that relatively short-term relationships are a sign of gay neuroses. As we have pointed out, there are many mitigating circumstances, not the least of which is rooted in the differences in function of gay and heterosexual long-term relationships. The counselor should be willing to explore with the client both the positive and negative consequences of terminating a given relationship. It is particularly important to help clients learn that ending a relationship is not a sign of failure either on the part of the individuals or of the couple as a whole.

LESBIAN PRIMARY RELATIONSHIPS
Relationship patterns

There are three major patterns for defining relationship boundaries in lesbian primary relationships: monogamous (sexually exclusive), non-monogamous (not sexually exclusive), and communal (may or may not include monogamy within identified couples). Lesbian relationships are typically classifiable according to one of these patterns, although a given relationship may change from one pattern to another over time, and one individual may follow different patterns in several different relationships. Monogamy is by far the most common of these relationship styles.[19]

Monogamy. Women raised in this culture are socialized and trained to fulfill the roles of wife and mother, marry for love, and live happily ever after. Lesbian women are no exception, and this is reflected in the approach many lesbians have to their love relationships.[20] The majority of lesbian relationships are monogamous, with the partners explicitly or implicitly sharing the understanding that their relationship is not only sexually but also emotionally exclusive.[21]

Monogamous couples are likely to live together in a situation that is similar to a heterosexual marriage, in some respects. Property may be jointly owned, the couple often shares a bed and bedroom, the home is jointly decorated and kept, and responsibilities are shared in some defined way. The couple generally spend the majority of their free time together and entertain and go out socially as a couple. They may belong to a circle of like-minded friends who play bridge, go dancing or drinking, have parties, and the like.

Differences in monogamous relationships. Women who belong to different ethnic, socio-economic, and geographical subcultures have different kinds of monogamous relationships. Some women live very traditional suburban lives. Marsha and Colette are typical of such a couple. They are two women in their late forties who live in an upper middle-class suburban neighborhood near a large West Coast city. They own an expensive ranch-style home with a pool, patio, and several acres of fruit trees. They also have two cars, three dogs, and a cat. Having lived together for 15 years, they are well accepted in the nongay community and are given little special attention. Both work at well-paying jobs, one in real estate, the other as a private duty nurse. They have a stable circle of gay friends, mostly women, and throw large parties several times a year for friends from all over the state. They have smaller parties for a circle of intimate friends about once a month and play bridge once a week with three other gay couples who live nearby. They do not go to gay bars and seldom go out except to an occasional movie.

Some couples, unlike Marsha and Colette who are fairly isolated, organize their lives almost exclusively around the gay community. Barbara and Wilma are a Black couple who live in a major metropolitan area. Barbara is in her late thirties, Wilma in her late twenties. Both have been married and have children, although neither is living with her children at this time. They have been together about 2 years and share an apartment in a middle-class neighborhood. They have a wide circle of gay and nongay friends and spend a lot of time socializing, having parties, visiting, and going to bars. Most weekends are spent in the city's numerous gay bars where there is dancing, and the couple can drink beer and enjoy their many friends. They are also involved in political activities in the Black gay community. Barbara has been involved in a number of gay relationships before this one, but this is only Wilma's second. Neither is convinced that it is her last, but they have agreed that as long as they are happy together, neither will get involved with anyone else.

Other couples spend their time in activities related to the women's community or the Metropolitan Community Church. Some spend much of their time watching or participating in sports activities. Most couples do some combination of activities within the gay or women's communities as well as other activities not related to either. A small minority of couples have almost no contact with the lesbian community and lead very independent lives.

Francis and Gwenn, for example, are two women who live in a northern university town. Both are in their thirties and have lived together for about 5 years. They each have well-paying but time-consuming jobs. Francis runs a small business school, and Gwenn is the Director of Women's Athletics at the university.

The gay community in their town is small and composed mostly of students and some faculty. Because of her position in the business community, Francis is afraid of being labeled as gay because she believes she would lose not only her student body but their prospective employers. Gwenn goes to great lengths to avoid meeting the lesbian stereotype or being seen in any "compromising" situations because she works in the field of women's athletics, traditionally supposed to attract a high proportion of gay women.

Francis and Gwenn have largely independent circles of nongay friends, and most of their socializing is business related. They never go to bars and only rarely appear in public together. Both have male escorts who will go with them to social functions where a male companion is expected. Both consider their relationship a permanent one, and neither is interested in changing it. Their lives are rather precariously balanced, and contacts with other lesbian women are kept to a minimum. The rare contacts they do have occur on vacations and out-of-town business trips where they are less afraid of being identified.

These examples are included to give an idea of the variety of lifestyles that monogamous couples can choose to live.[22] There are couples who live together for years without ever becoming involved in the lesbian community, whereas others are immersed in the political and social life of the gay community and repudiate anything that suggests acceptance of sexist and heterosexist norms and traditions.

Types of monogamous dyads. Within monogamous relationships, particularly those in which the partners share housing, there are several ways a relationship can be structured. Tanner, in her study of 24 lesbian women, identified three types of lesbian dyads: traditional-complementary, flexible nurturing-caretaking, and negotiated-egalitarian.[23] These are similar to what we have observed within the lesbian community, but a word of caution is appropriate.

In the first place, any typology of relationship styles is synthetic and oversimplified. Second, patterns of relating change as couples change and grow. Eventually, as a couple becomes comfortable with a particular way of relating, the partners evolve patterns of interaction that are unique and idiosyncratic. Finally, the notion of relationship styles is obviously not limited to lesbians. However, the fact that the partners in a lesbian couple are both women makes for differences between lesbian and nongay relationships.

We do not want to encourage readers to attempt to "pigeonhole" lesbian relationships by our discussion of relationship styles. We are presenting them so the reader will have a general idea of the kinds of relationships that are likely to occur in the lesbian community. Furthermore, an understanding of the kinds of relationship patterns characteristic of lesbian women is helpful in assessing areas where intervention is likely to be needed and those where it is not. It also gives readers unfamiliar with the lesbian community a better idea of the diversity of partnership patterns within the community.

Traditional relationships.[24] Traditional relationships are those in which economic, role distribution, and other variables are split between the partners in a way similar to the traditional, stereotyped husband-wife pattern found in many heterosexual marriages. Although some sources disagree,[25] our observation of the lesbian community suggests that such relationships are relatively rare, and there is evidence to support our observation.[26]

In a traditional style of relating, each partner has a different role to perform so that one is responsible for major financial decisions, may earn a higher salary, and is considered "dominant." This partner is not as likely to be expected to do certain kinds of household tasks such as laundry, dishes, and housekeeping. The other partner is responsible for those tasks usually assigned to the woman in a nongay relationship. In cases where role differentiation is taken to the extreme, the partners may enact "butch" and "femme" roles in behavior and dress as well.[27]

This traditional pattern of relating was certainly more common at one time than it is now,[28] and this is probably responsible for the belief held by many nongays that all lesbian couples take masculine and feminine roles. There is some indication that role taking is more common among lesbians in groups with lower socioeconomic status,[29] lesbians in their teens and early twenties,[30] and those over 45 or 50 who were young when butch/femme role taking was still common.[31]

Helping professionals must be careful, however, not to make unverified assumptions about the roles lesbian partners play on the basis of such things as physical characteristics. Both gays and nongays have grown up in a world in which the visible couples are heterosexual, and partners are usually discriminable on the basis of size, apparel, mannerisms, voice tone, and age, with the man almost always being older, larger, dressed exclusively in pants and tailored clothes, having short hair, and so forth. It is not surprising that in a lesbian couple, people often make assumptions about partners' roles on the basis of such physical characteristics and behavior. So the partner who is older or taller or larger, who dresses in a more ''masculine'' fashion, who has short hair or ''masculine'' mannerisms may be taken to be the more masculine-typed of the pair in all respects. This is very often not the case, and helping professionals should be careful to check out their assumptions before beginning any intervention.

This kind of social expectation can also affect a couple's interaction. It is difficult for two people to break away from societal expectations about role behaviors as strongly held as those about the physical manifestations of gender and gender role. Furthermore, it is not uncommon to find that within a couple, the partners will perform complementary tasks, with one doing most of the cooking and the other doing ''heavier'' tasks like mowing the lawn and washing the car. This does not mean that the two couples necessarily relate in a butch/femme style in any other sphere of their relationship. Both gays and nongays are often too quick to assume that a lesbian couple is taking roles that mimic heterosexual roles on the basis of a few clues.

Betty and Felice frequently confound those who don't know them. Betty is the older, taller, more ''masculine'' in appearance of the two. Felice has long hair, wears earrings, and dresses in very feminine attire. Betty is a highly paid legal secretary, does most of the cooking and housecleaning, collects guns, and is a carpenter in her spare time. Felice holds a black belt in karate, is an associate professor in sociology at a leading university, and by far the more assertive of the two. In physical appearance, they give every indication of conform-

ing to rigid roles, but in their behavior, they do not conform to societal expectations at all.

Gays have typically been somewhat defensive about the butch/femme stereotype, and for good reason. Both nongay feminists and some lesbians are opposed to role taking by lesbian couples. Nongays view it as a symptom of pathology; some lesbians view it as a cop-out to the heterosexist establishment.[32] What is important is that mental health professionals avoid judging gay clients' mental health on the basis of whether they conform to someone's stereotype or ideal of appropriateness. Some couples may feel constrained by roles and want help in changing them, others may function very well in a structured relationship. We support the concept of role flexibility and believe in encouraging individuals to fulfill their own potential in whatever way seems best to them. We do not believe, however, that individuals or couples who take butch/femme roles in all or part of their relationship should be considered ''sick,'' any more than we consider heterosexual couples ''sick'' who take these roles based on gender.

Status differential relationships. These are relationships in which, for reasons not connected to gender roles, the partners perceive themselves to be in different status positions on some dimension. These kinds of relationships are common in the lesbian community. Tanner[23] refers to them as *flexible nurturing-caretaking* relationships, a label we are not using because we find it too limiting.

Many couples have differential statuses on the basis of age, income, education, background, health, ability, and the like. Issues relevant to a relationship are, first, the way the couple perceives the status difference, and second, the way the difference affects the couple's functioning. Some status differences are temporary or specific to only one area, some are permanent; some are minimal in effect, some are sufficiently important that the entire relationship may be organized around them. Some common variables that may be permanent yet have little effect on a relationship are age, education, and socioeconomic background. Variables that may have a greater effect are income, health, job status, and race.

A relationship fits this pattern only if the particular difference is one that matters to the couple and therefore affects the way the partners relate. As Tanner points out, many such differences are ones that will change in time, but may temporarily cause the couple problems. An example would be a relationship in which one partner has an advanced degree and well-paying job while the other is still in school.

Temporary status differences. If the status difference is temporary, the effect on the couple may also be temporary yet difficult to handle. For example, if one member of the couple is making more money than the other, the majority of the couple's financial responsibilities may fall on her and she may resent the burden. Conversely the partner who is bringing in less money may feel guilty. This kind of situation can create tension for two women who would otherwise experience little strain by creating a status differential that neither may want nor believe is appropriate.

The strain of such a situation is likely to be greater for couples who have started out approximately as equals and then find the situation changed or who have started out with one partner in a financially better position only to have the circumstances reversed. Maggie and Beth are one such couple. When they first became involved, Maggie had a master's degree in social work and was employed by a family service agency at a job she did not particularly enjoy. Beth was in school part-time working on a doctorate in mathematics. Because of Maggie's good financial situation, they decided it would be best if Beth were to go to school full-time on a loan. They decided that they could manage their limited finances for the time it would take Beth to finish school. When she finished, Maggie would return to school to get her doctorate in public health, and Beth would help her financially.

The initial strain of supporting the two of them was handled reasonably well. At the end of 3 years, Beth had completed her doctorate and received a job offer at a northern university. Although the job required a change of location for the couple, they decided it would be a good opportunity for Beth. Since the university also had a public health program, Maggie would apply for admission there the following year. During that year, however, the strain became severe. Maggie, used to a job that paid well and gave her reasonable social status, suddenly found herself unemployed and without an income. She had been used to providing for two people, and now found herself dependent on Beth, alone in an unfamiliar city, and very unhappy.

In cases such as these, strain is often caused because the unwanted status difference may appear to be forcing one woman into the traditional feminine role. If, for example, one of the women is making less money, is working at a job that carries less social status, is going to school, or otherwise thinks of herself as a less contributing or less important member of the dyad, she may think it is expected that she do household tasks such as cooking, laundry, and housekeeping. These are traditionally the tasks of women in marriages. Many lesbian women do not like these jobs but undertake them on a shared basis. The woman who feels compelled to do them may strongly resent her position, particularly if it is a shift from an egalitarian or dominant status in the couple.

The second point of strain in such situations is likely to be based on the learned association between economic and job status and dominance. There may be an unspoken assumption on the part of one or both women that the person bringing home the greater amount of money should be responsible not only for financial, but other major life decisions for the pair. Because financial dependence or any kind of unwanted status differential can be depressing, the partner who finds herself in a lower status position may also find herself increasingly emotionally dependent while her lover becomes (or appears to be) increasingly emotionally independent.

A major danger in many nongay assumptions about lesbian dyads that include an expectation of role differentiation is that they see such differentiation when it occurs as, first, expected, and second, intentionally patterned after a heterosexual marriage. In a relationship like that of Maggie and Beth, where there were definite differences in tasks, income, and ultimately, in self-concept (as Beth became increasingly depressed), such a belief would lead a practitioner to assume that the role differences were an effect of some underlying predisposition rather than, in fact, the cause of Beth's depression and some serious difficulties for the couple. Although it is true that some couples do follow the traditional stereotype, most do not. In couples where there are clear-cut status differences, rather than assuming that this is intentional and desired by the couple, the helping professional should assess the extent to which this may, in fact, be problematic.

Permanent status differences. In some couples the difference in status is based on permanent factors such as health or age. In these instances, the couple needs to be helped to cope with the effects of the differences as any couple would. Again, helping professionals should remember that, although lesbians are women, they are not necessarily completely socialized into either the caretaking or the dependent roles so often defined for women. So a woman who is suffering from ill health is not liable to be as comfortable being dependent as many individuals assume women are.

Amy and Phyllis are a couple who have had to come to terms with these kinds of issues because of the difference in their ages. Amy is in her fifties, Phyllis is in her seventies, and they have lived together for 20 years. During the last 5 years, Phyllis' health has begun to fail, and she is increasingly experiencing the effects of age. Amy is still a relatively young and vigorous woman who is much more interested in and capable of activity than Phyllis. They are committed to each other and yet find that their age difference is making serious demands on the relationship.

Phyllis, chafing at enforced inactivity and tiredness, now spends increasing amounts of time alone while Amy goes out. In social settings where she used to be the life of the party, Phyllis is now more often quiet. She seldom dances, rarely makes new friends, often sits alone. Old friends come to visit her at home, and Amy is always gracious and attentive to Phyllis when they are seen together. They obviously still share a deep and abiding love and affection, but the strain of the changes in their relationship is also clear.

In a case like this, just as with a nongay couple, the older or more infirm partner must be given support in doing as much as she possibly can for herself. The younger or more able partner needs permission as well not to be consumed by the role of caretaker. Both must be helped to face the reality of their circumstances in order to develop a more functional and satisfactory way of conducting their relationship.

Such a couple may want to renegotiate their relationship contract. For example, if it has always been assumed that they will share most social activities, they might want to discuss the possibility that Amy will now go out by herself once or twice a week. They might also increase the amount of entertaining they do at home so Phyllis will get enough social stimulation. In all respects, they should be treated as a committed and loving couple, not like two ''friends'' or two ''old maids,'' as some people are inclined to think of and treat such women.

Summary. Status differences that are not related to gender roles and that the couple does not desire can be damaging to an otherwise well-functioning partnership. This is particularly true if the couple believes these differences are unavoidable. This can occur when one partner is alcoholic, addicted to drugs, chronically unemployed, severely depressed, or suffering from a chronic difficulty in dealing with life.

Helping professionals should realize that status differentials can cause problems in a lesbian dyad different from those that might be caused in a nongay couple. Furthermore, contrary to much literature about lesbian couples, committed couples do not usually manifest status differences like those found in nongay relationships. In circumstances where role differentiation does take place, it is likely to be a result of the status difference and may be problematic for the couple, rather than a desired state of affairs.

Egalitarian relationships. Many lesbian couples strive for primary relationships in which the partners are equal in as many respects as possible.[32] This is not always easy to do, but many lesbian couples succeed remarkably well in the attempt. Egalitarianism, like status difference, permeates most aspects of such a relationship: finances, housekeeping chores, decision making, communication, sexual behavior, and so forth.

To say that a lesbian relationship is egalitarian means primarily that the two women involved see it that way. It does not mean that they necessarily behave in exactly the same manner.

Relationships that are objectively equal are rare indeed. Most relationships that the partners consider egalitarian would probably show some kinds of differences to the objective observer. The important point is that many lesbian women believe their relationships are more likely to be egalitarian than are nongay relationships, and find their equality gratifying.[11]

Many lesbian couples, even though they may not have achieved total equality and may never be able to do so, have achieved a satisfactory balance that allows both partners to think of themselves as equals. Thus, even in relationships where there are unavoidable differences between partners, the fact that two women are not bound by gender role constraints makes the likelihood of perceived equality fairly high.

Nonmonogamous dyads. Some women in the lesbian community do not subscribe to the notion of monogamy, although they may share a living relationship with another woman.[33] Some such couples have what is essentially an open contract in which they agree explicitly that, although they

are committed to each other as primary emotional partners, they are each free to have other, secondary relationships that include sexual and emotional involvement. This may happen between two women who love each other but do not consider themselves ''in love.'' It may happen between women who have been living together for a number of years and feel the need for sexual and emotional experimentation to keep their primary relationship alive. It may simply be the preferred relationship style for both partners. In some cases, having more than one sexual partner while in a primary lesbian relationship is a function of one partner's differing sexual needs or of prevailing circumstances. Sometimes only one partner takes other lovers with, or sometimes without, her partner's knowledge and consent.

Dana and Hilary have been involved for about 10 years. Both have responsible business positions that require extensive travel. Although they obviously love each other and enjoy their relationship, they have little sexual contact. As a result, when Dana is on business trips, she frequently has sexual relations with women she knows in other towns. She has also maintained an off-and-on sexual relationship with a married woman she has known for many years. She does not mention these affairs to Hilary and feels no guilt over not having done so. As far as she is concerned, their relationship is permanent and her sexual activity with other women is incidental.

Sylvia and Karla have also been involved for about 15 years. They do not live together, however, and never have. Sylvia has two children and believes that it would be improper to have another woman living in the house until they have left home. She and Karla are both in their fifties and have known each other since before Sylvia's marriage. They are close friends as well as lovers. Both think their relationship has lasted as long as it has because they keep separate households and only see each other about three nights a week. Each has had numerous lovers, and each insists that these lovers have in no way affected the depth and importance of their relationship together.

Lee and Katie have been involved for 6 years.

They belong to a large group of lesbian women who live in or near a large midwestern city. They live together and function as a couple, but each is interested in relationships with other women as well. Although both have been primarily monogamous in their relationships up to this time, they have decided to renegotiate an open contract. One of the difficulties they have encountered in doing this is that they are not always simultaneous in their involvements with other women. This means that one partner may be left home alone while the other is out with another woman. This has caused some difficulty and resentment with which the women are having trouble coping.

Problems with nonmonogamous relationships. As can be seen from these examples, a nonmonogamous style can be very successful for some couples, although there are often problems in making this kind of relationship work. Women in this culture are not taught to be able to carry on more than one relationship at a time, and those who attempt to do so may experience guilt and resentment.

Because of the lack of social pressure to keep lesbian relationships together, some women may look to multiple relationships as a way of salvaging a monogamous relationship that is in trouble. In the majority of cases, this is probably not a successful solution for several reasons.

First and most important, it means that the two women turn their attention outside the relationship rather than focusing on improving their functioning as a couple. Second, an increase in interaction with another individual or individuals almost automatically results in a decrease in interaction within the dyad. Whatever interaction takes place is not likely to improve the partnership. Such interactions frequently become either superficial or increasingly negative, or may alternate between the two. Third, the inclusion of another woman, or possibly two other women, if each member of the couple is involved with someone else, may bring about unrealistic comparisons and expectations.

What frequently occurs is that one woman (or occasionally both women) becomes involved in a sort of "honeymoon" relationship with another woman. This creates a situation in which the outside lover is likely to appear in an unrealistically rosy light as someone with few faults, no annoying habits, and many wonderful characteristics. Such relationships exist in the empyrean and have little in common with the ordinary, day-to-day relationships that develop after the initial infatuation is over. The consequence is often that the old relationship the two women are hoping to salvage begins to appear shabby and unromantic when compared with the new relationship. When this occurs, it may be only a matter of time before the couple splits up.

There is nothing sacred about monogamy to be sure. It is up to the practitioner to help an individual or couple determine the advantages and disadvantages of a particular lifestyle for them. Having grown up in this culture, lesbian women may believe in the American myth of the perfect mate. Some women find a person who fits this description for them and yet have quite satisfactory sexual encounters outside the relationships while maintaining a strong emotional commitment.[11] Some lesbian women, however, because there are no strong pressures to keep them from doing so, may keep looking for the "perfect" relationship by shifting from one relationship to another. There is nothing intrinsically wrong with this. It only becomes problematic if an individual or couple do not have the knowledge and skills for building a lasting relationship and so look toward the formation of outside attachments, or serial attachments, believing that the problem is external rather than internal.

Communal arrangements. A final type of relationship arrangement is one in which there are more than two people involved. Living in such settings may affect the kinds of problems an individual has. Sometimes communal relationships involve a number of couples with primary relationships who live together and are more or less sexually exclusive. Other arrangements do not involve sexual exclusiveness.

Problems may arise in such settings over a number of issues, including jealousy, shifting of partners, child care, job responsibilities, and financial matters. Communal arrangements are very satisfactory for many women who undertake them, however, in that they provide an extended family setting and may allow a number of women to be very nearly self-sufficient and to own large amounts of property jointly. In such settings, contracting between couples and among commune members is extremely important. Members must be clear about household management, financial responsibilities, private time and space, individual property arrangements, care of pets and children, and so forth.

Relationship variables

The major consequence of having two women in a dyadic relationship instead of a woman and a man is that the effect of gender is removed. Those effects on a partnership that are the result of gender-based inequities, expectations, and the like do not automatically exist, although they are sometimes artificially created. As a result, there are some immediately observable differences between most lesbian and nongay couples in many areas of the relationship, including economics, distribution of responsibilities, sexual behavior, and communication.

Role differentiation. Compared with even the most "liberated" nongay couples, most lesbian relationships are likely to appear egalitarian unless the couple chooses to adopt a traditional relationship style. If the couple is living together, chances are their relationship follows some variation of one of the patterns described in the preceding section, with tasks shared on the basis of competence, available time, and partners' preferences.

This means that both partners will be responsible for household tasks such as cleaning, cooking, dishes, and laundry. Both are also responsible for seeing to repairs on home and car, separate financial arrangements, income, and so forth. Un-less there is an area in which one partner is particularly adept (or incompetent), chores are likely to be split equally.

Effects of absence of gender differences. The absence of gender as a basis for making decisions regarding who does what means that both partners share in the responsibilities as well as the benefits of the relationship more equally than is often the case when gender is used as a determining factor. Tanner quotes one woman as saying:

☐ A relationship with a woman is less demanding than with a man. There is more freedom involved. . . . The responsibilities to the other person are the same and the feelings are the same as in a marriage. Except in a heterosexual relationship you are playing a role. If I were to be with a guy, there is a certain role that I would play as a wife, that in a gay relationship . . . you don't have. . . . You have two people on an equal level living together, sharing responsibilities.[34]

And she quotes another woman:

☐ I love this relationship for the fact that I don't have to deal in terms of the culture with what I am expected to be. A woman who is working who has a husband or children has to keep in mind, whatever she does professionally, and whatever she does socially, that she has to be somebody's wife. This "wifeness" is prescribed by the culture and the law. I am free from that.[35]

The butch/femme dichotomy. The belief on the part of the nongay community that lesbians enact butch and femme roles is, as we have noted, one of the most persistent myths about lesbian relationships. This belief may have persisted for several reasons. There was a period of time when lesbian women did enact roles, or at least, many women tried to. At that time, characterizing the lesbian community as one composed of butch/femme relationships would have been more accurate. Although the situation has changed radically over the last 15 or 20 years, the nongay community is still responding to the dated stereotype rather than the contemporary reality.

A second reason for the continuation of the stereotype may be that some women fit the "butch" stereotype. If nongays either know or assume that these are lesbian women, and these are the only women they label as lesbian, this may confirm the stereotype for them. Those lesbian women, and there are many, who do not fit the stereotype are generally not visible as lesbians. Of course, what many people do not realize is that it is possible to demonstrate both masculine and feminine qualities.

The third reason why nongays may subscribe to the butch/femme stereotype is that, having been raised in a society in which gender roles and love relationships are essentially dichotomous, nongays may just not believe that there can be any alternatives. They may assume that two people of the same gender would either have to or want to take roles, because that is all they have observed.

Reasons for role taking in lesbian relationships. The adoption of roles by lesbian couples was and is most likely the result of having been raised in a culture that offers only two alternative behavioral styles: masculine and feminine. Abbot and Love say that

> presumably role-playing among lesbians exists because lesbians are raised in a role-playing society. Most human beings seem more secure and content if the content and obligations of their relationships are clearly spelled out. Butch-and-femme "marriages" have offered this kind of security to older lesbians who have absorbed that a man wants a woman and a woman wants a man. . . . Roles were sometimes learned by living them or cultivated consciously through the acquisition of techniques. To many women, however, they seemed so unnatural as to end by provoking a new self-consciousness and a new kind of contradiction with self.[36]

Butch and femme roles, particularly as they existed 20 or 30 years ago, might have been considered by an observer to be caricatures of nongay male and female roles in that they occasionally involved exaggeration. To the outsider, both the exaggeration and the difficulty of fitting well into any type of role that is not "tailored" may have invested these portrayals with elements of the ludicrous. But to the women who were attempting to enact them, these roles were serious. Adair and Adair present an interview with Pat, a woman who

effectively describes the difficulties of fitting into the stereotyped male image:

☐ There *was* a lot of pressure to look butch if you were. And, of course, you wanted to, 'cause you wanted to be identified as a dyke. I was never too good at it. It was frightening because if you weren't really like that, then you were acting all the time. And there was no way to counter so you could really be yourself.[37]

And later she says:

☐ Femmes were few and far between. It was hard to get a good femme, because once she was around dykes for a while, she turned into a dyke anyway. It was fierce for me because I didn't belong either place, really. I might have belonged more in the traditional women's role, but who needs that? If you were going to be gay, you wanted to be like a guy because they were the ones who could get things on. The masculine role was the one to play—to do all the asking, all the picking and choosing.[38]

Similarly, Del Martin and Phyllis Lyon describe the difficulty they had in determining what was "butch" and what was "femme" and their solution to the problem.

☐ What confused us were the concepts of what was masculine and what feminine. Phyllis tended toward more tailored clothes—boys-type shirts and suits—was that masculine? Del was sensitive, emotional, romantic—was that feminine? Or weren't these words, *masculine* and *feminine,* culturally defined and socially scripted? Did they really have anything to do with the way people really were? We decided no and started acting as people, as ourselves, as women rather than as caricatures in a heterosexual marriage. But it took us a while.[39]

A second reason for the predominance of roles before the late 1960s and still in some areas of the country and some age groups may have been the fact that lesbians function without men and so inevitably find themselves doing things traditionally considered masculine, for example, having a steady job, being financially independent, and being responsible for things such as mowing the lawn, chopping wood, and moving furniture. In fact, women may enter the lesbian lifestyle because they find there the freedom to do many nontraditional things. Such women who find themselves functioning well in what is traditionally the male role have few models of women who could do masculine things and still be feminine. The apparent alternative may have been to be as much like a man as possible because, obviously if one were doing masculine things like hauling wood, one must be masculine in other ways too. *Feminine women don't do things like that!*

As the lesbian community has matured, lesbians have found that it is not necessary or desirable to mimic masculine behavior that is not functional, or to pattern their relationships so completely on nongay relationship styles. Furthermore, many women are as uncomfortable with traditionally masculine behavior as they are with traditionally feminine behavior. Lesbian women know quite well that they are women. It is not womanhood they object to but the restrictions on women's behavior that have been placed on them by societal expectations. As women have begun to question the necessity for these restrictions and to try out new behaviors and ways of relating, it has become less and less likely for a lesbian couple to take butch and femme roles.

The best thing the helping professional can do is to try to avoid being caught up in conventional interpretations of behavior. Some lesbian women look masculine, some look feminine, some look one way one time and different another time. The appearance of the two partners in a relationship is far from indicative of anything other than the way they appear at the moment. This does not mean that lesbians don't have trouble making roles fit in relationships, or feeling comfortable in their own gender role behavior. Some women may think, incorrectly, that since they are not comfortable in the stereotyped feminine role, they must really want to be men. Young lesbians especially may be confused not only about their identity as lesbians,

but about their gender role identity and their place within the lesbian community. Lesbian couples may have difficulty developing and maintaining a relationship when there are no clear guidelines for appropriate roles. All of these are possible problems that lesbian women may encounter and for which they may seek help. The helping professional needs to be able to look beyond the stereotypes about lesbians and lesbian couples to the individual women who are asking for help.

Communication

Differences between lesbian and nongay couples. Lesbian women believe that communication is better in lesbian than in heterosexual relationships.[40] Women are more likely to have the skills for talking about feelings than men because it is culturally expected that women are more feeling. It is also considered more appropriate for women to focus on and express feelings, so they are more likely to do so. Women are also socialized to see to it that a relationship runs smoothly and to focus on the needs of others, even to the exclusion of their own needs.

Because women learn to value emotional expression, commitment, and intimacy, they may be more willing than men to make long-term commitments, to believe these are worth working for, and to assume a large part of the responsibility for seeing to it that a relationship continues. Also, because two women share the same background and experiences as women, they can often understand each other more easily than a man and woman can. They share the same gender-related values, goals, and relationship skills, although these are not developed in all women equally, of course. For all these reasons, communication between two women is often different from, and may be experienced as better than, communication between a man and a woman.

Communication problems. Although lesbian women may start out with a better chance of good communication, there are still a number of possible difficulties. Like nongay lovers, lesbian lovers can fall into the trap of assuming that they should be aware of each other's feelings without being told. This may be an even more frequent problem for lesbian than for nongay couples precisely because women are expected, and so may expect each other, to be more "sensitive," "intuitive," and "responsive to feelings" than men. A woman may also expect that another woman will be accepting of her feelings at all times.

A lesbian may assume that, because her lover is a woman, she does not need to articulate her thoughts and feelings. She may also believe that, because she is a woman, she should *always* be sensitive to and supportive of her lover's feelings. Partners may thus have unrealistic expectations of what they should do about feelings and may become angry and threatened if feelings are not understood without talking.

If anything, communication is more important in gay than nongay relationships because of the added strains imposed upon gay couples by society and the necessity for either maintaining a fictional relationship or of dealing with negative reactions from the outside world. The demands of family, friends, and co-workers on a lesbian couple's energy sometimes make it difficult for them to function smoothly. Furthermore, a great many lesbian relationships involve two women who are earning independent incomes and have independently developing careers. The demands of work and career on both women may also put a strain on the relationship unless both women are clear in their communications and expectations of each other.

Lack of assertiveness. The communication of needs is often difficult for women because they are not taught to be assertive about getting what they want.[41] Although it may be true that lesbian women are, in general, more assertive than nongay women in some areas of their lives, this may not be true in personal relationships. Because lesbian women have been socialized as women, as we have repeatedly noted, and are not unlike nongay women in their demonstration of nurturing and supportiveness, they may be equally as susceptible as nongay women to being supportive and protective when it would be more appropriate and functional to be assertive.

Independence/dependence. A major area of concern for many lesbians, and one requiring good communication, is the resolution of conflicting needs for emotional closeness and independence.[42] Sang comments that

> by far, the most frequent theme in lesbian couple relationships has to do with time together and time alone. Many lesbians feel that if they are in a committed relationship they will not have time to be by themselves. . . . Female socialization fosters togetherness. Having more in common often makes it difficult for lesbians to separate from the relationship to pursue their own interests.[43]

Peplau et al.[44] also found the issue of independence to be of concern to many of the women in their sample. The women in their sample who emphasized dyadic attachment ("concerns with having a close-knit, exclusive, and relatively permanent relationship"[45]) were less likely to see their own independence or their partner's dependence as a problem than those women who emphasized personal autonomy ("concerns with independence and equality"[45]).

Since this is likely to be an issue for a lesbian couple, it is important that the helping professional realize and point out to the couple that some of the problems they encounter are exacerbated by the realities of the lesbian lifestyle, but that a great many problems can be solved by talking about them and by each partner being very clear about her own needs. A contract can then be drawn up specifying the couple's agreement about independent social, leisure, and private time for each partner as well as arrangements for mutually satisfactory time spent together. If the relationship is to work, it is important that both partners' needs are met for both time spent apart and time spent together. It is often the case that clear contracting to meet these needs will demonstrate that there is a quality issue about time spent together as well as a quantity one. If a contract is arranged, neither party need feel resentment or guilt about either independent or mutually shared time, and this may make the quality of both kinds of time more satisfactory.

Forming relationships. Unfortunately, lesbian women do not get the kind of practice at forming and maintaining relationships that most nongay women get during adolescence. This often means that as young adults, they do not have the skills necessary to form satisfactory relationships. Heterosexual dating and courtship rituals provide young, nongay women with practice in forming relationships under the watchful eye of peers, parents, and other family members. Although this certainly does not ensure good relationship skills, it at least makes it more likely that nongays will learn how to fulfill later married roles.

The kinds of relationship experiences that are important to nongay adolescents are often irrelevant to young lesbians. For one thing, adolescent relationships give young heterosexual women practice in being appropriately feminine in relation to a male; they provide training in deference and correct feminine demeanor and in the cultivation and care of the male ego. Adolescent girls also get feedback and training from female peers on the appropriateness of various kinds of relationship behaviors, both public and private.

By moving back and forth from the male-oriented, sex-obsessed confines of an adolescent heterosexual relationship to the socially strict world of the adolescent female peer group, the young nongay woman learns what men want from her and what society expects her to do in response. She learns the skills necessary to "catch" a man and what to do to make him happy once he is "caught."

The adolescent lesbian, meanwhile, is learning relatively little that will help her form satisfactory relationships with other women as an adult. The kinds of relationship skills she will need are very different from those of her nongay sisters. The kinds of skills that lesbian women need to learn are those necessary to function in a relationship in which there is neither gender-based status nor gender-based division of roles.

There is another important kind of learning that takes place in early nongay relationships that lesbian women are liable to miss. In the likely event that her first relationships are not permanent ones, a young nongay woman learns about forming and breaking intense emotional bonds. She also learns to differentiate among her feelings and to experiment with what she wants and needs from another person. Ideally, she learns what qualities she is looking for in a mate and how to recognize someone who possesses these qualities. In essence, a nongay woman practices falling in love, and as she does, she learns what the consequences are not only of falling in love but of falling in love with particular kinds of people. Obviously, the kind of practice that nongay adolescents get does not make them expert at picking partners or forming relationships. Even so, they are likely to be ahead of their lesbian counterparts in that they obtain practice in situations that approximate those they will encounter as adults.

Young lesbians, on the other hand, are in a milieu that differs radically from what they will experience as adults. Furthermore, if an adolescent is already experiencing attraction to other women, she is unlikely to take relationships with men very seriously. Adolescent and early adult heterosexual dating is common among lesbian women, but it is unlikely to provide the kind of practice she needs either in relationship skills or in emotional involvement.

Another source of difficulty for young lesbians is the lack of a peer support group. Adolescent and many young adult lesbians who have not found or are not within reach of a lesbian community may think of themselves as different and feel isolated and alone. They also have no opportunity to learn about different kinds of lesbian women and lesbian relationships. As a result, lesbian women who are just coming out, especially very young women, may be inclined to fall in love with the first person they meet who is interested in them, even though the possibility of a good relationship may be negligible. So gay women may end up learning about relationships at a much later age than nongays, simply because they have not had an adequate chance to form adolescent lesbian relationships and thus practice relationship skills as nongays are able to do.

For women who have not had the chance to form adolescent lesbian relationships and who may have tried heterosexual dating without much enjoyment of success, the transition to a lesbian relationship may be extraordinary. It is common for women entering a lesbian relationship for the first time to find that things suddenly feel "right," that they feel "high" or especially beautiful or "whole."

☐ Finally things came together [with a woman] and it was great. I was amazed. I was in heaven. I was just—yipee! I know now I could never go back. My coming out meant years of being wiped out were over. Suddenly everything opened up and there I was, and this was where I was going after twenty-five years. . . . It's incredible. . . . It's the first time in my life I've been able to have a total relationship with someone who—instead of negating parts of myself—brought everything out. Everything I want to be I can be. Now I feel good. I feel beautiful. But it's not merely physical; it's just feeling so good there is no way you're not going to look good. It's wham, wham, wham—every morning I just wake up and wonder, "What's it going to be like today?"[46]

Maintaining relationships

Absence of roles and role models

Absence of roles. The absence of clear-cut roles within lesbian relationships creates some difficulties while it removes others:

☐ I think now the attempt is being made to be women together rather than man and woman [in lesbian relationships]. Kids today say, "There's no need for role playing in modern society." But it's terribly confusing. The longest relationships were the butch-femme ones. They were the ones that lasted twenty, thirty years. Everybody knew what she had to do. Now we say, "I'm not butch or femme; I'm just me." Well, who the hell is me? And what do I do? And how am I to behave? At least in role playing you knew the rules. You knew your mother and father. You knew what

they did and what their lives were like. You tried to do the same thing: you got a house, right? Now nobody knows how to behave in a lot of areas. It's harder.[47]

Absence of role models. The major difficulties couples face are probably caused by the absence of role models for relationships without clear-cut gender role differences as well as the fact that conceptions of "good" or "successful" relationships are based on the traditional heterosexual marriage model. This means that two women living together will usually have to develop a functional style of living without any model or pattern to use for reference. In order to successfully maintain a relationship over a long period of time, two women must somehow come to grips with the inevitable problems inherent in coordinating and making interdependent two potentially independent lifestyles.

Many of the problems encountered in doing this are also encountered by nongay couples, but are usually solved by reference to gender. Thus, for example, the problems of differing salaries, accommodations to one partner's job requirements, housekeeping arrangements, and the like are usually based on gender. Men make higher salaries, usually get the first choice of job and job location, and can almost always expect that their female partner will take care of most housekeeping arrangements. In many marriages, one partner or the other is responsible for certain kinds of tasks on the basis of gender: mowing the lawn, taking care of the car, doing the laundry, cooking, and the like. Even in those homes in which the man does some tasks traditionally reserved for women, close observation often indicates that the division of labor is still not equal and is gender based. As nongay couples move away from gender roles, they will certainly encounter some of the kinds of problems that gay couples experience in attempting to develop functional, long-term relationships.

Although the opportunity to have an equal division of labor as well as equality in other respects is certainly one of the most positive aspects to lesbian relationships, it may also bring about friction in a number of areas. Any couple striving for an egalitarian relationship is bound to have difficulty because this is essentially new ground and there is not much advice available on how to be successful at it. As time goes on and more is learned about such relationships, it is to be expected that egalitarian relationships will be more easily managed.

Changes within the relationship. All relationships change over time as the individuals involved accommodate to each other. The changes that are probably most critical in the maintenance of a relationship are those taking place in the areas of communication, sexuality, and perceived closeness of the two partners. Although no research has been done on this, it seems likely that one of the most difficult periods of time for all lesbian couples is during the transition from the "honeymoon" period to a more stable, less romantic type of relationship.

Making it past the honeymoon. Lesbian relationships are probably more vulnerable to post-honeymoon crises than nongay relationships for a number of reasons. First, the absence of any sanctifying ritual makes the initial period of intimacy between two women especially important. This is because the necessity for establishing the relationship as both special and binding lies almost completely with the couple. Although the lesbian community will provide some support and recognition for a new couple, the fact that couples form and split fairly often can make this recognition perfunctory.

Newly involved couples are often so completely immersed in each other that energy is taken away from other nonromantic friendships. As a result, the couple's circle of acquaintances may be somewhat impatient for the two women to settle down and stop being so exclusive. In contrast, a nongay married couple has the blessings of church and state, and usually, family and social convention supports a brief and clearly delineated honeymoon period before the couple returns to "normal" behavior. This period of time is often publicly announced and celebrated. The couple may take time off from work and are expected to spend a period of time alone together. The reader can imagine the reaction that would greet a lesbian woman who came waltzing in to work to announce that she has fallen deeply in love and has decided to commit her life to another woman and is planning to take time off from work for a honeymoon trip to the beach! This means that lesbian couples must severely circumscribe their joy and have no clearly delimited period of intense romance.

Furthermore, a heterosexual marriage union is often established with long-term goals in mind: the purchase of a home, raising of children, and acceptance and advancement within the community and in the workplace. These expectations give the nongay couple a long-term view of where their relationship is headed on the basis of reasonably concrete expectations. They make it not only necessary but desirable for the newlyweds to make a transition from the honeymoon to a more settled relationship, and they provide incentives for this transition. This is not meant to imply that nongay couples do not have difficulty making such a transition or that all have the aforementioned goals. However, these goals are probably fairly typical of the majority of nongay marriages, and it is believed they may provide an easing of the transition that is not available for lesbian couples.

Finally, lesbian couples inevitably face more uncertainty about the future of their relationship than nongay couples do. There is the continual reminder of the relative transience of lesbian relationships. There may also be less of a sense of joint endeavor than in nongay couples. There is rarely any expectation that a lesbian couple will adopt children or build toward some specific future as a couple. Most communities do not provide for the inclusion of admitted lesbians as established or respected members, let alone as community leaders, and there is still little encouragment for women to plan realistically for professional advancement and development. This means that most of what occurs in lesbian relationships must consistently be based in the present without any clear expectation of what the future holds. In a society built on a general disregard of here-and-now reality, this is a difficult task.

Changes in relationships with others. Another area in which lesbian couples may encounter problems making it past the honeymoon involves the couples' relationships with other women in the gay community. Again, there is a contrast here between nongay and lesbian couples that is likely to make for differences in both the type and extent of problems encountered and in the type of intervention required.

Relationships between individuals in this country are frequently among individuals of the same gender, regardless of sexual orientation. Both nongays and gays are likely to spend much of their social time with members of the same gender. Among nongay couples, the woman and man may each have separate groups of same-gender friends with whom they socialize. During the honeymoon period, the man and woman may spend more time with each other than with these groups of friends, but after the honeymoon, the husband and wife will usually resume these same-gender relationships. They may also have groups of friends with whom they socialize as a couple. These may or may not include their same-gender friends. Whatever the case, the same-gender peer group provides support for both men and women in entering and getting through the honeymoon phase. Within these groups, there is friendship, but no expectation of potential sexual relationships.

Within the lesbian community, it is also often the case that two women may have different sets of friends. Frequently, when the couple forms, they will pull away from extensive socializing with these friends for a period of time. When the couple is ready to begin socializing again, they almost always do so together rather than maintaining separate friendship groups. This is because, unlike nongays, the gay community setting is usually the only place where the couple is recognized as legitimate and is really the only place the couple has to go together to meet others where they can be treated as a pair. So if the two women have had separate groups of friends, one partner may either give up or substantially reduce contact with her friends, while entering the social group of her lover.

The consequence of this situation for gay women is that the process of forming an intimate relationship may jeopardize nonsexual relationships. In some cases, if the two partners have completely separate sets of friends, one partner may move away from these friends socially and, as the honeymoon period ends, may find herself feeling alone and lost. This feeling may be attributed to changes in the partnership, when in actuality, some of the distress may be the result of a loss of contact with a support group or a change in the quality of that contact. If one or both partners are threatened by contact with the lesbian community, the sense of isolation for both may deepen forcing them to turn increasingly to each other for support. This can ultimately have detrimental effects on the relationship by placing too many demands on it.

The helping professional who encounters this kind of situation should be aware of the different implications for gay and nongay couples of having same-gender friendship groups and take this into account in helping a couple assess the nature of their problem. The counselor should also explore with the couple their expectations about who they should interact with and how they should interact. If one or both women believe that friendships should be limited in some way, what are the implications of this for each of them? Is one woman being expected to give up her friends while the other is not? Are the women jealous of each other's past relationships or current friendships? What are the women's expectations about how much time they should spend together? Do they believe they should fulfill all of each other's needs? How possible is this, and what are the implications for their relationship in the long run if they try to do this?

As in so many other areas, it is often the case

that the counselor must teach women in a relationship to recognize, acknowledge, and assertively express their needs, and then negotiate with each other over how best to fill these. It may also be necessary to challenge a client's irrational beliefs about what she *should* do in a relationship.

Changes in the sexual relationship. The transition from the honeymoon stage of a relationship is likely to bring about changes in a couple's sexual relationship, and these changes can be problematic. In most relationships, it is expected that time will bring about a decrease in sexual activity. In lesbian relationships, such changes naturally occur but may be viewed as prophetic of other, more drastic changes and may thus have more severe consequences than necessary.

What may occur is that the two women view their increased sexual behavior during the initial stages of their relationship as "normal" and may thus expect that their sexual activity should stay at this level permanently. A decrease from this level of activity may be viewed as a move from "normal" to "abnormal" sexual activity, and one or both partners may then believe that this is indicative of relationship problems. In fact, all that may be happening is that the couple is moving from an atypical rate of sexual activity to a more typical and lower rate.

Although this may be true of heterosexual, gay male, and lesbian couples, lesbian women labor under an added burden. There is within the lesbian community a notion that being freed from the tyranny of male domination and sexual demands should somehow mean that one is free from cultural conditioning regarding female sexual behavior. The consequence of this is the myth that lesbians have "great sex all the time,"[48] a belief that Toder[48] considers one of the lesbian community's most destructive myths. Lesbian women may believe that they should be more sexually liberated than their nongay sisters: more sexual, more sensual, expert in sexual technique, breathtakingly and unfailingly orgasmic, and so forth. There is

also some inevitable response to the myth that all gay people are more interested in and more likely to engage in sexual activity than nongays. Gay women may believe they should want to have sex all the time. Education may be necessary in a therapeutic or counseling setting to combat these potentially harmful beliefs. Gay women must learn that sexual experience and level of sexual interest vary among individuals and according to circumstances.

In the early stages of a relationship, the focus on having a sexual relationship that meets gay cultural norms and expectations may lead to a severe letdown as sexual activity naturally decreases following a honeymoon for most couples. This decrease in activity, if viewed as abnormal and symptomatic, rather than normal, may lead one or both partners to worry that the relationship itself is in jeopardy.

Romance and sex. Because lesbian women are socialized as women, the perceived connection between romance and sexual behavior is a strong one, and a decrease in sexual behavior may be seen as a decrease in love or the romantic quality of the relationship. Another consequence of this pairing of romance and sexual behavior may be that a couple will believe their sexual encounters should always be romantic or that they should always be intense emotional experiences.

There are other problems that are dealt with in depth in Chapter 8. The main issue here is that lesbian women are vulnerable in viewing changes in sexual behavior as negative changes in the relationship when this is not in fact the case.

Changes in communication. Like everything else in a relationship, the communication behavior of couples alters with the passage of time. And, like changes in sexual behavior, such changes may be viewed as indications that something is "wrong" with the relationship when they may not mean that at all.

Lesbian couples start out like most couples, with a great deal of exclusive interaction. Naturally, not all couples communicate verbally, but most couples do spend a lot of their initial time together communicating in a variety of ways. Interaction between lovers is frequently intense and single-minded. Partners may drop all other friends, hobbies, and extracurricular activities during the early stages of a relationship. Everything but the relationship may be seen as irrelevant. This means that, aside from time spent working, lovers may spend all of their time together, paying continuous attention to each other, getting to know each other, sharing their life stories, and so forth.

As time passes and some of the novelty of the relationship wears off, the necessity and even desirability of this type of intense interaction will usually diminish. This change in focus naturally brings changes in behavior. The lovers may spend fewer hours together, and the hours they do spend together may be differently spent. The intensity of their interactions will undoubtedly lessen, the intensity and frequency of physical (not just sexual) contact may diminish, and so forth.

To women who live within the gay culture, any such changes can be viewed as upsetting because they may be interpreted as a loss of interest or a change in feeling. They may be taken as an indication that the couple is falling out of love or that something is wrong. If one partner feels the loss more than the other, she may be particularly threatened.

The practitioner must remember that lesbian couples are usually not willing to act like a couple in nongay public because of anticipated negative reactions.[11] This means that intimate behavior such as holding hands, kissing, hugging, and otherwise demonstrating affection are reserved for private circumstances. Because these kinds of demonstrations are taboo within nongay society, they may come to take on greater significance than they would with a nongay couple.

Implications for intervention. The changes that occur as a relationship develops and moves past the initial stage of infatuation may either be problematic in themselves or may precipitate other problems for a lesbian couple. In assessing these problems, the helping professional must keep in mind the issues discussed so far: the importance of the experience of intimacy in lesbian relationships, the lack of external support for these relationships,

and possible fears that lesbian women may have about the length of their relationships. Given these realities, intervention must then focus on the specific problem the lesbian couple is facing. They need to determine not only what they do not like about their current situation, but also what it is they would like to achieve.

If the couple, or one individual in the couple, is concerned about the occurrence of changes themselves, they can be reassured that changes are a natural and normal part of any relationship. More often, however, it will be the specific changes that have occurred that will be upsetting to one or both women.

First and foremost, the partners need to establish good communication. As women, they may have learned that it is not appropriate to express their desires or to be assertive about what they want. A woman is supposed to be supportive, nurturing, and nondemanding in a relationship. She is expected to figure out what her partner wants and provide it. If two women both attempt to take this kind of role, they will soon be at an impasse. So, partners may have to spend some time learning to express what they want from each other in all areas of the relationship: in time spent together, amount of private time, amount of sexual contact, the kinds of activities they will share, and the way they will relate to the gay community.

Other than the special problems that lesbian couples face that we have discussed that may call for unique solutions, most problems of lesbian couples are similar to and require the same kinds of interventive strategies as those of nongay couples. If the partners do not have good communication, assertiveness, or sexual skills, it will help to teach them these skills. If their expectations are that the early stages of their relationship should somehow continue permanently rather than being temporary, the practitioner may want to find out what the couple expects to happen as the relationship matures. If their expectations are unrealistic, these must be challenged and replaced with more realistic ones. If the couple believes that changes in a relationship are automatically signs that the relationship is in trouble, the practitioner should find out why they believe this is the case and help the two women test out their belief. If it does seem likely that they are incompatible, the counselor will need to either help them improve their relationship skills or separate.

Because of the unique kinds of strains and strengths that are often part of lesbian relationships, it is important that the counselor, particularly the nongay counselor, not be too quick to jump to conclusions about either the meaning of the presenting problem or the best solution to it. Lesbian women and lesbian couples have typically been viewed by the helping professions as childish, masochistic, neurotic, and so forth. These kinds of beliefs put lesbian couples in a bind. If they demonstrate mutual dependence because, as women, they have learned that this is appropriate, they may be viewed as having "neurotic dependency needs." If they have problems in a relationship that they attempt to work out while staying together, they may be seen as masochistic and overly dependent. If, on the other hand, a lesbian couple decides to end a relationship in a relatively short time, they run the risk of being viewed as hopelessly neurotic and incapable of long-term attachments. If a lesbian woman demonstrates nurturing in a relationship, she may be "accused" of mothering her partner, whereas a lesbian who is able to accept support from her partner is accused of taking a child's role. These kinds of characterizations are both pointless and ridiculous. They generally take features of typically feminine behavior that would be viewed as normal and desirable in a heterosexual context and make them appear neurotic because they occur between two women. Conversely, of course, lesbian women who show behavior that is not typically feminine are accused of being pseudo men or of rejecting their womanhood.

It may be difficult for a traditionally trained therapist to avoid these kinds of characterizations of lesbian couples. However, if the position of lesbian women is viewed logically within the context of the society as well as the lesbian community, we believe it can readily be seen that lesbians' responses in couples are appropriate, understandable, and usually quite functional. Those women who do have difficulty, who are, for example, dependent to the point of dysfunction or "masculine" to the point that their behavior is severely restricted can be helped best by treating them as women with relationship problems, not as women who are hopelessly neurotic because they do not fit society's preconception of how a woman should behave or because they are lesbian.

Terminating relationships

Lesbian relationships end for essentially the same reasons as nongay relationships: changes within the relationship, lack of necessary relationship skills, life demands, variables outside the relationship, or the death of one partner. This section discusses ways that the factors leading to termination in these areas may be different in lesbian and nongay relationships and the kinds of knowledge and skills that helping professionals will need in helping gay couples handle termination constructively.

Changes within the relationship. All relationships change over time, and part of the process of maintaining a relationship includes coping with those changes. What may be different about lesbian relationships are the kinds of couple conflicts, the partner's skill levels in working through a relationship if undesirable changes occur, and the amount of social support or pressure on a couple to stay together.

Lesbian women often get caught between their socialization as women and as members of the gay community. Like nongay women, lesbian women are raised to believe that there is one and only "true love" and that winning, or being won, is the answer to everything. If this is removed from the truth in the nongay community, it is almost never the truth in the gay community. Nonetheless, many gay women believe that this is what should happen to them. The collective wisdom of the gay women's community, however, makes it amply clear that this is not really the case. Many women believe, indeed, that it is both a sexist and heterosexist view of reality and so strive for more liberated relationships. Unfortunately, most women are not trained to carry out relationships that do not fit into the "happily ever after" mode. So the lesbian woman is often caught between her training within the nongay culture and what she knows is likely to occur based on observation and experience.

This cultural bind can lead to some relationships terminating when they need not as well as to some relationships continuing when separation might be better for both partners. First, as the relationship begins to change, one or both women may decide that this is not, after all, *the* relationship as they had hoped. The expectation may be that in "true love," little effort is required to keep romance going, and so, not knowing how to build and maintain a relationship, a couple may end their partnership because it is no longer meeting expectations.

As the relationship changes, partners who are expecting the honeymoon of true love to continue may begin looking about for other partners, and one or both may find someone who looks as though she may be Ms. Right. For some women, this search may be lifelong, frustrating, and futile. There is nothing neurotic or abnormal about this difficulty, although it is dysfunctional. In the nongay world, such searches also occur, but the number is undoubtedly reduced by the social pressures that help maintain relationships as well as by the establishment of gender-related behavior patterns in which each partner fits into a socially approved niche. Many nongay women may also wonder what ever happened to the Mr. Right they thought they married, but have neither means nor social support for looking for someone else.

A number of other changes may occur in relationships: changes in feelings, in behavior patterns, in the needs or desires of one or both partners, and the like. In some instances, changes internal to the relationship may be sufficient reason for the relationship to end, and both partners may agree to this. Often, however, one partner would

like to end while the other partner would like to continue the relationship. Occasionally, both partners may realize that there are problems and may wish to attempt to work these out. In any of these situations, the role of the practitioner is similar to what it would be in working with a nongay couple. The major differences to keep in mind are the potential lack of support systems for strengthening relationship bonds, the gay community "norm" of moderately short-term relationships, and the possible belief in one single perfect relationship. One or both partners may be unaware of the effect of these factors on them and on the relationship, and the helping professional may want to assess the extent to which any or all are operating in pushing the couple toward terminating their relationship.

Helping professionals must also be careful not to get caught in these traps. It is easy, for example, for a gay professional to become caught in the myth of perfect relationships and to urge a couple to separate (or stay together) to fulfill her or his own needs. It is also easy for a nongay professional to attempt to evaluate a lesbian relationship by nongay standards and to miss relevant issues or to dismiss the concerns of the clients as superficial.

Lack of relationship skills. In the case of lesbian couples, it is not so much that all relationship skills may be lacking as that, as we have noted earlier, gay women are unlikely to have learned skills for maintaining same-gender relationships. Although we believe it is important for all individuals to move beyond rigid gender role definitions of behavior, it is probably most important for lesbian women to do so in order for their relationships to work.

Lesbian women sometimes need to learn to be assertive with each other in their relationships and that it is neither necessary nor desirable to be sensitive, supportive, and caring all the time. It is neither possible nor functional for one individual to be continually concerned about another's feelings and desires to the exclusion of her own. Yet this is what many women believe.

If one or both women in a relationship believe any of these things, their beliefs can be challenged and more appropriate ones taught. The support and nurturing that two women can provide each other are some of the possible strengths of a lesbian relationship, but this support must be combined with the ability on the part of both partners to say "no," to take private time when it is needed, and to ask for what she wants. The helping professional may have to both legitimize and teach lesbian women these skills.

Life demands. These frequently take the form of professional demands on one or both partners that force a couple apart. Lesbian couples are inevitably going to be faced with these kinds of problems. The absence of a gender basis for career decisions means that lesbian couples may have careers that develop simultaneously and go in different directions. The freedom to develop without hindrance from gender role demands is a positive side of lesbian relationships. Its concomitant, however, is that a couple must often either decide to sacrifice one woman's career or to separate either temporarily or permanently.

Some lesbian couples are so interdependent that they believe it is worthwhile for one person to sacrifice temporarily for the other's career goals. But often, the sacrifice is too great for one partner, and the couple decides to split up. These kinds of separations are inevitably painful because they involve parting, and the partners' grief must be recognized.

Difficulties are more often likely to arise because one or both parties feel guilty and resentful. Women in this culture are taught that it is appropriate to give up everything for love, to follow one's lover to the ends of the earth, no sacrifice is too great, and so forth. This is scarcely true for any two people. When such a separation occurs, the partners must learn to separate the love they feel for each other from the right of each person to pursue her own personal goals, even though these may lead the partners in separate directions.

The tendency may be for each partner to tax the other, overtly or covertly, with a version of the "if you *really* loved me you would . . . " routine. The person leaving may think that if her partner *really* loved her, she would follow along. She may also feel guilt for having made the decision to move. The partner who is remaining may think that if her lover *really* cared, she would have refused the out-of-town job and stayed. She may also feel guilty for not going. So the two may separate with difficulty because they have internalized the cultural message that a woman who is really in love has nothing better or more important in life than her lover. Although each person's guilt and resentment are logical outgrowths of her beliefs, it is the counselor's responsibility to challenge the beliefs themselves and, ideally, help the couple separate with regret but without long-term resentment and guilt.

Variables outside the relationship. The most likely external intrusion is the appearance of another woman (or sometimes a man) on the couple's horizon. If one woman is attracted to another outside the relationship and decides to become involved with her, it is quite possible that the first relationship will terminate. In such cases, the lack of pressure from the gay community for a couple to stay together makes separation easier.

If a couple does break up because of another woman, the person most likely to seek help will probably be the woman who did not want to end the relationship. Again, influenced by what she has learned growing up in a heterosexual environment, she may believe that she is at fault, that she did something wrong or failed in some way. She should be reminded of the lack of support within the gay community for relationships to remain together and helped to realistically assess the relationship and her role in its termination. She must particularly be helped to be aware of and express any anger she is feeling toward her partner as soon as possible, particularly if she wants to have an ongoing friendship with this woman.

Because the lesbian community in which a couple moves is often circumscribed, the woman who is "left" in such a relationship may find herself in a quandary. If she continues to see her and her ex-partner's friends, she may run into her ex-partner and the woman's new lover. She may also encounter unwanted reactions from friends who may take sides with one or the other. The more readily and completely she can manage her feelings about the termination of the relationship and can work them out with her ex-partner, the less likely she will be to end up stranded without either her lover or the group of friends she is used to. Even though it may be difficult, she should probably be urged to continue to see these people if she really cares about them and to assertively handle any problems that arise.

Another problem that sometimes impinges on a couple is a combination of internal and external factors. Sometimes, the demands of one woman's life may make it desirable for her to begin to come out to others in her environment, or this may be something she thinks is in her best interest as a gay woman. If the woman decides to come out and her partner is in the closet, this may create a lot of friction. Even though it may not be an actual threat, the partner may be afraid that she will also be exposed as a lesbian. This is a sufficient problem to cause some couples to split up.

In such instances, both women's experiences and feelings should be accepted as valid. It may be a temptation, for a gay therapist particularly, to side with one person or the other. A gay professional who is out may believe that this is right and that the woman who is afraid is wrong. A gay professional who is still in the closet may be threatened by someone else's attempt to come out and may support the woman in the closet. Temptations may be similar for nongay professionals depending on their convictions. As with other issues, though, the decision must, of course, rest with the individual women.

The woman who wants to come out is very likely to be torn between her desire to take this step toward greater freedom and her real wish to maintain the relationship and avoid hurting the woman she loves. This is a very real, very painful conflict. Because the decision to come out is often a difficult one, the woman who wants to do so may find herself under a great strain.

Her partner, on the other hand, may perceive this as a threat to her job or career, to her nongay friendships, perhaps to her relationship with her parents. She may indeed overreact to the threat, but to her the danger is very real. She may be both resentful of her partner for putting her in an awkward and frightening position and ashamed of what she or her partner perceives as a lack of courage.

The reality may in fact be that if neither partner is willing to capitulate, they may have to end the relationship. This must be presented as a realistic possibility. Before accepting this as inevitable, however, the counselor can work with the couple to determine what the realistic threats are to the woman who does not want to come out. It is also wise to see if the partner who does want to come out may be willing to accept some sort of compromise, at least temporarily. It is sometimes the case that when a person gets ready to come out, he or she may be inclined to want to come out to *everyone,* when this really is not necessary, at least at first.

Whatever the partners decide to do individually, it is helpful if they can learn to separate their own needs and convictions from those of the partner, and from the issue of whether they actually love each other. If they do decide to separate, it will be good for them to each feel good about herself and about her decision, as well as about the other person and her decision. The issue of coming out must not be allowed to become one of absolute right or wrong, but can best be viewed according to what will serve each individual best under the circumstances.

Death of one partner. The death of one partner in a lesbian relationship is particularly difficult for the remaining partner because of the failure of society to recognize lesbian relationships. Except under unusual circumstances, the family of a lesbian may completely exclude her lover from the process. Because she is not legally family, she may not be allowed into an intensive care setting and may be kept away from her lover by family members. After her lover's death, she may be kept from retaining any of her lover's possessions, from attending the funeral, and may be prevented from being a beneficiary even though her partner has so specified in the will (see Chapter 3, ''Legal Rights of Gays''').

Under these circumstances, the grief process may be lengthened and made more severe. It may be difficult for the remaining partner to effectively terminate from her lover if she is unable to see her during an illness, to attend the funeral, or to participate in any of the events that provide for complete termination. We will not discuss the stages of the grief process here because they are the same for lesbians as for others. What may be different is the kind of intervention required to help a gay woman get through these stages.

In a nongay relationship, acknowledgment of the reality of the loved one's death is made easier by the entire cultural complex of events surrounding a death, from participation in the final illness in some cases to participation in funeral arrangements and the funeral itself, often including viewing the body. Friends of the family may support the bereaved individual, co-workers are informed and supportive, and leave may be granted from work. The widow or widower may complete the process by eventually disposing of the dead person's belongings, thus helping finish the termination process.

For some gay women, almost all these termination events are prevented. This may make it very difficult for the woman to accept the fact that her partner is dead. If she is not known to be gay at work, she cannot share her grief with others. There will be no immediate family support. She will have no leave of absence from her job. She may not have a chance to terminate with her lover while she is alive, and may not see her buried. In some cases, the family steps in and removes all the dead woman's effects.

In a situation like this, it is essential that the counselor help the client accept the reality of her partner's death and realize that if she has had the kinds of experiences detailed above, acceptance may take longer than it would otherwise. The client should be encouraged to talk about the death not only to the counselor but to friends. If possible, the counselor should urge the client's friends to discuss the subject with the bereaved woman, rather than avoiding it. The counselor may want to point out to the client that termination is more difficult because she has not had the kind of social support that a nongay person would have.

The lesbian community usually takes on the responsibilities of family at times like these. But there are differences between this extended family and the families of nongay couples. For one thing, it is quite possible that within a close group of lesbian friends, there may be others who have been involved in a love relationship with the deceased and who are also grieving. This may make it difficult for them to have the kind of semidetachment that is true of in-laws and friends of the family where a nongay married couple is concerned.

In general, the focus of treatment should be on helping the client through the grief process. The counselor must realize that the process may take longer and be more difficult with a gay client for the reasons given above.

GAY MALE PRIMARY RELATIONSHIPS

Gay men have male gender identities and are socialized as men. Their relationships are unlike nongay relationships in that they involve another man and, as with lesbian relationships, are enmeshed in a nonsupportive, sometimes antagonistic culture. They follow no general pattern and defy categorization beyond being same-gender relationships. Although some researchers have attempted to develop typologies,[49] the larger the sample, the more difficult that becomes. Jay and Young analyzed replies from over 2000 men who indicated that they were in a primary relationship, and could find no pattern.[50] We shall present some of the characteristics of gay male relationships, but we recognize that the immense variety means that we can focus only on the more common issues.

Characteristics of gay male relationships

Duration

Duration of relationships—myth. The most widely believed, prevalent myth relating to gay male relationships is the notion that gay men do not form long-term stable relationships. The findings of Bell and Weinberg,[51] Jay and Young,[52] and McWhirter and Mattison[53] refute the myth. However, until these findings become more widely known and accepted, the myth may continue to have the effect of a self-fulfilling prophecy. Some gay men, believing the myth and not knowing ways in which relationships can be developed and strengthened, use it as an excuse for breaking up a relationship when conflict exists.

Duration of relationships—reality. Tripp quite succinctly illustrates the reason for the myth and suggests the reality.

> Consider, for instance, the man who has had perhaps a hundred brief encounters, a number of short-range affairs, and one profound relationship which lasts for years or for the rest of his life. This combination of experiences is not at all unusual and it lends itself to three correct statements about the man: that he is highly promiscuous, that most of his relationships do not last, and that he clearly can and does maintain an important and substantial ongoing relationship.[54]

The reality, then, appears to be that gay men usually form short-term relationships *and* long-term stable ones. Saghir and Robins reported a similar pattern in the dating and going-steady behavior of nongay men, with the major difference being that genital activity was included in the gay male relationships and not in those of the nongay men.[55]

Those researchers who have included statistics on length of gay male primary relationships indicate that about one third lasted for more than 5 years.[56] McWhirter and Mattison, who studied 156 couples who were living together, found that the average length of relationships was almost 9 years, with 5 years being the most frequent, and the longest being over 37 years.[57]

The pattern presented by all the research appears to be, as Tripp indicated, an initial series of short-term, intense relationships lasting from 1 to 3 years, followed by longer-term relationships, with some lasting for over 30 years. As this pattern indicates, the initial relationships, the shorter ones, are a sort of trial-and-error education for the man, teaching him about his own needs and values and about establishing a primary relationship with another man, and preparing him for a more satisfactory, longer-term relationship at a later time.[58] This appears to be a necessity in that most men approach their first relationship with a rather idealistic, romanticized view,[59] developed as a result of living in a culture that promotes lifelong marriage, with a romantic beginning, as the relationship ideal.

It is possible that gay men do have trouble maintaining stable relationships *during their younger years,* but this is not unique to gay men. It is caused by a general lack of education about establishing and maintaining relationships combined with societal pressure to be in one. Nongay men have somewhat similar experiences, with three major differences. The gay man does not get the dating experience that the nongay man gets at equivalent ages; the gay man does not have to be concerned with filing for divorce if he and his partner decide that they are incompatible; and he does not have the concern of children who often arrive during the first 3 years of a heterosexual marriage. It is certainly possible that nongay men would follow the same pattern of relationships as gay men were it not for the marriage and children issues.

Counseling implications. If a gay man is concerned about the issue of duration, it may be necessary first to explain the myth and then explore the function of these early relationships as they apply to gay men, pointing out the similarity to the function of dating behavior of heterosexual men. It may also be necessary to explain the inherent differences between gay male and nongay relationships, including the issues of legal marriage and children, which are absent in the gay male couple.

The practice and educational aspects of these

shorter-term relationships do not decrease their intensity. As Bell and Weinberg indicate, the relationships of gay and nongay men are similar in their emotional involvement and commitment.[60] This similarity means that intervention techniques for gay couples who are in emotional conflict may be similar in many respects to those used with nongay couples.

Primary partner

Definition and characteristics of primary partner. A primary partner is someone with whom one feels a deep emotional attachment[61] either with or without sexual activity. We have used this term because it implies neither gender nor legality and acknowledges that people have many types of relationships but most have one that is considered to be most important emotionally. Many gay men use the term *lover* to describe this person.

There are no general characteristics beyond that definition. As Jay and Young indicated, "A 'lover' relationship for one couple would seem patently ridiculous to another pair of lovers and vice versa."[50] For example, one man describes his lover as a married man, living with his wife. They meet most often on a social basis. From the description, it appears that their homosexual activity is only with each other and infrequent.[62] Another lives apart from his lover, stating that both have very strong needs for solitude and are very independent. One likes living in the country, whereas the other prefers the city. They are sexual together once or twice a week, but that fluctuates depending on the strength of the need for solitude.[63] Another man describes a relationship that appears to mimic a more traditional marriage relationship, even to the point of one person being sexually exclusive and the other not.[64] There are many other variations described,[65] yet each one considers that he has a "lover" and therefore is in a primary relationship.

Counseling implications. This inability to characterize a lover may cause conflict for some men. One person may have a more traditional view, be-

lieving that a lover lives with you, shares in running a household, and spends most of his nonworking hours with you. The other may take a different view, indicating that his idea of a lover is based more on a feeling of commitment than where you live or who pays the bills or even how often you see each other. If these two men are attempting to build a relationship together, the counselor will have to help them explore those feelings, indicating the wide variety of possible patterns that exist, and helping them clarify their expectations for being considered a lover. It may be that neither alters his view, but both should be given the opportunity to explore the many possible alternatives, with acknowledgment from the counselor that a primary partner or lover designation depends entirely on the individuals involved.

Number of people. From the research, it would appear that all gay male primary relationships are dyads. However, from our observations, this is not totally true, because triads also exist. These are primary relationships that involve three men or two men and a woman. However, the overwhelming majority of gay male primary relationships are dyads; and our discussion, therefore, focuses on couples.

Characteristics of gay male couples

We mentioned that gay male primary relationships follow no single pattern. The men may be living together or apart, sexually exclusive or not, sexually active with each other or only with others, of the same or different socioeconomic status, age, or race, and so on with any variables except gender that one would like to examine. Although some researchers have acknowledged only men living together as being "coupled," the counselor cannot be so restrictive in viewpoint. For example, using that definition would have eliminated over half the men who reported in Jay and Young that they currently had a lover. In this section we will discuss some of the more common characteristics of gay male couples and the concerns that may be presented to the counselor.

The declaration of "couplehood". There is no single event that is used by all or even most gay men to indicate that a primary relationship has been established. Some use the act of buying a house together or moving into a shared house or apartment as the significant event. Others may exchange rings, usually worn on the right hand, to declare the existence of a couple. There are also some who go through a wedding ceremony to declare to each other and to friends that they are in a primary, committed relationship.

First sexual experience together, first meeting, or first declaration of love are also some of the many events that gay couples use as the anniversary of the beginning of their primary relationship. Each of these events provides a measure of time together and gives a date for anniversary celebrations. One couple we know has two anniversaries each year, their first meeting and their moving in together. Their twice-a-year anniversaries are seen as times of reaffirmation of their relationship. Whatever the event, it has special meaning for the men, similar to the significance of the engagement ring or marriage ceremony for the heterosexual couple, being a declaration that a primary relationship has been established.

Couples living together. Bell and Weinberg studied men who were living together in a "quasi marriage" that included a sexual relationship. They used three variables to separate these couples into two groups: numbers of sexual problems, numbers of sexual partners, and amount of time spent looking for sexual partners (cruising). If the men had low standard scores on all three variables, they were assigned to a group identified as "close-coupled" (67 men). If they scored high on any *one* of the three variables, they were assigned to the category, "open-coupled" (120 men).[66]

Bell and Weinberg found that those who lived together and met the three criteria for close-coupled status had fewer worries and concerns about cruising or establishing and maintaining a primary relationship, had "less regret about their homosexuality and [were] more sexually active" than their average respondents.[66] Those who were living together and met criteria for the open-coupled category experienced more concern about cruising and had "more regret about their homo-

sexuality." They also report that the most common sexual problem for the open-coupled group was the partner's unwillingness or inability to respond to sexual requests.[67]

McWhirter and Mattison also studied only couples who were living together. They chose their criteria because early clinical experience indicated that the dynamics of a couple living under the same roof were in some ways different from those of a couple living apart, and they wanted to focus primarily on the former. They found that couples go through stages of development as a couple, from a romantic, idealized "enthrallment" beginning to a settled, comfortable, more mature enthrallment stage after about 20 years together.[57]

Sonenschein found that those couples who began with a "romantic conception of ideally unending love," including a ritual ceremony and exchange of rings, were less likely to remain as a couple than were those who had a less formalized relationship. In other words, the more the couple mimicked the heterosexual marriage stereotype, the less likely that the relationship would last.[68]

Jay and Young indicated that 93% of the men who were living together gave essentially two reasons for doing so: "we want to" and "we love each other." The second reason is an example of how effective the acculturation process is with regard to proper behavior for couples. One could easily imply that being in love necessarily meant wanting to live together. It is also interesting to note that no one living apart gave the reason, "we love each other."[69]

Weinberg and Williams, in their study of gay men in three societies, categorized subjects by living arrangements: living with a gay roommate, alone, with parents, or with wife.[70] This approach does not identify couples because it is possible that two men living together would not identify as a couple and two men, each living alone, might. In fact, men could be in any one of those four categories and either be or not be in a relationship. However, the findings of the Weinberg and Williams study with regard to living arrangements are of interest.

> Among many homosexuals, the ideal arrangement is to live with a homosexual partner, especially one who is loved and with whom one's life is shared. . . . Compared with those other living arrangements, homosexual respondents living with homosexual roommates anticipate or have experienced the least intolerance or rejection on account of their homosexuality, anticipate the least discrimination, are the least worried about exposure of their homosexuality, the least concerned with passing, and the most known about. . . . They are the least socially involved with heterosexuals (except in Denmark) and the most socially involved with other homosexuals.[71]

Thus living together appears to be generally very positive for many gay men. However, if two men are living together and wish to consider moving apart, the counselor must be careful to help them weigh all the advantages and disadvantages. If their desire to live apart is the result of some conflict that can be resolved satisfactorily with other solutions, then they should explore those. For example, sometimes there is a need for private space that is not being met by the current living arrangements. Some possibilities that other men have found helpful are separate bedrooms or a separate entrance and living quarters within the same house. However, the counselor must be aware of the cultural bias that couples "should" live together. In the next section, we discuss some of the reasons for couples living apart. These are valid for some individuals, and the fact that many couples do not live with each other is sufficient to suggest that living apart might be one solution that could help a relationship survive.

Couples living apart. Research on the dynamics of gay male couples who live apart is limited. Some men live apart because of the need to maintain secrecy about their sexual orientation. They may work in situations in which discovery would mean loss of employment, because there is no guarantee that an employer must ignore a person's sexual orientation in job performance evaluation. The men may be married and believe that discovery would result in dissolution of that marriage. This is certainly true in some cases, but not in all. There are gay men who are married, whose wives know of the orientation, and who have managed to maintain an agreeable marital relationship. Other couples live apart because they both have a strong need for private living arrangements. As we have mentioned, this need can be met to some extent while living together, but for some, living apart is the best solution.

Whatever the reason, living apart from one's primary partner is contrary to the cultural dictates for being a couple. Thus, these men have to overcome the pressures of those dictates and may need support for the notion that living apart can be healthy for a relationship. Jay and Young indicate that the gay male community is supportive in that living apart is viewed as being an acceptable model for men in a primary relationship, emphasizing the importance of the gay community in helping men develop alternatives to the marriage model. If the gay man is separated from other gay men, his view of possibilities for establishing relationships may be limited. Only by exposure to the many possible alternatives can he find validation for his own needs, and that exposure may have to come from the counselor's exploration.

The counselor should indicate that many gay male couples live apart and that living arrangements are not necessarily an indication of commitment to the relationship or love for the partner. The men may have to explore their expectations for the partner's behavior. This will depend greatly on the reasons for their living apart. For example, if both are married and do not wish their wives to know, then their obligations to the family may take precedence over obligations to the partner. One man might wish to be with his partner but cannot because the family situation makes it impossible at that time.

If the men are living apart because of strong needs for solitude and independence, then they should explore the ways in which such needs sometimes are expressed in behavior. For example, if one is beginning to feel that his personal time is insufficient, he may start an argument with his partner in order to force a separation, or he may take some other action that is designed to separate them. The counselor will need to help them set up signals or find some way to better communicate their needs, with an understanding that acknowledging those needs is an expression of love and caring for the partner and of commitment to the relationship.

Roles. As with lesbian couples, gay men who live together as couples are subjected to the notion that they fit into the roles of "husband" and "wife." No stereotype exists without some basis in reality, and there are some gay male couples who fit the pattern. However, they are in the minority.[72] Many of the reasons for the stereotype concerning gay male couples are identical to those for lesbian couples. There are some gay men who appear effeminate, albeit a minority. Society offers only one model for relating as a couple, the husband/wife, masculine/feminine model. For a long time, the only socially visible gay men were those who fit the effeminate stereotype. A young gay man had no other models available. It was not until he was old enough to be able to meet other gay men that he was able to see any evidence to the contrary, and even then the stereotype was often visible. If he were motivated sufficiently to go to the library to seek information, he discovered that gay male couples indeed played husband and wife and had short-term relationships.

At one time, there was a great deal of role playing in gay male couples, but that has substantially declined.[72] Whereas several years ago it was fairly common to hear one man talk about his partner as his wife and refer to him as "she," this is much less common today. This may be the result of the increasing variety of visible role models available. It may also be that gay men have become aware of the possible oppressiveness of husband/wife roles.

Whatever the reason, gay men have tended to lessen the masculine/feminine role playing as couples. In fact, if you walk down the street in the gay section of a large city or go into a gay bar, you are more likely to encounter couples who resemble a pair of lumberjacks or construction workers or cowboys. Although it is true that these may be "costumes" and not necessarily reflective of the dynamics of the everyday relationship, at least the visual models available are no longer primarily "butch/femme" ones.

If a counselor is working with a couple who appear to fit the butch/femme stereotype, caution must be exercised on two points. First, they may prefer role playing, and it may be a factor that helps them to maintain the relationship. Attempting to curtail that behavior might destroy the relationship. Second, it is necessary to distinguish between role playing and behavior that is an expression of personal preference. If one man prefers to do the cooking, laundry, and housecleaning, and the other prefers to work in the yard, repair the car, and maintain the outside of the house, then they are simply fulfilling their own needs and should be supported by the counselor. However, if there is conflict, then the counselor will have to help them sort out their individual needs and reach a compromise on an equal basis. For example, if neither likes washing dishes or mowing the lawn, then they should either share those chores, compromise by having each do the least objectionable to him, or hire someone to come in and do them. Husband/wife role playing occurs in a minority of relationships, but the stereotype is still prevalent. The counselor must be aware of the possibility that he or she accepts the stereotype and be cautious about confusing personality needs with role playing.

Roles and sexual activity. Generally, gay men do not exhibit stereotypical role behavior in sexual activity,[73] just as they generally do not exhibit such behaviors in their daily interactions. Hooker noted that gay men who were in long-term relationships were apt to engage in a wide variety of sexual techniques and to be versatile in switching sexual activity roles depending on their feelings and needs or on those of the partner.[74] Saghir and Robins found that about half their gay male sample interchanged sex roles and never considered themselves in either the giver or the receiver role, whereas many of the other group adopted role behavior only on a transient basis, depending on "personal and group expectations."[75]

Also, one cannot make assumptions about role behavior in sexual activity from role behavior in general. Couples who play out the husband/wife roles in the everyday dynamics of the relationship may or may not carry these roles into the sexual activity sphere. There might be total role reversal in sexual activity. The male who is less than superbutch might very well be the one who is taking the dominant or "husband" role in the sexual activity, with the one who is taking the masculine role in their daily interactions preferring to be in the more passive role during sexual activity. It may also be that the daily roles totally disappear when it comes to sexual activity, with each enjoying all aspects of giving and receiving.

If couples are concerned about the implications of preferring one sexual role to another, the counselor might explore two points. First is the individual's attitude about the meaning of a particular sex act to his own masculinity. There is no correlation, but some men do have concerns about the possibility of such implications. The man who prefers to be the receiver of anal intercourse might believe that he is exhibiting feminine qualities and find this uncomfortable. The counselor can help him understand the difference between enjoying sexual activity and gender role behavior in an attempt to lessen his discomfort.

The second area for exploration is one of possible dysfunction. The counselor should determine if the man has ever tried reversing the roles. If not, then exploring the possibility of reversal would be appropriate. If he has attempted it, and is unable to function in the other role, then determine if it is a matter of lack of knowledge or a sexual dysfunction requiring sex therapy. If it is a matter of lack of knowledge, the counselor should be able to educate. If it is a need for sex therapy, the counselor should be able to refer to a competent therapist.

Nonmonandry. Whether living together or apart, whether dyad or triad, most gay male primary relationships are not monandrous[76] (sexually active only with one other man).[77] Researchers such as Saghir and Robins[78] and McWhirter and Mattison[57] indicate that the expectation for sexual exclusiveness usually exists in the beginning of early relationships but lessens with age and consequent experience. As was explained by a gay man in Jay and Young's book:

☐ I feel that this is an issue which too many couples fail to face, simply accepting a societal norm of exclusiveness without examining their own needs and reasons. Some couples grow best together when they remain exclusive, some grow best when they share with others in one or another form of nonexclusiveness. The basic requirement is that the agreement, whatever it is, be mutual, loving, and deeply examined.[17]

An example of monandry as an issue is the case of John and Sam. They began their relationship when John was 19 and Sam was 20.[79] They both had very romantic notions about this relationship and swore to each other that it would last forever. As they report, they initially told each other, "We're not going to be like those other gay couples. We *really* love each other and we're going to be together forever." They also swore that they would not be "unfaithful" to each other.

During the first 3 years of what is now a 5-year relationship, they indeed managed to maintain sexual exclusivity. It was not easy, as both were very attractive men and often received offers to break that vow. They also received verbal pressure from other gay men, essentially in the form of, "no one is sexually faithful these days." They counted their anniversary date as the day they moved in together, and after about 2½ years, each began to feel that their sexual activity together was getting routine, a feeling they did not share with each other.

John was the first to break the vow of exclusivity. He had stopped in a public rest room to urinate.

Later, he admitted that he knew it was one in which an anonymous transitory sexual experience was possible, but at the time he swore that he had to urinate and that particular toilet just happened to be handy. While in the restroom, he did allow another man to perform fellatio on him and he found the experience very exciting, although he felt very guilty about it afterwards. He repeated this experience several times, each time as the passive recipient of fellatio. He finally felt an obligation to tell Sam, although he was apprehensive about doing so.

As expected, the information was received with much emotional reaction and accusations. Once relative calm had returned, they both talked about the meaning of the experiences, and John tried to persuade Sam that they meant nothing as far as their relationship was concerned, that he still loved Sam and still wanted to stay with him. Sam was unwilling to accept this plan. He was hurt because John had broken the agreement, and Sam felt that nothing could repair the damage. Sexual activity between them ceased for almost a month; during this time, Sam met someone in a bar and went home with him. According to Sam, the sexual activity was not very exciting. His partner for the night was "too uptight about sex" and only wanted to be the recipient of anal intercourse, which failed to meet Sam's desire for more variety and reciprocity.

Thus, Sam now had an experience outside of the relationship, but he found it neither exciting nor very pleasurable. However, he did discover that it did not affect his feelings for John in any way, either positively or negatively. When he came back and told John about the experience, John felt slightly uncomfortable, much to his surprise. They eventually talked about the possibility of maintaining their relationship, allowing for outside experiences, but they also agreed not to tell each other about them. This is where their relationship contract stands today. They do occasionally have sexual partners outside the relationship, but do not share information about those encounters with each other.

The case of John and Sam presents some common issues that might cause couples to seek counseling. Specifically, the issues are sexual boredom, the importance of sexual exclusiveness to the relationship and to the individuals (values clarification) and the reasons for its having that importance, the lack of any previously established method for discussing a desire to alter the contract, the breaking of the contract and the implications for trust in the future, and the clarification of a new contract for the future, including a negotiation clause.

John and Sam had a contract that indicated essentially that sexual exclusiveness was the most important aspect of their relationship, and breaking that aspect of the contract was tantamount to breaking the relationship. The counselor's task is to help them clarify their contract and to establish a means of negotiating for altering it. This can be accomplished through values clarification techniques. However, it is not enough simply to clarify the values. The beliefs behind those values and their implications must also be explored.

If John and Sam decided that they wanted to attempt another monandrous contract, then the counselor should help them explore each of the points we have suggested under the section titled "Monandry." If they wish to attempt a contract that includes nonmonandry, then the counselor should help them explore the possibilities that are suggested in the following section, including the solution that they finally reached. However, the most crucial issue that they need to resolve is one of communication. They lack any means of discussing a possible change in their contract, and the counselor may have to teach them communication as well as negotiation skills.

Counseling for nonmonandry. The cultural model of monogamy may make it difficult for some counselors to help gay men through the process of accepting sexual activity outside the relationship. The case of John and Sam is somewhat typical in that the process evolved by each partner's experiencing the other's outside activity without any preparation. This process can work but it is difficult.

Another approach would be to suggest that the couple establish some private time, as suggested by Myers and Leggitt.[80] Private time is time set aside for each partner to do what he wants without accounting for the time in any way. The amount of private time may vary according to individual needs, but it does provide for a method whereby partners can maintain a sense of individuality. If the counselor is going to suggest this as a means of dealing with the sexual exclusivity issue, the initial taking of private time should be approached cautiously. One suggestion might be that each partner first take his private time and do something nonsexual, to allow one partner time to deal with the feelings aroused by wondering what the other one is doing. Once that issue is worked through, then the private time should be entirely inviolate, allowing each partner to do whatever he wants. This approach has helped some men deal with the sexual exclusivity issue.

Another way that some men have solved this issue is best explained by presenting the case history of Jeremy and David as it relates to monandry.[79] This relationship began casually. Jeremy met David in a gay bar. They were mutually attracted to each other and went to David's motel room where they had a very pleasant sexual encounter. Jeremy had recently broken up with a lover of 3 years and was feeling no desire to get involved in another relationship. However, when David asked to see him again the next evening, Jeremy agreed. They continued to meet sporadically for about 6 months.

Jeremy began to sense that David was getting serious about their relationship, and although Jeremy enjoyed David's company and their sexual activity together, Jeremy felt very strongly about not getting into another relationship. They began seeing each other more frequently, socializing together and enjoying each other's company. Eventually, Jeremy began to realize that the relationship was developing and he felt that they needed to resolve some issues. He reports that he became most uncomfortable when David first said, "I love you," to which Jeremy replied that he wanted David to know that he really liked him but was not interested in establishing a relationship.

As the first year ended, Jeremy realized that a strong bond was developing between them, so he asked David if they could discuss their relationship and what was possible for them. Jeremy said that he liked David very much and was beginning to feel that he was willing to make a 1-year commitment but only under the condition that neither expect sexual exclusivity.

As Jeremy reports, "I told David that I really enjoyed sex with other men and that I wasn't willing to give that up. I also knew that the gay couples I saw who tried to be exclusive didn't last long, so I figured it couldn't work that way even if I wanted to, which I didn't."

David agreed to the condition and they continued to see each other and to further develop the relationship. However, David kept hinting at a desire for sexual exclusivity with Jeremy. As Jeremy reports, "David would say things like, 'I love you so much I'd be willing to give up other men just to have only you,' or if I was going away on a trip without him, he'd say, 'Save it for me,' meaning, 'Don't have sex with anyone while you're gone.'" At each of those statements, Jeremy felt uncomfortable and began to deal with it by trying to get David to see it in a different light. The conversation would go something like the following:

J: Do you really love me?

D: Yes, of course I do.

J: Then you want me to be happy?

D: Of course.

J: Then why do you want me to promise that I won't have sex with anyone while I'm gone? Suppose I meet some hunky number and he's interested in me. If I don't have sex with him, I'll be very unhappy and I'll probably either break my promise or resent you for placing that restriction on me. I might not have sex with anyone, but that should be my choice and not something you impose on me.

D: Oh, I hadn't thought of it that way.

J: Well, I wish you'd at least think about it. I told you I really enjoy sex with other men and I want to feel that you love me enough to want me to do what will make me happy. I want your support and to know that its OK with you if I do.

D: Well, I'll think about it, but the thought of you having sex with someone else is not pleasant.

Jeremy kept this general line of reasoning going for about a year. David attempted to change his own thinking and eventually did. Jeremy kept trying because he knew that he wanted the relationship with David, but also knew that what he was saying was absolutely true. The relationship might not have lasted had David maintained his attitude. Jeremy would probably have engaged in sex with others, and would then very likely have felt guilty and restricted, leading to a sense of resentment that might have destroyed the relationship. They now not only have each other's support in their outside activity but also often become sexually aroused when hearing the explicit details.

There were other dynamics in the relationship between David and Jeremy that required that Jeremy make some compromises, but their way of dealing with the monandry issue was successful, and it might be helpful for others.

The issue is one of attitude change, which is not always simple, especially when the attitude is related to self-esteem,[81] as was David's. In counseling, the professional can suggest that the client examine his attitudes from a variety of perspectives. As in the case of Jeremy and David, sexual activity outside a couple may be viewed as positive for both the individual and the relationship. Pointing out that a desire for the partner's happiness might include support for his enjoying sexual activity with someone else is a vast departure from the societal dictate.

The fact that one is dealing with two men makes the possibility easier to explore than were it two women, because of the differing socialization around sexual activity. Men are taught that their sexual activity can be separated from deep, emo-tional attachment. However, they also are socialized to expect that their primary partner will not want or need outside activity. This is based on a heterosexual model in which one partner (the woman) is socialized to view sexual activity as the ultimate signifier of a deep emotional attachment and the other (the man) to expect that his partner will not want any other sexual partner, and if she does, it would mean that she no longer cared for him. This is certainly not the case for all heterosexuals. In fact, some report that their marriages are improved by sexual activity outside the relationship,[82] but the cultural message and the general socialization of males and females into men and women still carries the message that sexual activity has different meanings for the two.

In general, gay male couples eventually have to deal with the monandry issue. Most of them begin to accept nonmonandry as the way to meet their needs for sexual activity. However, there does appear to be an initial expectation for monandry in a relationship, as is evidenced by the fact that younger gay male couples are more likely to be monandrous than are older gay couples.[83] How, then, do gays manage to develop this attitude toward sexual activity that allows outside sexual partners?

Initially they don't. Apparently they have to go through a period in their lives where they have to face the issue by breaking up a relationship because one or both are not monandrous and then come in contact with some couples who have a nonmonandrous relationship. There is little doubt that they meet these nonmonandrous couples before their own relationships break up, but they usually approach that from a somewhat romanticized view of "well, we don't have to be like they are." Again, we must caution the reader to remain aware that there are some monandrous gay male couples. But for the overwhelming majority, the value that the society places on sexual exclusivity in a relationship must be rejected.

The following conversation between a 19-year-old, Dan, and a 60-year-old, Tom, may help to illustrate the situation. Dan is not in a relationship at present, having ended one about 4 months before this conversation took place. Tom has been in a primary relationship with Charlie for the past 25 years. The conversation took place in a gay male discussion group.

Dan: Do you mean that you and Charlie have other sexual partners?

Tom: Certainly we do! [He hesitates for a few seconds] Oh, we started out being faithful to each other and that lasted for many years, but for the past, oh, 10 years or so, we have been having sex with other men.

Dan: I can't believe it. Was it easy to do?

Tom: No, not at all. Initially it was very difficult for me. Charlie did it first and didn't tell me. Then one day I found out and I went to pieces. I really felt that it was all over. But we talked about it. I wanted to know why he had done it and he said something like, "Oh, because it was fun." I accused him of not loving me and of destroying everything we had built together, and he kept saying that it didn't have anything to do with his love for me. He was right, but I couldn't see it at the time.

Dan: What did you do?

Tom: Well, I stayed angry for about a week and then I decided I'd go out and try it. Charlie said that it was fine with him as long as I didn't fall in love with anyone.

Dan: And did you?

Tom: Did I what?

Dan: Go out?

Tom: Yes, it was about a couple of months later when I got cruised by this nice looking number and decided it looked like it might be fun, so I went with him.

Dan: And . . . ?

Tom: Well, it just sort of went on from there. We've both tricked a lot since then and even shared some of them. I'm having more fun than ever and I really think it helped our relationship. I don't think Charlie would have stayed with me if I had tried to stop it, and I certainly would have missed out on a lot.

Dan: Well, I still don't believe it, and I *know* I couldn't live like that. I want someone who's going to be mine alone.

Dan continued to maintain his desire for a monandrous relationship throughout the 6 months that the group met. He will probably follow the pattern that many before him have, going through an initial stage of several relationships, each one beginning on a monandrous contract and then breaking up, providing him with skills for establishing a relationship that will more closely meet his own needs. But then, he may also find someone who shares his desires and establish a long-term monandrous relationship.

Monandry. The most difficult pattern for gay male couples to maintain is one of monandry, because of the relatively easy access to casual sexual partners. In order to maintain a monandrous relationship, several issues need to be explored and clarified. The first is the importance of monandry to the relationship. A monandrous couple usually views sex as that one aspect of the relationship that will not be shared with others. They may share their money, house, car, time, ideas, and other activities with people outside the relationship, but not sexual activity. This means that the sexual activity is being viewed as the most important aspect of the relationship.

They must also decide on the way in which they will deal with their sexual arousal toward others. Understanding that sexual arousal to others does not mean sexual activity with others is important. "Lusting in the mind" is not necessarily the same as engaging in sexual activity with someone else. For most men, it is unreasonable to expect that being in a relationship will mean loss of physical desire for others. They may want to share their feelings of attraction to others with the partner or to keep it secret, depending on their individual ability to accept the difference between attraction and acting upon the attraction, but they should realize that attraction will inevitably occur.

They must also explore their ability to withstand the pressures from other gay men to be nonexclusive. When many other relationships are in existence without being sexually exclusive, it might be difficult to maintain one that is. They should be made aware that the pressures will exist.

Their sexual activity together may develop as Sam and John's did; that is, it may get boring. If the counselor discovers that the two men have developed a pattern of sexual activity every Monday, Wednesday, and Friday after the evening news, then they should consider breaking that pattern. They should also be cautioned about the possibility of reestablishing a similar one later. If they are always engaging in the same activity, then it would be appropriate to suggest that they get a copy of *The Joy of Gay Sex*[84] and read it together for some ideas. One method for introducing variety is for each partner to take the book, read through it, and when he finds something he might like to try, jot down the page number on a piece of paper. After each one has done this, they can compare numbers to see if any match and then try that activity. If no page number match, then they can discuss a compromise by taking one from each person's list, a sort of "Let's try one of yours this afternoon and one of mine on Saturday morning" approach.

In trying a new sexual activity, the couple should be cautioned about the confounding factors in trying anything new. The first time there will be concerns about how to do it and whether the instructions are being followed correctly. It may be difficult to focus on the feelings associated with the activity. If either doesn't enjoy it the first time, they should be encouraged to give it at least two more tries before deciding that they don't like it. By the third time, they will have overcome the initial concerns and will be able to evaluate the activity itself.

Finally, they should discuss a plan of action for renegotiating their monandrous contract. The two men who are in the relationship today will change over time, and part of that change might be a different attitude toward the limits of the relationship. One or both might find that the value placed on sexual exclusivity has altered, lessening its importance. They both should agree on ways of discussing that change should it occur. Otherwise, it might be the source of conflict in the relationship and could lead to its dissolution.

It is possible for gay men to have a loving, long-term, primary relationship and include monandry as one aspect. However, they must be able to discuss each of the points we have just described and to understand the importance they have placed on sexual activity. It is simply a matter of individual values and attitudes.

Summary

Gay men's relationships, as with other aspects of their lives, are varied. They are more similar to nongay relationships than different. It is unfortunate that most studies tend to focus on sexual activity and its accompanying issues. A relationship is much more than the sexual activity or sexual concerns or problems of the individuals. Gay men in primary relationships have to work, eat, buy groceries, and take care of the car(s). They are involved in politics, community issues, entertaining friends, and each other. They have to decide on the brand of toothpaste to buy, what color to paint the living room, and where to get the money to repair the roof. We, too, have been guilty of spending time in this section discussing the sexual aspects, but they appear to be somewhat foreign to nongays, are likely to be among the several issues that cause gay couples to seek help, and are also the source of some of the myths about gay relationships. However, the sexual aspects are just one part of the primary relationship.

Gay men fall in and out of love with the same intensity as heterosexual men. Their relationships may be easier to end legally than are marriages, but the emotional components are no different. As Tripp indicates, with agreement from recent researchers and our own observations, the "settled-in qualities of the [effective] homosexual couple tend to be precisely those which characterize the stable heterosexual relationship."[85]

However, being in a relationship is seldom easy or simple for anyone. Being in one that is stigmatized is even more difficult. The counselor working with gay male couples should be familiar with male sexuality, gay male subcultures, the pressures of a homophobic society, and the problems associated with any primary relationship. He or she must discard any parameters of an ideal effective relationship other than those that best suit the individuals involved.

In addition, anyone working with gay male couples should be familiar with the "stages" approach to counseling as developed by McWhirter and Mattison.[53] Their research shows that gay male relationships go through classical stage development, and their successful clinical practice, which is theoretically based on their stage theory, attests to the validity of their conclusions. It is a unique approach to the process of relationship development and deserves careful attention by anyone who will be counseling or providing therapy for gay male couples.

If the counselor is familiar with all these aspects of being male, gay, and in a relationship, he or she will be better able to work with a gay male couple in a manner that will more adequately meet their unique needs.

END NOTES

1. Jay, K., & Young, A. *The gay report*. New York: Summit Books, 1979, pp. 316-318; 362-365.
2. Otto, H. "Introduction." In H. Otto (Ed.), *The family in search of a future*. New York: Appleton-Century-Crofts, 1970, p.1.
3. Jourard, S. "Reinventing marriage: The perspective of a psychologist." In H. Otto, 1970, p. 48.
4. Simmel, G. "The isolated individual and the dyad." In K. Wolff (Ed. and trans.), *The sociology of Georg Simmel*. London: Free Press, 1950, p. 123.
5. Simmel, 1950, pp. 123-124.
6. See Simmel's discussion of the special characteristics of dyads that are different from larger relationship groups, pp. 118-114.
7. We have inferred this from our own observations and from the data on couples' financial considerations as reported in Bell, A., & Weinberg, M. *Homosexualities: A study of diversity among men and women*. New York: Simon & Schuster, 1978, p. 323; and from the absence of any reference to finances as a reason for couples breaking up as

reported in Saghir, M., & Robins, E. *Male and female homosexuality: A comprehensive investigation*. Baltimore: Williams & Wilkins, 1973, pp. 58; 227.
8. Jay & Young, 1979, pp. 313-315; 355-357.
9. Simmel, 1950, pp. 130-132.
10. Myers, L., & Leggitt, H. *Adultery and other private matters: Your right to personal freedom in marriage*. Chicago: Nelson-Hall, 1975.
11. Moses, A. *Identity management in lesbian women*. New York: Praeger, 1978.
12. Bell & Weinberg, 1978, pp. 387-397.
13. Jay & Young, 1979, pp. 328-329.
14. Jay & Young, 1979, p. 357.
15. Jay & Young, 1979, p. 329.
15a. See Curry, H., and Clifford, D. *A legal guide for lesbian and gay couples*. Reading, Mass.: Addison-Wesley, 1980 for samples of contracts.
16. Levinger, G. "Sources of marital dissatisfaction among applicants for divorce." *American Journal of Orthopsychology*, 1966, *36*, 807.
17. Jay & Young, 1979, p. 359.
18. Jay & Young, 1979, p. 121.
19. Jay & Young, 1979, p. 323, estimate that there were probably about the same number of monogamous and nonmonogamous lesbians in their sample, but they have no direct statistics on the issue. Their conclusion appears a bit tenuous since it is based on extrapolation from the number of sexual contacts their respondents had during the previous year. Observation of the lesbian community suggests that most couples probably start out with an assumption of sexual exclusivity, although the arrangement may not remain that way.
20. Gagnon, J., & Simon, W. *Sexual conduct: The social sources of human sexuality*. Chicago: Aldine, 1973, pp. 176-216.
21. Albro, J., & Tully, C. "A study of lesbian lifestyles in the homosexual micro-culture and the heterosexual macro-culture." *Journal of Homosexuality*, 1979, *4*(4), 341-354; Bell & Weinberg, 1978, p. 100. For discussion of alternatives to monogamy in the lesbian community, see Dilno, J. "Monogamy and alternative lifestyles." In G. Vida (Ed.), *Our right to love: A lesbian resource book*. Englewood Cliffs, N.J.: Prentice-Hall, 1978, pp. 56-59; and Lewis, S. *Sunday's women: A report on lesbian life today*. Boston: Beacon Press, 1979, pp. 66-82.
22. For other descriptions of lesbian relationships, see Jay & Young, 1979; Martin, D., & Lyon, P. *Lesbian/woman*. New York: Bantam Books, 1972, esp. pp. 91-139; Lewis, 1979, pp. 66-82; 85-96; Vida, 1978b, pp. 48-63; and Tanner, D. *The lesbian couple*. Lexington, Mass.: D.C. Health, 1978.
23. Tanner, 1978.
24. Tanner, 1978, refers to these as "traditional-complementary prototype" relationships.

25. For example, Jensen, M. "Role differentiation in female homosexual quasi-marital unions." *Journal of Marriage and the Family,* 1974, *36*(2), 360-367.

26. Jay & Young, 1979, p. 319, report that 59% of their sample said they never role played during sexual activity, and another 24% said they did so only rarely; 56% said they never role played in situations other than those related to sexual activity and another 33% said they did so in nonsexual situations only rarely. For more discussion of role playing in lesbian relationships and lesbians' attempts to avoid doing so see Lewis, 1979, pp. 36-42; Martin & Lyon, 1972, pp. 62-90; and Whitlock, K. "Striving toward equality in loving relationships." In Vida, 1978b, pp. 63-66.

27. For example, see Pam and Rusty's story in Adair, N., & Adair, C. *Word is out: Stories of some of our lives.* New York: Dell, 1978, pp. 43-54.

28. For example, see Adair & Adair, 1978, pp. 57-64; Lewis, 1979, various places throughout the text; Martin & Lyon, 1972, pp. 75-139; 197-200; and Wolf, D. *The lesbian community.* Berkeley: University of California Press, 1979, pp. 40-43.

29. Gagnon & Simon, 1973, p. 198.

30. Lewis, 1979, pp. 40-42.

31. Lewis, 1979, pp. 40-42; Martin & Lyon, 1972, pp. 75-139; Wolf, 1979, pp. 40-43.

32. Whitlock, 1978.

33. See Jay & Young, 1979, for a description of some such relationships.

34. Tanner, 1978, p. 90.

35. Tanner, 1978, p. 91.

36. Abbott, S., & Love, B. *Sappho was a right-on woman.* New York: Stein and Day, 1973, pp. 92-93.

37. Adair & Adair, 1978, pp. 59-60.

38. Adair & Adair, 1978, p. 63.

39. Martin & Lyon, 1972, pp. 74-75.

40. Moses, 1978, found that in her sample, of whom 88% had at least some and 55% had a distinct amount of heterosexual experience, better communication with a woman than with a man was considered the most important advantage to lesbian as compared with heterosexual relationships.

41. Sang, B. *Lesbian relationships: A struggle towards couple equality.* Paper presented at the American Psychological Association, San Francisco, 1977.

42. Peplau, L., Cochran, S., Rock, K., & Padesky, C. "Loving women: Attachment and automony in lesbian relationships." *Journal of Social Issues,* 1978, *34*(3), 7-27.

43. Sang, 1977, p. 5.

44. Peplau et al., 1978.

45. Peplau et al., 1978, p. 14.

46. Adair & Adair, 1978, pp. 127-128.

47. Adair & Adair, 1978, p. 64.

48. Toder, N. "Sexual problems of lesbians." In Vida, 1978b, p. 105.

49. Bell & Weinberg, 1978, 132-134; 137-138. Note on pp. 132 and 346 that their criteria excluded 29% of their sample.

50. Jay & Young, 1979, p. 339.

51. Bell & Weinberg, 1978, pp. 102; 320.

52. Jay & Young, 1979, p. 340.

53. McWhirter, D., & Mattison, A. *Stages: A developmental study of male homosexual relationships.* New York: St. Martin's Press, in press. Also, McWhirter, D. Personal communication, 4 September 1980.

54. Tripp, C. *The homosexual matrix.* New York: McGraw-Hill, 1975, p. 150.

55. Saghir & Robins, 1973, p. 55.

56. Saghir & Robins, 1973, p. 76; Bell & Weinberg, 1978, p. 370; Jay & Young, 1979, p. 340.

57. McWhirter, personal communication, 1980.

58. Saghir & Robins, 1973, p. 56; Bell & Weinberg, 1978, p. 92.

59. Sonenschein, D. "The ethnography of male homosexual relationships." *Journal of Sex Research,* 1968, *4*(2), 81-82; see also description of stage one of development in McWhirter & Mattison, in press.

60. Bell & Weinberg, 1978, pp. 102; 132.

61. Farrell, W. *The liberated man.* New York: Bantam Books, 1975, pp. xxix-xxx.

62. Jay & Young, 1979, p. 343.

63. Jay & Young, 1979, p. 346.

64. Jay & Young, 1979, p. 348.

65. Jay & Young, 1979, pp. 341-354.

66. Bell & Weinberg, 1978, p. 132.

67. Bell & Weinberg, 1978, p. 133.

68. Sonenschein, 1968, p. 81.

69. Jay & Young, 1979, p. 355.

70. Weinberg, M., & Williams, C. *Male homosexuals: Their problems and adaptations.* New York: Penguin Books, 1975, p. 334.

71. Weinberg & Williams, 1975, pp. 334-335.

72. Saghir & Robins, 1973, pp. 74-75; Bell & Weinberg, 1978, p. 325; Jay & Young, 1979, pp. 356-366.

73. Saghir & Robins, 1973, pp. 59-60; 64-65.

74. Hooker, E. "An empirical study of some relations between sexual patterns and gender identity in male homosexuals." In J. Money (Ed.), *Sex research: New developments.* New York: Holt, Rinehart & Winston, 1965, pp. 24-52.

75. Saghir & Robins, 1973, p. 60.

76. Saghir & Robins, 1973, p. 57; Tripp, 1975, pp. 154-155; Bell & Weinberg, 1978, pp. 102; Jay & Young, 1979, pp. 357-361.

77. McWhirter and Mattison have suggested the term *monandry* instead of *monogamy* because of the heterosexual marriage implications of the latter.

78. Saghir & Robins, 1973, p. 57.
79. From the case files of the authors.
80. Myers & Leggitt, 1975, pp. ix-x; 12-13; 50-63.
81. Katz, D. "The functional approach to the study of atti-
    tudes." *Public Opinion Quarterly,* 1960, *24,* 163-204.
82. Myers & Leggitt, 1975.
83. Saghir & Robins, 1973, p. 57; McWhirter, personal com-
    munication, 1980.
84. Silverstein, C., & White, E. *The joy of gay sex.* New York:
    Crown, 1977.
85. Tripp, 1975, p. 159.

PART THREE

Special issues in counseling gay clients

10

Third World[1] lesbians and gay men

There appears to be little research on Third World homoerotic people living in the United States. There are several possible reasons for this. One is a lack of understanding that Third World gays have some concerns and adaptations that are different from other gays. Another is that Third World gays are still very much hidden within their cultures and are not easily available for research. And still another is that most of the research on homoerotic people has been carried out by First World researchers who have been more concerned with First World homoerotic people. Whatever the reason, the fact remains that very little research is available on Third World gays.

GENERALITIES

There are several articles that either focus specifically on or include a discussion of Third World gays.[2-6] They all indicate that ethnic concerns are more important than sexual orientation. This is consistent with our belief that homoerotic people are socialized as men and women, within their cultural context, before they develop a lesbian or gay male identity. Third World gays are very much influenced by their own ethnic culture, and if they live in another country, then they must also be concerned with the ways in which members of their group are viewed in the predominant culture in which they live.

According to one report, there were 600 lesbians and gay men attending the National Gay/Lesbian Third World Conference in the winter of 1980.[7] The conference was organized to enable Third World gays to focus on issues that were important to them, such as sexuality, coming out, parenting, and health. Why a special conference for Third World homoerotic people? Primarily because they are concerned not only with the issue of gayness but also with the many issues associated with being a member of the Third World.[8]

BLACKS

Bell and Weinberg compared samples of Black lesbians and gay men to white lesbians and gay men and found some differences between the Black and white groups. Black gay men and lesbians were more likely to report feeling tension and loneliness but less likely to report feeling suicidal or seeking professional help for any emotional problems.[9] There were differences in frequency of specific sex acts and in preference for technique,[10] and Blacks were more religious.[11]

Weinberg and Williams compared their samples of Black and white gay men, and found that the Black men were more open about their homosexuality, less apt to expect discrimination because of their orientation, more apt to be in a sexually exclusive relationship, and were more self-accepting than were the white gay men.[12] Bass-Hass compared samples of Black and white lesbians and found that white lesbians entered a homoerotic relationship at an earlier age, were less likely to have had heterosexual contacts, and were less satisfied with their life situation than were Black lesbians.[13]

Acosta and Dyne found that the concerns of being Black were far more important to Black gays than were concerns of being gay. Acosta suggests that this is brought about by two very different forces. First is a very strong family tie. Blacks who had come out to their families had experienced little if any rejection. They were accepted as being family members first. However, he cautions against assuming that Blacks in general are tolerant or accepting of homoerotic behavior.[14] Those very families in which a lesbian or gay man was accepted still condemned homosexuality in general, viewing it as a white person's attempt to undermine the Black family.[15] Acosta suggests that the second force is one of fear, being afraid of being rejected by the Black community and subsequently forced into the white community where he or she would be unwelcome. Thus, the Black lesbian or gay man generally maintains a strong interest in his or her Black heritage.[16]

Dyne indicates that Black gays generally are not open about their gayness and are not likely to be involved in gay activism.[17] He agrees with Acosta's assessment of the strong intolerance for homoeroticism within the Black community. Mel Boozer, a Black sociologist who is openly gay, identifies two reasons for the intolerance toward Black gay males: a historical stereotype of inferiority for the Black male who then views the gay male as unmasculine, therefore inferior; and an existing shortage of marriageable males, which is further increased by those who are gay.[18]

Clayborne also discusses the extreme intolerance of homosexuality within the Black culture, identifying the source as twofold. First is the Black's acceptance of the "puritanical denunciation of homosexuality,"[19] based on the stereotype of homoerotic people as being inferior. Clayborne suggests that the prevalent stereotype of Blacks as inferior means that they need to find some other group to identify as inferior, and homoerotic people fill that need.[20] Second is the strong religiosity of Blacks. He indicates that Christian religions played a very positive role for Blacks for many years. Because those religions used the Bible to condemn homosexuality, Blacks were provided with a religious base for their intolerance.[19]

Cornwell's personal account of her experiences as a Black lesbian indicates further support for the notion that cultural influences override orientation. As she describes her feelings on becoming involved in the women's movement:

☐ It was a pleasant surprise to find that gay was considered good, by some womyn [sic] at least. Consequently, since I thought black was beautiful, I felt I had at last found my place under the sun. And so anxious was I to hold to that illusion, many months passed before I finally faced the truth—racism did exist in the movement.[21]

This attitude among white gays toward Black gays is also mentioned by Dyne,[17] indicating that the commonality of homoeroticism is insufficient to counteract the cultural attitude of racism.

MEXICAN-AMERICANS

Vasquez suggests that the problems of the Mexican-American homoerotic person depend on whether he or she is still living in a strongly Mexican culture with its polar-opposite gender role behavior. The more acculturated toward American values, the less problematic is the strict Mexican culture. She cites several examples of the ways in which the culture influences the lesbian or gay man. For example, those lesbians who are more acculturated into American ways are less likely to be involved in playing the "husband-wife" roles in their relationship.[22] Vasquez also cites several examples of the cultural influence on gay men, including one mother who would rather her son be homosexual than be married to a woman she didn't like; and several instances of men who are married but carry out the "macho" image by being the passive recipient of homosexual fellatio, engaging in it purely for the "physical" pleasure.[23]

SUMMARY

The literature available on Third World lesbians and gay men supports the notion that homoerotic behavior has little meaning outside of its cultural context. The counselor who is working with a

Third World homoerotic person must be familiar with not only the issues of being gay but also the issue of being gay *within a particular culture*.

The available research indicates that Black lesbian women and gay men experience little difficulty in acknowledging their orientation to family members, primarily because of the importance of the family within the Black culture, but do experience racism from gay whites. Mexican-Americans, however, are likely to experience very strong negative reactions if they come out to their families, especially if the family is still within the Mexican culture. We found no research on other Third World lesbians and gay men.

IMPLICATIONS FOR COUNSELING

Gochros, although focusing on the needs of Blacks, summarized the general responsibilities of the counselor in working with Third World lesbians and gay men.

> Race and sex are two of the most sensitive issues in our culture, and many White workers, saddled with both racial and sexual prejudice and misinformation, may well be functionally paralyzed in trying to deal with sexual issues with Black clients.[24]

We would like to add that "racial and sexual prejudice and misinformation" are not the sole province of white counselors. As Acosta indicates, Third World people, including counselors, may also possess those characteristics.[25] This means that in addition to evaluating his or her attitudes toward and information about homoerotic people, the counselor must also evaluate his or her racist attitudes and knowledge about the client's culture.[26]

If the counselor is white, the initial session(s) will primarily be one(s) in which the counselor will be tested to find out if there are any indications of prejudice. As Gochros points out, "Anger and resentment among clients runs very high. Suspicion of White workers is manifest."[27] Almost *any* gay client will approach a counselor from suspicion of prejudice, unless the client has reason to believe that the counselor is also homoerotic. The Third World gay client will have double suspicion. He or

she will expect the counselor to exhibit prejudice based on both orientation and race. It is the counselor's responsibility to be aware of being tested by the client and to be aware of personal indications of prejudice.

For example, if the counselor is white and the client is Black, ignoring that difference is tantamount to acknowledging the stereotype of inferiority. The counselor might try saying something such as "It's obvious from our skin color that we are different racially and for some people that, in itself, presents problems. I'm wondering if there are any ways you see that difference as affecting our interaction." This may sound a bit blunt to some counselors, but it certainly does not allow the issue to smolder and interfere, unacknowledged, at a later time.

If the Third World client is angry and resentful, that will have to be the initial focus of counseling before any other issues can be addressed. If the counselor perceives either of these feelings in the client, it is important to acknowledge that perception, find out if it is true, and then either work on that before beginning any work on the other concerns or work on both simultaneously.

Some counselors use techniques that require that the client "self-disclose." These will not usually work with the Third World person, especially if that person is Black and male. One social work professor, who describes himself as "a man of color," has the following sign on the wall in his office:

You Cannot Blackenize American Psychoanalytic Theories By Attempting to Give "Soul" to Freud.

Third World people have generally learned that self-disclosure makes them more vulnerabale than they already are by virtue of their skin color, and their self-protection requires that they not disclose "self."

Counseling Third World lesbians and gay men requires knowledge of female and male sexuality as it develops within their own culture as well as the ways in which the dominant culture affects that development. The counselor must also be cognizant of both cultures' attitudes toward homoeroticism.

GENERAL NOTE

An international directory of Third World lesbian and gay resources is being compiled and maintained by Dr. Billy Jones, Executive Director, The National Coalition of Black Gays, PO Box 57236, West End Station, Washington, D.C. 20037 (available after November 1981). In addition, Henry Weimhoff, 10 West 76th Street, Apt. 1C, New York, N.Y. 10023 has compiled and maintains a current bibliography on the topic, and it is available for a small fee ($1.00 at the time this book was printed).

END NOTES

1. The term *Third World* is an economic as well as ethnic term. The Third World countries are those in primary economy, such as Latin America, Asia, and Africa. They are essentially "underdeveloped" countries. Second World countries are the socialist and communist blocs, not including China, which is Third World. First World countries are the democracies and Europe. Third World people are those who come from those countries. They may be living in a First World country, such as the United States, but they are still considered Third World people.
2. Acosta, E. "Affinity for Black heritage: Seeking lifestyle within a community." Washington, D.C.: *The Blade,* 11 October 1979, pp. A-1; A-25. "Glimpses of Black gay lives—part II: Yearning for faith and love." Washington, D.C.: *The Blade,* 21 November 1979, pp. B-1; B-5. "Gay and Black in D.C.: Emerging dialogue between races." Washington, D.C.: *The Blade,* 6 December 1979, pp. B-1; B-5.
3. Vasquez, E. "Homosexuality in the context of the Mexican-American culture." In D. Kunkel (Ed.), *Sexual issues in social work: Emerging concerns in education and practice.* Honolulu: University of Hawaii School of Social Work, 1979, pp. 131-147.
4. Clayborne, J. "Blacks and gay liberation." In K. Jay & A. Young (Eds.), *Lavender culture.* New York: Jove/HBJ, 1978, pp. 458-465.
5. Dyne, L. "Is DC becoming the gay capitol of America?" *The Washingtonian,* September 1980, pp. 96-101; 133-141.
6. Carrier, J. " 'Sex-role preference' as an explanatory variable in homosexual behavior." *Archives of Sexual Behavior,* 1977, *6*(1), 53-65.
7. Jones, B. "Being black and gay—both issues must be faced." *Sexuality Today Newsletter,* 4 February 1980, pp. 2-3.
8. Jones, 1980, p. 3.
9. Bell, A., & Weinberg, M. *Homosexualities: A study of diversity among men and women.* New York: Simon & Schuster, 1978, pp. 207; 215.
10. Bell & Weinberg, 1978, pp. 108-110.
11. Bell & Weinberg, 1978, pp. 151-152.
12. Weinberg, M., & Williams, C. *Male homosexuals: Their problems and adaptations.* New York: Penguin Books, 1975, pp. 371-372.
13. Bass-Hass, R. "The lesbian dyad: Basic issues and value systems." *Journal of Sex Research,* 1968, *4*(2), 126.
14. Such assumption was made by Weinberg and Williams (1975, pp. 372; 387) based on their own findings of self-acceptance and openness of the Black gay male within his culture and based on the findings reported in Staples, R. "The sexuality of black women." *Sexual Behavior,* 1972, *2*(4), 4-15. However, Acosta and Dyne indicate that the assumption of general cultural acceptance from reports of familial acceptance is incorrect.
15. Acosta, 11 October 1979, p. A-25. See also Clayborne, 1978, pp. 458-465.
16. Acosta, 11 October 1979, pp. A-1; A-25.
17. Dyne, 1980, p. 138.
18. Boozer, M. Cited in Dyne, 1980, p. 138.
19. Clayborne, 1978, p. 459.
20. Clayborne, 1978, pp. 458-459.
21. Cornwell, A. "Three for the price of one: Notes from a gay Black feminist." In Jay & Young, 1978, p. 470.
22. Vasquez, 1979, p. 144.
23. Vasquez, 1979, pp. 139-142.
24. Gochros, J. "Sex and race: Some further issues for social work practitioners." In Kunkel, 1979, p. 168.
25. Acosta, 6 December 1979, p. B-5.
26. As an example of the influence of folklore on Black gay men within a Black subculture, see Money, J., & Hosta, G. "Negro folklore of male pregnancy." *Journal of Sex Research,* 1968, *4*(1), 34-50.
27. Gochros, 1979, p. 170.

11

The special problems of rural gay clients

A. ELFIN MOSES and JANET A. BUCKNER

Homosexuals have won a certain degree of acceptance in the large cities. But the final victory for homosexual freedom will have to be won in the small towns. It is easy enough to grant acceptance to a group of people one sees oneself as never having to associate closely with. It calls for a greater degree of understanding, for a true change of mind, to welcome such a group of people into the intimate society of a small town.[1]

There are special problems encountered in working with gay clients in rural settings that are caused by the special features of rural heterosexual communities and the gay communities within them. A number of authors have pointed out that rural areas are likely to be characterized by conservatism, traditionalism, religious fundamentalism, isolation of atypical or deviant members, resistance to change, high visibility, lack of confidentiality, and a tendency to view problems as personal rather than system based.[2] Two major studies of attitudes toward gays have found that attitudes are most likely to be negative among rural individuals, especially those in the rural South and Midwest.[3] Although these features of rural areas certainly affect intervention with nongay clients,

Reprinted from *Human Services in the Rural Environment* **5**(5): 22-27, September-October 1980.

they have an even greater impact on intervention with rural gays. To be effective, helping professionals working with gay clients must take account of the realities of rural living and modify their interventions accordingly.

IMPACT OF THE HETEROSEXUAL COMMUNITY

Rural people have "a strong moralistic sense of what is desirable behavior and belief,"[4] and it is considered desirable to uphold established tradition and the institutions of family, church, and school.[5] It is hard for gay people to find a place within these traditions and institutions where they are accepted. In fact, a gay lifestyle would be seen by most rural heterosexuals as being in complete contradiction to all they value. Gay people do not get married, so they do not fit into traditional family life; and they are considered to be highly immoral and sinful, so they certainly are not welcome in church. Furthermore, some gay individuals don't conform to "appropriate" gender role stereotypes, another breach of rural tradition.

Lack of acceptance

Gay people are rarely well accepted within a rural nongay community. Because of the conservatism of the rural milieu, those working with gay clients must realize that many of the community support systems relied upon in treatment with non-gays, such as those discussed by Nooe,[6] are not available to gay clients. Family, nongay friends, church members, and neighbors are unlikely to rally to the aid of a gay client if they know she or he is gay as they would for a nongay person. In fact, they may be actively hostile. The anticipation of hostility causes most rural gays to try not to be identified and to be afraid of what will happen if they are identified.[7]

Fear of discovery

☐ No one who has not had the experience of discovering he is homosexual in a tightly knit community, where traditional values are the only values and moral issues sort themselves tidily into black and white, can quite grasp how difficult it is. Mere survival is hard; survival with a semblance of self-esteem is harder, since one has grown up with the same values that now condemn one. And standing up to be counted—alone—to face seemingly universal opprobrium is more than can be expected of most people. I know I would never have had the courage to do it if I had settled in Ravenna—or almost any other small town in America. Smalltown life imposes conformity; I am certain I would have succumbed and spent my whole life trying to pass as straight.[8]

Rural gays are understandably likely to be worried about being discovered to be gay. The conservatism of rural communities, combined with small size and consequent lack of anonymity, gives the gay person reason to be anxious. Gays are often afraid that someone will figure out their sexual preference by seeing them in the "wrong" place (such as a gay bar) or with the "wrong" kind of people, namely, people known to be gay. One person describes such a situation:

☐ I live in a town of about 200 people. I work in a city of about 5,000. I live in fear that someone will find out that I am gay. I am an elementary school teacher. . . . I love my work with a passion and would be lost away from the classroom and children. . . . I am professional in my work. I avoid any involvement with my students that would be construed as sexual. . . . I want to

actively seek other homosexuals in this area, but I have had to be painfully careful. One false move could lead to a disgrace to my family who could never accept such a thing. My career would be destroyed.[9]

Since this is a common experience for rural gays, counselors should not be surprised to find gay clients demonstrating high anxiety. Clients may be particularly anxious about entering treatment, fearing that if they do, their sexual preference will become known. Although urban gays also worry about being found out, they are more likely to be anonymous and less likely to be dependent on the nongay community for support.

Generalized anxiety

The fear of discovery that rural gays experience may be so generalized that almost all social situations become difficult. Contacts with nongays are frightening because of the possibility of somehow giving oneself away and because of the constant strain of attempting to be someone one is not, of hiding a part of oneself. Contacts with other gays are threatening because of the fear that a nongay person will observe the individual in a compromising situation, and the word will be out. Even though anxiety may be overgeneralized, mental health workers should realize that this is an appropriate survival response to a hostile environment rather than a symptom of an underlying disturbance.

It is up to the counselor to help the client learn to tell the difference between those situations that require caution about revealing sexual preference and those that do not and to teach the client survival skills for functioning in a nongay milieu that do not involve anxiety. For example, gay clients often worry that they can be easily identified as gay by their co-workers when this often is not the case. In all likelihood, an adult gay person who has been functioning within a community for a period of time has either been identified as gay and is accepted or is passing successfully. The ideal situation is for the client to be realistic about the dangers of being identified without driving herself or himself crazy with worry about it.

Isolation from the nongay community

Rural gays are very likely to feel isolated from the surrounding nongay community. The problems that Rhenisch[10] reports for rural feminists exist for gays as well, and particularly for gay women: intense isolation, lack of communication with other gays, feelings of hopelessness and of having no options combine with other social limitations to create a difficult situation. This sense of isolation and the hopelessness that may spring from it have several causes. For native residents of a given area, the most important cause is the exclusion of the gay person from the primary sources of social support such as family and church.

Even gays who remain unidentified are likely to feel isolated. The attempt to appear nongay often causes the gay individual to avoid or limit contacts with other gays. Being gay also means that a person doesn't share many interests and activities that nongays have in common, such as the whole social complex built around marriage and family. As a rule, gay people raised in rural areas naturally share the values of the nongay community, and this probably means that they share the attitudes of heterosexuals toward gays. It is lonely and frightening to know that others view people like oneself negatively, to share some of those negative views, and to be shut off not only from other gays but from the nongay community as well.[11]

Isolation is, in some degree, an almost unavoidable reality for members of any minority in a rural area, and particularly so for gays. However, there are some steps that helping professionals can take that may help. One important thing to do is to point out to the client that a feeling of isolation does not mean that there is anything wrong with him or her, but is rather a fact of life for anyone in a rural area who is seen as different.

If there is a gay community, it will be helpful for the worker to be familiar with contact persons within the community to use as referral sources. The gay individual does need to realize, however, that the gay community will not necessarily solve the problem of isolation (see also pp. 177-179).

For lesbian women, local women's groups may prove to be places where they can find social contacts with other women. They should be careful in being open about their lesbianism in such groups, however, because in rural areas, women's organizations may not be as receptive to openly gay members as they are in more tolerant urban areas.

Gays should certainly consider the option of leaving a rural area for a more accepting urban location. This may be a frightening idea for someone raised in a rural area, and it may be unpleasant to think of moving to an urban environment. Gay clients should be encouraged to travel to nearby cities or larger urban areas if at all possible to see what it is like and to be better able to weigh the advantages of rural and urban gay lifestyles. The practitioner who works with gay clients will ideally have contacts within the local gay community who can suggest resources within the larger urban areas so that a gay client is not left completely on his or her own. Men's and women's bars, restaurants, women's coffeehouses and bookstores, as well as gay switchboards, the Metropolitan Community Church, and various university-based organizations usually advertise in gay publications, and some, such as switchboards, hotlines, and the MCC are listed in the phone book. Information on many of these resources is usually available through any gay community contact.

Some gay clients want to live in a rural area but have trouble because they live in the town or region where they grew up. If this is the case, a move to another rural area away from immediate family and childhood friends may solve the problem of social isolation. If the client is not continually worrying that parents or childhood friends will discover her or his gayness, then integration into both nongay and gay communities may be easier.

We cannot stress enough the importance of helping rural gays find out that there are options open to them. For some, experiencing the hectic pace of urban living for a few weekends is enough to convince them that it is preferable to create a positive

176

lifestyle in a rural location. Others feel better knowing that there are support groups available in urban areas if they want to use them. There are some, however, who will want to leave a rural area and will feel better knowing that this is something they can plan to do.

Lack of information on the part of the nongay community

This is much more of a problem in rural than in urban areas and is closely related to rural conservatism and the relative isolation of rural areas. Neither gays nor nongays in rural areas are as likely to be aware of and have knowledge about alternative lifestyles as their urban counterparts. In the first place, rural areas simply do not support the lifestyle diversity that urban areas do. There is instead a "homogeneity of history, identity and lifestyle . . . [that] often translates into a strong orientation to conformity and an intolerance of deviation."[4]

Second, because of the lack of support for lifestyle diversity, deviations from the norm that do exist are not readily visible. Media coverage of events concerning gays may either be totally absent, or if available, biased in a negative way. Rural nongays may be unwilling to read or learn about the problems gays face or to believe information that does not confirm beliefs already held. Furthermore, those gay men and women who would be most likely to be visible are likely to leave or be driven out of the community.

Third, there is a lack of books, movies, magazines, and other sources of information about gays. Rural bookstores and libraries are undoubtedly less likely to carry controversial material about gays and gay lifestyles, and there are not usually gay or women's bookstores available in rural areas. Films that present gay people accurately may be ignored by or run only briefly in rural theatres. Even if literature and films are made available, those gays who most need the information may be afraid to use these sources, and nongays are likely to avoid them as well.

This lack of information contributes to the sense of isolation of gays in a real way, as well as to poor self-image and lack of awareness of possible alternative gay lifestyles and of the positive aspects to being gay. Fortunately, there are a number of resources available to gays that will help provide both contacts and information, among them national organizations, magazines, books, and travel guides. Helping professionals should be able to direct gays to these.[12]

National organizations and resources for gays

Rural gay professionals particularly may find contacts through professional gay organizations that will help them feel less isolated. Many professionals do not realize that a number of professions now have gay organizations or caucuses. Some of these are: Association of Gay Psychologists, Caucus of Gay and Lesbian Counselors, Caucus of Gay Public Health Workers, Gay Academic Union, Gay Anthropologists, Gay Nurses' Alliance, National Lawyers Guild Gay Caucus, the Task Force on Gay Liberation of the American Library Association, and the Association of Gay Social Workers.

Gay clients who feel particularly isolated from their church, as many rural clients do, can be referred to the Metropolitan Community Church (MCC), a national church originated to serve the gay community. The MCC has branches in many cities, and members are willing to provide outreach services to gays. There are also a number of other religious organizations that address the spiritual needs of gays. Among them are organizations from many of the major denominations, including Baptist, Episcopalian, Roman Catholic, Eucharistic Catholic, Friends, Mennonite, Methodist, Mormon, Lutheran, Presbyterian, and Unitarian.

THE RURAL GAY COMMUNITY

The impact of rural culture on individual gays naturally extends to the gay community as a whole. Many of the problems rural gays face are exacerbated by the small size, lack of diversity, and extreme secretiveness of the gay community. In places where such communities exist, they may consist almost entirely of small, isolated, and exclusive groups of men and women. There may be no local gathering place, such as a bar, restaurant, or coffee house, where gays can go to socialize openly. Like the rural nongay community, the rural gay community does not have as much diversity of lifestyles as would be found in an urban community. There are few rural gays who are open about their sexual preference, and they are often excluded from groups of gays who are "in the closet" and are generally socially avoided by them.

Isolation from the gay community

Gay clients may be isolated from both the nongay and gay communities. Isolation from the gay community can occur for a couple of reasons. First, the individual gay person who is just identifying herself or himself as gay or the newcomer to a rural area may have difficulty finding a group of people with whom to establish social ties. The size of the rural gay community is limited, and many members may be so well hidden that they are difficult for an individual to identify. Second, the limited number of gay people may make it difficult for a gay person to find others with whom there is much in common except the fact of gayness. This, combined with social isolation from the nongay community, can understandably lead to depression.

The helping professional must realize several things about this situation before he or she can be of help. Being out of contact with other gay people is a lonely experience. Most gay people spend a large amount of their social time with other gays, especially those of the same gender.[13] Not being able to be around other gay people often means that one is seldom able to completely relax and be open about one's sexual preference. It is not unreasonable for a gay person to want very much to make contact with other gays and to be anxious and depressed if that contact is not available.

Helping professionals must also understand that, contrary to popular heterosexual belief, all gays are not alike, and gay people are not consumed with interest in sexual activity.[14] It is not enough for a gay person just to have contact with others

who are gay. Like nongays, gay people have friendship preferences and are not satisfied just having sexual contacts with other gay people. Helping professionals should not expect that contact with other gays will automatically solve all of a client's social needs.

Isolation from other gays is a potentially serious problem for rural gay clients. Along with fear of discovery, isolation in one form or another is probably one of the major causes of depression and anxiety among rural gays. The worker should be prepared to help the client assess the extent of his or her isolation and what it is based on, and understand that being isolated from other gay people who are compatible is a realistic cause for both anxiety and depression. Gay clients sometimes think that there is something wrong with *them* when they can't make social contacts that they enjoy, and do not realize that it is a lack of gay people to choose from that is at least part of the problem.

Related to the problem of general social isolation is the inevitable shortage of appropriate partners. The consequence is that some people end up without partners while others end up forming relationships out of desperation or staying in relationships that are no longer functioning well.

The role of the counselor in helping the client cope with social isolation is twofold. First, the client's ability to utilize available resources must be assessed. Because of appropriate role models, lack of visible gays to emulate, and fear about being discovered, rural gay clients may be lacking in appropriate social skills necessary to meet other gay people. A gay man, for example, may be afraid to go to a gay bar to meet other men because he does not know what will happen or how to act. Once in a bar, he may be afraid to speak to other men there. A lesbian woman may be afraid to go to a local gay women's coffee house or other meeting place because she thinks she will be observed going in or because, like her male counterpart, she does not know how to act or how to introduce herself to others. If these kinds of social skills are lacking, a gay client will not be able to take advantage of any resources that are available. It is then up to the counselor to help the client learn appropriate social skills for meeting others in the gay community.

The counselor's second function is to help the client realistically assess and come to terms with the realities of rural gay community life. In some cases, the best solution is for the person to move to an area with a larger gay population. If the client cannot or does not want to do this, there are other options, some of which were mentioned earlier. As far as social contacts are concerned, the client should be encouraged to explore resources in the closest city with a gay community, to attempt to contact other gays in the immediate area, and to form friendships within the nongay community.

The problem of finding a satisfactory love relationship may be more difficult to solve. It is always a good idea to find out whether the client is actually ready for a long-term love relationship or is feeling pressured by loneliness, a sense of personal inadequacy, or by friends who believe everyone should be involved with someone. The pressures exerted by the heterosexual marriage model are such that gays may believe they should be involved in love relationships when what they really want most are friendships and perhaps sexual contacts. Sometimes pointing this out is sufficient to allow the client to relax and take some time seeking out and forming friendships rather than rushing into or hanging onto a dysfunctional relationship.

Effect on self-image

Although there is no information comparing the self-image of rural and nonrural gays, our experiences in rural settings indicate that rural gays, particularly those raised in rural areas, may suffer from poor self-image. The lack of information about gays and gay culture in rural settings means that gays who live in these areas are subject to all the negative myths and misconceptions traditionally held about gay people by nongays. If they are exposed only to the sensationalism of the news

media or traditional religious, legal, medical, psychiatric, and lay opinions, they will have an exceedingly negative and quite incorrect view of what it means to be gay.

Rural gay men may believe that gay men are child molesters, instinctively or innately "mannered," sex-obsessed, and sadomasochistic. Lesbian women may worry that they are oversexed or undersexed, that they must automatically take either a "butch" or "femme" role in relationships, or that they secretly want to go to bed with their mothers. Both men and women may believe that they are sinful, sick, neurotic, unable to maintain relationships, and so forth.

To combat such misconceptions and the lack of accurate information (and plethora of prejudiced material) from which they grow, it is imperative that the counselor be familiar with the current available literature on gays, be prepared to educate gay clients about what it *really* means to be gay, and feel comfortable with the conception of homosexuality and lesbianism as potentially normal, functional, and healthy. It is our belief, and the belief of other mental health professionals, that if the worker does not feel as comfortable helping someone become a healthy gay person as she or he does helping someone become a healthy heterosexual, that person should not be working with gay clients.[15]

LACK OF ORGANIZATIONS AND SERVICES FOR RURAL GAYS

Health and mental health services for rural gays are usually either poor or nonexistent. Davenport and Davenport have pointed out that a major problem in helping rural rape victims is provision of services, because rural communities may not perceive such services as necessary and desirable.[16] The same is true for rural gay clients. The rural gay community is seldom large enough or sufficiently well organized to provide its own health and mental health services, and it is highly unlikely that rural nongay communities will see special services for gays as desirable or that they would have the resources to provide them if they did. Mental health professionals with the skills and training to work effectively with gay clients are scarce. Some may be unwilling to work with gay clients because they fear guilt by association. Most nongays are certainly unwilling to advocate openly for gay rights or gay services, and gay helping professionals are often even less likely to want to do so because of their own fear of exposure.

There is also a lack of organizations and services provided by and for gays in rural areas. In larger urban areas, there are inevitably bars, restaurants, coffeehouses, businesses, and cultural events either specifically for or clearly accepting of gay clientele. There is also a wide variety of and ease of access to various types of information about gays in bookstores, libraries, record stores, and the like. This is rarely the case in rural areas. Not only are there fewer gays in rural areas to provide economic support for gay services, but those in residence are sometimes afraid to provide such support or even to patronize gay services and social or cultural events for fear of being identified.

One consequence of this is that members of the gay community, particularly those who remain "in the closet," are likely to be out of touch with the rapidly growing gay rights movement, the larger national gay community, and the increasing amount of information and literature about gays. The national lesbian community, for example, produces books, magazines, and records that speak directly to gay women. Gays in rural areas who do not have available, do not know how to find, or are afraid to participate in available gay activities not only miss out on information, but are also deprived of the sense of gay culture, pride, and community that these resources provide.

Ideally, of course, mental health professionals in rural areas would be advocates of and spokespersons for gay rights, and this may be happening slowly in some areas. Until gay rights are a reality, however, and until rural attitudes change, services for gays in rural areas will be minimal, and gay people will continue to be afraid to use those that exist. For some gays, the risk of coming out of the closet even far enough to attend a concert or buy a book about gay people is too threatening, and their preference should be respected. For other gay clients, however, the most healthy alternative may indeed be to begin to be more open about their gayness in small ways, such as increased participation in gay activities, getting up the nerve to buy a book about gay people, or going to a gay bar. In whatever way the gay client handles this, one of the main objectives should be for the client to develop a positive image of self as a gay person.

SUMMARY AND CONCLUSIONS

We have painted a rather gloomy picture of the rural gay lifestyle, and we have done so for a reason. In order to work effectively with rural gay clients, helping professionals must understand the kinds of problems and pressures that both they and their clients can expect to face in a rural setting. Ignorance of these problems and pressures can easily lead counselor and client into unjustified assumptions about the client's mental health and into nonproductive attempts at intervention.

Problems and pressures notwithstanding, however, many rural gay clients are happy with their lifestyle and are highly functional within the rural setting. The goal of the worker should not simply be for the client to "get by" or to learn to adjust. It is quite possible for gay clients who really want to live in rural areas to enjoy doing so, not just to tolerate it.

We certainly advocate helping clients who want to leave rural areas to do so. For some, the thought of being able to move to a different location provides a positive and exciting goal to work toward. Those gay people who want to stay in rural locations should be strongly encouraged and helped to create as satisfactory a lifestyle as possible. We believe that gay people belong in rural areas and can fit into rural community life. We have tried to suggest some ways that helping professionals can make this possible by being willing to view gayness as a positive life choice and by providing information, resources, and support to rural gay clients.

180

END NOTES

1. Brown, H. *Familiar faces, hidden lives*. New York: Harcourt Brace Jovanovich, 1976, p. 107.

2. Denman, J. "Problems of rural areas." In H. Johnson (Ed.), *Rural human services: A book of readings*. Itasca, Ill.: F.E. Peacock, 1980; DiNitto, D., & Hernandez, S. "Alcoholism services in rural areas: Implications for social work education." In J. Davenport III, J.A. Davenport, & R. Wiebler (Eds.), *Social work in rural areas*. Laramie: University of Wyoming School of Social Work, 1980; Johnson, L. "Human service delivery patterns in non-metropolitan communities." In Johnson, 1980; Kirkland, J., & Irey, K. "Confidentiality: Issues and dilemmas in rural practice." In E. Buxton (Ed.), *2nd National Institute on Social Work in Rural Areas Reader*. Madison: University of Wisconsin Extension, 1977; Rhenish, L. "Is a feminist mood arising in rural America?" In Johnson, 1980; Schott, M. "Casework: Rural." In Johnson, 1980; Weber, G. "Preparing social workers for practice in rural social systems." In Johnson, 1980.

3. Levitt, E., & Klassen, A., Jr., "Public attitudes toward homosexuality: Part of a 1970 survey by the Institute of Sex Research." *Journal of Homosexuality*, 1974, *1*(1), 29-43; Nyberg, K., & Alston, J. "Analysis of public attitudes toward homosexual behavior." *Journal of Homosexuality*, 1976/1977, *2*(2), 99-107.

4. DiNitto & Hernandez, 1980, p. 112.

5. Kaplan, B. *Blue Ridge: An Appalachia community in transition*. West Virginia University, Office of Research and Development, Appalachian Center, 1971; Weber, 1980.

6. Nooe, R. "De-institutionalization in rural areas." *Human Services in the Rural Environment*, 1980, *5*(1), 17-20.

7. Crew, L. "Just as I am: Growing up gay." *Southern Exposure*, 1977, *5*(1), 59-65.

8. Brown, 1976, p. 107.

9. Jay, K., & Young, A. *The gay report*. New York: Summit Books, 1979, p. 705.

10. Rhenisch, 1980, p. 35.

11. Crew, 1980.

12. Perhaps the best single source of information on services, churches, organizations, publications, bars, businesses, and accommodations for gays is the *Gayellow Pages, National Edition*. This volume, published twice yearly, is continually updated and provides a remarkable national listing of resources for the gay community. The publication is also invaluable for the helping professional who works with gay clients. The volume is published by Renaissance House, Box 292, Village Station, New York, N.Y. 10014, and costs approximately $5.00. Another excellent source with which helping professionals should be familiar is the National Gay Task Force (NGTF), 80 Fifth Avenue, New York, N.Y. 10011. NGTF publishes, among other things, a *Gay and Lesbian-Feminist Organizations* list, *Gay Professional Organizations and National Caucuses* list, and is also a source of information on religious organizations, groups for gay parents, and for parents of gays. Lists of *Gay Bookstores and Mail Order Services, U.S. and Canada (25¢)* and *Student Gay Groups, U.S. and Canada (50¢)* are available prepaid from National Gay Student Center, 2115 S St., NW, Washington, D.C. 20008.

13. Jay & Young, 1979, pp. 218-220; 232-233; Bell, A., & Weinberg, M. *Homosexualities: A study of diversity among men and women*. New York: Simon & Schuster, 1978, pp. 171-179.

14. See Chapter 8, "Lesbian and Gay Male Sexual Activity," in this book.

15. Davison, G. "Homosexuality and the ethics of behavioral intervention." *Journal of Homosexuality*, 1977, *2*(3), 195-204; Silverstein, C. "Homosexuality and the ethics of behavioral intervention: Paper 2." *Journal of Homosexuality*, 1977, *2*(3), 205-211.

16. Davenport, J., & Davenport, J. III. "The rural rape crisis center: A model." *Human Services in the Rural Environment*, 1979, *1*(1), 29-39; Davenport, J., & Davenport, J. III. "Training volunteers for rural rape crisis services." In T. Morton and R. Edwards (Eds.), *Training in the human services* (Vol. 2). Knoxville: University of Tennessee, Office of Continuing Social Work Education, 1980.

12

Confidentiality

J.L. BERNARD

You have been seeing Mrs. Myra Harris in individual psychotherapy for the past 3 months, during which time she has made good progress on her complaint of chronic, if mild, depression. It has become apparent that a major factor in this depression has been a singularly unhappy marriage to a man who drinks heavily and is often abusive toward her. Mrs. Harris has been secretly involved in a lesbian affair with a neighbor for some time, and recently decided to file for divorce. She has realized that her sexual orientation is gay, but is afraid to "come out" until after the divorce, because she is determined to gain custody of her 3-year-old daughter. To this end, she has asked you to testify in court as to her "fitness" as a mother. Because there is little question in your mind that Mrs. Harris would clearly be the better single parent, you have agreed.

You are on the witness stand, where Mrs. Harris' lawyer has just finished eliciting your expert testimony to the effect that she would make an excellent mother. The judge has intervened with several questions, and it is your impression that he is sympathetic to Mrs. Harris' position. Her husband's lawyer approaches the witness stand, smiles warmly and says, "To the best of your knowledge, isn't Mrs. Harris a lesbian, and isn't she in fact sexually involved with another woman at this time?"

Will you have to answer, or can Mrs. Harris'

lawyer successfully object that anything his client may have told you about her sexual behavior and/or preferences was said in confidence?

Most mental health professionals are aware of, and committed to, a belief that what clients tell them is confidential. Many of them would be surprised to learn that their ethical concept of confidentiality may have no significance whatever in a court of law. Whether you will be required to answer the lawyer's question depends on your professional affiliation (for example, marriage counselor, physician, social worker, psychologist), the state in which you practice, and a host of other considerations.

CONFIDENTIALITY AND PRIVILEGE

The concept of confidentiality has its roots in ethical standards, and in a tradition of the mental health professions that certain matters discussed in the privacy of a psychotherapeutic relationship should never be repeated. This is unquestionably a sound therapeutic principle because it is improbable that many clients would feel free to discuss the most secret aspects of their private lives without some assurance that what is said would go no further. However, as important as confidentiality may be in a therapist's office, the concept is without meaning in a court of law. Rather, the controlling principle is "privilege."

In our system of justice there is a fundamental

belief that if all the facts are submitted truthfully to the court, the case will be decided fairly, and that, to the extent that certain facts are concealed, justice may well be thwarted. However, this same system of justice also recognizes that certain communications should be considered so private and intimate that to reveal them in court would probably do more harm than good. Thus, there is a tension between two governing principles: the need to know all the facts, and the need to protect certain communications. As is the case with most conflicts of principle, our legal system has evolved a compromise position in which certain communications are considered privileged (that is, they need not be revealed in court) whereas others are not. It is important for members of the various mental health professions to know on which side of the line they fall.

Well before the colonies were settled, the origins of our legal system were developing in England as the "common law." Common law refers to traditional principles of jurisprudence that slowly evolved out of the decisions of the courts in a time when very little law was being set down by legislatures. In common law, the only communications recognized as privileged were those between an attorney and client. *All* other privileged communications are the result of statutes enacted by the various state legislatures.

Several observations should be made at this point. No communication is privileged unless that privilege has been affirmatively granted by statute (often as part of a licensing statute for the profession). In those instances in which this statutory grant has been made, the extent and conditions of the privilege vary considerably from state to state. As noted earlier, the fact that a profession's ethical standards mandate confidentiality is unlikely to impress a court in the absence of a statutory grant of privileged communication. All states now recognize by statute (in addition to the common law principle) the attorney-client privilege, and most recognize communications between a clergyman

and penitent as privileged. However, Schwitzgebel notes that only slightly over half the states recognize communications between a psychologist and client as privileged, and far fewer extend the privilege to such professions as social work and counseling.[1]

The rule governing the privilege of witnesses in the federal courts leaves considerable discretionary power with the individual judge. These courts are directed to decide whether or not a witness's testimony should be privileged in terms of "the principles of the common law as they may be interpreted in the light of reason and experience."[2] However, this same rule adds that in civil (noncriminal) proceedings, if a state statute grants privileged communications, the federal courts in that state should follow that statute. Thus, if your state grants privileged communication to your profession, and you are called to testify in a federal court in that state, communication between your client and yourself should be privileged if the matter is civil (for example, a divorce proceeding, a personal injury case) but may well not be if it is criminal.

By this point it should be apparent that individual mental health professionals must determine whether or not their states have granted their professions privileged communications, and if so, to what extent and under what conditions. As an example of how complex these matters can become, consider the laws of California on the subject. California grants a "psychotherapist-patient" privilege, and goes on to define psychotherapists quite broadly. The term includes physicians who practice as psychiatrists if they are licensed by any state, along with psychologists and clinical social workers (although it points out that the social workers must be doing therapy of a "nonmedical nature") if they are licensed by California. Finally, school psychologists credentialed by the state, and marriage, family, and child counselors licensed by California are also included.[3] However, this broad grant of privilege is limited by other statutes, such that if the proceedings are criminal, only the psychiatrists and psychologists are protected,[4] and if the victim of the crime is a child under the age of 16, there is no psychotherapist-patient privilege for any profession.[5] Thus, in California, the defendant in a criminal case could not claim privileged communication if damning information has been revealed to a family counselor, but could if the same information had been revealed to a psychologist. And if the victim of the crime were under 16, the defendant could not claim it at all.

The prospect of attempting to determine what the law says about the privilege for a given profession may tend to needlessly intimidate the nonlawyer. Yet, every state has a compilation of all the statutes governing its citizens, typically referred to as a *Code,* and the Code for a given state can usually be found in the reference section of the nearest public library. Codes are thoroughly indexed, and although the wording may be legalistic, the careful consideration of a statute will usually make its meaning reasonably clear.

As an example, assume that a hypothetical licensed clinical psychologist in the state of Tennessee wants to determine if privileged communication has been extended to his or her profession, and if so, to what extent and under what conditions. The statutes of Tennessee are compiled in the Tennessee Code Annotated. Its 29 volumes include three indexes, and by turning to this index and looking up "psychologist," one is directed to Chapter 11 of Title 63. This Chapter of the Code provides the reader with all the statutes governing the practice of psychology in this state. Within Title 63, Chapter 11, Section 1117 discusses privileged communication, stating:

> For the purpose of this chapter, the confidential relations and communication between licensed psychologist . . . and client are placed upon the same basis as those provided by law between attorney and client, and nothing in this chapter shall be construed to require any such privileged communication to be disclosed.

Note that if we are to determine the extent and limitations of the privilege, we must learn what the law says about the attorney-client privilege. Returning to the index under "attorney" reveals that Chapter 3 of Title 29 defines it in Section 305 thus:

> No attorney . . . shall be permitted, in giving testimony against a client, or person who consulted him professionally to disclose any communication made to him as such by such person, during the pendency of the suit, before or afterwards, to his injury.

The attorney-client standard is the most potent example of privileged communication, and applied to the psychologist in Tennessee, it says, in simpler language, that a psychologist cannot repeat anything said by a client, before, during, or after a lawsuit, if it would injure the client.

The Tennessee statute granting privileged communication to the clergy does not mention the attorney-client standard, but the wording makes it clear that it is to be construed in that manner.[6] If one looks in the Tennessee Code Annotated for a statute granting privileged communication between psychiatrist and patient, one can be found, but with an interesting limitation. The statute states that communication between a psychiatrist and patient is privileged, but unlike that granted to attorneys, clergy, and licensed psychologists, it can be withheld if the judge decides that to do so is "in the interests of justice."[6] Finally, if one attempts to delineate the extent to which communications with such professionals as social workers or marriage counselors are privileged in Tennessee, it quickly becomes apparent that the practice of these two professions is not regulated by the state, licensure has not been granted, and there is no privileged communication.

Assuming that an examination of the Code for your state reveals that the legislature has granted the privilege to communications made by a client to a member of the profession to which you belong, there are several points that need further consideration. These come under the heading of "rules of evidence," which, although probably not stated explicitly as part of the statute, will affect the court's interpretation of any witness privilege.

1. The privilege belongs to the client, not the therapist. It may be waived by the client, in

which case the therapist will be required to testify, whether or not it seems to be in the client's best interest. The client (or the client's attorney) must affirmatively assert the privilege in order to block the therapist's testimony, and a failure to do so amounts to a waiver. The therapist cannot claim the privilege for the client. In a 1970 California case,[8] a psychiatrist refused to answer questions posed during a deposition because they concerned one of his patients and he believed the communication to be privileged. The patient had not appeared at the deposition (and thus could not assert the privilege). The psychiatrist's well-intentioned refusal to answer resulted in his being jailed for contempt, and on appeal to the Supreme Court of California, the sentence was upheld.

2. Only that information communicated in a professional relationship can be considered privileged. If an individual casually remarks to his psychologist neighbor over the back fence about personal involvement in criminal activities (such as cocaine distribution), and if he subsequently becomes a defendant in a criminal trial, an assertion of privileged communication will not be heard by the court. A wife who, in conversation with her therapist at a cocktail party, admits to an extramarital affair would not be able to assert privileged communication should her husband sue for divorce, and subpoena the therapist as a witness.

3. In most cases, the presence of a third party as a witness to the communication (for example, a friend of the client, the client's employer, the client's lover) destroys the privilege. The rationale here is that if the information communicated were really all that private, it would not have been said in front of a third party. If the third party is professionally associated with the therapist (for example, a psychiatrist's nurse, a psychologist's psy-

chological examiner) the privilege is not voided, because these people can reasonably be seen as necessary adjuncts to the treatment. This third-party issue raises serious questions about confidentiality and privilege in such areas as couples counseling or group psychotherapy. Although it would seem possible to contend that the members of a psychotherapy group are a necessary part of the treatment, the law in this area is ill defined.

4. When clients place their own mental status at issue during the proceeding, as when using an insanity defense, in doing so, they waive any right to claim privileged communication. This might conceivably have application to the case presented earlier. The client had asked the therapist to testify in a custody hearing on the issue of her fitness as a parent. If her husband's lawyer is sufficiently persuasive, the court may well rule that she has placed her mental status in issue, and in doing so, waived her right to assert privileged communication when the therapist is asked about her sexual preference.

5. Finally, when a client sues a therapist for malpractice, this waives the right to assert privileged communication. To have it otherwise could permit the client to make any conceivable assertion about misconduct or negligence, and then refuse to allow the therapist to testify in response.

The issues surrounding confidentiality and its legal parallel, privileged communication, are extensive and complex.[9] Returning to the question raised by Mr. Harris' attorney at the beginning of this discussion, in Tennessee the following would seem to be the answers. If you are a clergyman or licensed psychologist, you would probably be allowed the privilege by the court and not be required to answer. If you are a psychiatrist, you would not be required to answer unless the court held that your answer is required "in the interests of justice." If you are a social worker or marriage counselor, your answer would be required, and a refusal could result in your being jailed for civil contempt.

The concerned therapist of whatever persuasion owes it to clients to become cognizant of what protection, if any, the state legislature has granted. Further, it seems reasonable for a reputable therapist to advise clients presenting problems in which litigation seems likely in the future (such as divorce actions and child custody suits) that, although professional ethics mandate confidentiality, the courts may or may not be persuaded to recognize a communication with you as privileged, depending on what the state Code says on the subject.

END NOTES

1. Schwitzgebel, R.L., and Schwitzgebel, R.K. *Law and psychological practice.* New York: John Wiley & Sons, 1980.
2. Rule 501, Rules of Evidence for the United States District Courts and Magistrates (1975).
3. West's Annotated California Evidence Code, Article 7, P.1010.
4. West's Annotated California Evidence Code, Article 7, P.1028.
5. West's Annotated California Evidence Code, P.1027.
6. Tennessee Code Annotated, 24-109.
7. Tennessee Code Annotated, 24-112.
8. In Re Lifshutz, 497 P. 2d 557 (1970).
9. See for example Schwitzgebel & Schwitzgebel, 1980, p. 202.

13

The rights of gay students on the college campus

J.L. BERNARD

In 1965, America was deeply engaged in an increasingly unpopular war, fault lines were developing in our society, and emotions were running high. At the university level, unrest was being manifest in violent demonstrations. Mary Beth Tinker and her brother John felt deeply that the war was wrong and decided to join the protest movement. So they went to their high school in Des Moines, Iowa one day wearing black armbands as a symbolic expression of their concerns. They were sent home from school and suspended until they would return without the armbands.

They took their case to the federal courts and lost at the district and circuit levels. However, the Supreme Court was sympathetic to their position,[1] and its decision contained several formidable statements on the rights of all students. Speaking for the court, Mr. Justice Fortas said:

> The District Court concluded that the action of the authorities was reasonable because it was based on a fear of a disturbance from the wearing of the armbands. But, in our system, undifferentiated fear or apprehension of disturbance is not enough to overcome the right to freedom of expression. (at 1242)

And further:

> [Students] may not be confined to the expression of those sentiments that are officially approved. In the absence of a specific showing of constitutionally valid reasons to regulate their speech, students are entitled to freedom of expression of their views. (at 1243)

A few years later, this line of reasoning faced a far more substantial challenge in *Healy v. James*.[2] A chapter of the Students for a Democratic Society (SDS) applied for recognition as a campus organization at Central Connecticut State College and was refused by school officials on the grounds that the group was likely to cause "violent acts of disruption." When this case reached the Supreme Court, the position the Court had taken in *Tinker* did not waver. Further, an important legal issue was clarified in this case. Whereas the federal district court had held that the SDS chapter had the burden of proving that it would not be disruptive to normal school activities, the Supreme Court held that the burden rested with the school officials to prove that the student group would be disruptive. Once again, freedom of expression, as guaranteed by the First Amendment to the United States Constitution carried the day.

These two cases came to form the foundation on which the rights of gay students on the college campus stand. The operant concepts are the First Amendment guarantees of freedom of expression, assembly, and petition. However, an important distinction must be drawn at the outset; that between speech and behavior. Although significant strides have been made by gay students where speech is the issue, in the roughly one half of our states that still have "sodomy laws," homosexual intercourse remains a criminal act. As recently as 1976, the Supreme Court rejected an attempt by two citizens of Virginia to overturn that state's sodomy law (see *Doe v. Commonwealth's Attorney*[3]).

In the early 1970s, the Gay Student's Organization (GSO) at the University of New Hampshire applied for, and was granted, recognition as a campus organization. Soon afterwards, they sponsored a dance that, although it took place without incident, received considerable media coverage. This led to criticism by the Governor, which in turn prompted the university's Board of Trustees to reconsider their earlier recognition of the GSO. The Trustees filed suit in a local court to clarify their rights (and those of the GSO), and while awaiting judgment banned any further social activities by the GSO.

The students promptly countered by filing suit in federal district court, claiming their constitutional rights were being violated, and asking the court to order the Trustees to grant them the same rights and privileges as any other formally recognized campus group. This court held for the students, and the university appealed. On appeal, the federal circuit court, citing *Healy* as precedent, affirmed the lower court's ruling, noting that the university had failed to show any legitimate state interest in restricting the activities of this particular group.[4]

A short time later, the Gay Alliance of Students (GAS) at Virginia Commonwealth University applied for recognition as a campus organization and was refused. They too, turned to the federal courts. At the district court level, school officials argued that recognition of a gay student group would "increase sodomy," and that it would both make the school more attractive to gay students while hindering recruitment of nongay students. This court was not persuaded and, citing *Healy*, held for the students, ordering the university to grant the GAS recognition. Virginia Commonwealth appealed this decision and found to their chagrin that

the circuit court of appeals not only affirmed the lower court's ruling, but took it a step further by ordering the university to afford all privileges to the GAS that are given to any other recognized campus group.[5] As a reminder of the importance of the earlier mentioned distinction between speech and behavior, it should be noted that this circuit court was the same one that upheld Virginia's "sodomy law" in *Doe* while that case was wending its way to the Supreme Court.

A momentary digression seems warranted at this point to answer those students who ask, "Is it really worth all that trouble just to get recognition?" Although this is obviously a question that every gay student will have to answer as an individual, it should be noted that recognition carries with it a package of perquisites that can be quite significant. Among others, this package may include the right to hold meetings in campus facilities, the right to post notices on campus bulletin boards, the right to a listing in the student organization directory, the right to hand out literature on campus, the right to coverage in the school annual, the right to hold social events on campus, and perhaps most important, to the extent that the school administration has funds budgeted for the support of campus organizations, the right to a fair share of those funds.

A few years after the Virginia Commonwealth case, the University of Missouri denied recognition of a campus gay student organization called Gay Lib. These students, too, turned to the federal judiciary for relief only to lose at the district court level. This court accepted the university's assertion that recognition would result in "the commision of felonious acts of sodomy in violation of Missouri law." On appeal, the circuit court reversed that decision, citing not only the New Hampshire and Virginia cases, but once again, *Healy*, noting that:

none of the purposes or aims of Gay Lib . . . evidences advocacy of present violations of state law or

188

of university regulations. . . . The district court . . . made no findings that Gay Lib would, ". . . infringe reasonable campus rules, interrupt classes, or substantially interfere with the opportunity of other students to obtain an education." *Healy v. James,* 189.[6]

More recently, a federal district court in Tennessee has once again upheld the right of gay students to organize and demand formal recognition as a campus organization.[7] Austin Peay State University took a novel tack when confronted with an application for recognition by a gay student group. The school officials admitted the students' right, under the federal Constitution, to organize but still refused to grant recognition. The hollowness of this recognition of a right to organize (while refusing formal recognition as a campus group) is best illustrated by the fact that school policy absolutely prohibited any activity of any kind by an unrecognized group. In federal district court, the university brought out many of the same arguments that had been tried, and failed, before. They failed again.

One of the school's contentions was that recognition would give "credibility" to homosexual behavior and expand violations of state law prohibiting such activity (the same position taken earlier by the University of Missouri). The court rejected this position firmly, stating:

> Here we are not dealing with conduct, but with the *advocacy of the acceptability* of conduct. Defendants fear the potential harm of ideas, of information, of "recognition." All are speech in their purest form. Protection of even potentially harmful speech is grounded in the belief "that our people, adequately informed, may be trusted to distinguish between the true and the false. . . ." *Viereck v. United States,* 318 U. S. 236, 251 (1942). Denial of that choice substitutes paternalism for individual responsibility, Orwellian conformity for individual freedom. (at 1274)

Although the rights of gay students to organize and demand recognition as a campus organization have been consistently upheld by the federal courts, a closer examination is warranted at this point. It should be noted that all of these cases have involved state-supported institutions. The rights of the gay student in a private college are much less clear, and for a straightforward reason. The rights guaranteed each of us by our federal Constitution (freedom of religion, freedom of the press, freedom of expression, and so on) are intended to protect us from *government,* not from each other. Thus, when a state-supported institution discriminates against a student, or a group of students, the federal courts will view the institution as "an arm of the state" and intervene. The application of these constitutional guarantees to disputes between private citizens is much less clear. The federal courts are likely to view the relationship of the student at a private college to the school administrators as one between individuals, and turn to the law of contracts when disputes arise. For example, if a student enrolls at a private college that requires church attendance twice weekly, and if this information was made known to the student in advance, the federal courts might well decline to hear a later contention that this requirement abridges the student's freedom of religion. Rather, if this requirement were repugnant to the student, the court would probably suggest that he is free to leave the school and transfer to one that makes no such requirement. Thus, the right of gay students on a private college campus to organize and demand recognition remains an unsettled question.

Although the First Amendment guarantee of freedom of expression is staunchly defended by the federal courts (indeed, it is sometimes referred to as "the darling of the judiciary"), that right is by no means absolute. Supreme Court Justice Oliver Wendell Holmes once observed that freedom of speech does not grant the right to shout "fire" in a crowded theater; some forms of speech are beyond constitutional protection. The line in this area has been drawn in at least two cases, *Brandenburg v. Ohio*[8] and *Tinker*. In *Brandenburg,* the Supreme Court held that the abridgment of free speech is justified only if that speech is directed at producing or likely to incite "imminent lawless action." *Tinker* modified this reasoning slightly in applying it to an academic environment, noting that unacceptable behavior need not be defined solely by the criminal code, speaking instead to the "disruption" of normal campus activities, such as the process of education. The Court held here that if school officials have actual evidence that leads them to "reasonably . . . forecast" (*Tinker,* at 514) that a substantial disruption of school activities is imminent, they may act to interfere. Obviously, what constitutes "substantial disruption" (or, for that matter "actual evidence") is open to interpretation, and the future may well see litigation on these questions. One area open to speculation is disruption caused by the reaction of militant nongay students to the activities of a recognized gay campus group (harassment). It seems probable that were such an incident to occur it would be the responsibility of the school officials to deal with the cause of the disruption, that is, the nongay students.

In closing, we have seen that federal litigation over the right of gay student groups to recognition at state-supported institutions has consistently upheld the First Amendment. In light of this, it might seem reasonable to expect school officials to accept this and routinely grant recognition to gay student groups in the future. However, administrators of state-supported institutions are notoriously sensitive to the attitudes of the taxpayers who support them (although federal courts have repeatedly said that this concern is irrelevant when the issue is freedom of expression). When confronted with this dilemma, school officials may see their safest course of action to lie in refusing recognition to gay student groups until they are "forced" to do so by the courts. Gay students who are denied recognition as a campus organization and turn to the federal courts for relief should realize that before the suit is adjudicated all of the original plaintiffs may well have earned their degrees and left the campus. It is not unusual for such cases (particularly where appeals are involved) to take several years. Yet, for those gay students to whom the issue is one of principle, the victory may be well worth the struggle.

END NOTES

1. *Tinker v. Des Moines Indep. Community School Dist.*, 393 U.S. 503 (1969).
2. *Healy v. James*, 408 U.S. 169 (1972).
3. *Doe v. Commonwealth's Attorney for City of Richmond*, 425 U.S. 901 (1976).
4. *Gay Students Org. of Univ. of New Hampshire v. Bonner*, 509 F 2d 652 (1st Cir. 1974).
5. *Gay Alliance of Students v. Matthews*, 544 F 2d 166 (4th Cir. 1976).
6. *Gay Lib v. University of Missouri*, 558 F 2d 848 (8th Cir. 1977) *cert denied sub nom.*
7. *Student Coalition, Etc. v. Austin Peay State U.*, 477 F. Supp. 1267 (1979).
8. *Brandenburg v. Ohio*, 395 U.S. 444 (1969).

14

Aging

The expression, *growing old,* is often interpreted negatively. In this culture, it has traditionally been viewed as a time of frailty, illness, loneliness, and preparing for death; all with wrinkled, sagging bodies that are neither appropriate for nor interested in sexual activity. As with other aspects of cultural stereotypes, gays and nongays internalize all, some, or none of these views.

Decisions about what constitutes "old age" are subjective. A teenager may consider someone who is 35 as "old," whereas the 35-year-old may view "old" as 55 or 60. There is no age at which one becomes "old." Porcino, in her book on older women, uses 40, identifying that age as the beginning of the "second half of life."[1] Some programs for older people use 55 or 60 as the minimum age for eligibility, and retirement from employment may occur at age 65 or 70. Regardless of the age, the process of growing older presents some special concerns for many people. The specificity of those concerns for older homoerotic people is unclear, because research is so limited, with no reported studies exclusively on gays over 60.

Those few studies that do exist are encouraging in many respects. They hint that homoerotic individuals may have a more successful response to aging than do many nongays. The stereotype of the lonely, desperate, sexless lesbian or gay man appears to fit only a small minority. As Bell and Weinberg indicate in their Epilogue:

> The homosexual who is afraid that he might end up a "dirty old man," desperately lonely, should be assured that such plight is not inevitable, and that, given

our society's failure to meet the needs of aging people, heterosexuality hardly guarantees well-being in old age.[2]

Based on the available research, we believe that "such plight" does not appear likely. In support of our belief, we will include in this section not only the research on older gays but also attitudes toward aging, behaviors of younger gay men and lesbians that might affect aging, our own observations of older gay men and lesbian women, and the observations of Chris Almvig,[3] who has been working with lesbians and gay men over 50 since 1975.

ATTITUDES TOWARD AGING
Lesbians' attitudes toward aging

Research on younger lesbians' attitudes toward aging indicates that they are positive. In addition, for themselves and their partner, they emphasize interest in qualitites that are not likely to be affected by the aging process.

Saghir and Robins' oldest female respondent was 54 (mean age of sample, 31),[4] so their research provided no data on lesbians over 60; however, they did ask respondents about concerns related to growing old. Some indicated that they expected to have a stable relationship during their later years, while the largest percentage were neither apprehensive about aging nor had any identifiable fantasies about it, indicating that they expected to "grow old gracefully, involved, and interested . . . [with] increased interest in non-sexual activities and relationships."[5]

Jay and Young also had little information on

older lesbians, because only 4 of their 962 women were over 60, with an additional 22 indicating that they were 50 to 60.[6] However, they also investigated attitudes toward aging, and reported that only one quarter of their respondents indicated negativeness.[7]

From both Saghir and Robins and Jay and Young, there appear to be two groupings of younger lesbians with regard to concerns about aging: the majority, who are not apprehensive about it, and the minority, who are. The apprehensive group generally seem to worry about physical appearance and loneliness, the two concerns that are also expressed by many nongay women.[8]

Concerns about appearance. Most of the respondents in Jay and Young indicated that they were more interested in personality, intellect, and hygiene, and that ''looks in general'' did not play an important part in their attraction to another woman.[9] One could infer from this that age, therefore, is of little concern to the women studied.

The nongay woman, however, is subjected to all the media messages emphasizing youth, suggesting that she must meet a physical standard of youthful attractiveness if she is to have a male partner. This is one instance in which not having lesbian couples portrayed in advertising may be an advantage. Although a few of the women in Jay and Young were concerned about physical appearance, it was primarily concern with obesity and not with the body changes that occur because of the aging process.[10] The emphasis on personality, intellect, and hygiene rather than on physical appearance means that the aging process for most lesbians may be more acceptable than for their nongay counterparts, who are constantly reminded of the emphasis on youthful appearance.

Concerns about loneliness. As Jay and Young point out, being alone is not the same as being lonely.[11] However, their lesbian respondents who expressed concern about being lonely were often expressing concern about being alone. The fact that they are in the minority may be explained by another difference between lesbians and nongay women. Lesbians do not have the same source of apprehension about being alone in their later years as heterosexual women.

Men die at earlier ages than do women. Thus the heterosexual woman can expect that she will outlive her husband and be without a partner for several years. Although this could happen to the lesbian, she is less likely to view it as a certainty. Either partner has an equal probability of living longer. In addition, the fact that women live longer than men means that an older lesbian is more likely to find an affectional relationship partner among her peers than is her heterosexual counterpart.

Gay men's attitudes toward aging

Younger gay men also indicate a generally positive attitude toward aging. They differ from lesbians in that they place more emphasis on youthful appearance in their sexual partner choice, but the majority do not report apprehension about aging.

Saghir and Robins suggest that apprehension about growing older is more prevalent among gay men than among lesbians. They write, ''It was not surprising to find that homosexual men approached the subject of old age with some apprehension, uncertainty, and wishful thinking.''[12] Although Saghir and Robins infer a generally negative attitude among gay men to aging, their data are open to a different interpretation. Almost half (44%) of the men indicated that they ''will grow old gracefully—involved and interested,'' and an additional 28% believe they ''will grow old in a stable homosexual relation[ship].''[12] Perhaps Saghir and Robins interpret this latter group as belonging to the ''wishful thinking'' category, but there are no adequate studies of the older gay man on which to base that assumption. In fact, the few studies available suggest that it is not wishful thinking at all.

Kelly's study[13] showed that the majority of his subjects over age 45 were in a relationship. For those who were not, the primary reasons were either the death of the partner or a rejection of the notion of living one's life with only one partner.[14] Berger's study of 112 gay men, ages 41 to 77, also indicated that the majority were not living alone.[15] It may be "wishful thinking" to look forward to growing older in a relationship, but with the negative stereotype of the lonely older gay so pervasive, even among gays themselves,[16] it is also possible to interpret that response as a positive attitude toward aging, in that it is not in accord with the expectations of the stereotype of growing old alone.

The majority of the men in Jay and Young indicated either a positive or neutral feeling about aging.[17] However, they differed from the lesbian sample in indicating that age is important in choosing a partner, leading Jay and Young to conclude that, "most gay men are likely to feel very aware of their age."[18] Bell and Weinberg also found an emphasis on youthfulness in their gay male sample and not in their lesbian sample.[19]

One of Jay and Young's respondents summed up the majority's positive approach in the following way:

☐ Aging? Who can avoid it? Why not make it good, maybe even a happy process? Why not call it maturing, and forget the derogatory connotations? I am 69 and am busier than I ever was when employed, and (I hope) my life is perhaps even slightly more meaningful because I can do my own thing, not just someone else's.[20]

In the studies of Kelly,[21] Saghir and Robins,[12] and Jay and Young,[17] only a minority of the gay men expressed an apprehensive attitude toward aging. For that minority, the apprehension was usually based on fears related to inability to attract a sexual partner (physical appearance), loneliness, and being alone.[22]

Concerns about appearance. So long as there is an emphasis on youthfulness and a glorification of the "body beautiful" within the gay community, physical appearance will continue to be of concern to the gay man. This may be positive in that he is likely to be concerned with maintaining physical fitness as he ages. However, it is also possible that his preoccupation with physical attractiveness can be a source of concern about aging.

Don Clark suggests several techniques for helping a gay man focus on aspects of an individual other than the physical.[23] For example, he suggests picking out a stranger who is unattractive and fantasizing qualities that would make that person an acceptable sex partner, or increasing the amount of touching and hugging with someone who has been deemed physically unattractive.[24] These exercises are not meant to be, nor are they, attempts to extinguish an extant attraction to visual cues. They simply help expand a person's options.

Concerns about loneliness. According to the available research, older gay men are generally neither alone nor lonely.[25] The majority of men in Kelly's study indicated that they were "socially and sexually active and satisfied in interpersonal relationships."[26] Berger indicates that "the great majority of respondents lived with a lover, family, or one or more roommates and had many friends . . . [and] were sexually active."[27] In her work with gay men over 50, Almvig has found that even those men who live alone and have only their Social Security check for income do not appear to be lonely. They have friendship networks, and their varied interests provide them with different types of stimulation, which in turn motivate them to stay active. She cites the case of Jerry as an example.[28]

Jerry is 72. He lives in a rent-subsidized apartment building with other older people in a large city. Jerry is gay and is one of the few gay men in the building. He has no money in the bank and he lives on his Social Security of $300 a month. There are other men in the building who are in similar circumstances, except that Jerry is gay and they aren't. Jerry is very active. Through his friends, he manages to go out to parties, and occasionally gets a free ticket to the theater. He takes bus rides to the zoo, the botanical gardens, and to many places where he can meet other people or just enjoy the sights. He goes to the flea market, and often goes to the many free events that are offered throughout the city. He reads a great deal, using his library card often. On a particular Saturday, Jerry will probably be off for some adventure, while approximately 25 nongay men sit in the lobby of the building watching television. Jerry talks about a variety of subjects. The other men in the building talk mostly of the baseball, basketball, or football game that was on television. Jerry has learned to be resourceful. He has also learned how to be stimulated in many ways. He is much "younger" at 72 than any other man over 60 in the building.[28]

BEHAVIORS THAT MAY AFFECT AGING

Another possible indicator of successful aging is the leisure-time interests of the adult. Saghir and Robins found that the vast majority (90%) of the gay men had no interest in being either participant in or spectator for football and baseball, whereas over two thirds of the heterosexual men were interested. More of the gay men were "engaged in individual sports like swimming, golf, tennis, and skiing"[29] and in "artistic pursuits" than were the nongay men. The gay men also were more interested in intellectual pursuits and "constructional hobbies like carpentry."[30] In comparing gay and nongay women, Saghir and Robins found that the gay women were significantly more involved in leisure time activities such as artistic pursuits and individual sports.[31]

All of this indicates that during their early and middle adult years, gay men and women are more involved in leisure activities that would be appropriate for their later years than are nongay men and women. However, whether this early difference in interests is maintained into the later years of life has yet to be studied. Our observations indicate that it does.

COUNSELING THE YOUNGER HOMOEROTIC INDIVIDUAL

For the younger gay person who is concerned about being alone and lonely during old age, the counselor should first discuss the difference between the two, pointing out that they are not necessarily synonymous. There should also be an exploration of ideas about being an older lesbian or gay man, to find out how much of the stereotype is believed. If the client knows any older lesbians or gay men who do not fit the stereotype, it may be necessary to suggest that these are perhaps typical

rather than atypical. The counselor should also discuss ways in which one can plan for the future, both financially and psychologically, and explore the person's ability to make friends and his or her interests and hobbies, suggesting activities that can be sources of pleasure during later years.

OTHER FACTORS AFFECTING AGING IN HOMOEROTIC PEOPLE

Our observations, those of Almvig, and the research of Kelly, Berger, and Wolf,[32] combined with the research on the attitudes and behavior of younger gay women and men, suggest that homoerotic individuals, especially those whom Bell and Weinberg describe as coupled or functional (the majority),[33] make a successful transition from middle to old age. They do not fit the stereotype of lonely and desperate,[34] and they apparently have fewer problems with the aging process than do most nongays. This is a result of many factors in their lives beyond their tendency to maintain positive attitudes toward aging and to develop interests that will provide stimulation in their later years. Among those factors are three that affect gays but do not appear significant for nongays: the advantage of stigmatization, friendship networks, and the freedom of retirement.

The advantage of stigma

Johnson and Kelly,[35] Steinman,[36] and others point out that being old and gay is a double stigma in this society. If one is old, gay, and Black, the stigma is tripled.[37] Kelly suggests that some older gay people indeed internalize the stigma and maintain a very negative self-image.[38] However, the research and our observations indicate that these are in the minority, and one possible explanation for this is that stigmatization may have some positive side effects.

The homoerotic person is stigmatized for sexual orientation, and in some cases for race, long before she or he is stigmatized for age. If that person is able to overcome the initial stigma, then the additional one of age will be less likely to have a negative effect. Lemert confirms this idea by noting that a person who has a strong positive self-concept is not likely to accept the negative label of deviant that society imposes.[39] This implies that the stigma associated with being gay may be advantageous in that it prepares a person for ignoring the social stigma of aging.

One younger woman interviewed in preparation for this book summarized this "advantage" outlook toward aging and other aspects of her life.

☐ I'm so glad I'm 33 and gay. Being a lesbian has taught me one really valuable lesson. Taboos can be broken, providing a source of strength. I found that when I broke the one about being gay, I could break the ones about my roles. Now I'm looking forward to breaking the ones about old age. I am not going to be a lonely, old lesbian. I'm going to be an interested, alive, older lesbian.[40]

She views the stigma of lesbianism as beneficial, in that overcoming that stigma gave her the skills to overcome others.

It is important to note that the nongay person is apt to find that aging is the first social stigma to be faced. The supportive societal messages that the nongay person has received for over 50 years of his or her life may make it difficult to ignore the negative societal messages associated with aging. Older gay people of today, in contrast, have had to cope with social stigma throughout their lives, and if successful, have developed enough self-acceptance[41] and self-confidence to permit them to manage the stigma of aging successfully. Thus, it is less likely to affect older homoerotic people than older heteroerotic people.

Friendship networks

Another aspect of lesbian and gay male lifestyles that is different from many nongay ones and appears to make the aging process easier is the establishment of friendship networks. Research indicates that gay men and women are likely to

have more close friends than are heterosexual men and women.[42] As Bell and Weinberg suggest, this is a reflection of the fact that most heterosexuals are involved in family interaction and do not seek outside friendships for support.[42]

Gays generally do not depend on blood relations for support. Instead, they choose their friends and support systems and have more opportunity to develop new friendships throughout their lives than may be the case with nongays. Although some gays are parents, most are not concerned with raising a family, but place their energies into each other and into their friends. They have more opportunity for socializing outside the home, and therefore more opportunity for learning the skills necessary for making new friends.

Berger indicates that the friendship network is important not only because it provides general support for the older gay person but also because of its composition. The network often includes gays who are much younger. Their presence serves two very positive functions: helping to intellectually stimulate the older person and preventing expressions of self-deprecation.[43]

For many nongay people, the friendship network that exists is closely linked to occupation. If a person has been accustomed to sharing family concerns, talking about the children or the spouse or the garden, and generally sharing personal information with work colleagues, at retirement the absence of those contacts will be felt. What initially may be a feeling of "thank heaven I don't have to go to work tomorrow" may turn into one of missing those contacts. Gays find that they are less likely to share personal information with work colleagues, and some go to great lengths to prevent such information from being known. Their personal sharing is often with friends outside of work, and that network will not change at retirement.

The freedom of retirement

Most lesbians and gay men work and at some time retire. The older gay person today has lived for many years in a society in which discovery of a homoerotic orientation meant loss of a job. They managed to find many ways to keep from having to publicly admit or deny their orientation in order to earn a living and establish some financial security for retirement. For those individuals, retirement can be a very positive event, freeing them from those daily concerns. Many gays approach retirement as the time when they will be able to do things they could previously do only on weekends or vacations and do them without fear of losing a job.

The majority of gay men and lesbians do not have children and therefore do not have the same expectations for or problems associated with raising children as do nongay men and women. There is no expectation that children will take care of them during their retirement years, and therefore no consequent disappointment when that does not occur. There is no crisis to be faced when the last child leaves home. There essentially are very few dynamics in the gay couple to precipitate the "post-retirement identity crisis" that often occurs in the nongay couple.[44] This suggests that retirement for the homoerotic person can be a crisis-freeing event rather than a crisis-producing one. As Wolf indicates, "Retirement [does] not mean loss but rather enrichment of life."[45]

COUNSELING THE OLDER HOMOEROTIC INDIVIDUAL

The foregoing discussion presents a rather pleasant picture for the older gay man and lesbian woman. The research evidence and observational information indicate that this is true for the majority. However, there are some who have problems that might require intervention, such as belief in the stereotype, communication difficulties with health professionals, inability to live on a fixed income, and dealing with dying and death.

Belief in the stereotype

There are older homoerotic people who are lonely and alone. They sometimes believe the stereotype and view their gayness as responsible for their situation. If someone with this attitude seeks help, the counselor can explore that causal reasoning, discussing both the research findings that indicate otherwise and the concept of self-fulfilling prophecy. It is likely that the client will not be comfortable with his or her gayness, and the initial counseling can focus on increasing that comfort level.

It may then be necessary to teach the person some social skills and to explore the client's interests in order to suggest activities that will allow for meeting others, both gay and nongay. It may be that the initial focus will be toward meeting other gay people. This has the advantage of allowing the client to meet older gays who do not fit the stereotype and younger gays who can offer the kinds of support that Berger reported.[46] It has a possible disadvantage in that it tends to further focus on orientation. In exploring the client's interests and suggesting ways in which these may be expanded, the counselor may also wish to explore the issue of risk taking, and help the client separate real from imagined risks.

These suggestions are primarily approaches for helping anyone, gay or nongay, deal with feelings of loneliness. However, the gay client may tend to ascribe the genesis of those feelings to his or her sexual orientation, whereas the nongay person is not likely to do that. The counselor must, therefore, first help the client separate the two issues: orientation and loneliness. It is not appropriate to suggest changing orientation. It is appropriate to suggest changing behavior to increase the probability of meeting other people and to support changing attitudes to gain more personal satisfaction from others and self.

Communication difficulties with health professionals

As Bell and Weinberg noted, societal concerns for the elderly are sadly lacking.[47] Butler suggests that health care for the elderly is lacking as well. He describes it as being dominated by a "Peter Panism" in which students are taught to diagnose as if there were always a "[single] cause for a variety of symptoms,"[48] an approach that is inappropriate for older people, because the older person is likely to have an average of "five diseases or

. . . five medications acting together at one time."[48]

This means that the older homoerotic person will need to communicate with a health professional at some time. Some older gays may be reluctant to do this, either because of negative past experiences with health care professionals or because of a general wariness about discussing themselves with any authority figure. There might also be a tendency to withhold information, especially about orientation-related matters. It is unlikely that someone would seek counseling specifically because of an inability to communicate with a health professional, but it is possible that a counselor who is working with older gay people would discover this reluctance in a client.

The counselor should explore the necessity for health care and should encourage the client to take an assertive role in seeking care. This would include asking questions as well as answering them, refusing to accept an attitude that indicates that aging is responsible for whatever symptoms exist, and confronting any homophobic attitudes that arise.

Inability to live on a fixed income

Some gay people are faced with living out their lives on a seemingly inadequate, fixed income, especially those who find Social Security to be their only income source. They will be more concerned with problems of everyday living than will others who have carefully planned the financial aspect of retirement. These men and women may need help in developing a plan for living on a fixed budget.

There are some resources available, such as rent subsidy, but the individual may need help in acquiring those resources, in budget control, and in finding inexpensive or free ways to pursue personal interests. Jerry, whose situation we outlined previously, is an example of someone who has successfully managed his life as an older person on a fixed income. We presented his situation because sometimes knowing about a success helps provide alternatives for those who are having problems.

Dying and death

We have already discussed some of the issues involved with the death of a partner. (See section entitled "Death of One Partner" in Chapter 9.) The death of a lover is traumatic, and the emotions involved in a mourning period are not lessened by a homoerotic orientation. In fact, the mourning period for a gay person may be longer and more severe because of the lack of societal support for gay primary relationships.

In addition, the issues of institutionalization and inheritance rights are different for gays. A gay person whose lover is dying in an institution may have difficulty visiting and/or spending time in the institution. Some institutions impose a "family members only" policy, and the lover is not legally a family member. Helping professionals must be made aware of the emotional needs of both partners in this situation, and may have to take an advocacy role in intervening in institutional policies and procedures to enable the lover to spend time with her or his dying partner.

SUMMARY

From evidence that exists concerning the attitudes and behavior of younger adults, it appears that lesbians and gay men have a better chance of successful aging than do nongay men and women. The limited amount of research on older homoerotic people suggests that this is true. There are problems for some, but other than the special issues of self-fulfilling prophecy, inheritance, and dealing with health professionals and institutions, these problems are more related to the society's failure to meet the needs of its aged population than to the issue of being a homoerotic individual.

END NOTES

1. Porcino, J. *A handbook for women in the second half of life*. Manuscript in preparation.
2. Bell, A., & Weinberg, M. *Homosexualities: A study of diversity among men and women*. New York: Simon & Schuster, 1978, p. 231.

3. Chris Almvig has compiled data on 310 lesbians and gay men over 50. However, as of this writing, she has not yet analyzed the data. She talked to us about her observations derived from working with homoerotic people over the age of 50 since 1975. She may be contacted through SAGE: Senior Action in a Gay Environment, Inc., 487-A Hudson Street, New York, N.Y. 10014.

4. Saghir, M., & Robins, E. *Male & female homosexuality: A comprehensive investigation*. Baltimore: Williams & Wilkins, 1973, p. 12.

5. Saghir & Robins, 1973, p. 312.

6. Jay, K., & Young, A. *The gay report*. New York: Summit Books, 1979, p. 809.

7. Jay & Young, 1979, pp. 205-206.

8. Tavris, C. "The sexual lives of women over 60." *Ms.*, July 1977, pp. 62-65.

9. Jay & Young, 1979, pp. 203-204.

10. Jay & Young, 1979, p. 204.

11. Jay & Young, 1979, p. 332.

12. Saghir & Robins, 1973, p. 174.

13. Kelly, J. "Homosexuality and aging." In J. Marmor (Ed.), *Homosexual behavior: A modern reappaisal*. New York: Basic Books, 1980, pp. 176; 181.

14. Kelly, 1980, pp. 184-185.

15. Berger, R. "Psychological adaptation of the older homosexual male." *Journal of Homosexuality,* 1980, *5*(3), 161-175.

16. Johnson, M., & Kelly, J. "Deviate sex behavior in the aging: social definitions and the lives of older gay people." In O. Kaplan (Ed.), *Psychopathology of aging*. New York: Academic Press, 1979, pp. 252-253.

17. Jay & Young, 1979, pp. 287-288.

18. Jay & Young, 1979, p. 276.

19. Bell & Weinberg, 1978, p. 105.

20. Jay & Young, 1979, pp. 206; 287-291.

21. Kelly, 1980, pp. 186-187.

22. Kelly, 1980, p. 187; Jay & Young, 1979, pp. 288-291.

23. Clark, D. *Loving someone gay*. Millbrae, Calif.: Celestial Arts, 1977, pp. 125-127.

24. Clark, 1977, p. 126.

25. Saghir & Robins, 1973, p. 58; Berger, 1980, p. 172; Kelly 1980. p. 185.

26. Kelly, 1980, pp. 185-186.

27. Berger, 1980, pp. 171-172.

28. Almvig, C. Personal communication, 28 August 1980.

29. Saghir & Robins, 1973, pp. 175-176.

30. Saghir & Robins, 1973, p. 176.

31. Saghir & Robins, 1973, p. 312.

32. Wolf, D. "Life cycle change of older lesbians and gay men." Paper presented at annual convention of The Gerontological Society, San Diego, Calif., 1980. Wolf's research on older lesbians and gay men will be available as *Growing older: Lesbians and gay men*. Berkeley: University of California Press, in press.

33. Bell & Weinberg, 1978, pp. 132-133; 135-136.

34. Berger, 1980, p. 171; Johnson & Kelly, 1980, pp. 247-248.

35. Johnson & Kelly, 1980.

36. Steinman, R. "Gray and gay." In R. Skeist (Ed.), *To your good health*. Chicago: Chicago Free Press, 1980, pp. 199-200.

37. Binstock, R. "Interest group liberalism and the politics of aging." *The Gerontologist,* Autumn, p. 265.

38. Kelly, 1980, pp. 181-182.

39. Lemert, E. *Social pathology*. New York: McGraw-Hill, 1951.

40. From authors' files.

41. Weinberg, M. "The male homosexual: Age-related variations in social and psychological characteristics." *Social Problems,* 1970, *17,* 527-537; Tripp, C. *The homosexual matrix*. New York: Signet, 1975, pp. 255-265; Berger, 1980, p. 169.

42. Bell & Weinberg, 1978, p. 178.

43. Berger, 1980, pp. 172-173.

44. Steinman, 1980, p. 201.

45. Wolf, 1980, p. 5.

46. Berger, 1980, p. 173.

47. Bell & Weinberg, 1978, p. 231.

48. Butler, R. "Meeting the challenge of health care for the elderly." *Journal of Allied Health,* 1980, *9*(3), 164.

15

Gay parents

Riddle calculates that "of the estimated 20 million gay persons in this country . . . probably at least one-third of the lesbians and around 10% of the gay males have children, though not all have custody."[1] Although exact figures are not known, there appear to be a far greater number of lesbian mothers than gay fathers, as indicated by the number of child custody cases and the focus of most of the research done to date on gay parents.[2] Discussions with mental health professionals, as well as knowledge about the comparative statuses and incomes of men and women, suggest that lesbians probably face more difficulties as parents than men do.[3] Because of this emphasis on lesbian mothers in custody cases, literature, and public awareness, much of our discussion will focus on them. We have assumed that many of the issues are the same for gay fathers, who also have to contend with societal prejudices against men as single parents.

CHILD CUSTODY ISSUES

There is every indication that the problems gay parents face and the differences between gay and nongay parents are not inherent in their sexual preference, but are the result of societal reaction.[4] Nowhere is this more apparent than in the case of child custody. Having the custody of her or his children contested is undoubtedly one of the most stressful experiences a gay person can undergo.

Our national homophobia and the myths and misinformation on which this homophobia is partly based become blatant when child custody becomes an issue. Individuals who are otherwise tolerant, if not accepting, of gays become homophobic at the notion that a gay person would be allowed to raise children. The reasons for this specific homophobic reaction are related to the same fears and misconceptions about gay people that relate to other areas of their lives. Because so many people have this reaction, and because helping professionals may be called upon to give expert testimony and are often in positions where they can influence the beliefs of others, we will attempt to dispel some of the myths about gay parents.

Myths and misconceptions about gay parents

Gay parents will raise gay children. This is probably the major concern nongays, and some gays as well, have about gays as parents. Before we discuss the evidence relating to this myth, we want to point out that this concern in itself is clear evidence of homophobia. As a culture, we are so afraid of gay people and consider gayness so pathological that almost any kind of upbringing is considered preferable to the possibility that a child might turn out to be gay. Although it has been amply demonstrated that gays are no less healthy and may, in some respects, be healthier than nongays, the fear continues. It is our belief that even if gay parents were more likely to raise gay children, this in itself would not be a reason for denying a gay parent child custody.

Fortunately for gay parents, this does not appear to be an issue. There is absolutely no evidence to support the belief that gay parents are more likely to raise gay children than are nongay parents. As is often noted, the vast majority of lesbians and gay men are raised by heterosexual parents.[5] If parents' sexual preference were a variable that could predict a child's sexual preference, researchers would have discovered it long before this. Yet in all the studies we have reviewed that have attempted to determine the causes and correlates of homosexuality, not one has shown any indication that gay children are more likely to come out of gay than of nongay homes. Indeed, none of the studies even mention, and apparently none have found, gay children who grew up with gay parents.

This is not to say that gay parents do not raise gay children. Some of them do, but in approximately the same proportion as that found among nongay families.[6] As we have said before, there is no identifiable factor, including sexual preference of parents, that can be said to "cause" or even "predispose" someone to homosexuality or lesbianism.

Proselytizing. Another worry nongays have is that gay parents will attempt to convince their children to be gay. In the first place, there is no evidence to suggest that sexual preference (as distinct from having sexual relationships with those of the same gender) is something that an individual chooses. Although it is possible to choose whether and how to act on sexual preference, the preference itself does not seem to be a matter of choice for most people. Although there is no evidence to suggest that gay parents do attempt to persuade their children to be gay, and some evidence to the contrary,[7] it is unlikely that efforts at persuasion in either direction would have much effect. Parents of gay children often expend extraordinary amounts of energy in attempting to reverse their children's sexual preference, and the medical and psychological sciences have bent their efforts toward that end with remarkably little success.

Those who believe that gay parents could somehow override what appears to be an early and unalterable determination of sexual preference must believe either that the gay lifestyle is extraordinarily attractive and desirable or that gay people are supremely persuasive. In any event, there is no

evidence to indicate that gay parents are likely to proselytize for a gay sexual preference. Some, however, may hope that their children become nongay in order to avoid oppression, and many may simply be more tolerant of their child's sexual preference and experiences than is commonly true of nongay parents.[8]

Gay parents and their children's gender role development. As we noted earlier (Chapter 2), individuals who are homophobic are more likely to have strongly conformist attitudes regarding traditional gender roles than those who are not homophobic. It seems that these are the people most likely to worry about gender role conformity in the children of gay parents. Unless one is determined that children must enact rigidly stereotyped gender roles, there appears to be little reason for concern about children learning cross-gender behavior, no matter who their parents are.

The evidence on psychological androgyny presented in preceding chapters shows fairly clearly that an ability to express both masculine- and feminine-typed behaviors leads to greater self-esteem,[9] greater behavioral flexibility,[10] and higher scores on both the Social Ascendancy and Intellectuality scales of the Personality Research Form.[11] Androgynous individuals also receive more scholastic awards, date more, and have lower incidences of childhood illness (as compared with undifferentiated subjects).[11] Androgyny is associated with athleticism, scientific interests, and literary pursuits.[11] Masculine-typed individuals, whether male or female, usually fall second but are someimes equivalent to androgynous individuals, followed by female-typed and then undifferentiated individuals.[11]

Since gays are more likely than nongays to be either androgynous or masculine-typed (especially lesbians), it might appear that gay parents would be preferable as role models to nongays who model more restrictive gender-typed behavior patterns.[12] For better or worse, however, the acquisition of gender role behavior is neither simple enough nor sufficiently well understood to make this kind of prediction with any confidence. Most children still spend their early years in an environment largely peopled with female figures. In spite of this feminine influence, most boys grow up to be nongay, and almost half of all boys are masculine gender–typed.[13] It is still not clear what variables determine this.

At present, there is some empirical evidence indicating that children of gay parents show no difference in gender role behavior from children of nongay parents,[14] and there is no evidence to contradict this finding.[15] In fact, some lesbian mothers complain that in spite of their best efforts, their sons still show definite "sexist" tendencies learned, apparently, from peers, media, and other adults.[16] Gay mothers do make strong attempts in many cases to expose their sons to male models and, when feasible, allow their sons to have positive contacts with their fathers in order to prevent any potential negative effects from growing up in a home where the adults are of the same gender.[17] It is not known whether gay fathers make the same kinds of attempts, but presumably they do.

Children of gays will be damaged by growing up in "deviant" homes. Some people believe that growing up in a home with a parent who is gay is not in the best interests of the child because of the societal reaction to gayness. They are concerned that this reaction will be harmful to the child. We must certainly expect that the children of gay parents will have to cope with prejudice, misunderstanding, and possibly even negative peer reactions. But then, so may the children of Black parents, poor Appalachian parents, divorced parents, and parents with physical impairments such as blindness, deafness, or paraplegia. The fact that a child's parents are different from the majority of white, middle-class, unimpaired parents is not usually considered an appropriate reason for removing a child from the home. We see no reason why sexual preference should be any different in this respect, unless it can be shown that there is

some clear and consistent impairment because of this.

There is no evidence that gay children suffer disproportionately because of their parents' sexual preference.[18] Lewis[19] found that, in her study, the children expressed more difficulty with their parents' divorce than with their mothers' lesbianism. "Almost without exception, the children were proud of their mother for challenging society's rules and for standing up for what she believed. Problems between the mother and children seemed secondary to the children's respect for the difficult steps she had taken."[20] Lewis' conclusion is that "the parent's sexual preference does not matter as much as the love, caring and maturity of the adults and their effort to help their children become self-reliant and self-assured."[21]

Other concerns about gay parents. Riddle lists several other concerns that nongays have about gay parenting, none of which are justified as reasons to prevent gays from having custody of their children. She reports testimony and data that provide evidence that gay parents are as good at parenting as nongays.[4] The cities of Chicago, New York, and San Francisco, for example, have all used gay homes as foster homes for several years with no untoward results. In fact, Riddle notes that gay parents who are trying to get or keep custody of their children must be highly motivated. "Sexual orientation has little to do with whether or not one wants to be a parent, but it has a lot to do with motivation because of the high cost of being a gay parent at this time."[22]

Another issue sometimes raised is that gay parents might seduce or molest their children. This fear probably comes from the myths that gays are "oversexed" and will have sex with children if no adult is available. With regard to this belief, Riddle states that "97% of child molesters are heterosexual males (usually related to the child), and 87% of the victims are girls."[23] She states further that there is no evidence that gay parents are more likely than nongay parents either to seduce their children or allow them to be seduced.[4]

A final concern is that exposure to overt sexual expression between two people of the same gender will somehow be harmful to the child. Although one might wonder what harm will come to children from observing warm, loving relationships between two people, observation indicates that gays are every bit as careful about sexual indiscretion in front of their children as are nongays. Indeed, some gay parents go to the extent of almost stopping sexual relations because they are afraid this will somehow damage the child or because they have not yet come out to the child.[24]

Effects of myths and misconceptions on gay parents. Even though a gay parent may not really believe that he or she is harming a child by being gay, it may be extremely difficult to hold on to this belief in the face of the reactions of friends and associates whose "well-meaning" comments are consistently undermining the parent's self-confidence. One lesbian mother comments:

☐ The major concern my nongay friends have about my situation is that I will somehow damage *my* son by being open and honest about my relationships (insinuating and sometimes saying that I am not a good parent because I am not protecting him from a confusing, traumatic environment). The insinuation is also frequently expressed with reference to his sex—meaning it would not be so important were he a girl. "What kind of self-image will he have when he grows up seeing his mother rejecting men?" and so forth. When I was first coming out I thought they might be right—but even after having regained my senses I find that it still takes a lot of energy to deal with frequent (biweekly sometimes) encounters of this nature.[25]

These kinds of encounters will occur for many gay parents, but the parents who may suffer most are those who know of no other gay parents with whom to share their concerns, or have only friends who are as beset as they are. If it is possible, counselors can be very helpful by putting gay parents in touch with other parents in their area or, failing that, with the national networks available.

More directly, the client can be helped to develop some specific thoughts and self-statements to counteract the negative statements of others. The client must learn to combat these kinds of societal reactions on his or her own as well as possible. A good way to help the client do this is for the client to learn the *facts* about gay parenting, learn to repeat these facts to himself or herself so that they become a firm part of the client's belief system, and practice stress management techniques. Furthermore, clients will benefit from learning assertive responses to others who insist on making incorrect or upsetting remarks. The gay parent does not have to listen to derogatory, misinformed, homophobic conversations or comments about gay parents. There are several options open. The parent can turn and walk away or attempt to otherwise terminate the interaction. If it is not too stressful, she or he can counter assertively with accurate information and the sources of that information. The parent can request that the offensive party refrain from making those kinds of comments, and so forth.

Obviously, the kind of tactic a gay parent chooses will depend on whether or not she or he is openly gay. It is most likely that these comments will be made, however, if others do know that the individual is gay. It is essential to teach gay parents that they do not have to listen to stress-inducing comments, and that they can come up with workable solutions to handle others who attempt to engage them in derogatory conversations about the topic of gay parenting.

Gay parents, child custody, and the courts

Lesbian mothers and gay fathers live with a constant threat of losing their parental rights. Almost anyone can challenge an individual's custody of their children. Although the most common occasion for dispute is between parents during the dissolution of a marriage, the right to custody may also be challenged by other relatives or government authorities.[26]

Child custody disputes following divorce. If a child's parents are divorcing and cannot agree on the disposition of the children, the court is then called in to decide what to do in the child's "best interest." The presiding judge in such cases has complete discretion in determining what the child's best interests are. He or she may act in accordance with or completely contrary to testimony and recommendations given by expert witnesses. Even though a lesbian mother's social worker, psychiatrist, and physician all testify to her competence as a parent, motivation, mental health, and the health and well-being of her child(ren), the judge may simply decide that it is "in the best interest of the child" to give custody to the father or another relative. Riddle says that judges will frequently give custody to someone other than the gay parent in order not to be "responsible for the consequences."[27] She says:

☐ Personally, I have spent up to 5½ hours on the witness stand, with no opposing testimony, and still had the judge refuse to grant custody to a perfectly competent gay parent for these reasons. Never underestimate how much the misinformation present in the courts can influence a custody decision.[27]

Child custody disputes involving relatives. Even in cases in which a relative other than the natural parent sues for custody of the child, the gay parent's status as the natural parent of the child is not likely to account for much.

The courts retain the discretion to *presume* that it would be detrimental to the children to allow them to live with their lesbian mother and judges are free to apply their own value judgments in determining what is detrimental.[28]

As in disputes between parents, the judge may make her or his decision *regardless* of evidence that demonstrates the gay parent's mental health and competence as a parent.

Child custody disputes involving state intervention. When the state intervenes between parent and child, the situation is usually a serious one involving neglect or abuse. If the parent is also discovered to be gay, this may make it more difficult for the parent to get the child back. There are also situations in which the state may step in and remove a child because the mother has been re-

ported for lesbianism.[28] If the state decides that exposure to a lesbian relationship is potentially damaging to the child, the child may then be placed in a foster home.

Custody decisions favorable to gay parents. Riddle estimates that gay parents are winning (therefore losing) about 50% of the child custody battles they undertake.[1] Not very good odds. Unfortunately, even when a gay parent wins custody of a child, that does not mean that the problems are over.

Frequently, the awarding of custody to a lesbian mother, for example, is made with the condition that the mother not enter or continue a relationship with another women, or that she see her lover only under special circumstances. Martin and Lyon[20] present two cases, one in Seattle and one in San Jose, California, in which such conditions were attached to the custody decision. In the first, two women who shared a house and the responsibility for their six children were forced to separate because it was not considered in the best interests of the children to live in a home with "two mothers as models."[29] In the second case, a lesbian woman was awarded custody of her three children on the condition that she only see her lover when the children were in school or visiting their father.

Even after the decision has been made, the parent must be extremely careful about total compliance with any conditions the court has set. Failure to comply can be grounds for the case to be reopened and the custody orders changed.[30]

Summary. Gay parents facing child custody disputes in court are confronted by the tremendous obstacle of commonly held negative beliefs about gays. The major concerns nongays have about allowing gay parents to have custody of their children have all been shown to be unfounded, yet gay parents continue to lose many custody decisions. Even decisions in favor of a gay parent maintaining custody can result in continued trauma because of the conditions placed by the court. In all court decisions, the discretion of the judge is complete and final, and decisions against gay parents can be and frequently are made in the face of overwhelmingly positive testimony.

Although more research needs to be done, the small amount that exists demonstrates that gays as a group are competent, motivated parents and that their children do not usually suffer negative effects from their parent's lifestyle. The cost of fighting for and maintaining child custody and of raising children in a gay home may be high, yet the important qualities of love, openness, and parental consistency are as available in gay as in nongay families.

COPING WITH GAY PARENTHOOD

Being a gay parent can be stressful, and in this section we will discuss some of the major problems that gays face. But it is also a rewarding and fulfilling experience. Although we will talk primarily about the hardships, we do not want the positive side of gay parenting to be forgotten. Nor should parents be allowed to lose sight of the joys of raising children, which, after all, are the reasons gay men and women are willing to pay a high price for parenthood. It is easy for client and counselor to become so involved in working with problems that being a gay parent begins to look like unmitigated trauma. Every effort should be made to help gay parents have as many pleasurable experiences as possible, even during hard times. A conscious effort to spend some positive time every day with children, partner, and self can help clients cope more effectively and with less strain.

We cannot begin in this book to cover all the possible kinds of problems that gay parents may face. We have attempted to address the issues we believe to be of major importance. Both counselor and client are urged to read further and to make connections with gay parents in the community as well as with local and national gay parents' organizations. We will suggest further reading as it relates to specific areas covered below.

Gay parenthood as a new role

A surprisingly high percentage of lesbian women and gay men get married.[31] Of those who marry, about half have at least one child as a result of the marriage, although it is not known what percentage maintain custody or visiting rights after

dissolution of the marriage.[31] Interestingly, almost half of the white women who later identified as lesbian did not think of themselves as lesbian when they married (the proportion is much lower for Black men and women and white men).[31]

This means that for a significant number of gay parents, and particularly white lesbian women, the trauma of divorce may be coupled with the strain of coming out and of entry into a gay lifestyle. If child custody is also being contested at the same time, the stresses on such a person may appear almost unbearable and may affect all parts of the person's life: psychological, emotional, physical.

If the parent is just coming out as a gay person, he or she may need help in doing this as we discuss in Chapter 7. Furthermore, socialization being what it is, the newly divorced gay parent is liable to feel guilty and frightened. There is almost inevitably some social opprobrium connected with divorce. Many people still believe they should stay together "for the sake of the children," and when this proves impossible, may experience guilt over their failure as marital partners and parents. Gays are not exempt from these emotions. Coupled with these feelings there may be a host of feelings as well about being gay. There may be relief about being out of the marriage, joy at being able to express one's sexual and affectional feelings, guilt about feeling happy in a situation that is painful for others, fear of what it means to be gay, and confusion about all the feelings that the person is experiencing simultaneously.

The helping professional will want to help the client separate and identify each of her or his feelings. It is especially important to identify and validate positive feelings the client may be having and to help the client keep these feelings separate from other, negative feelings, to teach the client that it is possible to feel joy about the change in circumstances as well as pain, and that experiencing positive emotions does not mean that he or she is a "terrible" person. As with other clients who are coming out, and who may be uncertain about what it means to be gay, or who hold negative beliefs about gay people, one of the counselor's first tasks is to provide the client with valid information about being gay as well as support in her or his choice of a lifestyle.

Remember that many gay people, particularly those who are just coming out, share society's prejudices and misconceptions. They are every bit as likely as nongays to believe that gays are sick and that the gay lifestyle is wrong. Perhaps even more important, they may believe that gay parents cannot raise healthy, "normal" (that is, heterosexual) children. Even if the parent does not want to have custody or visiting rights, he or she may worry about having hurt the child as a "latent" homosexual.

In working with such clients, it is most important that the parent be assured that her or his sexual preference is not going to damage the children and that there is nothing wrong with being gay. As with any other gay person who is coming out, the counselor should provide accurate information about sexual preference and should, if possible, provide the gay parent with contacts with the gay community.

Helping gay parents through the child custody process

The two major parts of the child custody issue are deciding whether to attempt to gain custody and the custody fight itself. Lesbian mothers are much more likely to be involved in actual custody litigation than gay fathers, who are usually caught up in attempts to win visitation rights.[32] In either case, and whether the parent decides to fight for or relinquish parental rights, both emotional and psychological trauma are almost inevitable.

Deciding whether or not to attempt to gain custody. If the gay parent's ex-spouse has determined to contest custody rights, a very difficult and demanding decision must be made. The gay parent must realize that a court battle over custody

will be exhausting in every way and will take a toll on both parent and child. He or she must also realize that, although more cases are being won now than before, the odds are still not good. Even if custody is won, the conditions may be exacting and must be adhered to meticulously. Even so, the case can be reopened at any time and the custody decision altered or reversed. It is important that the helping professional stress the realities of the situation so that the gay parent can make an informed decision. It is especially important that the gay parent be put in touch with others who have been through the court process so that he or she can get a realistic picture of what it will be like from someone who has experienced it. The decision must be made out of a desire to raise the child or children, not out of spite, anger, guilt, or political conviction.

If the parent decides not to ask for custody, she or he will go through the normal processes of grief and separation that would be experienced by any divorced person, gay or nongay, under the circumstances. The helping professional can help the client manage these normal feelings, and should also be sensitive to possible negative beliefs on the client's part about self as a gay person. Women particularly are socialized to believe that their role as a mother is of primary importance in determining self-worth. Do not let the client confuse the decision to lead her own life as a lesbian with her value as a human being or as a woman.

If the parent decides to fight for custody, there are some things he or she should do. First, your client should have a good lawyer, preferably a feminist. Second, your client should be in contact with as many supportive groups and individuals as possible, such as the Lesbian Mothers' National Defense Fund.[33] Third, if your client can read, you can suggest some reading materials and should be able to tell your client where to find these locally or how to send for them.[34] If your client can't read or can't afford the materials, it will be helpful if you are familiar with their contents and can cover the material with the parent. Fourth, make every attempt to encourage your client to get the case settled out of court. Most cases involving lesbian mothers are decided this way and the odds are definitely better in the gay parent's favor.

In working with the client yourself, prepare the client to handle an extremely stressful and possibly extended process. In getting ready for this, you will certainly want to teach your client some good coping skills. Assertiveness training, stress management, and problem-solving skills will all be invaluable.[35] Your client can anticipate many situations both during and after the custody battle in which these coping skills will be severely tested. A good time to start learning them is before they are needed.

If a gay parent wins custody of the children, the trouble is still not necessarily over. Raising a child as a single parent is difficult enough. Raising a child as a gay parent may be more so because of societal attitudes. There are bright spots, however. Lesbian mothers are more likely to be "less religious, better educated and more often professionally employed, and more involved with the women's movement than the general female population."[36] Furthermore, "single lesbian mothers tend to share housing with other adults, to own their own homes, and to operate their own businesses more than do single heterosexual mothers."[37] But the major worries that distinguish gay from nongay mothers are really those related to their sexual preference and how it will affect their children and the process of child rearing.

Social adjustments of gay parents

Unless they live in a very supportive environment, gay parents probably worry much more about "passing" than do gays who are not parents.[37] Pagelow found that "with very few exceptions, the lesbian mothers (in her study) emphasized the necessity of 'passing' in order to avoid termination from employment, subsequent blackballing, eviction from residence or problems with child custody."[39] Furthermore, gay parents worry that their children's peers will find out and that the children will suffer because of this.[38]

There are indications that the effects on children are not as severe as lesbian mothers anticipate. Studies have found that there seem to be no deleterious effects to children from growing up in a gay environment,[4] that many children seem unaware of negative societal reactions toward their parents, and that those who are aware of these reactions are able to support their mother's lifestyle and to realize that the problem lies with society, not with their mother.[39]

As with other clients who are inappropriately anxious about being identified as gay, gay parents will benefit from learning to tell those situations that deserve caution from those that do not, and from learning the difference between realistic caution and unrealistic anxiety. With gay parents, however, the possibility of loss of custody may require a greater degree of caution than is true for other gays. Because of this necessity for passing, the importance of a support network for gay parents is magnified. Having children will often mean that the gay parent is forced to spend more time with nongays and more time passing than other gays. This can be stressful. Encourage gay parents to develop and use a local support network if at all possible, preferably one that includes other gay parents and their children. This will provide a place where both parents and children can relax in a supportive atmosphere.

Coping with children as a gay parent

Coming out to children. Berzon strongly advocates, and we concur, that lesbian mothers (and presumably gay fathers) come out to children as soon as possible.[40] There are a number of reasons for this. First, trying to keep sexual preference a secret, particularly from older children, is going to put a strain on the entire family, especially if the parent has a lover sharing the living space. In a situation in which open communication is especially desirable, hiding one of the most salient facts of the parent's life is going to make this almost impossible. Sexuality and sexual preference are not matters to be ashamed of, yet this is the message gay parents give their children when they avoid the issue.

Second, attempting to avoid the issue is going to create communication problems, especially with older children. It is almost inevitable that older children will be aware of differences between their home life and the lives of their friends. If the parent does not give permission for these differences to be discussed by broaching the subject, it tells the child that these are matters that should not be talked about. This may confirm the negative impression that children receive about gayness from other sources. It may prohibit the child from asking questions and sharing thoughts and feelings, not only about her or his parents, but about other related areas of concern such as the child's own sexuality and sexual preference, comments made by peers and other adults about "queers," lifestyle differences, and the like.

Third, if the parent does not bring up the subject of gayness at a planned time, the child may find out about it from others and be shocked and upset or afraid to discuss it. This means that the first impression the child gets about the parent's gayness will probably be a negative one. The longer a parent waits, the more likely it is that the child will be accumulating a weight of negative evidence and the more difficult it may become to present the child with a positive picture.

Finally, the strain of trying to keep gayness a secret, particularly if a couple is involved, may cause or become confused with other problems. If the children have not been told, a gay couple may feel constrained to be abnormally distant and circumspect, not feeling free to be even minimally affectionate or open with each other. This can create enormous pressure on the entire family, and particularly on the gay couple. It can lead to resentment of the children and a generally disrupted life. If there are other problems in the relationship, these can be masked or worsened by the pervasive strain of attempting to hide reality.

Parents who are resistant to sharing the fact of their sexual preference with their children may still be uncomfortable with it themselves. Go over carefully with a client the reasons he or she has for not wanting to come out to the children. There may be some good reasons, but these are usually temporary. If the person is completely opposed to it, talk over very carefully his or her own attitudes toward gayness. Also explore with the parent his or her fears about the child's reaction to the truth. Point out that the child will eventually become aware that something is different, even if the parent does not come out. It is far better to deal with this difference in the open where there is a chance it may be viewed as either neutral or good, rather than hiding it and increasing the chance that the difference will be viewed as something "wrong."

Helping professionals are themselves sometimes opposed to a parent's coming out to her or his children. If you find yourself strongly opposed, you may also still have some negative thoughts about gays or about gay parents. If you do, and you cannot change them, you should refer the client and attempt to resolve these issues yourself before working with other gay clients.

How to come out to children. The manner and content of coming out to children should probably be tempered by their ages. Younger children are less likely to understand what it means to be gay and are also less likely to be concerned with the social implications of gayness than older children. Younger children are more likely to want to know what it means in terms of their mother's or father's behavior toward them. Anything that decreases a parent's attention is going to be seen as undesirable. Very young children are probably the easiest to handle because they grow up in an atmosphere in which gayness is ordinary, and so will not be confronted with the trauma of an observable shift in circumstances. If the mother or father has a lover, this person's presence is also more likely to be taken in stride by a younger than an older child.

Older children are more likely to be worried about the fact that their home life is different from that of their peers. They may be embarrassed by their gay parent(s) in public, and may worry that their friends will find out.[41] These worries usually subside after an initial period of time, but they are worth anticipating. An atmosphere of openness and trust will make it easier for children to communicate their reactions directly.

Coming out to children should be planned the same way one plans coming out to other adults. The client should decide what to say and how and when to say it[42] and should practice with the counselor before attempting to talk to the children. It may be hard for a parent to anticipate a child's reaction, so it is best to have the client practice handling several kinds of responses. The parent should be ready for a negative reaction on the part of the child, even though he or she is not really expecting one. That way, if a child becomes upset or angry, the parent will already have practiced ways to cope with this.

In working with the client, it is crucial that you help the client present being gay as a positive reality. Coming out should not have the feeling of telling a guilty secret or of embarrassment or shame. If a parent is not sufficiently comfortable with being gay to talk about it comfortably and with assurance, then telling the children should be postponed until the client has become personally at peace with being gay.

If the client can be reasonably matter of fact in coming out and can communicate personal pleasure about being gay, it will be easier for the child to respond honestly. Just because the parent feels positive, however, does not ensure that the child will. Gay parents should be prepared to respond to their child's feelings as well as the content of what he or she says. If a child responds to a parent's talk about gayness by calling the parent a ''queer,'' or by an angry outburst, the parent should focus on the child's feelings of anger and hurt and talk about these rather than berate the child for being insulting or for using the word *queer*. Role playing in the counselor's office can help the client learn to respond appropriately to feelings.

Children's reactions to parent's sexual preference. Gay parents probably spend a lot of time worrying needlessly about their children's reactions to their sexual preference. All in all, children turn out to be surprisingly resilient and understanding. In most cases, children do not seem to have any long-term negative reactions.[43] In fact, most children prefer living with a gay parent to the situation that preceded their parents' divorce.[44]

Although children do respond with acceptance very often, they may also have concerns about their parent's sexual preference. Lewis found that children's main concerns were that they had to keep their mother's sexual preference a secret, worry about their own sexual preference, and various concerns about their mother's lover or about the relationship with their father.

Some of these worries may be answered, particularly for the older child who is more likely to be concerned, by presenting the child with facts and encouraging discussion of worries that the child has. In attempting to find out what a child worries about, do not neglect and be sure parents do not neglect to ask children about positive experiences. If a mother or father (or counselor) focuses only on what is going wrong or what the child is concerned about, this gives the child the message that he or she ought to be worrying and that attention is more likely to be given to talk about problems than about positive experiences. This is an outcome that should definitely be avoided because it may increase the likelihood that the child will think about and verbalize negative experiences.

Trying to pass with young children. A parent who is considering coming out to a very young child must keep in mind the child's limited capacity to understand the need for secrecy. One gay parent comments:

☐ My experience has been that with a young verbose offspring, "passing" is almost a joke. And if I'm attempting to "pass," I must be prepared to go to "Plan B" at the drop of a hat. [My son, a 4-year-old] knows no discretion and doesn't know he's telling anything he shouldn't. The best way I've found to cope with it all is to realize that "passing" is not really a viable option in most situations (e.g. school, neighbors, relatives, friends). This puts added fuel on the worry that custody *could* be challenged by *anybody* . . . any time.[45]

The helping professional should raise this as a consideration to the parent with a very young child. If the child is particularly bright, she or he may make observations and ask questions sufficiently astute to make passing difficult without excessive subterfuge. This is part of the reality that a gay parent must face. It is not pleasant, but the gay parent must be willing to cope with the possibility that his or her child may unwittingly ''blow the closet door wide open.'' If the parent is not willing to consider this option or is severely stressed by the possibility, it may be wise to discuss with him or her the idea of relinquishing custody or of moving to an area of the country where social, economic, and legal repercussions are least likely to occur.

Gay couples as parents

Unless prohibited by a court decision, most gay parents will probably become involved with a lover. Some are already involved at the time of divorce. Many will want to share living space. This will inevitably raise some problems, although the problems are not unlike those caused within a nongay family by the addition of a new authority figure. Shared parenting also has some very positive consequences, among them, increased support, love and companionship, shared responsibilities, and shared good times.

It is most important that, as a helping professional, you treat a gay couple and the children with them as a *two-parent family,* unless the natural parent specifically indicates that this is not the case. In many instances, at least where lesbian mothers are concerned, the mother's lover becomes a second parent.[46] She is not a father figure and should not attempt to be one. Nor is she an ''aunt'' or a ''friend.'' Although the lesbian couple may not, and probably will not, choose to use the word *lover* to refer to each other, the fact that

they are lovers in all senses of the word should not be disguised any more than it is in a nongay family. This does not mean that the couple should go into detail about their sexual relationship in front of the children, or that they should make love in front of the children. But it is important that the children see the relationship as exactly what it is: a healthy love relationship between two people of the same gender.

If the mother's or father's lover appears on the scene shortly after the divorce or comes into an already established single-parent family, it is natural for the children to be resentful, suspicious, and jealous. Another adult in the house means another authority figure. It also means competition for the natural parent's time and attention. Boys particularly may resent another woman living with their mother because they are afraid she will try to replace the father. As in other situations, open communication and an acceptance of the child's feelings are important. It is also helpful for gay couples to realize that many of the problems they face are faced by nongay couples as well.

Trying to incorporate a child or children into a gay relationship may also cause strain for the partners, and the mother's or father's lover may also experience jealousy and will certainly be under a strain at least at first. If possible, difficulties should be anticipated and discussed *before* the lover moves in. The relationship should not be suddenly forced on the children. Although they may have no ultimate choice in the matter, discussion with them before making final decisions will allow children a chance to negotiate matters and help them think of themselves as part of the family.

The couple will also benefit from deciding before they live together how they will handle such matters as discipline of the children, household responsibilities involving child care, finances, sleeping arrangements, private time separately and together, and their behavior in front of the children. The natural parent should be clear about expectations regarding the children, and both partners should be comfortable with their agreement before household arrangements are finalized. Both partners will benefit from knowing how to be assertive and how to share thoughts and feelings. They will need to be able to separate inevitable conflicts over the children from their love for each other, something that is not always easy to do.

Teaching children to cope with societal prejudice. Gay parents often worry about what will happen if a child's peers find out about the parent's sexual preference, about whether or not the child will tell the nongay parent or some other adult thus threatening the custody arrangement, and about the general affect of societal discrimination against gay people on their children. These are all reasonable concerns, but are not reasons for high anxiety or panic.

The response of a child's peers probably varies according to the same variables that affect adult homophobia. In more rural, religious, and conservative areas, gay people in general will experience more difficulty. So will their children, in all likelihood. This might be something for a gay parent to consider before taking custody of a child. Some parents manage without apparently encountering serious difficulty. Others, especially those in rural areas, have a difficult time. One lesbian mother found that her child's peers were no problem, but that some of the nongay mothers were.[47] Even so, the children seemed to handle this well.

No matter where a gay family lives, but particularly in highly homophobic areas, children of gay parents may have to learn "situational ethics."[48] The child learns that it is okay to be open about her or his parent's gayness with some people but not with others. Although this may be uncomfortable for a gay couple who would like to be open about their lifestyle, it is not a terrible thing for children to learn, and is not really that different from other kinds of discriminations children are required to make about when behavior is and is not appropriate. Most people teach their children a variety of situational discriminations concerning language, dress, and general behavior.

One positive way to do this with regard to gayness and prejudice is to teach children that people live and believe differently. Each person has a right to live and believe as he or she wants as long as other people aren't hurt. The parent can talk about the ways that their family differs from other families, and elicit the children's perceptions of how other families differ from each other. Care should be taken to elicit positive differences, as well as those that are negative or neutral. The children can be taught concurrently that some people are prejudiced against others because of differences in race, religion, sex, sexual preference, age, income, and so on. This may be a good way to begin teaching a child about prejudice and tolerance and showing her or him what the effects of prejudice can be.

SUMMARY

Being a gay parent, like being a nongay parent, is a mixture of joyous and painful experiences, although gay parenthood may require more effort, primarily because of societal intolerance. We have indicated that the societal concerns about gay parents are unfounded, yet they exist. Furthermore, they create challenges to a parent's custody or visitation rights, questions on the part of others about gay parents' ability to be responsible, loving, and effective in raising children, questions about how to come out to children, and the necessity for teaching children about prejudice and intolerance.

Many gay parents have met these challenges successfully, both for themselves and their children, whereas others are just beginning the process. We have suggested ways in which the challenges may be met in the best interests of the parent, lover, and children; and we have cautioned the counselor to be aware of the tendency to focus on the negative and forget the positive. Clients who are gay parents should be encouraged to view the positives of their unique position and given the opportunity to explore alternatives in an atmosphere that is supportive, recognizing that being a gay parent can, indeed be a joyous experience.

210

END NOTES

1. Riddle, D. *Gay parents and child custody issues.* Unpublished manuscript, Department of Psychology, University of Arizona, Tucson, 1977, p. 2.
2. Riddle, 1977, p. 2; Hitchens, D. "Social attitudes, legal standards, and personal trauma in child custody cases." *Journal of Homosexuality,* 1979/1980, *5*(1/2), 89.
3. Pagelow believes that evidence shows lesbian mothers have more difficulty than nongay single mothers. Single women with children generally may have more trouble with housing and employment and, as women, earn only 59¢ for every $1.00 earned by a man in a comparable job. See Pagelow, M. "Heterosexual and lesbian single mothers: A comparison of problems, coping, and solutions." *Journal of Homosexuality,* 1980, *5*(3), 189-204.
4. Riddle, 1977.
5. A number of writers mention this in passing, among them: Riddle, 1977, p. 8, who cites Kinsey; and Martin, D., & Lyon, P. "Lesbian mothers." *Ms.,* 1973, *2*(4), 79, who refer to their own experiences in having met "thousands" of lesbians, none of whom were raised by gay parents.
6. Bryant, B. *Lesbian mothers.* Unpublished manuscript, 1975. (Available from Lymar Associates, 330 Ellis St., Room 401, San Francisco, Calif.) cited in Nungesser, L. "Theoretical bases for research on the acquisition of social sex-roles by children of lesbian mothers." *Journal of Homosexuality,* 1980, *5*(3), 183; Lewis, S. *Sunday's women.* Boston: Beacon Press, 1979, p. 115 cites Richard Green as quoted in Pred, E. (Ed.). "Studies and surveys." *The Advocate,* 31 May 1978, no pages given.
7. Riddle, 1977, pp. 5; 8.
8. Bryant, cited in Nungesser, 1980, p. 183.
9. Spence, J., & Helmreich, R. *Masculinity and femininity: Their psychological dimensions, correlates, and antecedents.* Austin: University of Texas Press, 1978, 54-55. For a good summary of data supporting higher self-esteem among androgynous subjects see Kelley, J., & Worell, J. "New formulations of sex roles and androgyny: A critical review." *Journal of Consulting and Clinical Psychology,* 1977, *45*(6), 1101-1115.
10. Bem, S. "Sex role adaptability: One consequence of psychological androgyny." *Journal of Personality and Social Psychology,* 1975, *31*(4), 634-643.
11. Kelley & Worell, 1977, p. 1107.
12. Riddle, D. "Relating to children: Gays as role models." *Journal of Social Issues,* 1978, *34*(3), 38-57.
13. Spence & Helmreich, 1978, pp. 54-55.
14. Ostrow, D. *Gay and straight parents: What about the children?* Unpublished Bachelor's thesis, Hampshire College, 1977, cited in Nungesser, 1980, p. 85.
15. Riddle, 1977, p. 5.
16. Martin & Lyon, 1973, pp. 79-80; Riddle, 1977, p. 9. One lesbian mother in a personal communication commented of her son, "This happened at so early an age (2½ years) that I was stunned!"
17. Martin & Lyon, 1973, p. 80; Riddle, 1977, p. 9.
18. Riddle, 1977.
19. Lewis, K. "Children of lesbians: Their point of view." *Social Work,* 1980, *25*(3), 203.
20. Lewis, 1980, p. 199.
21. Lewis, 1980, p. 203.
22. Riddle, 1977, p. 6.
23. Riddle, 1977, pp. 8-9.
24. Riddle, 1977, p. 10; Mayadas, N., & Duehn, W. "Children in gay families: An investigation of services." *Homosexual Counseling Journal,* 1976, *3*(2), 76.
25. Personal communication.
26. Hitchins, D. "Social attitudes, legal standards, and personal trauma in child custody cases." *Journal of Homosexuality,* 1979/1980, *5*(1-2), 91.
27. Riddle, 1977, p. 4.
28. Hitchins, 1979/1980, p. 93.
29. Martin & Lyon, 1973, pp. 78-79.
30. Hitchins, 1979/1980, p. 94.
31. Bell, A., & Weinberg, M. *Homosexualities: A study of diversity among men and women.* New York: Simon & Schuster, 1978, pp. 160-170.
32. Hitchins, 1979/1980, p. 89.
33. Lesbian Mothers' National Defense Fund, 1446 Lorentz Place North, Seattle, Wash. 98109. Probably the best single resource agency for any kind of information about gays is the National Gay Task Force, 80 Fifth Avenue, New York, NY 10011. Also see Stevens, M. "Lesbian mothers in transition." In G. Vida (Ed.), *Our right to love: A lesbian resource book.* Englewood Cliffs, N.J.: Prentice-Hall, 1978, p. 211, for a list of other resources.
34. Stevens, 1978, recommends Gibson, G. *By her own admission: A lesbian mother's fight to keep her son.* New York: Doubleday, 1977; Women in Transition, Inc. *Women in transition.* New York: Scribner & Sons, 1976; and Hope, K., & Young, N. *Momma—The sourcebook for single mothers.* New York: New American Library, 1976. Also see Lewis, 1979, pp. 114-127; and Wolf, D. "The lesbian community." Berkeley: University of California Press, 1979, pp. 136-165, on lesbian motherhood in the gay community.
35. See Gambrill, E. *Behavior modification: Handbook of assessment, intervention and evaluation.* San Francisco: Jossey-Bass, 1977, pp. 530-601, on social skills and assertiveness training, pp. 438-529 on stress management, and pp. 394-402 on problem solving.
36. Nungesser, 1980, p. 183.
37. Pagelow, 1980, pp. 200-203.
38. Lewis, 1979, pp. 121-123.

39. Lewis, 1980, pp. 201; 203.
40. Berzon, B. ''Sharing your lesbian identity with your children.'' In Vida, 1978b.
41. Berzon, 1978, p. 71.
42. See Berzon, 1978, esp. pp. 72-73 for a good discussion of this point.
43. Lewis, 1980, p. 203.
44. Lewis, 1980, p. 199.
45. Personal communication.
46. Lewis, 1979; Wolf, 1979, p. 160; Vida, 1978, pp. 76-77.
47. Lewis, 1979, pp. 121-122.
48. Wolf, 1979, p. 155.

PART FOUR

Summation

16

Positive intervention with gay clients: a summation and conclusion

We have attempted to present sufficient discussion of empirical evidence to convince the reader, as we are convinced, that being gay is a normal, nonpathological form of human sexual and affectional expression. We have also tried to show that gay people experience distinct problems caused primarily by societal oppression, but arising as well from the lack of visible models for healthy gay lifestyles and relationships. A great many gays do lead enjoyable, highly effective lives; many have excellent relationships, but are seldom identifiable as gay and are probably less likely to be the people who seek professional help. Throughout the book, we have made suggestions for intervention as and where these have seemed relevant to the content under discussion. In this final chapter, we would like to summarize our opinions about intervention with gay clients and make some general recommendations for working positively with them based on our beliefs about gay people and gay lifestyles.

POSITIVE INTERVENTION

Truly effective intervention with gay clients requires that mental health professionals take a positive approach. This does not mean simply that the counselor is accepting of homoerotic people and lifestyles. It means being willing to work with clients in accordance with the realities of gay life, rather than with nongay interpretations of those realities. It was long ago time to stop trying to convert gays. It is now time to move beyond merely helping gays cope and adjust to helping them develop innovative and satisfying ways to grow as gay people.

In order to do this, helping professionals must learn to challenge some of their preconceptions about what is best for their clients, and some of their set ways of looking at the world. They must support gay clients in exploring and developing personally satisfactory ways of expressing sexuality and gender identity that may differ from traditional nongay expectations. For example, gay clients can be encouraged to move beyond stereotypical gender role definitions if they wish and taught ways of coping assertively with societal reactions. At the same time, gays who are comfortable with more gender-typed behavior can be reassured that they do not have to conform to either a "butch" or "femme" image in order to be gay. Such men and women may need to learn assertiveness skills to use with other gay people who expect gays to conform to gay stereotypes.

There has still been little written by either clinicians or researchers about counseling gay couples. At this point, it is somewhat avant garde to talk about doing couple counseling with gays, and yet that is often what is necessary, because most gays are involved in some type of couple relationship. Many helping professionals, however, are still using the heterosexual marriage model of intervention either for lack of any other or because they believe it to be the only appropriate model.

We have tried to show differences between gay and nongay primary love relationships. We believe that those differences require different intervention approaches. For example, it is fairly clear that, for reasons we have discussed, gay couples generally do not remain together as long as married heterosexual couples do. Gay couple counseling, to be effective, must take this into account. Helping professionals, both gay and nongay, must disabuse themselves of the notion that healthy people have lifelong relationships and are monogamous. This is a patently false assumption, and one that can render intervention useless at best, and damaging at worst, to people who simply cannot fit into the heterosexual marriage model. Because this model predominates, however, those people, both gay and nongay, who are experiencing difficulty with that model are unlikely to be aware of any other options.

Mental health professionals can be instrumental in helping gay couples develop personally satisfactory relationship styles. This will often mean urging couples to eschew the typical nongay approach to relationships that emphasizes total sharing of incomes, living space, checking accounts, and so forth. Some gay couples may find it preferable to develop more independent relationship styles in which the partners maintain separate accounts, possessions, bedroom, and even living arrangements. This contradicts everything people have learned about how two people who love each other are supposed to behave, but as we have attempted to show in this book, it is often much more consistent with the realities of gay life. This does not mean, however, that couples who prefer to attempt traditional relationships should be discouraged from doing so. Rather, those who are dissatisfied with traditional arrangements can be reassured that this does not mean there is something wrong with

them or with the relationship. Instead, the counselor can work with them to try to develop a situation that is mutually satisfactory.

There may also be times when the most effective intervention a counselor can make is to help a couple dissolve, rather than maintain, a relationship. Again, this may run contrary to what many counselors believe is appropriate. In gay relationships, however, where there are often pressures forcing couples apart, it may be necessary to focus more attention on helping couples dissolve their relationship satisfactorily than is the case in nongay relationships.

In addition to aiding the client in self-acceptance of orientation, counselors should be willing to help clients with problems related to coming out to others. Although we certainly advocate sensitivity to the client's current skill and motivational levels regarding this, we also believe it is time for helping professionals to encourage and support gay clients in coming out as soon as they are ready to do so. This means that the professional should consider the issue of sufficient importance to be willing to spend time with the client preparing him or her to come out to others, by using role playing, stress management, assertiveness training, or any other type of intervention that will make it easier for the client to come out and feel positive about the result. Gay counselors particularly need to be aware of their own concerns in this area. Some are so afraid of being identified personally that they frighten gay clients into staying in the closet. Others are convinced that coming out is so politically or morally correct that they are contemptuous of those who are afraid to do so. Gay counselors must be willing to start wherever the client is and move toward the client's goals. If the counselor, gay or nongay, finds the client's goals incompatible with her or his needs or convictions, the client should be referred elsewhere.

Another area of intervention that is often ignored, particularly by nongay therapists, is training gay clients to be effectively gay. This may include such things as providing information and counseling about where and how to make sexual, social, and other kinds of contacts, or providing information on health issues or referral to appropriate resources for such issues.

All in all, the attitude that we would most like to see helping professionals adopt is that, although nongay society can make it very difficult for a gay person, being gay is potentially a positive way to be. We would also like helping professionals to realize that being gay is different in some important ways from being nongay. Many of the differences can be viewed as positive options for gays, such as increased freedom from gender role behavior, innovative and less restrictive relationship styles, gender empathy, increased communication, and possibly more satisfactory sexual relationships. Positive intervention means helping clients capitalize on these while learning to overcome other possible negative consequences of living a socially disapproved lifestyle.

Being gay has both positive and negative repercussions in this society. The counselor who is interested in working with gay clients in a manner that will benefit the client must be aware of his or her own level of homophobia, understand the differences between being gay and being nongay, be aware of the many different alternatives available for healthy relationships, and critically examine intervention approaches to eliminate assumptions of heteroeroticism and monogamous marriage as the only healthy models. Once this is accomplished, he or she should be able to help lesbian women and gay men deal positively with any life issues that are problematic.

APPENDIX

Throughout this book we have suggested several approaches for helping lesbian women and gay men deal with issues of living that create problems for some of them. We have made these suggestions with an underlying assumption that changing a homoerotic orientation is not an appropriate goal.

Although we began with that assumption, there are some therapists and counselors who still maintain that a person who is uncomfortable with his or her homoerotic orientation should be given the option of altering that to a heteroerotic orientation, and intervention techniques should be available which will help those clients to change.

What help or intervention approach should a helping professional offer a client who is uncomfortable with or disturbed by his or her homoerotic orientation? The following article by Eli Coleman suggests some possible answers. In it he discusses some of the reasons behind our underlying assumption and indicates that helping professionals are beginning to deal with the issue in a manner that recognizes both the importance and validity of a homoerotic orientation.

Toward a new model of treatment of homosexuality: a review*

ELI COLEMAN

There is probably little agreement today about the treatment of homosexuality. Counselors and therapists are faced with theoretical, ethical, moral, and practical decisions as to how to treat homosexual clients. The traditional approach has been to treat homosexuality as an illness and to attempt to cause a heterosexual shift. Recently, there has been a growing body of knowledge that has criticized this illness model. A new model has been slowly emerging that treats homosexuality not as a definable entity but as an attitude and behavior that is compatible with one of a large variety of life-styles.

This paper will review the research on various treatment approaches to homosexuality. Most of the studies on treatment outcomes that have been reported and reviewed here have been on male homosexuals. Consequently, there exists a serious gap in our understanding of the treatment of lesbians. It will become evident that more research is needed in this area as well as more empirical research on therapeutic approaches that do not consider homosexuality an illness and in need of "cure."

---

*This article appeared in the *Journal of Homosexuality*, Summer 1978, *3*(4), 345-359. © 1978 by The Haworth Press. Reprinted with permission.

THE ILLNESS MODEL
Psychoanalytic

Many psychoanalysts contend that homosexuality is determined by early childhood experiences. For example, Bieber and his associates contend that the presence of a fairly specific family constellation and peer relationships results in a homosexual outcome.[1] In this constellation, the relationship between the mother and father is severely disturbed. In most cases, relationships with siblings, particularly with brothers, are hostile. Relationships between same-sex peer groups are unhappy, painful experiences. In many cases the mothers are close-binding, possessive, and overintimate. The mothers, apparently, attempt to fulfill what is lacking in their relationship with their husbands. The fathers, invariably, are either absent or detached and hostile. Consequently, the prehomosexual son develops a fear and hate of his father on the one hand and a yearning for his affection on the other. The individuals, Bieber et al. theorize, develop a homosexual orientation as a complex, substitutive adaption to preserve sexual gratification. They avoid heterosexual intercourse and competition for women as a way of defending against attack by aggressive males. They seek out homosexual contact as a way of diverting men from women and to gain acceptance and love from men.

Treatment involves individual or group therapy designed to uncover early childhood conflicts in disturbed parental relationships and, as a result, reduce the individual's neurotic fear of homosexuality. Special attention is given to the disturbed relationship with the individual's father and other men.

Bieber et al.'s premise of disturbed familial relationships has been strongly criticized. First of all, the population upon which they based their conclusions was a select patient population and not representative of the general homosexual population.[2] Second, all data collected consisted of judgments by the subjects' analysts. Gonsiorek[3] points out that all of the researchers and rating analysts were members of one particular psychoanalytic society and had considerable knowledge and input into the study. Inadvertently, they may have simply designed a study and collected data that were consistent with their current notions of homosexuality. Third, there has been difficulty trying to replicate the Bieber group findings (see Siegelman,[4] for a review of these studies). Bieber,[5] himself, claims that since 1962 he has examined 850 male homosexuals, and 50 pairs of parents whose sons were homosexual. Without presenting the data in any form, Bieber claims that his examinations of these homosexuals and their parents confirm his earlier research findings.

Individual treatment. Various psychoanalysts have treated homosexuality through individual, long-term therapy. The empirical studies on this form of treatment have been far from encouraging. Curran and Parr[6] reported practically no increase in heterosexual behavior in a large group of exclusively homosexual males. Woodward[7] found somewhat greater success in causing a heterosexual shift with a few of his male bisexual patients. Mayerson and Lief[8] report the greatest success: Half of their 19 male patients treated reported exclusive heterosexuality 4½ years after termination. The authors were quick to point out that most of their successful patients were bisexual at the be-

ginning of treatment. Little change occurred for exclusive homosexuals. The criterion for "success" in this report is highly questionable. First, the self-reports of the patients were interpreted by the authors without external validation. This method is insufficient in terms of objective data collection. Second, the authors assume that change in behavior reflects change in orientation, fantasy, or attitude. Our general knowledge about homosexuality is that behavior, attitude, and fantasy are not always congruent. Fantasy is probably the best estimate of an individual's sexual orientation because of suppressor variables that influence behavior. For example, the Kinsey Scale[9] is insufficient in understanding an individual's sexual orientation because it is based upon overt behavior. A comparable instrument needs to be developed to judge and compare fantasy with behavior.

The most comprehensive psychoanalytic treatment study was conducted by Bieber et al.[1] Twenty-nine of their 106 male homosexuals (27%) showed a significant shift to heterosexuality after 150 to 350 hours of therapy. Again, these results may be clarified. Only 18% of the exclusively homosexual patients "improved," whereas 50% of the bisexuals in the study showed significant change. The effects of failure to shift to heterosexual behavior after these lengthy hours of therapy were not reported. Based on this study, Bieber[10] concluded that the most critical variable found on which to base a prognosis of change is the degree of pathology of the father-son relationship. Careful examination of the data reveals that "change" occurred primarily for bisexuals; little "success" was obtained for homosexuals. Bieber's conclusion seem to go unchallenged in spite of the fact that 15 years have elapsed and an adequate follow-up of this study has not been reported.

Group psychotherapy. Two studies have been reported for group psychoanalytic psychotherapy. Hadden[11] studied homogeneous groups of male homosexuals (matched for age, intelligence, and socioeconomic class) who met weekly for varying periods up to 10 years. Hadden reported that 37% shifted to a heterosexual orientation based upon a sample of 32 homosexuals who came for treatment. Of the 12 "successful" patients, 5 reported "happy" marriages as a result of treatment. These results must be viewed cautiously because they relied simply on self-report of the participants. It is not clear whether these patients came for treatment to change their sexual orientation. It is known that Hadden encouraged group members to attack what he termed "defensive rationalizations" of some members who were "superficially" supporting a homosexual orientation. The remaining group members who were not "successful" in making heterosexual shifts improved slightly in terms of homosexual mannerisms and increased their ability to form social relationships. It is not clear how these "unsuccessful" patients adapted to their failure to meet the expectations of the group leader after years of effort.

Mintz[12] reported on a study of 10 male homosexuals who were treated with a combination of individual and group therapy. As in Hadden's[11] study, the goal in therapy was heterosexual shift. Unlike Hadden's groups, each of Mintz's groups was composed of heterosexual males and females and at least two homosexual males. Mintz claimed that the groups were able to eliminate rationalizations about homosexuality and increase contact with heterosexual women and heterosexual men. These results were anecdotal and were based upon the therapist's perceptions.

Behavior therapy designed to change sexual orientation

Behavior therapy designed to change sexual orientation is considered here under the illness model for several reasons. Although these behavior therapists would not use the term "illness" for homosexuality, most would treat it as maladaptive. There are certainly behavior therapists who do not see homosexuality as maladaptive, and some of this research is reported in a later section of this paper. However, the behavior therapy literature and research is dominated by ways of "curing" homosexuals of their sexual orientation.[13]

Behavior treatment designed to change sexual orientation, as reviewed below, involves individual therapy. It is clear that, similar to psychoanalytic therapies, the treatment goal is heterosexual shift. Failures are considered to be those who retain their homosexuality. In general, the results have not been that much better than those reported by psychoanalysts.[13]

Modifying sexual fantasies. McGuire, Carlisle, and Young[14] first proposed the use of reinforcement in masturbation fantasies to "cure" male homosexual behavior. Heterosexual fantasies were paired with masturbation while homosexual fantasies were extinguished. It was hypothesized that homosexual behavior is originally developed and maintained through fantasy. Davison[15] describes a case study where he successfully modified male homosexual behavior through this technique. Subsequent studies have also reported heterosexual shifts.[16] However, these reports are based upon individual case studies and are subject to criticism based upon experimenter bias, halo effect, reliance upon self-report and experimenter interpretation, lack of adequate follow-up, no reports of "unsuccessful" cases, and lack of external validation of results.

When these methods were put to more rigorous experimental procedures, subjective reports suggested improvement, but objective physiological and behavioral measures of arousal remained unchanged.[17] This illustrates the problem with most of the reported research which has been based upon subjective reports by the subjects and interpretive observations and conclusions made by the experimenters.

Anticipatory avoidance conditioning. Feldman[18] developed a different approach called anticipatory avoidance conditioning in which patients were allowed to avoid electrical shock under a variable interval reinforcement schedule when viewing slides of same-sex nudes. In a series of studies, Feldman and his associates treated a group of 43 subjects, most of whom were male homosexuals, and claimed that 58% were cured after a 2-year follow-up.[19] These individuals were "cured" after only 20 hours of behavior therapy.

224

The main criteria for success in these studies were suppression of homosexual behavior and increased heterosexual behavior. As indicated previously, these criteria are grossly inadequate.

Birk[20] also has questioned the stability of these results over time. Birk's study utilized a treatment that required 4 to 6 weeks of anticipatory avoidance conditioning similar to Feldman and Mac-Cullough's[21] study. Using change in Kinsey rating as a dependent measure of treatment, Birk found dramatic change in male homosexual behavior as a result of behavior over a placebo control (similar to findings by Feldman and MacCullough[21]). This difference was significant at the .009 level. However, 1 year later a comparison of the treatment and control groups showed that Kinsey *behavior* change ratings were not statistically significant. Birk concluded that anticipatory avoidance conditioning techniques have oversimplified the treatment of homosexuality.

Covert sensitization. Cautela[22] described a process of therapy called covert sensitization, which does not involve the use of shock or nausea-inducing drugs. Instead of the aversive stimulus such as shock or drugs, aversive imagery is used. First, the patient is given deep muscle relaxation training as in systematic desensitization. The therapist and the patient construct a hierarchy of attractive homosexual scenes. While the patient is deeply relaxed, the most appealing scene is evoked followed by the suggestion of nausea or equally repulsive thoughts. An alternative procedure has been developed so that when the patient approaches the "deviant" stimulus through imagery and feels sick, he's allowed to turn away from the stimulus and experience a great feeling of relief. These procedures are practiced in therapy as well as given as "homework assignments." Cautela presumes that after sufficient pairings, the pleasure and arousal that has resulted from the "deviant" stimulus is replaced by pain, anxiety, or nothing at all. The imagery is then presumed to generalize and eliminate any homosexual behavior.

Again, as with anticipatory avoidance condi-

tioning, the literature is characterized by anecdotal reports of single case studies of males.[23] Empirical research to affirm the efficacy of these treatments is nonexistent.

Desensitization. Proponents of systematic desensitization have been quite vocal in promoting this approach over other behavioral approaches. Langevin,[24] for example, has stated that aversion therapy is insufficient and that some positive adaptive behavior would be required to effect a heterosexual shift. Kraft,[25] Huff,[26] and Ramsey and Van-Velzen[27] have reported "successful outcomes" on individual case studies using systematic desensitization with male homosexuality. This approach is based upon the assumption that homosexuality has an anxiety component; thus, desensitization would be more appropriate than aversion therapy to produce heterosexual shift and reduce homosexual behavior.

However, two analogous studies have been conducted to test this notion and have failed to support the aversion or anxiety hypothesis of homosexuality. Using verbal ratings and penile tumescence, Freund, Langevin, Cibiri, and Sajac[28] tested responses to detailed descriptions of heterosexual intercourse. Although verbal reports of homosexuals showed aversion to the description, penile volume increased. In a similar study, Langevin, and Stanford, and Block[29] found that although male homosexual subjects' ratings of sexual arousal were significantly larger for same-sex slides than for those of the opposite sex, sexual arousal toward opposite-sex slides was significantly greater than with neutral slides. These results show more appropriate support for a preferential notion or choice notion of homosexuality rather than an aversion, phobic, or anxiety viewpoint. It should also be noted that in addition to questioning the theoretical base of behavior therapists who utilize desensitization techniques, Bieber's ideas about male homosexuality and his notions of fear of heterosexual intercourse are also questioned.

Eclectic treatments

Because of the lack of clear evidence of the ability to cure homosexuals by either learning or psychoanalytic approaches, some therapists have combined treatment approaches. However, once again, most reports are anecdotal and are based upon individual case studies of males.[30] Blitch and Haynes[31] report on the multiple behavioral techniques in a case of a lesbian.

Birk[20] described a group approach to the treatment of homosexuality that combined behavioral techniques and more traditional psychoanalytic notions. He found that half of 66 men seeking treatment made heterosexual shifts their treatment goal and stayed in treatment for 1½ to 6 years. Of these, 85% showed at least partial heterosexual shifts, and 52% showed nearly complete heterosexual shifts. Thus, approximately 25% of those who sought treatment showed nearly complete heterosexual shifts. The effects of "unsuccessful" treatment by 75% of the participants were not reported.

DEVELOPMENT OF A NEW MODEL OF TREATMENT

Attempts to "cure" homosexual behavior have been just that. Emphasis has been placed upon change in behavior, and consequently these studies have not sufficiently shown that any treatment modality can alter an individual's sexual orientation. Even attempts at altering behavior have had limited success and results have been transitory. In addition, a flood of literature has been forthcoming that has put to rest the notion that homosexuality is an illness in the first place. Consequently, there have been attempts at developing a new model of treatment for clients whose concerns are related to their homosexual orientation.

Challenging the illness model of homosexuality

In the first significant study that challenged the illness perspective, Hooker[32] compared nonpatient male homosexuals with matched heterosexual controls. Hooker matched the two groups on age, intelligence, and schooling and administered a battery of psychological tests. The two groups could not be distinguished, and there was no evidence of psychological maladjustment in either group. Hooker's studies probably did the most to bring to the attention of psychotherapists the importance of ethnographic studies to develop a more comprehensive theoretical understanding of homosexuality.

Many other studies have been conducted that have not found any psychopathology of male homosexuality as measured by psychological profiles.[33] Thompson, McCandless, and Strickland,[34] Wilson and Green,[35] and Loney[36] found similar results for both male and female homosexuals. Again, the only major difference found between groups of homosexuals and heterosexuals was choice of sexual object. Gonsiorek[3] provides an extensive review of these and other studies related to the psychological adjustment of homosexuals.

Psychotherapists would be wise to look toward studies and descriptions of normal and satisfying life-styles of homosexuals.[37] The fact that homosexuals who have been able to "come out" (to acknowledge their homosexuality) seem to be the healthiest psychologically as indicated by a more stable positive self-image, fewer anxiety symptoms, and less depression has also been confirmed by Hammersmith and Weinberg[38] and by Weinberg and Williams.[39]

Research on new treatment approaches

Johnsgard and Schumacher[40] were the first to describe a treatment approach that clearly did not have heterosexual shift as the treatment goal. The authors described a group therapy approach for male homosexuals that simply emphasized trust, expression of feelings, and intimacy. Their main objective was to increase the participants' ability to be more open, accepting, and fully functioning human beings. The authors' anecdotal reports claimed that after 1½ years of treatment, the group had adjusted in significant ways.

Truax and Tourney[41] studied a group of 30 male clients who were in group therapy based upon the Johnsgard and Schumacher[40] model. These clients were compared with an untreated control group. Truax and Tourney utilized a pre-post treatment effects design and found more satisfying sexual behavior and improvements on a variety of clinical ratings among the homosexuals in treatment than in the group of controls. These findings, however, have been severely criticized by Henrichsen and Katahn[12] because of design deficiencies and inadequate or inappropriate statistical analyses.

The research on new treatment approaches is as sparse and fraught with similar design deficiencies and inadequate data collection methodology as other research conducted on the treatment of homosexuality. Kohlenberg[43] reported a single case study of an adult male who was sexually attracted to male children. This report was one of the first reports in the behavior therapy literature that described a behavioral treatment program designed to increase sexual responsiveness to same-sex persons. Using in vivo desensitization and a sexual counseling program modeled after Masters and Johnson's,[44] the client increased his attraction to adult males and decreased his attraction to male children. Data were based upon written reports by the client of his fantasies, prowling incidents, and a number of encounters with adults.

In a rather unique case study of two lesbian couples, Pendergrass[45] described using marriage counseling techniques to improve the psychological functioning of these women in their relationships. The results, although positive, were clearly anecdotal. Clearly, more empirical studies of couples counseling of same-sex partners is drastically needed.

Two studies also have been reported that tested the effects of assertive training on homosexual groups. Duehn and Mayadas[46] discussed a single case study of a 26-year-old male who accepted his homosexual orientation and sought help with social interpersonal problems incurred in his decision to come out. They were able to demonstrate acquisition of assertive behavior as a result of a program of behavioral rehearsals and focused videotape feedback. The authors noted that this methodology needed to be tested with larger samples and other client populations.

Russell and Winkler[47] attempted to solve the methodological problem in the following way.

Twenty-seven subjects were randomly assigned to a behaviorally oriented assertive training group or a non-directive group offered by a homosexual guidance service. The subjects were given self-report measures before and after the two treatment conditions. Both groups improved; however, there were no between-group differences. Unfortunately, the authors did not have a control group to compare with the treatment groups. Some of the improvement could have been a function of time, test, retest procedures, and general "placebo" effect. However, there is still some suggestion that groups designed to improve homosexual functioning do have positive effects upon those participating. Additional research is needed that can compare procedures designed to improve functioning with control groups.

These studies represent a new and needed trend in the research on the treatment of homosexuals. It is clearly evident that this research is insufficient in helping us understand the impact of therapeutic procedures that are designed to facilitate a homosexual functioning.

The theoretical, ethical, moral, and practical decisions

Before the civil rights and gay liberation movements, there was not much question in the minds of counselors and therapists that homosexuals who sought help should be encouraged to change their sexual orientation. Because of the political and social climate, too, there were not many homosexuals who would come to therapists and ask that their sexual orientation be left intact. Neither were there many homosexuals who would request help to facilitate their homosexual functioning. Consequently it is not surprising that the research that has so far been reviewed in this paper has held "heterosexual shift" as the implicit or explicit treatment goal.

With the advent of the gay liberation movement, more theoretical, ethical, moral, and practical questions were being asked in terms of the existing treatment modalities and goals. These questions were raised, ironically, primarily by behaviorists who once boasted of "success" in treating their homosexual clients. Most notably, Davison[48] proposed that for ethical reasons therapists should stop offering therapy to help homosexuals change and should concentrate instead on improving the quality of their interpersonal relationships. He claimed that homosexuals who voluntarily seek change do so in an atmosphere of discrimination and condemnation. In the light of the research that has found homosexuality not to be an illness, Davison asked that therapists stop presenting a cure for something that is not even regarded as illness.

Silverstein[49] and Begelman[50] similarly recognized the social pressures and influences on persons who request a change in their sexual orientation. They concluded that society has been mistaken and has been unnecessarily harsh on homosexuals and that, as "moral agents of society," therapists should not participate in such persecution. Begelman stated that therapists should enlist the clients' aid in combating the social system that is responsible for their unjustified negative self-image. Davison, Silverstein, and Begelman all agreed that a homosexual's sexual orientation should be left intact and requests for change should be denied.

To offer a cure to homosexuals who request a change in their sexual orientation is, in my opinion, unethical. There is evidence, as reviewed in this paper, that therapists can help individuals change their behavior for a period of time. The question remains whether it is beneficial for clients to change their behavior to something that is inconsistent or incongruent with their sexual orientation. In most cases, I would say not. There are some situations, as Freund[51] points out, where attempts to help clients accept their homosexuality are simply not possible and counseling toward heterosexual adjustment is a "second-best choice." Several therapists would also help homosexuals increase their sexual repertoire to include heterosexual intercourse.[52] Binder[53] went further in advocating affection training which would teach individuals with an exclusive sexual preference (heterosexual or homosexual) to be aroused by members of the other half of the population as well as the original arousal gender.

The practical value of Binder's approach is questionable. Implicit in Binder's model is the fact that we should all be bisexual. This reminds me of the pressure placed upon some nonorgasmic women not only to be orgasmic but to be multiorgasmic! The danger is that helping homosexuals increase their sexual repertoire may be easily misunderstood as a nonacceptance or intolerance of their basic sexual orientation. This results in the same pressure and sense of failure that is generated by attempts to "cure" individuals of their homosexuality. More emphasis needs to be placed upon helping homosexuals accept and value their sexual orientation rather than helping them increase their sexual repertoire. Exploring heterosexual behavior should always be available as a treatment goal, but it should never be viewed as denying or changing sexual orientation.

CONCLUSION

The illness model of homosexuality is no longer viable. It has been put to rest by the flood of research that has found that homosexuality per se is not pathological.[3] The main difference between homosexuals and heterosexuals is their choice of affectional and sexual preference. In addition, treatment modalities based upon the illness model have not reported very convincing evidence of success in "curing" homosexuals.

On the other hand, there is supportive but insufficient evidence that therapists can have a positive impact on facilitating homosexual functioning. Further research on treatment programs designed in this fashion are needed. Some fruitful areas of investigation would be: the effect of "coming out groups" on self-esteem, psychological adjustment, and interpersonal skills; the effect of couple communication training on communication skills and relationship satisfaction in same-sex partners; the effects of sexual dysfunction groups in improving sexual satisfaction; and the effects of individual psychotherapy on measures of self-esteem and psychological adjustment. At present, homosexual counseling agencies are in a vantage position to conduct this research because they are already providing these types of programs. Although client services are their primary focus, I hope they will think about developing objective data collection methods to evaluate empirically the impact of such programs. In addition, because research with lesbians is practically nonexistent, much more work is needed in this area. It is very dangerous to extrapolate from findings based upon male homosexuals and apply such extrapolations to lesbians.

In the meantime, therapists are still faced with the ethical, moral, theoretical, and practical decisions of determining treatment goals. It is much too naive to think that we leave that decision completely up to our clients. We are not value-free agents. Nor do I feel, as Begelman[50] does, that we *must* be moral agents criticizing society. The treatment goals must be carefully worked out between the therapist and the client. The meaning and significance of these decisions must be clearly discussed as well as the external forces affecting the client's decision. Whether the client wishes to explore, expand, or increase his/her sexual repertoire, the emphasis must be in assisting homosexuals to recognize and accept their sexual identity and help them value this identity in a predominantly heterosexual society.

REFERENCES

1. Bieber, I., Dain, H.J., Dince, P.R., Drellich, M.G., Grand, H.G., Gundlach, R.H., Kremer, M.W., Rifkin, A.H., Wilbur, C.B., & Bieber, T.B. *Homosexuality: A psychoanalytic study*. New York: Vintage Books, 1962.
2. Churchill, W. *Homosexual behavior among males*. New York: Hawthorne Books, 1967; Hooker, E.A. "The homosexual community." In J.H. Gagnon & W. Simon (eds.), *Sexual Deviance*. New York: Harper & Row, 1967.
3. Gonsiorek, J. "Psychological adjustment and homosexuality." JSAS *Catalog of Selected Documents*, 1977, 7.
4. See Siegleman, M. "Parental background of male homosexual and heterosexuals." *Archives of Sexual Behavior*, 1974, 3, 31-38 for a review of these studies.
5. Bieber, I. "A discussion of homosexuality: The ethical challenge." *Journal of Consulting and Clinical Psychology*, 1976, 44, 163-166.
6. Curran, D., & Parr, D. "Homosexuality: An analysis of 100 male cases." *British Medical Journal*, 1957, 1, 797-801.
7. Woodward, M. "The diagnosis and treatment of homosexual offenders." *British Journal of Delinquency*, 1958, 9, 44-49.
8. Mayerson, P. & Lief, H.I. "Psychotherapy of homosexuals: A follow-up study of nineteen cases." In J. Marmor (ed.), *Sexual inversion*, New York: Basic Books, 1965.
9. Kinsey, A., Pomeroy, W., & Martin, C. *Sexual behavior in human males*. Philadelphia: W.B. Saunders, 1948.
10. Bieber, I. "The psychoanalytic treatment of sexual disorders." *Journal of Sex and Marital Therapy*, 1974, 1, 5-15.
11. Hadden, S.B. "Treatment of male homosexuals in groups." *International Journal of Group Psychotherapy*, 1966, 16, 13-22.
12. Mintz, E.E. "Overt male homosexuals in combined group and individual treatment." *Journal of Consulting Psychology*, 1966, 20, 193-198.
13. Acosta, F.X. "Etiology and treatment of homosexuality: A review." *Archives of Sexual Behavior*, 1975, 4, 9-29; Henrichsen, J.J., & Ratahn, M. "Recent trends and new developments in the treatment of homosexuality." *Psychotherapy: Theory, Research, and Practice*, 1975, 12, 83-92.
14. McGuire, R.J., Carlisle, J.M., & Young, B.G. "Sexual deviations as conditioned behavior: A hypothesis." *Behavior Research and Therapy*, 1965, 2, 185-190.
15. Davison, G.C. "Elimination of a sadistic fantasy by a client-controlled counterconditioning technique: A case study." *Journal of Abnormal Psychology*, 1968, 73, 84-89.
16. Marquis, J.N. "Orgasmic reconditioning: Changing sexual object choice through controlling masturbation fantasies." *Journal of Behavior Therapy and Experimental Psychiatry*, 1970, 1, 263-272; Marshall, W.I. "The modification of sexual fantasies: A combined treatment approach to the reduction of deviant sexual behavior." *Behavior Research and Therapy*, 1973, 11, 557-564; Marshall, W.L. "A combined treatment approach to the reduction of multiple fetish-related behaviors." *Journal of Consulting and Clinical Psychology*, 1974, 42, 613-616.
17. Conrad, S.R., & Wincze, J.P. "Orgasmic reconditioning: A controlled study of its effects upon the sexual arousal and behavior of adult male homosexuals." *Behavior Therapy*, 1976, 7, 155-166.
18. Feldman, M.P. "Aversion therapy for sexual deviation: A critical review." *Psychological Bulletin*, 1966, 65, 65-69.
19. Feldman, M.P., & MacCullough, M.J. "The application of anticipatory avoidance learning to the treatment of homosexuality: Theory, technique, and preliminary results." *Behavior Research and Therapy*, 1965, 2, 165-

183; Feldman, M.P., MacCullough, M.J., Orford, J.F., & Mellor, V., "The application of anticipatory avoidance learning to the treatment of homosexuality." *Acta Psychiatrica Scandinavica*, 1969, *45*, 109-117; MacCullough, J.J., & Feldman, M.P. "Aversion therapy in the management of 43 homosexuals." *British Medical Journal*, 1967, *2*, 594-597.

20. Birk, L. "Group psychotherapy for men who are homosexual." *Journal of Sex and Marital Therapy*, 1974, *1*, 29-52.

21. Feldman & MacCullough, 1965.

22. Cautela, J.R. "Treatment of compulsive behavior by covert sensitization." *Psychological Record*, 1966, *16*, 33-41; Cautela, J.R. "Covert sensitization." *Psychological Reports*, 1967, *2*, 459-468.

23. Callahan, E.J., & Leitenberg, H. "Aversion therapy for sexual deviation: Contingent shock and covert sensitization." *Journal of Abnormal Psychology*, 1973, *81*, 60-73; Maletzky, B.M. "Assisted covert sensitization: A preliminary report." *Behavior Therapy*, 1973, *4*, 117-119; Segal, B., & Simms, J. "Covert sensitization with a homosexual: A controlled replication." *Journal of Consulting and Clinical Psychology*, 1972, *39*, 259-263.

24. Langevin, R. "Modification of human sexual behavior." In J. Edwards (ed.), *Medical science and the criminal law*, Toronto: University of Toronto Press, 1974.

25. Kraft, T. "A case of homosexuality treated by systematic desensitization." *American Journal of Psychotherapy*, 1967, *21*, 815-821.

26. Huff, F. "The desensitization of a homosexual." *Behavior Research and Therapy*, 1970, *8*, 99-102.

27. Ramsey, R.W., & VanVelzen, V. "Behavior therapy for sexual perversions." *Behavior Research and Therapy*, 1968, *6*, 233.

28. Freund, K., Langevin, R., Cibiri, S., & Sajac, L. "Heterosexual aversion in homosexual males." *Archives of General Psychiatry*, 1973, *122*, 168; 169.

29. Langevin, R., Stanford, A., & Block, R. "The effect of relaxation instructions on erotic arousal in homosexual and heterosexual males." *Behavior Therapy*, 1975, *6*, 453-458.

30. Fox, B., & DiScipio, W.J. "An exploratory study in the treatment of homosexuals by combining principles from psychoanalytic theory and conditioning: Theoretical and methodological considerations." *British Journal of Medical Psychology*, 1968, *41*, 273-282; Hanson, R.W., & Adesso, V.J. "A multiple behavioral approach to male homosexual behavior: A case study." *Journal of Behavior Therapy and Experimental Psychiatry*, 1972 *3*, 323-325; Kraft, T. "A case of homosexuality treated by combined behavior therapy and psychotherapy: A total assessment." *Psychotherapy and Psychosomatics*, 1971, *19*, 342-358; Salter, L.G. & Melville, C.H. "A re-educative approach to homosexual behavior: A case study and treatment recommendation." *Psychotherapy: Theory, Research, and Practice*, 1972, *9*, 166-167.

31. Blitch, J.W., & Haynes, S.N. "Multiple behavioral techniques in a case of a female homosexuality." *Journal of Behavior Therapy and Experimental Psychiatry*, 1972, *3*, 319-322.

32. Hooker, E.A. "The adjustment of the male overt homosexual." *Journal of Projective Techniques*, 1957, *21*, 18-21.

33. Clark, T.R. "Homosexuality and psychopathology in non-patient males." *American Journal of Psychoanalysis*, 1975, *35*, 163-168; Dean, R.B., & Richardson, H. "Analysis of MMPI profiles of forty college-educated overt male homosexuals." *Journal of Consulting Psychology*, 1964, *28*, 483-486; Evans, R.B. "Childhood parental relationship of homosexual men." *Journal of Consulting and Clinical Psychology*, 1969, *33*, 135-139; Evans, R.B. "Sixteen personality factor questionnaire scores of homosexual men." *Journal of Consulting and Clinical Psychology*, 1970, *34*, 212-215; Evans, R.B. "Adjective check list scores of homosexual men." *Journal of Personality Assessment*, 1971, *35*, 344-349; Manosevitz, M. "Early sexual behavior in adult homosexual and heterosexual males." *Journal of Abnormal Psychology*, 1970, *76*, 396-402; Mundorff, J.E. "Personality characteristics of selected college male heterosexuals, homosexual activists, and non-activists." *Dissertation Abstracts*, 1973, *34*, 1137; Ohlson, E.L. "A preliminary investigation into the self-disclosing ability of male homosexuals." *Psychology*, 1974, *11*, 21-25.

34. Thompson, N.L., McCandless, B.R., & Strickland, B.R. "Personal adjustment of male and female homosexuals and heterosexuals." *Journal of Abnormal Psychology*, 1971, *78*, 237-240.

35. Wilson, M.L., & Green, R.L. "Personality characteristics of female homosexuals." *Psychological Reports*, 1971, *28*, 407-412.

36. Loney, J. "An MMPI measurement of maladjustment in a sample of normal homosexual males." *Journal of Clinical Psychology*, 1971, *27*, 486-488.

37. Cotton, W.L. "Role-playing substitutions among homosexuals." *Journal of Sex Research*, 1972, *8*, 310-323; Cotton, W.L. "Social and sexual relationships of lesbians." *Journal of Sex Research*, 1975, *11*, 139-148; Dank, B.M. "The development of a homosexual identity: Antecedents and consequents." *Dissertation Abstracts*, 1973, *34*, 423-424; Freedman, M. *Homosexuality and Psychological Functioning*, Belmont, Calif.: Brooks/Cole, 1971; Freedman, M. "Homosexuals may be healthier than straights." *Psychology Today*, 1975, *8*, 23-32; Greenberg, J.S. "A study of male homosexuals (predominantly college students)." *American College Health Association Journal*, 1973, *22*, 56-60; Hedblom, J.H. "Dimensions of lesbian sexual experience." *Archives of Sexual Behavior*,

1973, *2*, 329-341; Myrich, F.L. "Homosexual types: An empirical investigation." *Journal of Sex Research*, 1974 *10*, 226-237; Neuhring, E.M., Fein, S.B., & Tyler, M. "The gay college student: Perspective for mental health professionals." *Counseling Psychologist*, 1974, *4*, 64-72; Sonnenschein, D. "The ethnography of male homosexual relationships." *Journal of Sex Research*, 1968, *4*, 69-83; Weinberg, M.S. "Homosexual samples: Differences and similarities." *Journal of Sex Research*, 1970, *6*, 312-325.

38. Hammersmith, S.K., & Weinberg, M.S. "Homosexual identity: Commitment, adjustment, and significant others." *Sociometry*, 1973, *36*, 56-79.

39. Weinberg, M.S., & Williams, C.S. *Male homosexuals: Their problems and adaptations*. New York: Oxford Press, 1974.

40. Johnsgard, K.W., & Schumacher, R.M. "The experience of intimacy in group psychotherapy with male homosexuals." *Psychotherapy: Theory, Research, and Practice*, 1970, *7*, 173-176.

41. Traux, R., & Tourney, G. "Male homosexuals in group psychotherapy." *Diseases of the Nervous System*, 1971, *32*, 707-711.

42. Henrichsen & Katahn, 1975.

43. Kohlenberg, J. "Treatment of homosexual pedophiliac using in vivo desensitization: A case study." *Journal of Abnormal Psychology*, 1974, *83*, 192-195.

44. Masters, W.H., & Johnson, V.E. *Human sexual inadequacy*. Boston: Little, Brown, 1970.

45. Pendergrass, V.E. "Marriage counseling with lesbian couples." *Psychotherapy: Theory, Research, and Practice*, 1975, *12*, 93-96.

46. Duehn, W.D., & Mayadas, N.S. "The use of stimulus/modeling videotapes in assertiveness training for homosexuals," *Journal of Homosexuality*, 1976, *1*(4), 373-381.

47. Russell, A., & Winker, R. "Evaluation of assertiveness training and homosexual guidance service groups designed to improve homosexual functioning." *Journal of Consulting and Clinical Psychology*, 1977, *45*, 1-12.

48. Davison, G.C. "Homosexuality and the ethics of behavioral intervention: Paper 1—Homosexuality, the ethical challenge." *Journal of Homosexuality*, 1977, *2*(3), 195-204.

49. Silverstein, C. "Homosexuality and the ethics of behavioral intervention: Paper 2." *Journal of Homosexuality*, 1977, *2*(3), 205-211.

50. Begelman, D.A. "Homosexuality and the ethics of behavioral intervention: Paper 3." *Journal of Homosexuality*, 1977, *2*(3), 213-219.

51. Freund, K. "Should homosexuality arouse therapeutic concern?" *Journal of Homosexuality*, 1977, *2*(3), 235-240.

52. Feldman, P. "Helping homosexuals with problems: A commentary and a personal view." *Journal of Homosexuality*, 1977, *2*(3), 241-249; McConaghy, N. "Behavioral intervention in homosexuality." *Journal of Homosexuality*, 1977, *2*(3), 221-227; Money, J. "Bisexual, homosexual, and heterosexual: Society, law, and medicine." *Journal of Homosexuality*, 1977, *2*(3), 229-233.

53. Binder, C.V. "Affection training: An alternative to sexual reorientation." *Journal of Homosexuality*, 1977, *2*(3), 251-259.

Bibliography

Aaronson, B., & Grumpelt, H. "Homosexuality and some MMPI measures of masculinity-femininity." *Journal of Clinical Psychology,* 1961, *17*(3), 245-247.

Abbitt, D., & Bennett, B. "Being a lesbian mother." In B. Berzon & R. Leighton (Eds.), *Positively gay.* Millbrae, Calif.: Celestial Arts, 1979.

Abbott, S. "Lesbians and the women's movement." In G. Vida (Ed.), *Our right to love: A lesbian resource book.* Englewood Cliffs, N.J.: Prentice-Hall, 1978.

Abbott, S., & Love, B. *Sappho was a right-on woman.* New York: Stein & Day, 1973.

Achilles, N. "The development of the homosexual bar as an institution." In J. Gagnon & W. Simon (Eds.), *Sexual deviance.* New York: Harper & Row, 1967.

Acosta, E. "Affinity for Black heritage: Seeking lifestyle within a community." Washington, D.C.: *The Blade,* 11 October 1979, pp. A-1; A-25. (a)

Acosta, E. "Glimpses of Black gay lives—part II: Yearning for faith and love." Washington, D.C.: *The Blade,* 21 November 1979, pp. B-1; B-5. (b)

Acosta, E. "Gay and Black in D.C.: Emerging dialogue between races." Washington, D.C.: *The Blade,* 6 December 1979, pp. B-1; B-5. (c)

Acosta, F. "Etiology and treatment of homosexuality: A review." *Archives of Sexual Behavior,* 1975, *4,* 9-29.

Adair, N., & Adair, C. *Word is out: Stories of some of our lives.* New York: Dell, 1978.

Albro, J., & Tully, C. "A study of lesbian lifestyles in the homosexual micro-culture and the heterosexual macro-culture." *Journal of Homosexuality,* 1979, *4*(4), 341-354.

Aldrich, A. *We walk alone.* New York: Fawcett, 1955.

Aldrich, A. (Ed.). *Carol in a thousand cities.* Greenwich, Conn.: Fawcett, 1960.

Allen, C. *Homosexuality: It's nature, causation, and treatment.* London: Staples Press, 1958.

Allen, C. "The aging homosexual." 1959. Reprinted in I. Rubin (Ed.), *The third sex.* New York: New Book, 1961.

Allen, F. "Homosexuality in relation to the problem of human differences." *American Journal of Orthopsychiatry,* 1940, *10*(1), 129-135.

Allison, R. *Lesbianism: Its secrets and practices.* Los Angeles: Medico Books, 1967.

American Foundation for the Prevention of Venereal Diseases, Inc. *The new venereal disease prevention for everyone.* Pamphlet available from 335 Broadway, New York, N.Y.

Anderson, E. "The elusive homosexual: A reply to Stone & Schneider." *Journal of Personality Assessment,* 1975, *39*(6), 580-582.

Angrist, S. "The study of sex roles." *Journal of Social Issues,* 1969, *25*(1), 215-232.

Anomaly (pseud.) (Introduction by R. Thouless). *The invert and his social adjustment: To which is added a sequel by the same author* (2nd ed.). Baltimore: Williams & Wilkins, 1948.

Ariete, S. "Sexual conflict in psychotic disorders." In C. Wahl (Ed.), *Sexual problems: Diagnosis and treatment in medical practice.* New York: Free Press, 1967.

Armon, V. "Some personality variables in overt female homosexuality." *Journal of Projective Techniques,* 1960, *24,* 292-309.

Armstrong, C. "Diversities of sex." *British Medical Journal,* 1955, *4923,* 1173-1177.

Aschaffenburg, A. "Relationship therapy with a homosexual: A case history." *Pastoral Counselor,* 1966, *4*(1), 4-12.

Ashworth, A., & Walker, W. "Social structure and homosexuality: A theoretical appraisal." *British Journal of Sociology,* 1972, *23,* 146-158.

Aslin, A. "Feminist and community mental health center psychotherapists' expectations of mental health for women." *Sex Roles,* 1977, *3*(6), 537-544.

Atkins, M., Fischer, M., Prater, G., Winget, C., & Zaleski, J. "Brief treatment of homosexual patients." *Comprehensive Psychiatry,* 1976, *17*(1), 115-124.

Atkinson, T. *Amazon odyssey.* New York: Links Books, 1974.

Bacon, C. "A developmental theory of female homosexuality." In A. Lorand & M. Balint (Eds.), *Perversions: Psychodynamics and therapy.* New York: Random House, 1956.

Bailey, R., & Brake, M. (Eds.). *Radical social work.* New York: Pantheon, 1975.

Bandura, A. "Psychotherapy as a learning process." *Psychological Bulletin*, 1951, *58*(2), 143-159.

Bandura, A. "Social-learning theory of identificatory process." In D. Goslin (Ed.), *Handbook of socialization theory and research*. Chicago: Rand McNally, 1969.

Bandura, A. "Psychotherapy based upon modeling principles." In A. Bergin & S. Garfield (Eds.), *Psychotherapy and behavior change*. New York: Wiley, 1971.

Bandura, A., & Walters, R. *Social learning and personality development*. New York: Holt, Rinehart & Winston, 1963.

Barahal, H. "Female transvestism and homosexuality." *Psychiatric Quarterly*, 1953, *27*(3), 390-438.

Bardwick, J. (Ed.). *Feminine personality and conflict*. Belmont, Calif.: Brooks/Cole, 1970.

Bardwick, J., & Doran, E. "Ambivalence: The socialization of women." In V. Gornick & B. Moran (Eds.), *Woman in sexist society*. New York: Basic Books, 1971.

Barker, D., & Allen, S. (Eds.). *Sexual divisions and society: Process and change*. London: Tavistock, 1976.

Barnette, W. "Study of an adult male homosexual and Terman-Miles M-F scores." *American Journal of Orthopsychiatry*, 1942, *12*, 346-352.

Barr, R., & Catts, S. "Psychiatric opinion and homosexuality: A short report." *Journal of Homosexuality*, 1974, *1*(2), 213-215.

Barry, H., Bacon, M., & Child, I. "Cross-cultural survey of some sex differences in socialization." *Journal of Abnormal and Social Psychology*, 1957, *55*, 327-332.

Bartell, G. "Group sex among the mid-Americans." In J. Smith & L. Smith (Eds.), *Beyond monogamy: Recent studies of sexual alternatives in marriage*. Baltimore: Johns Hopkins University Press, 1974.

Baruch, G. "Female self-esteem, self-ratings of competence and maternal career commitment." *Journal of Counseling Psychology*, 1973, *20*(5), 478-488.

Bass-Hass, R. "The lesbian dyad: Basic issues and value systems." *Journal of Sex Research*, 1968, *4*(2), 108-126.

Bauer, A. "A study of self-concept in women who identify with either a gay liberation or a women's liberation organization." (Doctoral dissertation, University of Northern Colorado, 1973) *Dissertation Abstracts International*, 1974, *34*, 3613A-5380A. (University Microfilms No. 74-1600)

Beach, F. (Ed.). *Sexual behavior*. New York: Wiley & Sons, 1965.

Beaton, S., & Guild, N. "Treatment for gay problem drinkers." *Social Casework*, 1976, *57*(5), 302-308.

Beauvoir, S. "The lesbian." 1952. Reprinted in A. Aldrich (Ed.), *Carol in a thousand cities*. Greenwich, Conn.: Fawcett, 1960. Also in H. Ruitenbeek (Ed.), *The problem of homosexuality in modern America*. New York: Dutton, 1963.

Beck, A., & Greenberg, R. "Cognitive therapy with depressed women." In V. Franks & V. Burtle (Eds.), *Women in therapy*. New York: Brunner/Mazel, 1974.

Becker, H. *Outsiders: Studies in the sociology of deviance*. New York: Free Press of Glencoe, 1963.

Begelman, D. "Homosexuality and the ethics of behavioral intervention." *Journal of Homosexuality*, 1977, *2*(3), 213-219.

Bell, A. "Human sexuality—A response." *International Journal of Psychiatry*, 1972, *10*, 99-102.

Bell, A., & Weinberg, M. *Homosexualities: A study of diversity among men and women*. New York: Simon & Schuster, 1978.

Bell, J. "Public manifestations of personal morality: Limitations on the use of solicitation statutes to control homosexual cruising." *Journal of Homosexuality*, 1979-1980, *5*(1-2), 97-114.

Belote, D., & Joesting, J. "Demographic and self-respect characteristics of lesbians." *Psychological Reports*, 1976, *39*, 621-622.

Bem, S. "Psychology looks at sex-roles: Where have all the androgynous people gone?" Paper presented at University of California, Los Angeles, Symposium on Women, May 1972.

Bem, S. "The measurement of psychological androgyny." *Journal of Consulting and Clinical Psychology*, 1974, *42*, 155-162.

Bem, S. "Sex role adaptability: One consequence of psychological androgyny." *Journal of Personality and Social Psychology*, 1975, *31*(4), 634-643.

Bem, S., Martyna, W., & Watson, C. "Sex typing and androgyny: Further explorations of the expressive domain." *Journal of Personality and Social Psychology*, 1976, *34*(5), 1016-1023.

Bene, E. "On the genesis of female homosexuality." *British Journal of Psychiatry*, 1965, *111*, 815-821.

Bentham, J. (L. Cromptom, ed.). "Offenses against one's self: Paederasty." *Journal of Homosexuality*, 1978, *3*(4), 389-405.

Berg, C. "The problem of homosexuality." *American Journal of Psychotherapy*, 1956, *10*(4), 696-708; and 1957, *11*(1), 65-79.

Berger, R. "Report on a community-based venereal disease clinic for homosexual men." *The Journal of Sex Research*, 1977, *13*(1), 54-62.

Berger, R. "Psychological adaptation of the older homosexual male." *Journal of Homosexuality*, 1980, *5*(3), 161-175.

Bergin, A., & Garfield, S. (Eds.). *Psychotherapy and behavior change*. New York: Wiley, 1971.

Bergler, E. "The respective importance of reality and phantasy [sic] in the genesis of female homosexuality." *Journal of Criminal Psychopathology*, 1943, *5*, 27-48.

Bergler, E. "Eight prerequisites for psychoanalytic treatment of homosexuality." *Psychoanalytic Review*, 1944, *31*, 253-286.

Bergler, E. "Differential diagnosis between spurious homosexuality and perversion homosexuality." *Psychiatric Quarterly*, 1947, *21*(3), 399-409.

Bergler, E. "Lesbianism: Facts and fiction." *Marriage Hygiene*, 1948, *1*(4), 197-202. (a)

Bergler, E. "The myth of a new national disease: Homosexuality and the Kinsey report." *Psychiatric Quarterly*, 1948, *22*(1), 66-88. (b) Reprinted as "Homosexuality and the Kinsey report." In A. Krich (Ed.), *The homosexuals as seen by themselves and thirty authorities*. New York: Citadel, 1954.

Bergler, E. *Homosexuality: Disease or way of life?* New York: Hill and Wang, 1956.

Bergler, E. *Counterfeit sex: Homosexuality, impotence, frigidity* (2nd ed.). New York: Grune & Stratton, 1958. (a)

Bergler, E. "D.H. Lawrence's *The Fox* and the psychoanalytic theory of lesbianism." *Journal of Nervous and Mental Disease*, 1958, *126*(5), 488-491. (b)

Bergler, E. *1000 homosexuals: Conspiracy of silence on curing and deglamorizing homosexuality*. Patterson, N.J.: Pageant Books, 1959.

Bergler, E., & Kroger, W. *Kinsey's myth of female sexuality: The medical facts*. New York: Grune & Stratton, 1954.

Bergmann, M. "Homosexuality on the Rorschach test." *Bulletin of the Menninger Clinic*, 1945, *9*, 78-84.

Bernard, L., & Epstein, D. "Androgyny scores of matched homosexual and heterosexual males." *Journal of Homosexuality*, 1978, *4*(2), 169-178.

Bernstein, B. "Legal and social interface in counseling homosexual clients." *Social Casework*, 1977, *58*(1), 36-40.

Bernstein, I. "Homosexuality in gynecologic practice." *South Dakota Journal of Medicine*, 1968, *21*, 33-39.

Berzon, B. "Sharing your lesbian identity with your children." In G. Vida (Ed.), *Our right to love: A lesbian resource book*. Englewood Cliffs, N.J.: Prentice-Hall, 1978.

Berzon, B. "Achieving success as a gay couple." In B. Berzon & R. Leighton (Eds.), *Positively gay*. Millbrae, Calif.: Celestial Arts, 1979.

Berzon, B. "Developing a positive gay identity." In B. Berzon & R. Leighton (Eds.), *Positively gay*. Millbrae, Calif.: Celestial Arts, 1979.

Berzon, B. "Telling the family you're gay." In B. Berzon & R. Leighton (Eds.), *Positively gay*. Millbrae, Calif.: Celestial Arts, 1979.

Berzon, B., & Leighton, R. (Eds.). *Positively gay*. Millbrae, Calif.: Celestial Arts, 1979.

Bettelheim, B. "Growing up female." In H. Ruitenbeek (Ed.), *Psychoanalysis and contemporary American culture*. New York: Dell (Delta), 1964.

Bieber, I. "On treating male homosexuals." *Archives of General Psychiatry*, 1967, *16*, 60-63.

Bieber, I. "The psychoanalytic treatment of sexual disorders." *Journal of Sex and Marital Therapy*, 1974, *1*, 5-15.

Bieber, I. "A discussion of homosexuality: The ethical challenge." *Journal of Counseling and Clinical Psychology*, 1976, *44*(2), 163-166.

Bieber, I., Dain, H., Dince, P., Drellich, M., Grand, H., Gundlach, R., Kremer, M., Rifkin, A., Wilbur, C., & Bieber, T. *Homosexuality: A psychoanalytic study*. New York: Basic Books, 1962.

Bijon, S., & Baer, D. "Socialization—The development of behavior to social stimuli." In E. McGinnies & C. Ferster (Eds.), *The reinforcement of social behavior*. Boston: Houghton Mifflin, 1971.

Binder, C. "Affection training: An alternative to sexual reorientation." *Journal of Homosexuality*, 1977, *2*(3), 251-259.

Binstock, R. "Interest group liberalism and the politics of aging." *The Gerontologist*, 1972, Autumn, p. 265.

Birk, L. "Group psychotherapy for men who are homosexual." *Journal of Sex and Marital Therapy*, 1974, *1*(3), 29-52.

Blair, R. "Counseling and homosexuality." *Homosexual Counseling Journal*, 1975, *2*(3), 94-106.

Blanton, S. "Phallic women." *Psychoanalytic Quarterly*, 1947, *16*(2), 214-224.

Blitch, J., & Haynes, S. "Multiple behavioral techniques in a case of female homosexuality." *Journal of Behavior Therapy and Experimental Psychiatry*, 1972, *3*, 319-322.

Block, D. "The thrust of infanticide and homosexual identity." *Psychoanalytic Review*, 1975-1976, *62*(4), 579-599.

Blumer, H. "Society as symbolic interaction." In J. Manis & B. Meltzer (Eds.), *Symbolic interaction: A reader in social psychology*. Boston: Allyn & Bacon, 1967.

Bogarth, R., & Gross, A. "Homosexuality: Sin or sickness? A dialogue." *Pastoral Psychology*, 1962, *13*(129), 35-42.

Boggan, E., Lister, M., & Rupp, J. *The rights of gay people: An American civil liberties handbook*. New York: Avon, 1975.

Boozer, M. As quoted in L. Dyne, "Is D.C. becoming the gay capitol of America?" *The Washingtonian*, September 1980.

Boston Women's Health Book Collective. *Our bodies, ourselves* (2nd ed.). New York: Simon & Schuster, 1976.

Boswell, J. *Christianity, social tolerance and homosexuality*. Chicago: The University of Chicago Press, 1980.

Botwinick, J., & Machover, S. "A psychometric examination of latent homosexuality in alcoholism." *Quarterly Journal of Studies on Alcohol*, 1951, *12*, 268-272.

Braaten, L., & Darling, C. "Overt and covert homosexual problems among male college students." *Genetic Psychology Monographs*, 1965, *71*(2), 269-310.

Bradley, M. *Third sex*. London: G. Gold & Sons, 1963.

Brake, M. "I may be queer, but at least I am a man." In D. Barker & S. Allen (Eds.), *Sexual divisions and society: Process and change*. London: Tavistock, 1976.

Branson, H. *Gay bar*. San Francisco: Pan-Graphic Press, 1957.

Brecher, E. *The sex researchers*. Boston: Little, Brown, 1969.

Brick, B. "Judaism in the gay community." In B. Berzon & R. Leighton (Eds.), *Positively gay*. Millbrae, Calif.: Celestial Arts, 1979.

Brody, E. "From schizophrenic to homosexual: A crisis in role and relating." *American Journal of Psychotherapy*, 1963, *17*(4), 579-595.

Brogan, C. "Changing perspectives on the role of women." *Smith College Studies in Social Work,* 1972, *42*(2), 155-173.

Bromberg, W. "Sex offense as a disguise." *Corrective Psychiatry and Journal of Social Therapy,* 1965, *11*(6), 293-298.

Broverman, I., Broverman, D., Clarkson, F., Rosenkrantz, P., & Vogel, S. "Sex role stereotypes and clinical judgments of mental health." *Journal of Consulting and Clinical Psychology,* 1970, *34*(1), 1-7.

Broverman, I., Vogel, S., Broverman, D., Clarkson, F., & Rosenkrantz, P. "Sex-role stereotypes: A current appraisal." *Journal of Social Issues,* 1972, *28*(2), 54-78.

Brown, D. "Sex-role development in a changing culture." *Psychological Bulletin,* 1956, *55*(4), 232-242.

Brown, D. "Sex-role preference in young children." *Psychological Monographs,* 1956, *70*(14), Whole No. 421.

Brown, D. "Masculinity/femininity development in children." *Journal of Consulting Psychology,* 1957, *21*(3), 197-202.

Brown, D. "Inversion and homosexuality." *American Journal of Orthopsychiatry,* 1958, *28*, 424-429.

Brown, H. *Familiar faces, hidden lives.* New York: Harcourt Brace Jovanovich, 1976.

Brown, P. "On the differentiation of homo- or heteroerotic interest in the male: An operant technique illustrated in a case of motorcycle fetishist." *Behavior Research and Therapy,* 1964, *2*(1), 31-35.

Brown, R. *Rubyfruit jungle.* Plainfield, Vt.: Daughters, 1973.

Brudnoy, D. "Homosexuality in America: At 200 years." *Homosexual Counseling Journal,* 1976, *3*(1), 10-22.

Bryant, B. *Lesbian mothers.* Unpublished manuscript, 1975. (Available from Lymar Associates, 330 Ellis St., Room 401, San Francisco, Calif.)

Bullough, V. "Homosexuality and the medical model." *Journal of Homosexuality,* 1974, *1*(1), 99-110.

Bullough, V. *Sexual variance in society and history.* Chicago: University of Chicago Press, 1976.

Bullough, V. "Variant lifestyles: Homosexuality." In B. Murstein (Ed.), *Exploring intimate lifestyles.* New York: Springer, 1978.

Bullough, V., Elcano, B., Legg, W., & Kepner, J. (Eds.). *An annotated bibliography of homosexuality.* 2 vols., New York: Garland Publishing, 1976.

Burgess-Kohn, J. "Why parents worry about homosexuality." *Parents Magazine,* January 1977, pp. 40-41; 64.

Burk, M. "Coming out: The gay identity process." In B. Murstein (Ed.), *Exploring intimate lifestyles.* New York: Springer, 1978.

Burns, D., & Beck, A. "Cognitive behavior modification of mood disorders." In J. Foreyt & D. Rathjen (Eds.), *Cognitive behavior therapy: Research and application.* New York: Plenum, 1978.

Burton, A. "The use of the masculinity-femininity scale of the MMPI as an aid in the diagnosis of sexual inversion." *Journal of Psychology,* 1947; *24,* 161-164.

Butler, R. "Meeting the challenge of health care for the elderly." *Journal of Allied Health,* 1980, *9*(3), 161-168.

Butts, W. "Boy prostitutes of the metropolis." *Journal of Clinical Psychopathology,* 1947, *8*(4), 673-681.

Buxton, E. (Ed.). *2nd national institute on social work in rural areas reader.* Madison: University of Wisconsin—Extension, 1977.

Bychowski, G. "The structure of homosexuals acting out." *Psychoanalytic Quarterly,* 1954, *23*(1), 48-61.

Bychowski, G. "Homosexuality and psychosis." In S. Lorand & M. Balint, (Eds.), *Perversions: Psychodynamics and therapy.* New York: Random House, 1956.

Bychowski, G. "The ego and the object of the homosexual." *International Journal of Psycho-Analysis,* 1961, *42*(3), 255-259.

Byrne, T., Jr., & Mulligan, F. "Psychopathic personality and sexual deviation: Medical terms or legal catch-alls—Analysis of the status of the homosexual alien." *Temple Law Quarterly,* 1967, *40*(4), 328-347.

Cain, A. "Homosexuality and alcohol." *Sexology,* 1963, *30*(5), 296-298.

Califia, P. "Lesbian sexuality." *Journal of Homosexuality,* 1979, *4*(3), 255-266.

Califia, P. *Sapphistry: The book of lesbian sexuality.* Tallahassee, Fla.: Naiad Press, 1980.

Callahan, E., & Leitenberg, H. "Aversion therapy for sexual deviation: Contingent shock and covert sensitization." *Journal of Abnormal Psychology,* 1973, *81,* 60-73.

Callahan, S. "Feminine responses to function." *Humanitas,* 1971, *6*(3), 295-310.

Cantor, D. "The homosexual revolution: A status report." 1967. Reprinted in *Social Progress,* 1967, *58*(2), 5-12.

Caprio, F. *Female homosexuality: A psychodynamic study of lesbianism.* Chapter 16, "Therapeutic management: Preventive measures." New York: Citadel Press, 1954, pp. 285-298. Reprinted as Preventive measures. In A. Aldrich (Ed.), *Carol in a thousand cities.* Greenwich, Conn.: Fawcett, 1960.

Caprio, F. "Female homosexuality." *Sexology,* 1955, *21*(8), 494-499.

Caprio, F. "Homosexual women." *Sexology,* 1956, *22*(9), 560-565.

Carlson, R. "Understanding women: Implications for personality theory and research." *Journal of Social Issues,* 1972, *28*(2), 17-31.

Carrier, J. " 'Sex-role preference' as an explanatory variable in homosexual behavior." *Archives of Sexual Behavior,* 1977, *6*(1), 53-65.

Carrier, J. "Homosexual behavior in cross-cultural perspective." In J. Marmor (Ed.), *Homosexual behavior: A modern reappraisal.* New York: Basic Books, 1980.

Cass, V. "Homosexual identity formation: A theoretical model." *Journal of Homosexuality,* 1979, *4*(3), 219-237.

Cattell, R., & Morony, J. "The use of the 16 PF in distinguishing homosexuals, normals, and general criminals." *Journal of Consulting Psychology*, 1962, *26*(6), 531-540.

Cautela, J. "Treatment of compulsive behavior by covert sensitization." *Psychological Record*, 1966, *16*, 33-41.

Cautela, J. "Covert sensitization." *Psychological Reports*, 1967, *2*, 459-468.

Chafetz, J., Sampson, P., Beck, P., & West, J. "A study of homosexual women." *Social Work*, 1974, *19*(6), pp. 714-726.

Chalus, G. "An evaluation of the validity of the Freudian theory of paranoia." *Journal of Homosexuality*, 1977, *3*(2), 171-188.

Chapman, A., & Reese, D. "Homosexual signs in Rorschachs of early schizophrenics." *Journal of Clinical Psychology*, 1953, *9*(1), 30-32.

Chodorow, N. "Being and doing: A cross-cultural examination of the socialization of males and females." In V. Gornick and B. Moran (Eds.), *Woman in sexist society*. New York: Basic Books, 1971.

Churchill, W. *Homosexual behavior among males*. New York: Hawthorne Books, 1967.

Clarenbach, K., as quoted in J. Edgar, E. Sweet, & M. Thom, *The decade of women: A Ms. history of the seventies in words and pictures*. New York: Paragon, 1979, p. 67.

Clark, D. *Loving someone gay*. Millbrae, Calif.: Celestial Arts, 1977.

Clark, D. "Being a gay father." In B. Berzon & R. Leighton (Eds.), *Positively gay*. Millbrae, Calif.: Celestial Arts, 1979.

Clark, T. "Homosexuality and psychopathology in nonpatient males." *American Journal of Psychoanalysis*, 1975, *35*, 163-168.

Clayborne, J. "Blacks and gay liberation." In K. Jay & A. Young (Eds.), *Lavender culture*. New York: Jove/HBJ, 1978.

Cleckley, H. *The caricature of love: A discussion of social, psychiatric and literary manifestations of pathologic sexuality*. New York: Ronald Press, 1957.

Cloward, R. "Illegitimate means, anomie, and deviant behavior." *American Sociological Review*, 1959, *24*, 164-176.

Cohen, M. "Personal identity and sexual identity." *Psychiatry*, 1966, *29*, 1-14.

Cohen, S., & Young, J., (Eds.). *The manufacture of news: Deviance, social problems and the mass media*. London: Constable, 1973.

Coleman, E. "Toward a new model of treatment of homosexuality." *Journal of Homosexuality*, 1978, *3*(4), 345-359.

Conrad, S., & Wincze, J. "Orgasmic reconditioning: A controlled study of its effects upon the sexual arousal and behavior of adult male homosexuals." *Behavior Therapy*, 1976, *7*, 155-166.

Coons, F. "Ambisexuality as an alternative adaptation." *Journal of the American College Health Association*, 1972, *21*(2), 142-144.

Corbett, S., Troiden, R., & Dodder, R. "Tolerance as a correlate of experience with stigma: The case of the homosexual." *Journal of Homosexuality*, 1977, *3*(1), 3-13.

Cornwell, A. "Three for the price of one: Notes from a gay Black feminist." In K. Jay & A. Young (Eds.), *Lavender culture*. New York: Jove/HBJ, 1978.

Cory, D. *The homosexual in America: A subjective approach*. New York: Greenberg, 1951.

Cory, D. "Homosexual attitudes and heterosexual prejudices." 1952. Reprinted in D. Cory (Ed.), *Homosexuality: A cross-cultural approach*. New York: Julian Press, 1956.

Cory, D. (Ed.). *Homosexuality: A cross-cultural approach*. New York: Julian Press, 1956.

Cory, D. "The language of the homosexual." *Sexology*, 1965, *32*(3), 163-165. (a)

Cory, D. *The lesbian in America*. New York: Macfadden Bartell, 1965. (b)

Cory, D., & LeRoy, J. *The homosexual and his society: A view from within*. New York: Citadel, 1963.

Cory, D., & LeRoy, J. "Homosexual marriage." *Sexology*, 1963, *29*(10), 660-662.

Cotton, W. "Role-playing substitutions among homosexuals." *Journal of Sex Research*, 1972, *8*, 310-323.

Cotton, W. "Social and sexual relationships of lesbians." *Journal of Sex Research*, 1975, *11*(2), 139-148.

Cowan, G. "Therapist judgments of clients' sex-role problems." *Psychology of Women Quarterly*, 1976, *1*(2), 115-123.

Crew, L. "Just as I am: Growing up gay." *Southern Exposure*, 1977, *5*(1) 59-65.

Cruikshank, M. "Lesbians in the academic world." In G. Vida (Ed.), *Our right to love: A lesbian resource book*. Englewood Cliffs, N.J.: Prentice-Hall, 1978.

Curran, D. "Sexual perversions and their treatment." *Practitioner*, 1947, *158*(946), 343-348.

Curran, D., & Parr, D. "Homosexuality: An analysis of 100 male cases seen in private practice." *British Medical Journal*, 1957, *5022*, 797-801.

Dailey, D. "Adjustment of heterosexual and homosexual couples in pairing relationships: An exploratory study." *Journal of Sex Research*, 1979, *15*(2), 143-157.

Dalsemer, T. "Counseling lesbians." *Women: A Journal of Liberation*, 1977, *5*(2), 22-26.

D'Andrade, R. "Sex differences and cultural institutions." In E. Maccoby (Ed.), *The development of sex differences*. Stanford, Calif.: Stanford University Press, 1966.

Daniel, S. "The homosexual woman in present day society." *International Journal of Sexology*, 1954, *7*(4), 223-223.

Dank, B. "Coming out in the gay world." *Psychiatry*, 1971, *34*, 180-197.

Dank, B. "The development of a homosexual identity: Antecedents and consequents." *Dissertation Abstracts*, 1973, *34*, 423-424.

Davenport, J., & Davenport, J. III. "The rural rape crisis center: A model." *Human Services in the Rural Environment,* 1979, *1*(1), 29-39.

Davenport, J., & Davenport, J. III. "Training volunteers for rural rape crisis services." In T. Morton & R. Edwards (Eds.), *Training in the human services* (Vol. 2). Knoxville: University of Tennessee Press, 1980.

Davenport, J. III, Davenport, J., & Wiebler, R. (Eds.). *Social work in rural areas.* Laramie: University of Wyoming School of Social Work, 1980.

David, H., & Rabinowitz, W. "Szondi patterns in epileptic and homosexual males." *Journal of Consulting Psychology,* 1952, *16*(4), 247-250.

Davids, A., Joelson, M., & McArthur, C. "Rorschach and TAT indices of homosexuality in overt homosexuals, neurotics and normal males." *Journal of Abnormal and Social Psychology,* 1956, *53*(2), 161-172.

Davis, K., & Kopp, M. *Factors in the sex life of twenty-two hundred women.* New York: Harper Brothers, 1929.

Davison, G. "Elimination of a sadistic fantasy by a client-controlled counter conditioning technique: A case study." *Journal of Abnormal Psychology,* 1968, *73,* 84-89.

Davison, G. "Homosexuality: The ethical challenge." *Journal of Consulting and Clinical Psychology,* 1976, *44*(2), 157-162.

Davison, G. "Homosexuality and the ethics of behavioral intervention." *Journal of Homosexuality,* 1977, *2*(3), 195-204.

Davison, G., & Wilson, G. "Attitudes of behavior therapists toward homosexuality." *Behavior Therapy,* 1973, *4,* 686-696.

Dean, R., & Richardson, H. "Analysis of MMPI profiles of forty college-educated overt male homosexuals." *Journal of Consulting Psychology,* 1964, *28*(6), 483-486.

Dean, R., & Richardson, H. "On MMPI high-point codes of homosexual *vs* heterosexual males." *Journal of Consulting Psychology,* 1966, *30*(6), 558-560.

DeCecco, J., & Figliulo, M. "Methodology for studying discrimination based on sexual orientation and social sex role stereotypes." *Journal of Homosexuality,* 1978, *3*(3), 235-241.

DeCecco, J., & Freedman, M. "A study of interpersonal conflict in homosexual relations." *Homosexual Counseling Journal,* 1975, *2*(4), 146-149.

DeCecco, J., & Shively, M. "A study of perceptions of rights and needs in interpersonal conflicts in homosexual relationships." *Journal of Homosexuality,* 1978, *3*(3), 205-216.

DeCrescenzo, T. "Group work with gay adolescents." *Social Work with Groups,* 1979, *2*(1), 35-44.

DeCrescenzo, T., & Fifield, L. "The changing lesbian social scene." In B. Berzon & R. Leighton (Eds.), *Positively gay.* Millbrae, Calif.: Celestial Arts, 1979.

DeCrescenzo, T., & McGill, C. *Homophobia: A study of the attitudes of mental health professionals toward homosexuality.* Unpublished manuscript, University of Southern California, School of Social Work, 1978.

DeLora, J., & Warren, C. *Understanding sexual interaction.* Boston: Houghton Mifflin, 1977.

Delph, E. *The silent community: Public homosexual encounters.* Beverly Hills, Calif.: Sage, 1978.

DeLuca, J. "The structure of homosexuality." *Journal of Projective Techniques and Personality Assessment,* 1966, *30*(2), 187-191.

DeLuca, J. "Performance of overt male homosexuals and controls on the Blacky test." *Journal of Clinical Psychology,* 1967, *23*(4), 497.

Demaria, L. "Homosexual acting out." *International Journal of Psycho-Analysis,* 1968, *49*(2), 219-220.

Dengrove, E. "Homosexuality in women." 1957. Reprinted in I. Rubin (Ed.), *The third sex.* New York: New Book, 1961.

Denman, J. "Problems of rural areas." In H. Johnson (Ed.), *Rural human services: A book of readings.* Itasca, Ill.: F.E. Peacock, 1980.

Denniston, R. "Ambisexuality in animals." In J. Marmor (Ed.), *Homosexual behavior: A modern reappraisal.* New York: Basic Books, 1980.

Denzin, N. "Symbolic interactionism and ethnomethodology." In J.D. Douglas (Ed.), *Understanding everyday life.* Chicago: Aldine, 1970.

DeRiner, J. *The sexual criminal: A psychoanalytic study.* Springfield, Ill.: Charles C Thomas, 1949.

Deutsch, H. "On female homosexuality." *Psychoanalytic Quarterly,* 1932, *1,* 484-510.

Dickey, B. "Attitudes toward sex roles and feelings of adequacy in homosexual males." *Journal of Consulting Psychology,* 1961, *25*(2), 116-122.

Dilno, J. "Monogamy and alternative lifestyles." In G. Vida (Ed.), *Our right to love: A lesbian resource book.* Englewood Cliffs, N.J.: Prentice-Hall, 1978.

DiNitto, D., & Hernandez, S. "Alcoholism services in rural areas: Implications for social work education." In J. Davenport III, J. Davenport, & R. Wiebler (Eds.), *Social work in rural areas.* Laramie: University of Wyoming School of Social Work, 1980.

Dinitz, S., Dynes, R., & Clark, A. "Deviance, norms and societal reactions." In S. Dinitz, R. Dynes, & A. Clark (Eds.), *Deviance: Studies in the process of stigmatization and societal reaction.* New York: Oxford University Press, 1969.

"DOB questionnaire reveals some comparisons between male and female homosexuals." *Ladder,* 1960, *12*(4), 4-25.

"DOB questionnaire reveals some facts about lesbians." *Ladder,* 1959, *12*(3), 4-26.

Douglas, J.D. "Conceptions of deviant behavior: The old and the new." *Pacific Sociological Review,* 1966, *9*(1), 9-14.

Douglas, J.D. (Ed.). *Understanding everyday life.* Chicago: Aldine, 1970.

Douglas, J.D. "Observing deviance." In J.D. Douglas (Ed.), *Research on deviance*. New York: Random House, 1972. (a)

Douglas, J.D. (Ed.). *Research on deviance*. New York: Random House, 1972. (b)

Douvan, E. "New sources of conflict in females at adolescence and early adulthood." In J. Bardwick (Ed.), *Feminine personality and conflict*. Belmont, Calif.: Brooks/Cole, 1970.

Duehn, W., & Mayadas, N. "The use of stimulus/modeling videotapes in assertive training for homosexuals." *Journal of Homosexuality*, 1976, *1*(4), 373-381.

Dunbar, J., Brown, M., & Amoroso, D. "Some correlates of attitudes toward homosexuality." *Journal of Social Psychology*, 1973, *89*, 271-279.

Dyne, L. "Is DC becoming the gay capital of America?" *The Washingtonian*, September 1980, pp. 96-101; 133-141.

D'Zurilla, T., & Goldfried, M. "Cognitive processes, problem solving and effective behavior." In T. D'Zurilla & M. Goldfried (Eds.), *Behavior change through self-control*. New York: Holt, Rinehart & Winston, 1975.

Eastman, P. "Consciousness raising as a resocialization process for women." *Smith College Studies in Social Work*, 1973, *43*(3), 153-183.

Edgar, J., Sweet, E., & Thom, M. *The decade of women: A Ms. history of the seventies in words and pictures*. New York: Paragon Books, 1979.

Edwards, J. (Ed.). *Medical science and the criminal law*. Toronto: University of Toronto Press, 1974.

Eisenberg, M. "The process of homosexual identity and the effect of homosexual subculture on the lifestyle of the homosexual." (Doctoral dissertation, University of Massachusetts, 1974). *Dissertation Abstracts International*, 1975, *35*(9-B), 4648B. (University Microfilms No. 75-6016).

Ellis, A. "The influence of heterosexual culture on the attitudes of homosexuals." *International Journal of Sexology*, 1951, *5*(2), 77-79. Reprinted as "The influence of heterosexual culture." In D. Cory (Ed.), *Homosexuality: A cross-cultural approach*. New York: Julian, 1956.

Ellis, A. "Are homosexuals necessarily neurotic?" 1955. Reprinted in D. Cory (Ed.), *Homosexuality: A cross-cultural approach*. New York: Julian, 1956.

Ellis, A. "Are homosexuals really creative?" *Sexology*, 1962, *29*(2), 88-93.

Ellis, A. "The truth about lesbians." *Sexology*, 1964, *30*(10), 652-655.

Ellis, A. "The ambiguity of contemporary sex attitudes." In E. Sagarin and D. MacNamara (Eds.), *Problems of sex behavior*. New York: Thomas Crowell, 1968. (a)

Ellis, A. "Homosexuality: The right to be wrong." *Journal of Sex Research*, 1968, *4*(2), 96-107. (b)

Ellis, A., & Allen, C. "On the cure of homosexuality." *International Journal of Sexology*, 1952, *5*(3), 135-142.

Erikson, K. "Notes on the sociology of deviance." *Social Problems*, 1962, *9*, 307-314.

Erikson, K. "Patient role and social uncertainty." In E. Rubington & M. Weinberg (Eds.), *Deviance: The interactionist perspective*. London: Macmillan, 1968.

Escoffier, J. "Stigmas, work environment, and educational discrimination against homosexuals." *Homosexual Counseling Journal*, 1975, *2*(1), 8-17.

Evans, R. "Childhood parental relationships of homosexual men." *Journal of Consulting and Clinical Psychology*, 1969, *33*, 135-139.

Evans, R. "Sixteen personality factor questionnaire scores of homosexual men." *Journal of Consulting and Clinical Psychology*, 1970, *34*, 212-215.

Evans, R. "Adjective Check List scores of homosexual men." *Journal of Personality Assessment*, 1971, *35*, 344-349.

Fabian, J. "The hazards of being a professional woman." *Professional Psychology*, 1972, *3*(4), 324-326.

Fabian, J. "The role of the therapist in the process of sexual emancipation." *Psychiatric Opinion*, 1973, *10*(4), 31-33.

Fairchild, B. "For parents of gays: A fresh perspective." In B. Berzon and R. Leighton (Eds.), *Positively gay*. Millbrae, Calif.: Celestial Arts, 1979.

Fairchild, B., & Hayward, N. *Now that you know: What every parent should know about homosexuality*. New York: Harcourt Brace Jovanovich, 1979.

Farberow, N. (Ed.). *Taboo topics*. New York: Atherton Press, 1963.

Farrell, R., & Nelson, J. "A causal model of secondary deviance: The case of homosexuality." *Sociology Quarterly*, 1976, *17*(1), 109-120.

Farrell, W. *The liberated man*. New York: Bantam Books, 1975.

Feldman, M. "Aversion therapy for sexual deviation: A critical review." *Psychological Bulletin*, 1966, *65*, 65-79.

Feldman, M., & MacCullough, M. "The application of anticipatory avoidance learning to the treatment of homosexuality. 1. Theory, technique, and preliminary results." *Behavior Research and Therapy*, 1965, *2*, 165-183.

Feldman, M., MacCullough, M., Orford, J., & Mellor, V. "The application of anticipatory avoidance learning to the treatment of homosexuality." *Acta Psychiatrica Scandinavica*, 1969, *45*(2), 109-117.

Feldman, P. "Helping homosexuals with problems: A commentary and a personal view." *Journal of Homosexuality*, 1977, *2*(3), 241-249.

Ferguson, K., & Finkler, D. "An involvement and overtness measure for lesbians: Its development and relation to anxiety and social zeitgeist." *Archives of Sexual Behavior*, 1978, *7*(3), 211-227.

Ferleman, M. "Homosexuality." *Menninger Perspective*, 1974, *5*(2), 24-27.

Ferster, C. "Classification of behavioral pathology." In L. Krasner & L. Ullman (Eds.), *Research in behavior modification*. New York: Holt, Rinehart & Winston, 1965.

Ferster, C. "Reinforcement and punishment in the control of human behavior by social agencies." In E. McGinnies & C.

Ferster (Eds.), *The reinforcement of social behavior*. Boston: Houghton Mifflin, 1971.

Figliulo, M., Shively, M., & McEnroe, F. "The relationship of departure in social sex-roles to the abridgement of civil liberties." *Journal of Homosexuality,* 1978, *3*(3), 249-255.

Fink, P. "Homosexuality: Illness or life style?" *Journal of Sex and Marital Therapy,* 1975, *1*(3), 225-233.

Fitzgerald, T. "A theoretical typology of homosexuality in the US." *Corrective Psychiatry and Journal of Social Therapy,* 1963, *9*(1), 28; 35.

Foreyt, J., & Rathjen, D. (Eds.). *Cognitive behavior therapy: Research and application.* New York: Plenum Press, 1978.

Fort, J., Steiner, C., & Conrad, F. "Attitudes of mental health professionals toward homosexuality and its treatment." *Psychological Reports,* 1971, *29,* 347-350.

Foster, J. *Sex variant women in literature: A historical and quantitative analysis.* Oakland, Calif.: Diana Press, 1975.

Fox, B., & DiScipio, W. "An explanatory study in the treatment of homosexuals by combining principles from psychoanalytic theory and conditioning: Theoretical and methodological considerations," *British Journal of Medical Psychology,* 1968, *41,* 273-282.

Fraker, S., & Barnes, J. "Of human bondage." *Newsweek,* 26 April 1976, p. 35.

Franks, V., & Burtle, V. (Eds.). *Women in therapy.* New York: Brunner/Mazel, 1974.

Freedman, M. "Homosexuality among women and psychological adjustment." *Dissertation Abstracts International.* 1968, *28,* 4294B-4295B. (University Microfilms No. 86-3308).

Freedman, M. *Homosexuality and psychological functioning.* Belmont, Calif.: Brooks/Cole, 1971.

Freedman, M. "Far from illness: Homosexuals may be healthier than straights." *Psychology Today,* March 1975, *8,* 28-32.

Freeman, J. "Growing up girlish." *Trans-Action,* 1970, *8*(42), 36-43.

French, E., & Lesser, G. "Some characteristics of the achievement motive in women." *Journal of American Society of Psychologists,* 1964, *68*(2), 119-128.

Freud, S. "Psychogenesis of a case of homosexuality in a woman" (B. Low & R. Gambler, trans.). 1920, *Standard Edition,* London: Hogarth Press, 1955, *18,* 147-172.

Freud, S. "Some neurotic mechanisms in jealousy, paranoia and homosexuality" (J. Strachey, trans.). 1922. *Standard Edition,* London: Hogarth Press, 1955, *18,* 223-232.

Freud, S. "The psychology of the female." *New Introductory Lectures on Psychoanalysis* (J. Strachey, Ed. and trans.). New York: W. W. Norton, 1933.

Freund, K. "Should homosexuality arouse therapeutic concern?" *Journal of Homosexuality,* 1977, *2*(3), 235-240.

Freund, K., Langevin, R., Cibiri, S., & Sajac, L. "Heterosexual aversion in homosexual males." *Archives of General Psychiatry,* 1973, *122,* 168-169.

Freund, K., Langevin, R., Satterberg, J., & Steiner, B. "Extension of the gender identity scale for males." *Archives of Sexual Behavior,* 1977, *6*(6), 507-519.

Friedan, B. *The feminine mystique.* New York: Norton, 1963.

Friedman, M. "Lesbian as teacher, teacher as lesbian." In G. Vida (Ed.), *Our right to love: A lesbian resource book.* Englewood Cliffs, N.J.: Prentice-Hall, 1978.

Fromm, E., & Elonen, A. "Projective techniques in a case of female homosexuality." *Journal of Projective Techniques,* 1951, *15,* 185-230.

Gagnon, J. *Human sexualities.* Glenview, Ill.: Scott, Foresman, 1977.

Gagnon, J., & Simon, W. (Eds.) *Sexual deviance.* New York: Harper & Row, 1967. (a)

Gagnon, J., & Simon, W. "The sociological perspective on homosexuality." *Dublin Review,* 1967, *512,* 96-114. (b)

Gagnon, J., & Simon, W. *Sexual conduct: The social sources of human sexuality.* Chicago: Aldine, 1973. (a)

Gagnon, J., & Simon, W. (Eds.). *The sexual scene.* New Brunswick, N.J.: Transaction Books, 1973. (b)

Galana, L., & Covina, G. *The new lesbians: Interviews with women across the U.S. and Canada.* Berkeley, Calif.: Moon Books, 1977.

Gambrill, E. *Behavior modification: Handbook of assessment, intervention and evaluation.* San Francisco: Jossey-Bass, 1977.

Garfinkle, E., & Morin, S. "Psychotherapists' attitudes toward homosexual psychotherapy clients." *Journal of Social Issues,* 1978, *34*(3), 101-112.

Gartrell, N, Kraemer, H., & Brodie, H. "Psychiatrists' attitudes toward female homosexuality." *Journal of Nervous and Mental Disease,* 1974, *159,* 141-144.

Gayellow pages: National edition: New York: Renaissance House, 1980.

Gaylin, W. "The homosexual act as a symptom." *Psychiatry Digest,* 1964, *25,* 25-30.

Gearhart, S. "The spiritual dimension: Death and resurrection of a hallelujah dyke." In G. Vida (Ed.), *Our right to love: A lesbian resource book.* Englewood Cliffs, N.J.: Prentice-Hall, 1978.

Gebhard, P. "Homosexual socialization." *Experpta Medica International Congress Series,* 1966, *150,* 1028-1031.

Gemme, R., & Wheeler, C. (Eds.). *Progress in sexology.* New York: Plenum Press, 1977.

George, K. "Etiology and treatment of sexual dysfunction in gay male clients." Paper presented at Pre-Institute Workshop, "The Counseling Needs of Lesbians and Gay Men," American Association of Sex Educators, Counselors, and Therapists, Washington, D.C., April 1979.

George, K. "Etiology and treatment of sexual dysfunction in gay (homosexual) male patients." Paper presented at 5th World Congress of Sexology, Jerusalem, 25 June 1981.

Gershman, H. "Considerations of some aspects of homosexuality." *American Journal of Psychoanalysis,* 1953, *13,* 82-83.

Gershman, H. "Homosexuality and some aspects of creativity." *American Journal of Psychoanalysis,* 1964, *24,* 29-38.

Gershman, H. "The effects of group therapy on compulsive homosexuality in men and women." *American Journal of Psychoanalysis,* 1975, & *35*(4), 303-312.

Giannell, A. "Gianell's criminosynthesis theory applied to female homosexuality." *Journal of Psychology,* 1969, *64*(2), 213-222.

Gibbs, J. "Issues in defining deviant behavior." In R. Scott & J. Douglas (Eds.), *Theoretical perspectives on deviance.* New York: Basic Books, 1972.

Gibson, G. *By her own admission: A lesbian mother's fight to keep her son.* New York: Doubleday, 1977.

Giese, H. "Differences in the homosexual relations of men and women." *International Journal of Sexology,* 1954, *7*(4), 225-227.

Gilbert, L., Deutsch, D., & Strahan, R. "Feminine and masculine dimensions of the typical, desirable, and ideal woman and man." *Sex roles,* 1978, *4*(5), 767-778.

Gillespie, W. "Notes on the analysis of sexual perversions." *International Journal of Psycho-Analysis,* 1952, *33*(4), 397-402.

Ginsburg, K. "The 'meat-rack': A study of the male homosexual prostitute." *American Journal of Psychotherapy,* 1967, *21*(2), 170-185.

Gittings, B., & Tobin, K. "Lesbians and the gay movement." In G. Vida (Ed.), *Our right to love: A lesbian resource book.* Englewood Cliffs, N.J.: Prentice-Hall, 1978.

Glenn, N. & Weaver, C. "Attitudes toward premarital, extramarital, and homosexual relations in the U.S. in the 1970's." *The Journal of Sex Research, 1979, 15*(2), 108-118.

Glick, B. "Homosexual panic: Clinical and theoretical considerations." *Journal of Nervous and Mental Disease,* 1959, *129*(1), 20-28.

Glover, E. "The social and legal aspects of sexual abnormality." *Medico-Legal and Criminological Review,* 1945, *13*(3), 133-148.

Gluckman, L. "Lesbianism: A clinical approach." *New Zealand Medical Journal,* 1966, *65*(407), 433-439.

Glueck, B., Jr. "Psychodynamic patterns in the homosexual sex offender." *American Journal of Psychiatry,* 1956, *112*(8), 584-590.

Gochros, H. "Teaching more or less social work students to be helpful to more or less gay people." *Homosexual Counseling Journal,* 1975, *2*(2), 58-67.

Gochros, H., & Schultz, L. *Human sexuality and social work.* New York: Association Press, 1972.

Gochros, J., "Sex and race: Some further issues for social work practitioners." In D. Kunkel (Ed.), *Sexual issues in social work: Emerging concerns in education and practice.* Honolulu: University of Hawaii School of Social Work, 1979.

Goffman, E. *Stigma.* Englewood Cliffs, N.J.: Prentice-Hall, 1963.

Goldberg, S. "What is normal: Logical aspects of the question of homosexual behavior." *Psychiatry,* 1975, *38*(3), 227-243.

Goldstein, F. "Sex identity and inversion." In G. Seward & R. Williams (Ed.), *Sex roles in a changing society.* New York Random House, 1971.

Goleman, D., & Bush, S. "The liberation of sexual fantasy." *Psychology Today,* October 1977, pp. 44-52; 104-107.

Gonsiorek, J. "Psychological adjustment and homosexuality." JSAS *Catalog of Selected Documents in Psychology,* 1977, 7.

Goodall, K. "Homosexuality: No target for behavior modification." *Psychology Today,* May 1975, p. 59.

Gordon, F., & Hall, D. "Self-image and stereotypes of femininity: Their relationship to women's role conflicts and coping." *Journal of Applied Psychology,* 1974, *59*(2), 241-243.

Gornick, V., & Moran, B. (Eds.). *Woman in sexist society.* New York: Basic Books, 1971.

Goslin, D. (Ed.). *Handbook of socialization theory and research.* Chicago: Rand McNally, 1969.

Gould, L. "Stories for free children: X—A fabulous child's story." *Ms.,* December 1972, pp. 74-76; 105-106.

Gould, L. *X—A fabulous child's story.* Houston: Daughters Publishing, 1978.

Gould, R. "Measuring masculinity by the size of a paycheck." In J. Pleck & J. Sawyer (Eds.), *Men and masculinity.* Englewood Cliffs, N.J.: Prentice-Hall, 1974.

Green, E., & Jounson, J. "Homosexuality." *Journal of Criminal Psychopathology,* 1944, *5*(3-4), 467-480.

Green, R. "Sissies and tomboys: A guide to diagnosis and management." In C. Wahl (Ed.), *Sexual problems: Diagnosis and treatment in medical patients.* New York: Free Press, 1967.

Green, R. "Homosexuality as a mental illness." *International Journal of Psychiatry,* 1972, *10,* 77-128.

Green, R. *Sexual identity conflict in children and adults.* New York: Basic Books, 1974.

Green, R. (Ed.). *Human sexuality: A health practitioner's text.* Baltimore: Williams & Wilkins, 1975.

Green, R. "Patterns of sexual identity in childhood: Relationship to subsequent sexual partner preference." In J. Marmor (Ed.), *Homosexual behavior: A modern reappraisal.* New York: Basic Books, 1980.

Green, R. " 'Sissies' and 'tomboys.' " *SIECUS Report,* 1979, *7*(3), 1-2; 15.

Greenberg, J. "A study of female homosexuals (predominantly college students)." *American College Health Association Journal,* 1973, *22,* 56-60.

Greenblatt, D. "Semantic differential analysis of the 'triangular system' hypothesis in 'adjusted' overt male homosexuals." Unpublished doctoral dissertation, University of California, Berkeley, 1966.

Greenspan, H., & Campbell, J. "The homosexual as a personality type." *American Journal of Psychiatry*, 1945, *101*(5), 682-689.

Gregory-Lewis, S. "Lesbians in the military." In G. Vida (Ed.), *Our right to love: A lesbian resource book*. Englewood Cliffs, N.J.: Prentice-Hall, 1978.

Gundlach, R., & Riess, B. "Lesbianism." *International Mental Health Research Newsletter*, 1963, *5*(3-4), 14-15.

Gundlach, R., & Riess, B. "Birth order and sex of siblings in a sample of lesbians and non-lesbians." *Psychological Reports*, 1967, *1*(20), 61-62.

Gundlach, R., & Riess, B. "Self and sexual identity in the female: A study of female homosexuals." In B. Riess (Ed.), *New directions in mental health*. New York: Grune & Stratton, 1968.

Gunnison, F., Jr. *An introduction to the homophile movement*. Hartford, Conn.: Institute of Social Ethics, 1967.

Guth, J. "Invisible women: Lesbians in America." *Journal of Sex Education and Therapy*, 1978, *4*(1), 3-6.

Hadden, S. "Treatment of male homosexuals in groups." *International Journal of Group Psychotherapy*, 1966, *16*, 13-22.

Hadden, S. "Homosexuality: Its questioned classification." *Psychiatric Annals*, 1976, *6*(4), 38-46.

Haeberle, E. *The sex atlas*. New York: Seabury Press, 1978.

Haist, M., & Hewitt, J. "The butch-fem dichotomy in male homosexual behavior." *Journal of Sex Research*, 1974, *10*(1), 68-75.

Hall, M. "Lesbian families: Cultural and clinical issues." *Social Work*, 1978, *23*(5), 380-385.

Halleck, S. "Another response to 'Homosexuality: The ethical challenge.'" *Journal of Consulting and Clinical Psychology*, 1976, *44*(2), 167-170.

Hamilton, W. *Christopher and gay: A partisan's view of the Greenwich Village homosexual scene*. New York: Saturday Review Press, 1973.

Hammer, M. "Homosexuality and the reversed Oedipus complex." *Corrective Psychiatry Journal of Social Therapy*, 1968, *14*(1), 45-47.

Hammersmith, S., & Weinberg, M. "Homosexual identity: Commitment, adjustment, and significant others." *Sociometry*, 1973, *36*, 56-79.

Hammond, H., & Damon, B. "Lesbian artists." In G. Vida (Ed.), *Our right to love: A lesbian resource book*. Englewood Cliffs, N.J.: Prentice-Hall, 1978.

Hampson, J. "Determinants of psychosexual orientation." In F. Beach (Ed.), *Sexual behavior*. New York: Wiley & Sons, 1965.

Hanson, R., & Adesso, V. "A multiple behavioral approach to male homosexual behavior: A case study." *Journal of Behavior Therapy and Experimental Psychiatry*, 1972, *3*, 323-325.

Hariton, B. "The sexual fantasies of women." *Psychology Today*, March 1973, pp. 39-44.

Harnick, N., & Boskey, J. "Lesbians and the left." In G. Vida (Ed.), *Our right to love: A lesbian resource book*. Englewood Cliffs, N.J.: Prentice-Hall, 1978.

Harper, R. "Can homosexuals be changed?" In I. Rubin (Ed.), *The third sex*. New York: New York, 1961.

Harris, B. "Lesbian literature: An introduction." In G. Vida (Ed.), *Our right to love: A lesbian resource book*. Englewood Cliffs, N.J.: Prentice-Hall, 1978.

Harris, D. *Social-psychological characteristics of ambisexuals*. Unpublished doctoral dissertation, University of Tennessee, 1977.

Hartman, B. "Comparison of selected experimental MMPI profiles of sexual deviants and sociopaths without deviation." *Psychological Reports*, 1967, *20*(1), 234.

Hassell, J., & Smith, E. "Female homosexuals' concepts of self, men and women." *Journal of Personality Assessment*, 1975, *39*(2), 154-159.

Havelin, A. "Political attitudes towards homosexuals and homosexuality." *Sociological Abstracts*, 1970, *18*(6), 1195.

Hawkins, R. "The Uppsala connection: The development of principles basic to education for sexuality." *SIECUS Report*, 1980, 8(3), 1-2; 12-16.

Hawkins, R., & Friedman, E. "Human sexuality: A content area for continuing medical education." *The P.A. Journal*, 1978, *8*(4), 219.

Hedblom, J. "Dimensions of lesbian sexual experience." *Archives of Sexual Behavior*, 1973, *2*(4), 329-341.

Hedblom, J., & Hartman, J. "Research on lesbianism: Selected effects of time, geographic location, and data collection technique." *Archives of Sexual Behavior*, 1980, *9*(3), 217-234.

Hedgpeth, J. "Employment discrimination law and the rights of gay persons." *Journal of Homosexuality*, 1979-1980, *5*(1-2), 67-78.

Heersema, P. "Homosexuality and the physician." *Journal of the American Medical Association*, 1965, *193*(10), 815-817.

Heidensohn, F. "The deviance of women: A critique and an enquiry." *British Journal of Sociology*, 1968, *19*(2), 160-175.

Heilbrun, A., Jr. "Sex role, instrumentality, expressive behavior and psycho-pathology in females." *Journal of Abnormal Psychology*, 1968, *73*, 131-136.

Heilbrun, A., Jr. "Measurement of masculine and feminine sex role identities as independent dimensions." *Journal of Consulting and Clinical Psychology*, 1976, *44*(2), 183-190.

Heilbrun, A., Jr., & Thompson, N. "Sex-role identity and male and female homosexuality." *Sex Roles*, 1977, *3*(1), 65-79.

Heilbrun, C. *Toward a recognition of androgyny*. New York: Alfred Knopf, 1975.

Heiman, J. "Women's sexual arousal." *Psychology Today*, April 1975, pp. 93-94.

Henley, N., & Pincus, F. "Interrelationship of sexist, racist, and antihomosexual attitudes." *Psychological Reports*, 1978, *42*, 83-90.

Henrichsen, J., & Katahn, M. "Recent trends and new developments in the treatment of homosexuality." *Psychotherapy: Theory, Research, and Practice,* 1975, *12*(1), 83-92.

Henry, G. "Psychogenic factors in overt homosexuality." *American Journal of Psychiatry,* 1937, *93*, 889-908.

Herman, M., & Wortis, S. "Aberrant sex-behavior in humans." *Annals of the New York Academy of Science,* 1947, *47*, 639-645.

Hewitt, C. "On the meaning of effeminancy in homosexual men." *American Journal of Psychotherapy,* 1961, *15*(4), 592-602.

Hiltner, S. "Homosexuality and the churches." In J. Marmor (Ed.), *Homosexual behavior: A modern reappraisal.* New York: Basic Books, 1980.

Hitchens, D. "Social attitudes, legal standards, and personal trauma in child custody cases." *Journal of Homosexuality,* 1979/1980, *5*(1-2), 89-96.

Hite, S. *The Hite report.* New York: Macmillan, 1976.

Hoffman, M. *The gay world: Male homosexuality and the social creation of evil.* New York: Basic Books, 1962.

Hoffman, M., & Hoffman, L. (Eds.). *Review of child development research* (vol. 1). New York: Russell Sage Foundation, 1964.

Hogan, R., Fox, A., & Kirchner, J. "Attitudes, opinions, and sexual development of 205 homosexual women." *Journal of Homosexuality,* 1977, *3*(2), 123-136.

Holeman, R., & Winokur, G. "Effeminate homosexuality: A disease of childhood." *American Journal of Orthopsychiatry,* 1965, *35* 48-56.

Holmes, K. "Sexually transmitted diseases." (USDHEW Monograph, U.S. Public Health Service Publication No. 00-2908) Washington, D.C.: U.S. Govt. Printing Office, 1976, p. 23.

Hooker, E. "A preliminary analysis of group behavior of homosexuals." *Journal of Psychology,* 1956, *42*, 217-225.

Hooker, E. "The adjustment of the male overt homosexual." *Journal of Projective Techniques,* 1957, *21*, 18-21.

Hooker, E. "Male homosexuality in the Rorschach." *Journal of Projective Techniques,* 1958, *22*, 33-54.

Hooker, E. "The case of El: A biography." *Journal of Projective Techniques and Personality Assessment,* 1961, *25*(3), 252-267.

Hooker, E. "The adjustment of the male overt homosexual." In H. Ruitenbeek (Ed.), *The problem of homosexuality in modern America.* New York: Dutton, 1963. (a)

Hooker, E. "Male homosexuality." In N. Farberow (Ed.), *Taboo topics.* New York: Atherton, 1963. (b)

Hooker, E. "An empirical study of some relations between sexual patterns and gender identity in male homosexuals." In J. Money (Ed.), *Sex research: New developments.* New York: Holt, Rinehart & Winston, 1965. (a)

Hooker, E. "Male homosexuals and their worlds." In J. Marmor (Ed.), *Sexual inversion: The multiple roots of homosexuality.* New York: Basic Books, 1965. (b)

Hooker, E. "The homosexual community." In J. Gagnon &

W. Simon (Eds.), *Sexual deviance.* New York: Harper & Row, 1967.

Hooker, E. "Homosexuality." In *International Encyclopedia of the Social Sciences* (Vol. 14). New York: Macmillan, 1968.

Hooker, E. "Parental relations and male homosexuality in patient and nonpatient samples." *Journal of Consulting and Clinical Psychology,* 1969, *33*(2), 140-142.

Hooker, E., & Chance, P. "Facts that liberated the gay community." *Psychology Today,* July 1975, pp. 52-55; 101.

Hope, K., & Young, N. *Momma—The sourcebook for single mothers.* New York: New American Library, 1976.

Hopkins, J. "The lesbian personality." *British Journal of Psychiatry,* 1969, *115*, 1433-1436.

Hopkins, J. "Lesbian signs on the Rorschach." *British Journal of Projective Psychology and Personality Study,* 1970, *15*(2), 7-14.

Horowitz, M. "The homosexual's image of himself." *Mental Hygiene,* 1964, *48*(2), 197-201.

Hotvedt, M. "Parenting concerns of homosexual parents." Paper presented at Pre-Institute Workshop, American Association of Sex Educators, Counselors, and Therapists, Washington, D.C., April 1979.

"How gay is gay?" *Time,* 23 April 1979, pp. 72-76.

Huff, F. "The desensitization of a homosexual." *Behavior Research and Therapy,* 1970, *8*, 99-102.

Humphries, L. *The tearoom trade: Impersonal sex in public places.* Chicago: Aldine, 1970.

Humphries, L., & Miller, B. "Identities in the emerging gay culture." In J. Marmor (Ed.), *Homosexual behavior: A modern reappraisal.* New York: Basic books, 1980.

Huntington, G. "History of pornographic films." Paper presented at Institute for Sex Research, Summer Program, Indiana University, Bloomington, July 1973.

Hyde, J. *Understanding human sexuality.* New York: McGraw-Hill, 1979.

Irwin, P., & Thompson, N. "Acceptance of the rights of homosexuals: A profile." *Journal of Homosexuality,* 1977, *3*(2), 107-121.

Israel, A., Raskin, P., & Pravder, M. "Gender and sex-role appropriateness: Bias in the judgment of disturbed behavior." *Sex Roles,* 1978, *4*(3), 399-413.

Jaco, E. (Ed.). *Patients, physicians and illness* (2nd ed.). New York, Free Press, 1972.

Jacobs, M. "The treatment of homosexuality." *South African Medical Journal,* 1969, *43*(37), 1123-1126.

Jacobson, N., & Margolin, G. *Marital therapy: Strategies based on social learning and behavior exchange principles.* New York: Brunner/Mazel, 1979.

Jacobson, R. "Gay issues in financial planning." In B. Berzon & R. Leighton (Eds.), *Positively gay.* Millbrae, Calif.: Celestial Arts, 1979.

Jay, K. "Coming out as process." In G. Vida (Ed.), *Our right to love: A lesbian resource book.* Englewood Cliffs, N.J.: Prentice-Hall, 1978.

Jay, K., & Young, A. (Ed.). *After you're out: Personal experiences of gay men and lesbian women.* New York: Links, 1975.

Jay, K., & Young, A. (Eds.). *Out of the closets: Voices of gay liberation.* New York: Jove/HBJ, 1977.

Jay, K., & Young, A. (Eds.). *Lavender culture.* New York: Jove/HBJ, 1978.

Jay, K., & Young, A. *The gay report.* New York: Summit Books, 1979.

Jeffery, C. "The historical development of criminology." In H. Mannheim (Ed.), *Pioneers in criminology* (2nd ed.). Montclair, N.J.: Patterson Smith, 1972.

Jensen, M. "Role differentiation in female homosexual quasi-marital unions." *Journal of Marriage and the Family,* 1974, *36*(2), 360-367.

Johnsgard, K., & Schumacher, R. "The experience of intimacy in group psychotherapy with male homosexuals." *Psychotherapy: Theory, Research, and Practice,* 1970, *7,* 173-176.

Johnson, B. "Protestantism and gay freedom." In B. Berzon & R. Leighton (Eds.), *Positively gay.* Millbrae, Calif.: Celestial Arts, 1979.

Johnson, H. (Ed.). *Rural human services: A book of readings.* Itasca, Ill.: F.E. Peacock, 1980.

Johnson, L. "Human service delivery patterns in nonmetropolitan communities." In H. Johnson (Ed.), *Rural human services: A book of readings.* Itasca, Ill.: F.E. Peacock, 1980.

Johnson, M., & Kelly, J. "Deviant sex behavior in the aging." In O. Kaplan (Ed.), *Psychopathology of aging.* New York: Academic Press, 1979.

Johnston, J. *Lesbian nation: The feminist solution.* New York: Simon & Schuster, 1973.

Jones, B. "Being black and gay—Both issues must be faced." *Sexuality Today Newsletter,* 4 February 1980, pp. 2-3.

Jones, E. "Early development of female homosexuality." *International Journal of Psychoanalysis,* 1927, *8,* 458-472.

Jourard, S. "Reinventing marriage: The perspective of a psychologist." In H. Otto (Ed.), *The family in search of a future.* New York: Appleton-Century-Crofts, 1970.

Judson, F., Miller, K., & Schaffert, T. "Screening for gonorrhea and syphilis in the gay baths—Denver, Colorado." *American Journal of Public Health,* 1977, *67*(8), 741.

Kagan, J. "Acquisition and significance of sex-typing and sex-role." In M. Hoffman & L. Hoffman (Eds.), *Review of child development research* (Vol. 1). New York: Russell Sage Foundation, 1964.

Kaplan, B. *Blue Ridge: An Appalachia community in transition.* West Virginia University, Office of Research and Development, Appalachian Center, 1971.

Kaplan, H. *The new sex therapy: Active treatment of sexual dysfunctions.* New York: Brunner/Mazel, 1974.

Kaplan, O. (Ed.). *Psychopathology of aging.* New York: Academic Press, 1979.

Karlen, A. *Sexuality and homosexuality: A new view.* New York: W.W. Norton, 1971.

Karlen, A. "A discussion of 'Homosexuality as a mental illness.' " *International Journal of Psychiatry,* 1972, *10,* 108-113.

Karlen, A. "Homosexuality in history." In J. Marmor (Ed.), *Homosexual behavior: A modern reappraisal.* New York: Basic Books, 1980.

Karr, R. "Homosexual labeling and the male role." *Journal of Social Issues,* 1978, *34*(3), 73-83.

Katchadourian, H., & Lunde, D. *Fundamentals of human sexuality* (2nd ed.). New York: Holt, Rinehart & Winston, 1975.

Katz, D. "The functional approach to the study of attitudes." *Public Opinion Quarterly,* 1960, *24.* 163-204.

Katz, J. (Ed.). *A gay news chronology: 1969-1975 index and abstracts of articles from the New York Times.* New York: Arno Press, 1975.

Katz, J. *Gay American history.* New York: Thomas Crowell, 1976.

Kaye, H., Berl, S., Clare, J., Eleston, M., Gershwin, B., Gershwin, P., Kogan, L., Torda, C., & Wilbur, C. "Homosexuality in women." *Archives of General Psychiatry,* 1967, *17*(5), 626-634.

Kaye, J. "The effect of group therapy on compulsive homosexuality in men and women: A discussion." *American Journal of Psychoanalysis,* 1975, *35*(4), 313-316.

Keiser, S., & Schaffer, D. "Environmental factors in homosexuality in adolescent girls." *Psychoanalytic Review,* 1949, *36,* 283-295.

Keller, S. "The female role: Constants and change." In V. Franks & V. Burtle (Eds.), *Women in therapy.* New York: Brunner/Mazel, 1974.

Kelly, J. "Homosexuality and aging." In J. Marmor (Ed.), *Homosexual behaviors: A modern reappraisal.* New York: Basic Books, 1980.

Kelly, J., & Worell, J. "Parent behavior related to masculine, feminine, and androgynous sex-role orientation." *Journal of Consulting and Clinical Psychology,* 1976, *44,* 843-851.

Kelly, J., & Worell, J. "New formulations of sex roles and androgyny: A critical review." *Journal of Consulting and Clinical Psychology,* 1977, *45*(6), 1101-1115.

Kempe, G. "The homosexual in society." *British Journal of Delinquency,* 1954, *5*(1), 4-20.

Kemph, J., & Schwerin, E. "Increased latent homosexuality in a woman during group therapy." *International Journal of Group Psychotherapy,* 1966, *16,* 217-224.

Kendrick, D., & Clark, R. "Attitudinal differences between heterosexually and homosexually oriented males." *British Journal of Psychiatry,* 1967, *113*(494), 95-99.

Kennedy, E. *Sexual counseling.* New York: Seabury Press, 1977.

Kenyon, F. "Physique and physical health of female homosexuals.'' *Journal of Neurology, Neurosurgery and Psychiatry,* 1968, *31*(5), 487-489. (a)

Kenyon, F. ''Studies in female homosexuality. IV. Social and psychiatric aspects. V. Sexual development, attitudes, and experience.'' *British Journal of Psychiatry,* 1968, *114,* 1337-1350. (b)

Kenyon, F. ''Studies in female homosexuality. VI. The exclusively homosexual group.'' *Acta Psychiatrica Scandinavica,* 1968, *44*(3), 224-236. (c)

Kenyon, F. ''Studies in female homosexuality: Psychological test results.'' *Journal of Consulting and Clinical Psychology,* 1968, *38,* 510-513. (d)

Khan, M. ''The role of infantile sexuality and early object relations in female homosexuality.'' In I. Rosen (Ed.), *The pathology and treatment of sexual deviation: A methodological approach.* London: Oxford University Press, 1964.

Kimmel, D. ''Adult development and aging: A gay perspective.'' *Journal of Social Issues,* 1978, *34*(3), 113-130.

Kimmel, D. ''Adjustment to aging among gay men.'' In B Berzon & R. Leighton (Eds.), *Positively gay.* Millbrae, Calif.: Celestial Arts, 1979.

Kinsey, A., Pomeroy, W., & Clyde, E. ''Homosexual outlet.'' In J. McCaffrey (Ed.), *The homosexual dialectic.* Englewood Cliffs, N.J.: Prentice-Hall, 1972.

Kinsey, A., Pomeroy, W., & Martin, C. *Sexual behavior in the human male.* Philadelphia: W.B. Saunders, 1948.

Kinsey, A., Pomeroy, W., Martin, C., & Gebhard, P. *Sexual behavior in the human female.* Philadelphia: W.B. Saunders, 1953.

Kirkland, J., & Irey, K. ''Confidentiality: Issues and dilemmas in rural practice.'' In E. Buxton (Ed.), *2nd national institute on social work in rural areas reader.* Madison: University of Wisconsin Extension, 1977.

Kirsh, B. ''Consciousness-raising groups as therapy for women.'' In V. Franks & V. Burtle (Eds.), *Women in therapy.* New York: Brunner/Mazel, 1974.

Kitsuse, J. ''Societal reaction to deviant behavior.'' *Social Problems,* 1962, *9*(3), 247-256.

Kittrie, N. *The right to be different: Deviance and enforced therapy.* Baltimore: Johns Hopkins Press, 1971.

Klaf, F., & Davis, C. ''Homosexuality and paranoid schizophrenia: A survey of 150 cases and controls.'' *American Journal of Psychiatry,* 1960, *116*(12), 1070-1075.

Klaich, D. *Woman plus woman.* New York: Simon & Schuster, 1974.

Klein, F. *The bisexual option: A concept of one-hundred percent intimacy.* New York: Arbor House, 1978.

Kling, S. ''Homosexual behavior.'' In S. Kling (Ed.), *Sexual behavior and the law.* New York: Bernard Geis Associates, 1965.

Knapp, J., & Whitehurst, R. ''Sexually open marriage and relationships: Issues and prospects.'' In B. Murstein (Ed.), *Exploring intimate lifestyles.* New York: Springer, 1978.

Knutson, D. ''Job security for gays: Legal aspects.'' In B. Berzon & R. Leighton (Eds.), *Positively gay.* Millbrae, Calif.: Celestial Arts, 1979.

Knutson, D. '''Introduction' to special issue: 'Homosexuality and the law.''' *Journal of Homosexuality,* 1979-1980, *5*(1-2), 5-24.

Kohlenberg, J. ''Treatment of a homosexual pedophiliac using in vivo desensitization: A case study.'' *Journal of Abnormal Psychology,* 1974, *83,* 192-195.

Kollar, M. ''A comparison of the satisfaction with a residence hall living situation of gay/lesbian residents with heterosexual residents as measured by the University Residence Environment Scale and a Gay/Lesbian Awareness Workshop Program for university residence hall assistants.'' Unpublished doctoral dissertation, University of Tennessee, Knoxville, August 1980.

Kraft, T. ''A case of homosexuality treated by combined behavior therapy and psychotherapy: A total assessment.'' *Psychotherapy and Psychosomatics,* 1971, *19,* 342-358.

Krasner, L., & Ullman, L. (Eds.). *Research in behavior modification.* New York: Holt, Rinehart & Winston, 1965.

Kremer, M., & Rifkin, A. ''The early development of homosexuality: A study of adolescent lesbians.'' *American Journal of Psychiatry,* 1969, *126*(1), 91-96.

Krich, A. (Ed.). *The homosexuals as seen by themselves and thirty authorities.* New York: Citadel, 1954.

Kunkel, D. (Ed.). *Sexual issues in social work: Emerging concerns in education and practice.* Honolulu: University of Hawaii School of Social Work, 1979.

Kurt, E., & Lief, H. ''Why sex education for medical students?'' In R. Green (Ed.), *Human sexuality: A health practitioner's text.* Baltimore: Williams & Wilkins, 1975.

Lachman, L. ''Electoral politics: An interview with Elaine Noble.'' In G. Vida (Ed.), *Our right to love: A lesbian resource book.* Englewood Cliffs, N.J.: Prentice-Hall, 1978.

Laner, M. ''Growing older female: Heterosexual and homosexual.'' *Journal of Homosexuality,* 1977, *4*(3), 267-276. (a)

Laner, M. ''Permanent partner priorities: Gay and straight.'' *Journal of Homosexuality,* 1977, *3*(1), 21-39. (b)

Langevin, R. ''Modification of human sexual behavior.'' In J. Edwards (Ed.), *Medical science and the criminal law.* Toronto: University of Toronto Press, 1974.

Langevin, R., Stanford, A., & Block, R. ''The effect of relaxation instruction on erotic arousal in homosexual and heterosexual males.'' *Behavior Therapy,* 1975, *6*(4), 453-458.

Larkin, J. ''Coming out.'' *Ms.,* March 1976, pp. 72-74; 84; 86.

Lee, J. ''Going public: A study in the sociology of homosexual liberation.'' *Journal of Homosexuality,* 1977, *3*(1), 49-78.

Legg, W. ''Blackmailing the homosexual.'' *Sexology,* 1967, *33*(8), 554-556.

Lehman, J. ''What it means to love another woman.'' In G. Vida (Ed.), *Our right to love: A lesbian resource book.* Englewood Cliffs, N.J.: Prentice-Hall, 1978.

Lehne, G. ''Gay male fantasies and realities.'' *Journal of Social Issues,* 1978, *34*(3), 28-37.

Leighton, R. "For men: New social opportunities." In B. Berzon & R. Leighton (Eds.), *Positively gay*. Millbrae, Calif.: Celestial Arts, 1979.

Lemert, E. *Social pathology*. New York: McGraw-Hill, 1951.

Lemert, E. *Human deviance: Social problems and social control* (2nd ed.). Englewood Cliffs, N.J.: Prentice-Hall, 1972.

Leo, J. "Homosexuality: Tolerance vs approval." *Time*, 8 January 1979, pp. 48-49.

Levine, M. "Gay ghetto." *Journal of Homosexuality*, 1979, *4*(4), 363-378.

Levinger, G. "Sources of marital dissatisfaction among applicants for divorce." *American Journal of Orthopsychology*, 1966, *36*, 803-807.

Levitt, E., & Klassen, A., Jr. "Public attitudes toward homosexuality: Part of a 1970 national survey by the Institute of Sex Research." *Journal of Homosexuality*, 1974, *1*(1), 29-43.

Lewis, K. "Children of lesbians: Their point of view." *Social Work*, 1980, *25*(3), 203.

Lewis, S. *Sunday's women: A report of lesbian life today*. Boston: Beacon Press, 1979.

Lewis, V. "Androgen insensitivity syndrome: Erotic component of gender identity in nine women." In R. Gemme & C. Wheeler (Eds.), *Progress in sexology*. New York: Plenum, 1977.

Leznoff, M. "Interviewing homosexuals." *American Journal of Sociology*, 1956, *62*(2), 202-204.

Leznoff, M., & Westley, W. "The homosexual community." In J. Gagnon & W. Simon (Eds.), *Sexual deviance*. New York: Harper & Row, 1967.

Liazos, A. "The poverty of the sociology of deviance: Nuts, sluts, and preverts." *Social Problems*, 1972, *19*, 103-120.

Liddicoat, R. "A study of non-institutionalized homosexuals." *Journal of the National Institute of Personnel Research*, 1961, *8*, 217-249.

Lidz, R., & Lidz, T. "Homosexual tendencies in mothers of schizophrenic women." *Journal of Nervous and Mental Disease*, 1969, *149*(2), 229-235.

Liljestrand, P., Gerling, E., & Saliba, P. "The effects of social sex-role stereotypes and sexual orientation on psychotherapeutic outcomes." *Journal of Homosexuality*, 1978, *3*(4), 361-373.

Liljestrand, P., Peterson, R., & Zellers, R. "The relationship of the assumption and knowledge of the homosexual orientation to the abridgment of civil liberties." *Journal of Homosexuality*, 1978, *3*(3), 243-248.

Lindner, R. "Homosexuality and the contemporary scene." In H. Ruitenbeek (Ed.), *The problem of homosexuality in modern America*. New York: Dutton, 1963.

Lofland, J. *Deviance and identity*. Englewood Cliffs, N.J.: Prentice-Hall, 1969.

Loney, J. "An MMPI measurement of maladjustment in a sample of normal homosexual males." *Journal of Clinical Psychology*, 1971, *27*, 486-488.

Loney, J. "Background factors, sexual experiences, and attitudes toward treatment in 2 'normal' homosexual samples." *Journal of Consulting and Clinical Psychology*, 1972, *38*, 57-65.

Loney, J. "Family dynamics in homosexual women." *Archives of Sexual Behavior*, 1973, *2*(4), 343-350.

Lorand, A., & Balint, M. (Eds.). *Perversions: Psychodynamics and therapy*. New York: Random House, 1956.

Lorde, A. "I've been standing on this street corner a hell of a long time." In G. Vida (Ed.), *Our right to love: A lesbian resource book*. Englewood Cliffs, N.J.: Prentice-Hall, 1978.

Lotman, L. "Gay + art = renaissance." In B. Berzon & R. Leighton (Eds.), *Positively gay*. Millbrae, Calif.: Celestial Arts, 1979.

Luger, N. "Detection and management of other sexually transmitted diseases." *Bulletin of the New York Academy of Medicine*, 1976, *52*(8), 897-905.

Lumby, M. "Homophobia: The quest for a valid scale." *Journal of Homosexuality*, 1976, *2*, 39-47.

Luria, Z., & Rose, M. *Psychology of human sexuality*. New York: Wiley & Sons, 1979.

Lyness, J. "An experiential report of androgynous spousal roles." In B. Murstein (Ed.), *Exploring intimate lifestyles*. New York: Springer, 1978.

Lyon, P., & Martin, D. "Reminiscences of two female homophiles." In G. Vida (Ed.), *Our right to love: A lesbian resource book*. Englewood Cliffs, N.J.: Prentice-Hall, 1978.

Maccoby, E. (Ed.). *The development of sex differences*. Stanford, Calif.: Stanford University Press, 1966.

MacCullough, J., & Feldman, M. "Aversion therapy in the management of 43 homosexuals." *British Medical Journal*, 1967, *2*, 594-597.

MacDonald, A., Jr. "Identification and measurement of multidimensional attitudes toward equality between the sexes." *Journal of Homosexuality*, 1974, *1*(2), 165-182.

MacDonald, A., Jr. "Homophobia: Its roots and meanings." *Homosexual Counseling Journal*, 1976, *3*(1), 23-33.

MacDonald, A., Jr., & Games, R. "Some characteristics of those who hold positive and negative attitudes toward homosexuals." *Journal of Homosexuality*, 1974, *1*(1), 9-27.

MacDonald, A., Jr., Huggins, J., Young, S., & Swanson, R. "Attitudes toward homosexuality: Preservation of sex morality or the double standard?" *Journal of Consulting and Clinical Psychology*, 1973, *40*, 161.

MacKinnon, J. "The homosexual woman." *American Journal of Psychiatry*, 1947, *103*(5), 661-664.

Magee, B. *The gays among us: A study of homosexuality in men and women*. New York: Stein & Day, 1978.

Mager, D. "Out in the workplace." In K. Jay & A. Young (Eds.), *After you're out: Personal experiences of gay men and lesbian women*. New York: Links Books, 1975.

Maletzky, B. "Assisted covert sensitization: A preliminary report." *Behavior Therapy*, 1973, *4*, 117-119.

Manis, J., & Meltzer, B. (Eds.). *Symbolic interaction: A reader in social psychology.* Boston: Allyn & Bacon, 1967.

Mannheim, H. (Ed.). *Pioneers in criminology* (2nd ed.). Montclair, N.J.: Patterson Smith, 1972.

Mannion, K. "Female homosexuality: A comprehensive review of theory and research." JSAS *Catalog of Selected Documents in Psychology,* 1976, *6*(2), 44. (Ms. No. 1247).

Manosevitz, M. "Early sexual behavior in adult homosexual and heterosexual males." *Journal of Abnormal Psychology,* 1970, *76,* 396-402.

Marlowe, K. "The life of the homosexual prostitute." *Sexology,* 1964, *3*(1), 24-26. (a)

Marlowe, K. *Mr. Madam: Confessions of a male madam.* Los Angeles: Sherbourne Press, 1964. (b)

Marlowe, K. *The male homosexual.* Los Angeles: Sherbourne Press, 1965.

Marmor, J. (Ed.). *Sexual inversion: The multiple roots of homosexuality.* New York: Basic Books, 1965.

Marmor, J. "Homosexuality: Mental illness or moral dilemma?" *International Journal of Psychiatry,* 1972, *10,* 114-117.

Marmor, J.: "Clinical aspects of male homosexuality." In J. Marmor (Ed.), *Homosexual behavior: A modern reappraisal.* New York: Basic Books, 1980.

Marmor, J. "Epilogue: Homosexuality and the issue of mental illness." In J. Marmor (Ed.), *Homosexual behavior: A modern reappraisal.* New York: Basic Books, 1980.

Marmor, J. "Overview: the multiple roots of homosexual behavior." In J. Marmor (Ed.), *Homosexual behavior: A modern reappraisal.* New York: Basic Books, 1980.

Marmor, J. (Ed.). *Homosexual behavior: A modern reappraisal.* New York: Basic Books, 1980.

Marquis, J. "Orgasmic reconditioning: Changing sexual object choice through controlling masturbation fantasies." *Journal of Behavior Therapy and Experimental Psychiatry,* 1970, *1,* 263-272.

Marshall, W. "The modification of sexual fantasies: A combined treatment approach to the reduction of deviant sexual behavior." *Behavior Research and Therapy,* 1973, *11,* 557-564.

Marshall, W. "A combined treatment approach to the reduction of multiple fetish-related behaviors." *Journal of Consulting and Clinical Psychology,* 1974, *42,* 613-616.

Martin, D., & Lyon, P. *Lesbian/woman.* New York: Bantam Books, 1972.

Martin, D., & Lyon, P. "Lesbian mothers." *Ms.,* 1973, *2*(4), pp. 78-80.

Martin, D., & Lyon, P. "The older lesbian." In B. Berzon & R. Leighton (Eds.), *Positively gay.* Millbrae, Calif.: Celestial Arts, 1979.

Masters, W., & Johnson, V. *Human sexual inadequacy.* Boston: Little, Brown, 1970.

Masters, W., & Johnson, V. *Homosexuality in perspective.* Boston: Little, Brown, 1979.

Matza, D. *Delinquency and drift.* New York: John Wiley & Sons, 1964.

Matza, D. *Becoming deviant.* Englewood Cliffs, N.J.: Prentice-Hall, 1969.

Mayadas, N., & Duehn, W. "Children in gay families: An investigation of services." *Homosexual Counseling Journal,* 1976, *3*(2), 70-83.

Mayerson, P., & Lief, H. "Psychotherapy of homosexuals: A follow-up study of nineteen cases." In J. Marmor (Ed.), *Sexual inversion: The multiple roots of homosexuality.* New York: Basic Books, 1965.

McCaffrey, J. (Ed.). *The homosexual dialectic.* Englewood Cliffs, N.J.: Prentice-Hall, 1972.

McCaghy, C., & Skipper, J. "Occupational predisposition and lesbianism." In E. Rubington & M. Weinberg (Eds.), *Deviance: The interactionist perspective.* London: Macmillan, 1973.

McCauley, E., & Ehrhardt, A. "Role expectations and definitions: A comparison of female transexuals and lesbians." *Journal of Homosexuality,* 1977, *3*(2), 137-147.

McConaghy, N. "Behavioral intervention in homosexuality." *Journal of Homosexuality,* 1977, *2*(3), 221-227.

McCormack, W. "Sexually transmitted conditions other than gonorrhea and syphilis." (USDHEW monograph, U.S. Public Health Service Publication No. 00-2765). Washington, D.C., U.S. Govt. Printing Office, 1974.

McCrary, J., & Gutierrez, L. "The homosexual person in the military and in national security employment." *Journal of Homosexuality,* 1979-1980, *5*(1-2), 115-146.

McDonald, G., & Moore, R. "Sex-role self-concepts of homosexual men and their attitudes toward both women and male homosexuality." *Journal of Homosexuality,* 1978, *4*(1), 3-15.

McGinnies, E., & Ferster, C. (Eds.). *The reinforcement of social behavior.* Boston: Houghton Mifflin, 1971.

McGuire, R., Carlisle, J., & Young, B. "Sexual deviations *vs* conditioned behavior: An hypothesis." *Behavior Research and Therapy,* 1965, *2,* 185-190.

McIntosh, M. "The homosexual role." *Social Problems,* 1968, *16*(2), 182-192.

McKee, J., & Sherriffs, A. "The differential evaluation of males and females." *Journal of Personality,* 1957, *25,* 356-371.

McKinlay, T., Kelly, J., & Patterson, J. "Teaching assertive skills to a passive homosexual adolescent." *Journal of Homosexuality,* 1977, *3*(2), 163-170.

McNaught, B. "Gay and Catholic." In B. Berzon & R. Leighton (Eds.), *Positively gay.* Millbrae, Calif.: Celestial Arts, 1979.

McWhirter, D., & Mattison, A. *Stages: A developmental study of homosexual male couples.* New York: St. Martins, in press.

Mead, M. "Marriage in two steps." In H. Otto (Ed.), *The family in search of a future.* New York: Appleton-Century-Crofts, 1970.

Menow, J. "Gay sex in the schools." *Parents Magazine,* 1977, *70*(9), 66; 100; 104-106.

Meyer, R. "Legal and social ambivalence regarding homosexuality." *Journal of Homosexuality,* 1977, *2*(3), 281-287.

Mileski, M., & Black, D. "The social organization of homosexuality." *Urban Life and Culture,* 1972, *1,* 187-202.

Miller, W., & Hannum, T. "Characteristics of homosexually involved incarcerated females." *Journal of Consulting Psychology,* 1963, *27*(3), 277.

Miller, J. *Toward a new psychology of women.* Boston: Beacon Press, 1976.

Millet, K. *Sita.* New York: Farrar, Straus, & Giroux, 1977.

Millham, J., San Miguel, C., Christopher, L., & Kellog, R. "A factor-analytic conceptualization of attitudes toward male and female homosexuals." *Journal of Homosexuality,* 1976, *2*(1), 3-10.

Millham, J., & Weinberger, L. "Sexual preference, sex-role appropriateness and restriction of social access." *Journal of Homosexuality,* 1977, *2,* 343-357.

Milligan, D. "Homosexuality: Sexual needs and social problems." In R. Bailey & M. Brake (Eds.), *Radical social work.* New York: Pantheon, 1975.

Mills, C. "The professional ideology of social pathologists." *American Journal of Sociology,* 1943, *49*(2), 165-180.

Minnigerode, F. "Attitudes toward homosexuality: Feminist attitudes and sexual conservatism." *Sex Roles,* 1976, *2,* 347-352.

Mintz, E. "Overt male homosexuals in combined group and individual treatment." *Journal of Consulting Psychology,* 1966, *20,* 193-198.

Mischel, W. "Sex typing and socialization." In P. Mussen (Ed.), *Manual of child psychology* (Vol. 2). New York: Wiley & Sons, 1970.

Monchy, R. "A clinical type of male homosexuality." *International Journal of Psycho-Analysis,* 1965, *46*(2), 218-225.

Money, J. "Factors in the genesis of homosexuality." In G. Winokur (Ed.), *Determinants of human sexual behavior.* Springfield, Ill.: Charles C Thomas, 1963.

Money, J. (Ed.). *Sex research: New developments.* New York: Holt, Rinehart & Winston, 1965.

Money, J. "Human behavior cytogenetics: Review of psychopathology in three syndromes—47,XXY; 47,XYY; and 45,X." *Journal of Sex Research,* 1975, *11*(3), 181-200.

Money, J. "Genetic and chromosomal aspects of homosexual etiology." In J. Marmor (Ed.), *Homosexual behavior: A modern reappraisal.* New York: Basic Books, 1980.

Money, J., & Ehrhardt, A. *Man and woman, boy and girl.* Baltimore: Johns Hopkins University Press, 1972.

Money, J., Hampson, J.G., & Hampson, J.L. "An examination of some basic sexual concepts: The evidence of human hermaphroditism." *Bulletin of the Johns Hopkins Hospital,* 1955, *97,* 301-319. (a)

Money, J., Hampson, J.G., & Hampson, J.L. "Hermaphroditism: Recommendations concerning assignment of sex, change of sex, and psychologic management." *Bulletin of the Johns Hopkins Hospital,* 1955, *97,* 284-300. (b)

Money, J., & Hosta, G. "Negro folklore of male pregnancy." *Journal of Sex Research,* 1968, *4*(1), 34-50.

Money, J., & Tucker, P. *Sexual signatures: On being a man or a woman.* Boston: Little, Brown, 1975.

Monteflores, C. de, & Schultz, S. "Coming out: Similarities and differences for lesbians and gay men." *Journal of Social Issues,* 1978, *34*(3), 58-72.

Morgan, M. *The total woman.* Old Tappan, N.J.: Fleming H. Revell, 1973.

Morin, S.F. "Educational programs as a means of changing attitudes about gay people." *Homosexual Counseling Journal,* 1974, *1,* 160-165.

Morin, S.F. "An annotated bibliography of research on lesbianism and male homosexuality (1967-1974)." JASA *Catalog of Selected Documents in Psychology,* 1976, *6,* 15. (Ms. No. 1191)

Morin, S.F. "Heterosexual bias in psychological research on lesbianism and male homosexuality." *American Psychologist,* 1977, *32*(8), 629-637.

Morin, S.F. "Psychology and the gay community: An overview." *Journal of Social Issues,* 1978, *34*(3), 1-6.

Morris, P. "Doctors' attitudes to homosexuality." *British Journal of Psychiatry,* 1973, *122,* 435-436.

Morse, B. *The lesbian: A frank and revealing study of women who turn to their own sex for love.* Derby, Conn.: Monarch Books, 1961.

Morton, T., & Edwards, R. (Eds.). *Training in the human services* (Vol. 2). Knoxville: University of Tennessee, Office of Continuing Social Work, 1980.

Moses, A. *Identity management in lesbian women.* New York: Praeger, 1978.

Mozes, E. "The lesbian." *Sexology,* 1951, *18*(5), 294-299.

Mundorff, J. "Personality characteristics of selected college male heterosexuals, homosexual activists, and non-activists." *Dissertation Abstracts,* 1973, *34,* 1137.

Murstein, B. (Ed.). *Exploring intimate lifestyles.* New York: Springer, 1978.

Mussen, P. "Early sex-role development." In D. Goslin (Ed.), *Handbook of socialization theory and research.* Chicago: Rand McNally, 1969.

Mussen, P. (Ed.). *Manual of child psychology* (Vol. 2). New York: Wiley & Sons, 1970.

Myers, L., & Leggitt, H. *Adultery & other private matters: Your right to personal freedom in marriage.* Chicago: Nelson-Hall, 1975.

Myrich, F. "Homosexual types: An empirical investigation." *Journal of Sex Research,* 1974, *10,* 266-237.

Myron, N., & Bunch, C. (Eds.). *Women remembered.* Baltimore: Diana Press, 1974.

Myron, N., & Bunch, C. (Eds.). *Lesbianism and the women's movement.* Baltimore: Diana Press, 1975.

Nash, J., & Hayes, F. "The parental relationships of male homosexuals: Some theoretical issues and a pilot study." *Australian Journal of Psychology,* 1965, *17*(1), 35-43.

Nixon, J., & Berson, G. "Women's music." In G. Vida (Ed.), *Our right to love: A lesbian resource book.* Englewood Cliffs, N.J.: Prentice-Hall, 1978.

Nooe, R. "De-institutionalization in rural areas." *Human Services in the Rural Environment,* 1980, *5*(1), 17-20.

Norris, L. "Comparison of two groups in a southern state women's prison: Homosexual behavior vs. nonhomosexual behavior." *Psychological Reports,* 1974, *34,* 75-78.

Norton, H. *The third sex.* Portland, Ore.: Facts Publishing, 1949.

Norton, J. "Counseling on homosexuality." *Journal of Sex Education and Therapy,* 1977, *3*(2), 29-30.

Nuehring, E., Fein, S., & Tyler, M. "The gay college student: Perspective for mental health professionals." *Counseling Psychologist,* 1974, *4,* 64-72.

Nungesser, L. "Theoretical bases for research on the acquisition of social sex-roles by children of lesbian mothers." *Journal of Homosexuality,* 1980, *5*(3), 177-188.

Nyberg, K. "Sexual aspirations and sexual behavior among homosexually behaving males and females: The impact of the gay community." *Journal of Homosexuality,* 1976, *2*(1), 29-38.

Nyberg, K., & Alston, J. "Analysis of public attitudes toward homosexual behavior." *Journal of Homosexuality,* 1976/1977, *2*(2), 99-107.

Oberstone, A., & Sukoneck, H. "Psychological adjustment and life style of single lesbians and single heterosexual women." *Psychology of Women Quarterly,* 1976, *1*(2), 172-188.

Ohlson, E. "A preliminary investigation into the self-disclosing ability of male homosexuals." *Psychology,* 1974, *11,* 21-25.

Orbach, W. "Homosexuality and Jewish law." *GALA Review,* 1980, *3*(2), 6-9; 22: *3*(3), 18-22; 24: *3*(4), 10-14; 19-20; 22; *3*(5), 15-21: *3*(7), 8-12.

Osman, S. "My stepfather is a she." *Family Process,* 1972, *11*(2), 209-218.

Ostrow, D. *Gay and straight parents: What about the children?* Unpublished Bachelor's thesis, Hampshire College, 1977. Cited in Nungesser, 1980, p. 85.

Otto, H. (Ed.). *The family in search of a future.* New York: Appleton-Century-Crofts, 1970.

Pagelow, M. "Heterosexual and lesbian single mothers: A comparison of problems, coping, and solutions." *Journal of Homosexuality,* 1980, *5*(3), 189-204.

Paine, M. "Views of a hidden homosexual." *Social Progress: A Journal of Church and Society,* 1967, *58*(2), 22-25.

Pardes, H., Steinberg, J., & Simons, R. "A rare case of overt and mutual homosexuality in female identical twins." *Psychiatric Quarterly,* 1967, *41,* 108-130.

Parker, W. *Homosexuality: A selective bibliography of over 3,000 items.* Metuchen, N.J.: Scarecrow Press, 1971.

Parsons, T. "Definitions of health and illness in the light of American values and social structure." In E. Jaco (Ed.), *Patients, physicians, and illness* (2nd ed.). New York: Free Press, 1972.

Pattison, E. "Confusing concepts about the concept of homosexuality." *Psychiatry,* 1974, *37*(4), 340-349.

Pearce, F. "How to be immoral and ill, pathetic and dangerous, all at the same time: Mass media and homosexuality." In S. Cohen and J. Young (Eds.), *The manufacture of news: Deviance, social problems and the mass media.* London: Constable, 1973.

Pendergrass, V. "Marriage counseling with lesbian couples." *Psychotherapy: Theory, Research and Practice,* 1975, *12*(1), 93-96.

Peplau, L., Cochran, S., Rook, K., & Padesky, C. "Loving women: Attachment and autonomy in lesbian relationships." *Journal of Social Issues,* 1978, *34*(3), 7-27.

Phares, E. "A social learning theory approach to psychopathology." In J. Rotter, J. Chance, & E. Phares (Eds.), *Application of a social learning theory of personality.* New York: Holt, Rinehart & Winston, 1972.

Pleck, J. "Masculinity—femininity: Current alternative paradigms." *Sex Roles,* 1975, *1*(2), 161-178.

Pleck, J., & Sawyer, J. (Eds.). *Men and masculinity.* Englewood Cliffs, N.J.: Prentice-Hall, 1974.

Plummer, K. *Sexual stigma: An interactionist account.* London: Routledge and Kegan Paul, 1975.

Pollack, S., Huntley, D., Allen, J., & Schwartz, S. "The dimensions of stigma: The social situation of the mentally ill person and the male homosexual." *Journal of Abnormal Psychology,* 1976, *85*(1), 105-112.

Ponse, B. "Secrecy in the lesbian world." In C. Warren (Ed.), *Sexuality: Encounters, identities and relationships.* Beverly Hills, Calif.: Sage Publications, 1977.

Ponse, B. "Lesbians and their worlds." In J. Marmor (Ed.), *Homosexual behavior: A modern reappraisal.* New York: Basic Books, 1980.

Poole, K. "The etiology of gender identity and the lesbian." *Journal of Social Psychology,* 1972, *87,* 51-57.

Popkess, A. "Some criminal aspects of abnormalities of sex." *Practitioner,* 1954, *172,* 446-450.

Porcino, J. *A handbook for women in the second half of life.* Manuscript in preparation.

Propper, A. "Lesbianism in female and coed correctional institutions." *Journal of Homosexuality,* 1978, *3*(3), 265-274.

Querlin, M. *Women without men* (M. McGraw, trans.). New York: Dell, 1965.

Ramsay, R., & Van Velzen, V. "Behavior therapy for sexual perversions." *Behavior Research and Therapy,* 1968, *6*(2), 233.

Rancourt, R., & Limoges, T. "Homosexuality among women." *Canadian Nurse,* 1967, *63*(12), 42-44.

Regardie, F. "Analysis of a homosexual." *Psychiatric Quarterly,* 1949, *23*(3), 548-566.

Reitzell, J. "A comparative study of hysterics, homosexuals, and alcoholics using content analysis of Rorschach responses." *Rorschach Research Exchange and Journal of Projective Techniques,* 1949, *13*(2), 127-141.

Rhenish, L. "Is a feminist mood arising in rural America?" In H. Johnson (Ed.), *Rural human services: A book of readings.* Itasca, Ill.: F.E. Peacock, 1980.

Richards, D. "Homosexual acts and the constitutional right to privacy." *Journal of Homosexuality,* 1979-1980, *5*(1-2), 43-66.

Riddle, D. *Gay parents and child custody issues.* Unpublished manuscript, University of Arizona Department of Psychology, Tucson, 1977.

Riddle, D. "Relating to children: Gays as role models." *Journal of Social Issues,* 1978, *34*(3), 38-58.

Riddle, D., & Sang, B. "Psychotherapy with lesbians." *Journal of Social Issues,* 1978, *34*(3), 84-100.

Riess, B. (Ed.). *New directions in mental health.* New York: Grune & Stratton, 1968.

Riess, B. "New viewpoints on the female homosexual." In V. Franks & V. Burtle (Eds.), *Women in therapy.* New York: Bruner/Mazel, 1974.

Riess, B., Safer, J., & Yotive, W. "Psychological test data on female homosexuality: A review of the literature." *Journal of Homosexuality,* 1974, *1*(1), 71-85.

Rochlin, M. "Becoming a gay professional." In B. Berzon & R. Leighton (Eds.), *Positively gay.* Millbrae, Calif.: Celestial Arts, 1979.

Romano, R. "Sexually transmitted diseases in the gay community." *Suffolk County [N.Y.] Medical Society Bulletin,* 1979, *57*(1), 20-21.

Romm, M. "Sexuality and homosexuality in women." In J. Marmor (Ed.), *Homosexual behavior: A modern reappraisal.* New York: Basic Books, 1980.

Rosen, A., Rekers, G., & Friar, L. "Theoretical and diagnostic issues in child gender disturbances." *Journal of Sex Research,* 1977, *13*(2), 89-103.

Rosen, D. *Lesbianism: A study of female homosexuality.* Springfield, Ill.: Charles C Thomas, 1974.

Rosen, I. (Ed.). *The pathology and treatment of sexual deviation: A methodological approach.* London: Oxford University Press, 1964.

Rosenfeld, H. "Remarks on the relation of male homosexuality to paranoia, paranoid anxiety and narcissism." *International Journal of Psycho-Analysis,* 1949, *30*(1), 36-47.

Ross, H. "Modes of adjustment of married homosexuals." *Social Problems,* 1971, *18*, 385-393.

Ross, M. "The relationship of perceived societal hostility, conformity and psychological adjustment in homosexual males." *Journal of Homosexuality,* 1978, *4*(2), 157-168.

Ross, M., & Mendelsohn, F. "Homosexuality in college: A preliminary report of data obtained from one hundred thirty-three students seen in a university student health service and review of pertinent literature." *Archives of Neurology and Psychiatry,* 1958, *80*(2), 253-263.

Ross, M., Rogers, L., & McCulloc, H. "Stigma, sex and society: A new look at gender differentiation and sexual variation." *Journal of Homosexuality,* 1978, *3*(4), 315-330.

Rotter, J., Chance, J., & Phares, E. (Eds.). *Application of a social learning theory of personality.* New York: Holt, Rinehart & Winston, 1972.

Rowse, A. *Homosexuals in history: A study of ambivalence in society, literature and the arts.* New York: Macmillan, 1977.

Rubin, I. (Ed.). *The third sex.* New York: New Book, 1961.

Rubington, E., & Weinberg, M. (Eds.). *Deviance: The interactionist perspective.* London: Macmillan, 1968.

Ruitenbeek, H. (Ed.). *The problem of homosexuality in modern America.* New York: Dutton, 1963.

Ruitenbeek, H. (Ed.). *Psychoanalysis and contemporary American culture.* New York: Dell (Delta), 1964.

Ruitenbeek, H. *The new sexuality.* New York: New Viewpoints, 1974.

Russell, A., & Winkler, R. "Evaluation of assertive training and homosexual guidance service groups designed to improve homosexual functioning." *Journal of Consulting and Clinical Psychology,* 1977, *45*(1), 1-13.

Rutner, I. "A double-barrel approach to modification of homosexual behavior." *Psychological Reports,* 1970, *26*, 355-358.

Ryder, R. "Androgynous and contract marriage." In B. Murstein (Ed.), *Exploring intimate lifestyles.* New York: Springer, 1978.

Safer, J., & Reiss, B. "Two approaches to the study of female homosexuality: A critical and comparative review." *International Mental Health Research Newsletter,* 1975, *17*(1), 11-13.

Sagarin, E. *Structure and ideology in an association of deviants.* New York: Arno Press, 1975.

Sagarin, E. "Thieves, homosexuals and other deviants: The high personal cost of wearing a label." *Psychology Today,* March 1976, pp. 25-31.

Sagarin, E., & MacNamara, D. (Eds.). *Problems of sex behavior.* New York: Thomas Crowell, 1968.

Sagarin, E., & MacNamara, D. "The homosexual as a crime victim." *International Journal of Crime and Penology,* 1975, *3*(1), 12-25.

Saghir, M., & Robins, E. "Homosexuality: Sexual behavior of the female homosexual." *Archives of General Psychiatry,* 1969, *20*(2), 192-201.

Saghir, M., & Robins, E. *Male and female homosexuality: A comprehensive investigation.* Baltimore: Williams & Wilkins, 1973.

Salter, L., & Melville, C. "A re-educative approach to homosexual behavior: A case study and treatment recommendation." *Psychotherapy: Theory, Research, and Practice,* 1972, *9*, 166-167.

Sang, B. *Lesbian relationships: A struggle towards couple equality*. Paper presented at the American Psychological Association, San Francisco, 1977.

Sang, B. "Lesbian research: A critical evaluation." In G. Vida (Ed.), *Our right to love: A lesbian resource book*. Englewood Cliffs, N.J.: Prentice-Hall, 1978.

San Miguel, C., & Millham, J. "The role of cognitive and situational variables in aggression toward homosexuals." *Journal of Homosexuality*, 1976, *2*(1), 11-27.

Satir, V. "Marriage as a human-actualizing contract." In H. Otto (Ed.), *The family in search of a future*. New York: Appleton-Century-Crofts, 1970.

Saul, L., & Beck, A. "Psychodynamics of male homosexuality." *International Journal of Psycho-Analysis*, 1961, *42*(1-2), 43-48.

Schafer, S. "Sexual and social problems of lesbians." *The Journal of Sex Research*, 1976, *12*(1), 50-69.

Schafer, S. "Sociosexual behavior in male and female homosexuals: A study in sex differences." *Archives of Sexual Behavior*, 1977, *6*(5), 355-364.

Scheff, T. "The societal reaction to deviance." *Social Problems*, 1964, *11*, 401-413.

Scheff, T. *Being mentally ill: A sociological theory*. Chicago: Aldine, 1966.

Schofield, M. *The sexual behavior of young people*. Boston: Little, Brown, 1965. (a)

Schofield, M. *Sociological aspects of homosexuality: A comparative study of three types of homosexuals*. Boston: Little, Brown, 1965. (b)

Schott, M. "Casework: Rural." In H. Johnson (Ed.), *Rural human services: A book of readings*. Itasca, Ill.: F.E. Peacock, 1980.

Schur, E. *Crimes without victims: Deviant behavior and public policy*. Englewood Cliffs, N.J.: Prentice-Hall, 1965.

Schur, E. *Labeling deviant behavior*. New York: Harper & Row, 1971.

Schwarz, B. "Homosexuality: A Jewish perspective." *United Synagogue Review*, Summer 1977, pp. 4-5; 23-27.

Schwitzgebel, R.L., & Schwitzgebel, R.K. *Law and psychological practice*. New York: Wiley & Sons, 1980.

Scott, P. "Homosexuality with special reference to classification." *Proceedings of the Royal Society of Medicine*, 1957, *50*(9), 659-660.

Scott, R. "A proposed framework for analyzing deviance as a property of social order." In R. Scott & J.D. Douglas (Eds.), *Theoretical perspectives on deviance*. New York: Basic Books, 1972.

Segal, B., & Simms, J. "Covert sensitization with a homosexual: A controlled replication." *Journal of Consulting and Clinical Psychology*, 1972, *39*, 259-263.

Seward, G., & Williams, R. (Eds.). *Sex roles in a changing society*. New York: Random House, 1971.

Sex Information and Education Council of the U.S. "The SIECUS/Uppsala principles basic to education for sexuality." *SIECUS Report*, 1980, *8*(3), 8-9.

Shapiro, J. "Socialization of sex roles in the counseling setting: Differential counselor behavioral and attitudinal responses to typical and atypical female sex roles." *Sex Roles*, 1977, *3*(2), 173-184.

Shavelson, E., Biaggio, M., Cross, H., & Lehman, R. "Lesbian women's perceptions of their parent-child relationships." *Journal of Homosexuality*, 1980, *5*(3), 205-216.

Sherman, J. *On the psychology of women*. Springfield, Ill.: Charles C Thomas, 1971.

Shively, M., & DeCecco, J. "Components of sexual identity." *Journal of Homosexuality*, 1977, *3*(1), 41-48.

Shively, M., Rudolph, J., & DeCecco, J. "The identification of the social sex-role stereotypes." *Journal of Homosexuality*, 1978, *3*(3), 225-234.

Shrum, R. "Gay baiting in the classroom: Sexual politics in California." *New Times*, 4 September 1978, pp. 21-27.

Siegelman, M. "Adjustment of homosexual and heterosexual women." *British Journal of Psychiatry*, 1972, *120*, 477-481. (a)

Siegelman, M. "Adjustment of male homosexuals and heterosexuals." *Archives of Sexual Behavior*, 1972, *2*(1), 9-25. (b)

Siegelman, M. "Parental background of homosexual and heterosexual women." *British Journal of Psychiatry*, 1974, *124*, 14-21. (a)

Siegelman, M. "Parental background of male homosexuals and heterosexuals." *Archives of Sexual Behavior*, 1974, *3*(1), 3-18. (b)

Silverstein, C. "Even psychiatry can profit from its past mistakes." *Journal of Homosexuality*, 1976/1977, *2*(2), 153-158.

Silverstein, C. *A family matter: A parents' guide to homosexuality*. New York: McGraw-Hill, 1977.

Silverstein, C. "Homosexuality and the ethics of behavioral intervention: Paper 2." *Journal of Homosexuality*, 1977, *2*(3), 205-211.

Silverstein, C., & White, E. *The joy of gay sex*. New York: Crown, 1977.

Simmel, G. "The isolated individual and the dyad." In K. Wolff (Ed. and trans.), *The sociology of Georg Simmel*. London: Free Press, 1950.

Simon, W., & Gagnon, J. "Femininity in the lesbian community." *Social Problems*, 1967, *15*(2), 212-221. (a)

Simon, W., & Gagnon, J. "Homosexuality: The formulation of a sociological perspective." *Journal of Health and Social Behavior*, 1967, *8*(3), 177-185. (b)

Simon, W., & Gagnon, J. "The lesbians: A preliminary overview." In J. Gagnon & W. Simon (Eds.), *Sexual deviance*. New York: Harper & Row, 1967. (c)

Simon, W., & Gagnon, J. "On psychosexual development." In D. Goslin (Ed.), *Handbook of socialization theory and research*. Chicago: Rand McNally, 1969.

Simpson, R. *From the closets to the courts*. New York: Viking Press, 1976.

Sisley, E., & Harris, B. *The joy of lesbian sex*. New York: Crown, 1977.

Skeist, R. (Ed.). *To your good health*. Chicago: Chicago Free Press, 1980.

Skolnick, A. "The myth of the vulnerable child." *Psychology Today*, February 1978, pp. 56-65.

Slovenko, R. (Ed.). *Sexual behavior and the law*. Springfield, Ill.: Charles C Thomas, 1965.

Slovenko, R. "Homosexuality and the law: From condemnation to celebration." In J. Marmor (Ed.), *Homosexual behavior: A modern reappraisal*. New York: Basic Books, 1980.

Smith, J., & Smith, L. (Eds.). *Beyond monogamy: Recent studies of sexual alternatives in marriage*. Baltimore: Johns Hopkins University Press, 1974.

Snively, W., & Beshear, D. *Textbook of pathophysiology*. Philadelphia: Lippincott, 1972.

Sobel, H. "Adolescent attitudes toward homosexuality in relation to self concept and body satisfaction." *Adolescent*, 1976, *11*(43), 443-453.

Socarides, C. "Theoretical and clinical aspects of overt male homosexuality (panel report)." *Journal of the American Psychoanalytic Association*, 1960, *8*, 553-566.

Socarides, C. "Theoretical and clinical aspects of overt female homosexuality (panel report)." *Journal of the American Psychoanalytic Association*, 1962, *10*, 579-592.

Socarides, C. "The historical development of theoretical and clinical concepts of overt female homosexuality." *Journal of the American Psychoanalytic Association*, 1963, *11*, 386-414.

Socarides, C. "Female homosexuality." In R. Slovenko (Ed.), *Sexual behavior and the law*. Springfield, Ill.: Charles C Thomas, 1965.

Socarides, C. *The overt homosexual*. New York: Grune & Stratton, 1968. (a)

Socarides, C. "A provisional theory of aetiology in male homosexuality: A case of preoedipal origin." *International Journal of Psycho-Analysis*, 1968, *49*(1), Part 1. (b)

Socarides, C. "Homosexuality: basic concepts and psychodynamics." *International Journal of Psychiatry*, 1972, *10*, 118-125.

Solomon, D. "The emergence of associational rights for homosexual persons." *Journal of Homosexuality*, 1979-1980, *5*(1-2), 147-156.

Sonenschein, D. "The ethnography of male homosexual relations." *Journal of Sex Research*, 1968, *4*(2), 69-83.

Spence, J., & Helmreich, R. *Masculinity and femininity: Their psychological dimensions, correlates, and antecedents*. Austin: University of Texas Press, 1978.

Sprague, W. *The lesbian in our society*. New York: Tower Publications, 1962.

Staats, G. "Stereotype content and social distance: Changing views of the homosexual." *Journal of Homosexuality*, 1978, *4*(1), 15-18.

Stanley, J., & Robbins, S. "Lesbian humor." *Women*, 1976, *5*(1), 26-29.

Staples, R. "The sexuality of black women." *Sexual Behavior*, 1972, *2*(4), 4-15.

Stearn, J. *The sixth man*. Garden City, N.Y.: Doubleday, 1961.

Stearn, J. *The grapevine*. New York: Macfadden-Bartell, 1965.

Steffensmeier, D., & Steffensmeier, R. "Sex differences in reactions to homosexuality: Research on continuities and further developments." *Journal of Sex Research*, 1974, *10*(1), 52-67.

Stein, T. "Gay service organizations: A survey." *Homosexual Counseling Journal*, 1976, *3*(2), 84-97.

Steinman, R. "Gray and gay." In R. Skeist (Ed.), *To your good health*. Chicago: Chicago Free Press, 1980.

Stevens, M. "Lesbian mothers in transition." In G. Vida (Ed.), *Our right to love: A lesbian resource book*. Englewood Cliffs, N.J.: Prentice-Hall, 1978.

Stoller, R. "Gender-role change in intersexed patients." *Journal of the American Medical Association*, 18 May 1964, pp. 164-165.

Stone, W., Schengber, J., & Siegfried, F. "The treatment of homosexual women in a mixed group." *International Journal of Group Psychotherapy*, 1966, *16*(4), 425-433.

Storms, M. "Attitudes toward homosexuality and femininity in men." *Journal of Homosexuality*, 1978, *3*(3), 257-264.

Swanson, D., Loomis, S., Lukesh, R., Cronin, R., & Smith, J. "Clinical features of the female homosexual patient: A comparison with the heterosexual patient." *Journal of Nervous and Mental Disease*, 1972, *155*, 119-124.

Szasz, T. *The myth of mental illness*. New York: Harper & Row, 1961.

Szasz, T. *The manufacture of madness*. New York: Harper & Row, 1970.

Tanner, D. *The lesbian couple*. Lexington, Mass.: D.C. Heath, 1978.

Tanner, L. (Ed.). *Voices from women's liberation*. New York: New American Library (Signet), 1970.

Tavris, C. "Gay is beautiful at a distance." *Psychology Today*, January 1976, pp. 101-102.

Tavris, C. "The sexual lives of women over 60." *Ms.*, July 1977, pp. 62-65.

Taylor, I., Walton, P., & Young, J. *The new criminology*. London: Routledge and Kegan Paul, 1973.

Thompson, C. "Cultural pressures in the politics of women." *Psychiatry*, 1942, *5*, 331-339.

Thompson, C. "Changing concepts of homosexuality in psychoanalysis." *Psychiatry*, 1947, *10*(2), 183-189.

Thompson, C. "Some effects of the derogatory attitude toward female sexuality." *Psychiatry*, 1950, *13*, 349-354.

Thompson, G., & Fishburn, W. "Attitudes toward homosexuality among graduate counseling students." *Counselor Education and Supervision*, 1977, *17*, 121-130.

Thompson, N., Jr., McCandless, B., & Strickland, B. "Personal adjustment of male and female homosexuals and heterosexuals.'' *Journal of Abnormal Psychology,* 1971, *78*(2), 237-240.

Thompson, N., Jr., Schwartz, D., McCandless, B., & Edwards, D. ''Parent-child relationships and sexual identity in male and female homosexuals and heterosexuals.'' *Journal of Consulting and Clinical Psychology,* 1974, *41,* 120-127.

Toder, N. ''Sexual problems of lesbians.'' In G. Vida (Ed.), *Our right to love: A lesbian resource book.* Englewood Cliffs, N.J.: Prentice-Hall, 1978.

Toder, N. ''Lesbian couples: Special issues.'' In B. Berzon & R. Leighton (Eds.), *Positively gay.* Millbrae, Calif.: Celestial Arts, 1979.

Tourney, G. ''Hormones and homosexuality.'' In J. Marmor (Ed.), *Homosexual behavior: A modern reappraisal.* New York: Basic Books, 1980.

Tripp, C. *The homosexual matrix.* New York: New American Library, 1975.

Truax, R., & Tourney, G. ''Male homosexuals in group psychotherapy.'' *Diseases of the Nervous System,* 1971, *32,* 707-711.

Tuller, N. ''Couples: The hidden segment of the gay world.'' *Journal of Homosexuality,* 1978, *3*(4), 331-334.

Tully, C., & Albro, J. ''Homosexuality: A social worker's imbroglio.'' *Journal of Sociology and Social Welfare,* 1979, *6*(2), 154-167.

Turnage, J., & Logan, D. ''Sexual 'variation' without 'deviation'.'' *Homosexual Counseling Journal,* 1975, *2*(3), 116-119.

Twiss, H. (Ed.). *Homosexuality and the Christian faith: A symposium.* Valley Forge, Pa.: Judson, 1978.

Ullman, L., & Krasner, L. *A psychological approach to abnormal behavior.* Englewood Cliffs, N.J.: Prentice-Hall, 1969.

Van Gelder, L. ''Lesbian custody: A tragic day in court.'' *Ms.,* September 1976, *5*(3), 72-73.

Vasquez, E. ''Homosexuality in the context of the Mexican-American culture.'' In D. Kunkel (Ed.), *Sexual issues in social work: Emerging concerns in education and practice.* Honolulu: University of Hawaii School of Social Work, 1979.

Vetri, D. ''The legal arena: Progress for gay civil rights.'' *Journal of Homosexuality,* 1979-1980, *5*(1-2), 25-34.

Vida, G. ''The lesbian image in the media.'' In G. Vida (Ed.), *Our right to love: A lesbian resource book.* Englewood Cliffs, N.J.: Prentice-Hall, 1978. (a)

Vida, G. (Ed.). *Our right to love: A lesbian resource book.* Englewood Cliffs, N.J.: Prentice-Hall, 1978. (b)

Voeller, B. ''Society and the gay movement.'' In J. Marmor (Ed.), *Homosexual behavior: A modern reappraisal.* New York: Basic Books, 1980.

Wahl, C. (Ed.). *Sexual problems: Diagnosis and treatment in medical practice.* New York: Free Press, 1967.

Walfish, S., & Myerson, M. ''Sex role identity and attitudes toward sexuality.'' *Archives of Sexual Behavior,* 1980, *9*(3), 199-204.

Walker, C. ''Psychodrama: An experimental study of its effectiveness with the homosexual society.'' *Group Psychotherapy and Psychodrama,* 1974, *27*(1-4), 83-97.

Ward, D., & Kassebaum, G. *Women's prison: Sex and social structure.* Chicago: Aldine, 1965.

Warren, C. ''Observing the gay community.'' In J.D. Douglas (Ed.), *Research on deviance.* New York: Random House, 1972.

Warren, C. *Identity and community in the gay world.* New York: Wiley & Sons, 1974.

Warren, C. (Ed.). *Sexuality: Encounters, identities and relationships.* Beverly Hills, Calif.: Sage Publications, 1977.

Warrior, B. ''Sex roles and their consequences.'' In L. Tanner (Ed.), *Voices from women's liberation.* New York: New American Library, 1970.

Weber, G. ''Preparing social workers for practice in rural social systems.'' In H. Johnson (Ed.), *Rural human services: A book of readings.* Itasca, Ill.: F.E. Peacock, 1980.

Weinberg, M. ''Homosexual samples: Differences and similarities.'' *Journal of Sex Research,* 1970, *6,* 312-325.

Weinberg, M. ''The male homosexual: Age-related variations in social and psychological characteristics.'' *Social Problems,* 1970, *17,* 527-537.

Weinberg, M., & Bell, A. *Homosexuality: An annotated bibliography.* New York: Harper & Row, 1972.

Weinberg, M., & Williams, C. *Male homosexuals: Their problems and adaptations.* New York: Penguin Books, 1975. (Originally published by Oxford Press, 1974.)

Weinberg, T. ''On 'doing' and 'being' gay: Sexual behavior and homosexual male self-identity.'' *Journal of Homosexuality,* 1978, *4*(2), 143-156.

Weinberger, L., & Millham, J. ''Attitudinal homophobia and support of traditional sex roles.'' *Journal of Homosexuality,* 1979, *4*(3), 237-246.

Weinrich, J. ''Nonreproduction, homosexuality, transsexuals and intelligence: A systematic literature search.'' *Journal of Homosexuality,* 1978, *3*(3), 275-289.

West, D. *The other man: A study of the social, legal and clinical aspects of homosexuality.* New York: Whiteside and William Morrow, 1955.

West, D. ''Parental figures in the genesis of male homosexuality.'' *International Journal of Social Psychiatry,* 1959, *5*(2), 85-97.

West, J. *Homosexuality.* Chicago: Aldine, 1968.

Westwood, G. ''Problems of research into sexual deviations.'' *Man and Society,* 1961, *1*(1), 29-32.

Wheeler, W. ''Analysis of Rorschach indices of male homosexuality.'' *Journal of Projective Techniques,* 1949, *13,* 97-126.

Whitam, F. ''Childhood indicators of male homosexuality.'' *Archives of Sexual Behavior,* 1977, *6*(2), 89-96. (a)

Whitam, F. "The homosexual role: A reconsideration." *The Journal of Sex Research*, 1977, *13*(1), 1-11. (b)

Whitlock, K. "Striving toward equality in loving relationships." In G. Vida (Ed.), *Our right to love: A lesbian resource book*. Englewood Cliffs, N.J.: Prentice-Hall, 1978.

Wiesner, P. "Gonococcal pharyngeal infection." *Clinical Obstetrics and Gynecology*, 1975, *18*(1), 120-129.

Wilbur, C. "Clinical aspects of female homosexuality." In J. Marmor (Ed.), *Sexual inversion: The multiple roots of homosexuality*. New York: Basic Books, 1965.

Will, G. "How far out of the closet?" *Newsweek*, 30 May 1977, p. 92.

Williams, D. "Social aspects: Homosexuality and sexually transmitted diseases." Paper presented at conference on sexually transmitted diseases, Health Sciences Center, State University of New York at Stony Brook, 27 September 1978.

Willis, S. *Understanding and counseling the male homosexual*. Boston: Little, Brown, 1967.

Willy, A., Vander, L., & Fisher, O. *The illustrated encyclopedia of sex*. New York: Cadillac Publishing, 1961.

Wilson, G., & Davison, G. "Behavior therapy and homosexuality: A critical perspective." *Behavior Therapy*, 1974, *5*, 16-28.

Wilson, M., & Green, R. "Personality characteristics of female homosexuals." *Psychological Reports*, 1971, *28*, 407-412.

Winner, A. "Homosexuality in women." *Medical Press*, 1947, *217*, 219-220.

Winokur, G. (Ed.). *Determinants of human sexual behavior*. Springfield, Ill.: Charles C Thomas, 1963.

Wolf, D. *The lesbian community*. Berkeley: University of California Press, 1979.

Wolf, D. "Life cycle change of older lesbians and gay men." Paper presented at annual convention of The Gerontological Society, San Diego, Calif., 1980.

Wolf, D. *Growing older: Lesbians and gay men*. Berkeley: University of California Press, in press.

Wolff, K. (Ed. and trans.). *The sociology of Georg Simmel*. London: Free Press, 1950.

Women in Transition, Inc. *Women in transition*. New York: Scribner & Sons, 1976.

Wood, R. "New report on homosexuality." In I. Rubin (Ed.), *The third sex*. New York: New Book, 1961.

Woodward, M. "The diagnosis and treatment of homosexual offenders." *British Journal of Delinquency*, 1958, *9*, 44-49.

Wysor, B. *The lesbian myth*. New York: Random House, 1974.

Yankowski, J., & Wolff, H. *The tortured sex*. Los Angeles: Holloway House, 1965.

Yockey, J. "Role theory and the female sex role." *Sex Roles*, 1978, *4*(6), 917-927.

Young, T. *Women who love women*. New York: Pocket Books, 1977.

Young, W. "Prostitution." In J. Gagnon, & W. Simon (Eds.). *Sexual deviance*. New York: Harper & Row, 1967.

Zilbergeld, B. *Male sexuality*. Boston: Little, Brown, 1978.

Zimberg, N. "Changing stereotyped sex roles: Some problems for women and men." *Psychiatric Opinion*, 1973, *10*(2), 25-30.

Zucker, L. "Mental health and homosexuality." *Journal of Sex Research*, 1966, *2*(2), 111-125.

Index

A

Acceptance, lack of, 173-174
Adjustment, effect of gayness on, 56-57
Adolescence
  coming out to oneself in, 81-83
  cross-gender behavior in, 83
  lesbian, 142-143
Adolescents, intervention with, 82-83
Adult, coming out to oneself as, 83-84
Affectional factor in sexual orientation, 36
Aging, 190-197
  attitudes toward, 190-193
    gay men's, 191-193
      about appearance, 192
      about loneliness, 192-193
    lesbians', 190-191
      about appearance, 191
      about loneliness, 191
  behaviors that may affect, 193
  counseling older gay people about, 195-196
    and belief in stereotype, 195
    and communication with health professionals, 195-196
    and dying and death, 196
    and inability to live on fixed income, 196
  counseling younger gay people about, 193
  factors affecting, 193-196
    advantage of stigma as, 193-194
    freedom of retirement as, 194-195
    friendship networks as, 194
Alcoholism, gay, 72
  case study of, 75
Ambisexual bisexual, 37
Ambisexual heteroerotic, 37
Ambisexual homoerotic, 37
Ambisexuality, 38
Amebiasis, 116, 117
Anal intercourse, 110, 111
  inability to enjoy, 119
Analingus, 112
Androgen, 28
Androgen insensitivity syndrome, 29
Androgynous behavior, 58, 199
Androgyny, psychological, 31
Anniversaries of gay male couples, 155
Anorgasmia, 107
Another woman, in lesbian relationships, 150
Antecedents, etiology versus, 42-43
Anxiety
  about being found out, 67-69

Anxiety—cont'd
  in rural gay people, 174
Appearance
  gay men's attitudes toward, 192
  lesbians' attitudes toward, 191
Arousal pattern, 32-33
Art, lesbian, 76
Asexuals, 57
Assertiveness
  lack of, 141
  in lesbian relationships, 149-150
Assertiveness training, 83
Association of Gay Psychologists, 176
Association of Gay Social Workers, 176
Attitudes
  development of, within social sciences, 6-10
    in psychology, psychiatry, and psychotherapy, 7-10
    scientific approach in, 6-7
  societal, 15-16
  toward gay people, 3-14
    current, 15-20
Attorney-client privilege, 182
Availability for sexual contacts, 113
Aversion, sexual, 119

B

Bar, gay, 71-72
Becoming gay, 42-53
Bestiality, 112
Bible, interpretation of, 5-6
Biological factor in psychosexual development, 28-29
Biosociopsychological model of psychosexual development, 28-34
  biological factor in, 28-29
  psychological factor in, 31-34
  sociological factor in, 29-31
Bisexuality, 38
Black lesbians and gay men, 169-170
Blackmail, 113
Body contact in lesbian lovemaking, 106
Brandenburg v. Ohio, 188
Breast stimulation, 104
Breast tenderness, sensitivity to, 104
Butch/femme dichotomy, 139
Butch/femme stereotype, 133

C

Caucus of Gay and Lesbian Counselors, 176
Caucus of Gay Public Health Workers, 176
Changes in lesbians' relationships, 144-148
  as cause of termination, 148-149
Child custody, 24
  issues in, 198-203
    disputes following divorce as, 201-202
    disputes involving relatives as, 202
    favorable to gay parents, 202
    helping parents through process of, 204-205
Child molesting, 200
Children
  coming out to, 205-208
    children's reactions to, 207
  gay parents coping with, 205-208
Chromosomes, 28
Church
  Metropolitan Community, 93, 176
  position of, 5-6
Code, legal, 183
Coming out, 80-98
  after, 96-97
  as cause for termination of lesbian relationship, 151
  to children, 205-208
    children's reactions to, 207
    manner of, 206-207
    or trying to pass, 207-208
  in contracts, 127
  deciding to, 90-91
  to gay community, 89
  to heterosexuals, 89-90, 95-96
  to oneself, 80-87
    in adolescence, 81-83
    as adult, 83-84
    signification and, 85-87
    when difficult, 84-85
    when not difficult, 84
  to others, 87-96
    as adolescent, 87-89
      intervention for, 88-89
    as adult, 89-96
      intervention for, 93-96
  to parents, 91-95
    intervention for, 93-95
  as process, 80-96
  reasons for, 90

Communal arrangements, 137-138
Communication
  in lesbian relationships, 140-142
    changes in, 146-147
    importance of, 147
  during lovemaking, 102
Communication difficulties with health professionals, 195-196
Community, gay; see Gay community; Lesbian community
Confidentiality, 181-185
  example of, 181
  and privilege, 181-185
Contacts, sexual, 102, 113-114
Contract, "unspoken," 66
Contracting, 127-130
  content of, 127-128
  finances in, 128
  function of relationship in, 129-130
  as insurance, 128
  renegotiation of, 129
  sexual activity in, 128-129
Coprophilia, 112
Counseling; see Intervention
Couple interaction, 124-125
  problems in, 125
"Couplehood," declaration of, in gay male relationships, 154-155
Couples; see also Lesbian relationships
  gay, as parents, 208-209
    and helping children cope with prejudice, 209
  gay male, characteristics of, 154-163
    declaration of "couplehood" as, 154-155
    living apart as, 156-157
    living together as, 155-156
    monandry as, 162-163
    nonmonandry as, 158-162
      counseling for, 159-162
    roles in, 157
    sexual activity as, 157-158
  sexual activity in, 114-115
Courage, 67
Courts and child custody, 201-203
Crisco party, 112
Cross-dressing, 58-61
Cross-gender behavior, 30-31, 49-51
  in adolescence, 83
  in gay men, 49-51
  in lesbian women, 49
Culture, lesbian, 76

Cunnilingus in lesbian lovemaking, 105
  reluctance to engage in, 107-108
Custody, child; *see* Child custody

D

Darwinism, social, 6
Dating, 47
Death of partner in lesbian relationships, 151-152
Defecation, 112
"Degeneracy," causes of, 7
Deviance
  appreciative approach to, 11-12
  primary and secondary, 11
"Deviant" as label, 12
"Deviant" homes of gay parents, 200
Deviant identities, management of, 62-63
"Deviants," selection of, for study, 11-12
Discovery, fear of, in rural gay people, 174
Discrimination against gays, 22-24
Diseases, sexually transmitted, 116-117
Dissolution of relationship in contract, 128
Divorce, child custody disputes following, 201-202
Doe v. Commonwealth Attorney for Richmond, 22, 24, 187
Duration of gay male relationships, 153
Dyad, 124, 125
  monogamous, 132-136
  nonmonogamous, 136-137
Dying and death, 196
Dysfunction, sexual
  in gay male sexual activity, 118-120
  in lesbian sexual activity, 107
Dysfunctionals, 57

E

Egalitarian relationships, 136, 144
Ejaculation, premature, 118
Emotional commitment and sexual activity, 129
Empathy, intragender, 102
Employment, 22-23
Enemas, 112
English common law, 182
Erectile dysfunction, 118
Erotic variations, 112
Etiology versus antecedents, 42-43
Exclusive heteroerotic, 37
Exclusive homoerotic, 37
Exclusiveness in gay men's relationships, 158-162

Exclusivity, sexual, in gay male sexual activity, 117-118
Extended family, lesbian community as, 74-76

F

Family
  extended, lesbian community as, 74-76
  gay couple as, 208-209
Family in Search of a Future, 124
Family background, 44-46
  of gay men, 45
  implications of, 45-46
  of lesbian women, 44-45
Family members, relationships with, 64-65
Fantasy as factor in sexual orientation, 37, 38
Fear of discovery of rural gay people, 174
Fellatio, 111
  inability to enjoy, 119
Feminism and lesbianism, 76
Fetishisms, 112
Finances in contracts, 127, 128
Fist fucking, hazards of, 112
Fixed income, inability to live on, 196
Flexible nurturing-caretaking relationships, 137
"Free to Be You and Me," 50
Frequency of lesbian lovemaking, differences in, 109
Freud's impact on study of sexuality, 8
Friends
  coming out to, 95-96
  social relationships with, 65-66
Friendship networks, 194
Frottage, 111
Functioning
  personal, effect of gayness on, 57-58
  social, effect of gayness on, 62-69
Future, lack of ability to plan for, in lesbian relationships, 144-145

G

Gay
  becoming, 42-53
  experience of being, 54-56
    gay history in, 55-56
    role models in, 55
    social recognition in, 54-55
Gay Academic Union, 176
Gay alcoholism, 72

Gay Anthropologists, 176
Gay bar, 71-72
Gay children raised by gay parents, 198-199
Gay clients, positive intervention with, 215-217
Gay community, 70-72; *see also* Lesbian community
  gay bar in, 71-72
    and alcoholism, 72
  gender role behaviors in, 57-62
  gender role changes within, 62
  intervention implications for, 77
  social scene in, 71
  lack of support of, for long-term relationships, 150
Gay history, 55-56
Gay lifestyle, 54-79
Gay male community, 76-77
Gay male primary relationships, 152-164; *see also* Couples, gay male, characteristics of
  characteristics of, 153-154
    duration as, 153-154
      counseling implications for, 153-154
      myth and reality of, 153
    primary partner as, 154
Gay male sexual activity, 110-120
  counseling for, 115-120
    about promiscuity, 115-116
    about sexual dysfunction, 118-120
    about sexual exclusivity, 117-118
    about sexually transmitted diseases, 116-117
  sexual behavior in, 110-115
    anal intercourse as, 111
    fellatio as, 111
    frottage as, 111
    monandry as, 114
    mutual masturbation as, 111
    number of sexual partners in, 112
Gay men
  age of awareness of sexual orientation in, 48
  cross-gender behavior in, 49-51
  early sexual behavior of, 46-47
    dating as, 47
    gender of first partner in, 46
    heterosexual intercourse in, 47
    masturbation in, 46
  family backgrounds of, 45
Gay Nurses' Alliance, 176
Gay parents; *see* Parenthood, gay, coping with; Parent(s), gay

Gay people
  attitudes toward, 3-14
    current, 15-20
  rural; *see* Rural gay people
Gay sex, potential boredom in, 102
Gay social scene, 71
Gay students, rights of, 23, 186-189
Gaylord v. Tacoma School District, 21-22
Gayness
  correlates of, 16
  current attitudes toward, 15-20
  development of, intervention for, 51-52
  effect of, on personal functioning, 57-58
  historical attitudes toward, 3-14
  lack of cause of, 42-43
  as pathology, 8
  professional responses to, 16-18
  therapists' attitudes toward, 18
Gays
  attitudes toward
    current, 15-20
    historical, 3-14
  legal rights of, 21-24
Gender
  defined, 43
  of first partner, 46
Gender difference, effects of absence of, 138
Gender empathy, 104, 107
Gender identity, 29, 43
Gender role behavior, 30, 43
  in gay community, 57-62
  and sexual activity in gay male relationships, 157-158
  societal definitions of appropriate, 30-31
Gender role changes within gay community, 62
Gender role development of children of gay parents, 199-200
Genital manipulation, 102
Giardiasis, 116, 117
Golden shower, 112
Gonorrhea, 116
Granuloma inguinale, 116
Grief in separation in lesbian relationships, 150
Grief process in lesbian relationships, 152

H

Hands, use of, in lesbian lovemaking, 105-106
Health professionals, communication difficulties with, 195-196
Healy v. James, 186

Hepatitis, 116, 117
Heterosexual community, impact of, on rural gay people, 173-180
Heterosexual friends, coming out to, 89-90, 95-96
Heterosexual intercourse, 47
Heterosexual marriage model, 123
Historical bisexuality, 38
Historical overview of attitudes toward gay people, 4-6
    position of church in, 5-6
History
    gay, 55-56
    as part of sexual orientation, 38
Homoerotic orientation, development of, 44-52
    age of awareness of sexual orientation in, 47-48
    cross-gender behavior in, 49-51
    early sexual behavior in, 44-46
    family background in, 44-46
    intervention implications for, 51-52
Homophobia, 16, 209
    within helping professions, 18-19
Homosexual Behavior, 114
Homosexuality
    as clinical entity, 57
    psychiatric labeling of, 3
Homosexuality in Perspective, 118
Honeymoon in lesbian relationships, 144-145
"Honeymoon" relationship, 137
Hormones, 28-29
Housing, legal rights of gays and, 23

I

Identity
    deviant, management of, 62-63
    gender, 43
    sexual, 43-44
        development of, 27-41
"If you really loved me, you would . . . ," 150
Immigration, legal rights of gays regarding, 23
Income, fixed, inability to live on, 196
Independence/dependence, 141-142
Individuality, maintaining, 125-127
    private time in, 126-127
    social and leisure time in, 126
Inheritance, right of, 24
Insurance, contracting as, 128
Interaction
    couple, 124-125
        problems in, 125
    with friends, 65-66

Intercourse
    anal, 110, 111
    heterosexual, 47
Intervention
    with adolescents, 82-83
    for attitudes toward aging, 193, 195-196
    for changes in lesbian relationships, 147-148
    for child custody process, 204-205
    for coming out
        as adolescent, 88-89
        as adult, 93-96
        to parents, 93-95
    for development of gayness, 51-53
    for functioning as gay person, 67-69
    for gay community, 77
    for gay male sexual activity, 115-120
    for nonmonandry, 158-162
    positive, with gay clients, 215-217
    and self-labeling, 85-86
    with signification, 85-86
Intimacy, importance of, in lesbian relationships, 147
Isherwood, Christopher, 56
Isolation
    from gay community, 177-178
    from nongay community, of rural gay people, 175

J

Joy of Gay Sex, 110, 111, 163

K

Klinefelter's syndrome, 28
Klismaphilia, 112

L

Labeling theory, 10-12
Legal rights of gays, 21-24
Leisure time, 126
Lesbian community, 73-76
    concept of, 72-73
    as extended family, 74-76
    extended family networks in, 76
    identifying with, 73-74
    impact of, on lesbian women, 73
    intervention for, 77
    lesbian culture in, 76
Lesbian culture, 76
Lesbian lovemaking; *see* Lesbian sexual activity

Lesbian Mothers' National Defense Fund, 204
Lesbian relationships
    absence of roles in, 143
    absence of role models in, 143-144
    changes within, 144-148
        in communication, 146-147
        after honeymoon, 144-145
        intervention for, 147-148
        with others, 145-146
        in romance and sex, 146
        in sexual relationship, 146
    egalitarian, 136
    flexible nurturing-caretaking, 137
    forming, 142-143
    "honeymoon," 137
    importance of intimacy in, 147
    lack of ability to plan for future in, 144-145
    monogamous, 130-136
    patterns of, 130
    role differentiation in, 132-135
    status differential, 133-136
        permanent, 135
        temporary, 134-135
    termination of, 148-152
        because of changes, 148-149
        because of death of one partner, 151-152
        because of lack of relationship skills, 149-150
        because of life demands, 150
        because of variables outside relationship, 150-151
    traditional, 132-133
    variables in, 138-143
        communication as, 140-142
            differences in, 140
            independence/dependence in, 141-142
            lack of assertiveness in, 141
            problems in, 140-141
        role differentiation as, 138-140
            absence of gender differences as, 138-139
            butch/femme dichotomy as, 138-139
            role taking in, 139
Lesbian sexual activity, 104-110
    differences in desired frequency of, 109
    problems of, 106-110
        carrying gender empathy too far as, 107
        dysfunction as, 107
        reluctance to allow stimulation by partner as, 108-109

Lesbian sexual activity—cont'd
    problems of—cont'd
        reluctance to engage in stimulative techniques as, 107-108
    sexual behavior as, 104-106
        gender empathy in, 104
        stimulative techniques in, 104-105
            body contact as, 106
            cunnilingus as, 105
            use of hands as, 105-106
        stimulation to orgasm in, 105
Lesbian sexual response, physiology of, 104
Lesbian women
    age of awareness of sexual orientation in, 47-48
    cross-gender behavior in, 49
    early sexual behavior of, 46
    family backgrounds of, 44-45
    family pathology of, 45
Lesbianism
    as clinical entity, 57
    and feminism, 76
Levels
    of sexual activity, 100-103
    of sexual interest, 100-101
Life demands in lesbian relationships, 150
Lifestyle, gay, 54-79
Literature, lesbian, 76
Living apart of gay male couples, 156-157
Living together of gay male couples, 155-156
Loneliness
    gay men's attitudes about, 192-193
    lesbians' attitudes about, 191
"Lusting in the mind," 162

M

Manipulation in lesbian lovemaking, 105-106
Marriage between gays, 24
Masturbation, 33
    in development of homoerotic orientation, 46
    mutual, in gay male sexual activity, 110, 111
MCC, 93, 176
Meaningful relationships and sexual contacts, 114
Metropolitan Community Church, 93, 176
Mexican-American lesbians and gay men, 170
Military, legal rights of gay in, 23
Monandry in gay men's relationships, 162-163
Monogamous lifestyles, 131-132
Monogamy, 126
    in lesbian relationships, 130-136
Müllerian-inhibiting substance, 29
Music, lesbian, 76

Mutual masturbation, in gay male sexual activity, 110-111

My turn–your turn, 102

Myth(s)
  of duration of gay male relationships, 153
  about gay parents, 198-201

N

National Lawyers' Guild Gay Caucus, 176

National organizations and resources for gays, 176
  lack of, for rural gays, 178-179

Nature versus nurture, 7

Negotiation; *see* Contracting

Networks
  extended family, 76
  friendship, 194

Nipple stimulation in gay male sexual activity, 112, 115

Nongay friends, coming out to, 95-96

Nonmonandry in gay male relationships, 158-162

Nonmonogamous dyads, 136-137

Nurturing in lesbian relationships, 149-150

O

Object component, 36-40

Oral sex in lesbian lovemaking, 105
  reluctance to engage in, 107-108

Oral-genital activity in gay male sexual activity, 110, 111
  reluctance to engage in, 119

Organizations for gays, 176

Orgasm in lesbian lovemaking, 105

Orgies, 112

Orientation, sexual, 36-40, 43
  development of, early sexual behavior in, 46-47

"Oversexed" myth of gayness, 200

P

Parent(s)
  coming out to, 91-95
    helping children with, 93-94
    helping parents with, 94-95
  gay, 198-201
    child custody and courts and, 201-203
    myths and misconceptions about, 198-201
      and children's role development as, 199-200
      "deviant" homes as, 200
      effects of, 201
      proselytizing as, 199
      raising gay children as, 198-199
  reactions of, to coming out, 91-93
  sexual preference of, children's reactions to, 207

Parenthood, gay, coping with, 203-209
  and children, 205-208
  couples as parents and, 208-209
  as new role, 203-204
  social adjustments in, 205

Parents of Gays, 91, 92

Partner, primary, in gay male relationships, 154

Passing with young children, 207-208

Pathology
  attempts to find causes of, 8-10
  gayness as, 8

Peer support group, lack of, in adolescence of lesbians, 142-143

Personal functioning, effect of gayness on, 57-58

Physical factor in sexual orientation, 36

Poetry, lesbian, 76

Pornography, 112

Predominant heteroerotic, 37

Predominant homoerotic, 37

Preference
  gender, 37-38
  sexual, 36-40
    development of, 27-41

Prejudice, helping children cope with, 209

Premature ejaculation, 118

Primary deviance, 11

Primary partner in gay male relationships, 154

Primary relationships; *see* Gay male primary relationships; Lesbian relationships

Private time, 126-127
  in gay men's relationships, 160

Privilege, confidentiality and, 181-185

Privileged communication, 182

Promiscuity, 115-116

Proselytizing, 199

Protection
  in contracts, 127
  legal, for gays, 22-24

Proust, Marcel, 56

Psychological factor in psychosexual development, 31-33

Psychological health and adjustment, 56-57

Psychologist-client privilege, 182

Psychology, psychiatry, and psychotherapy
  societal pressures on, 8
  in study of sexuality, 7-10

Psychosexual development, table of, 35
  interpretation of, 34-36

R

Racial prejudice, 170
Reality of duration of gay male relationships, 153
Relationship skills, lack of, in lesbian relationships, 149-150
Relationships; *see also* Gay male primary relationships; Lesbian relationships
  characteristics of, 123-130
  duration of, 129-130
  formation of, 124
  with nongays, 69
  social, 63-67
  termination of, 129-130
Relatives, child custody disputes involving, 202
Religion as influence on attitudes toward gay people, 5-6
Renegotiation of contracts, 129
Resources for gays, 176
Retirement, freedom of, 194-195
Rimming, 112
Role differentiation in lesbian relationships, 132-135, 138-140
Role model, 55
  absence of, in lesbian relationships, 143-144
Role taking in lesbian relationships, 139
Roles
  absence of, in lesbian relationships, 143
  in gay male couples, 157
  and sexuality in gay male couples, 157-158
Romance and sex in lesbian relationships, 146
Rural gay community, 176-178
  effect of, on self-image, 178
  isolation from, 177-178
Rural gay people, 173-180
  anxiety and, 174
  fear of discovery and, 174
  impact of heterosexual community on, 173
  and isolation from nongay community, 175-176
  lack of acceptance of, 173-174
  lack of information of, 176
  organizations and resources for, 176
Rural prejudices, 173

S

Sadomasochism, 112
Sand, George, 55-56
Scat, 112
Scriptures, interpretation of, 5-6

Secondary deviance, 11
Self-concept aspect of sexual identity, 43-44
Self-identification, 43-44
Self-identity, 43-44
  case histories of, 39
Self-image, 178
Self-labeling, 80, 85-86
  intervention with, 85-86
Sequential bisexuality, 38
Sex and romance in lesbian relationships, 146
Sex role behavior, 43; *see also* Gender role behavior
Sex therapy, 103-104
Sexual activity; *see also* Gay male sexual activity; Lesbian sexual activity
  assumptions and realities about, 99-104
  in contracts, 128-129
  in couples, 114-115
  distinguished from sexual attraction, 129, 162
  and emotional commitment, 129
  levels of, 101-103
  and levels of sexual interest, 100-101
  myths and misconceptions about, 99-104
  and roles in gay male relationships, 157-158
Sexual attraction versus sexual activity, 129, 162
Sexual aversion, 118
Sexual behavior
  comparison of gay and nongay, 102-103
  early, in development of sexual orientation, 46-47
Sexual contact(s), 102
  frequency of, in lesbian lovemaking, 106
  and meaningful relationships, 114
  reasons for high number of, 113-114
Sexual desire, lack of, 118
Sexual dysfunction
  in gay male sexual activity, 118-120
  in lesbian sexual activity, 107
Sexual exclusivity, 114-115, 126
  in contracts, 127
  in gay male sexual activity, 117-118
Sexual goal, 32
Sexual identity, 36-40, 43-44
  and preference, development of, 27-41
Sexual interest, levels of, 100-101
Sexual object choice, 31-32
Sexual orientation, 36-40, 43
  age of awareness of, 47-48
    in gay men, 48
    in lesbian women, 47-48
  development of, early sexual behavior in, 46-47
Sexual preference, 36-40

Sexual problems
   of gay men, 118-120
   of lesbians; *see* Lesbian sexual activity, problems of
Sexual relationship, lesbian, changes in, 146
Sexual response, lesbian, physiology of, 104
Sexual self-identity, 43-44
   case histories of, 39
Sexuality, 27
Sexually transmitted diseases, 116-117
Shigellosis, 116
Signification, 80
   and helping process, 85-87
   positive effects of, case study of, 85-86
Singer v. U.S. Civil Service Commission, 22
Sissy behavior, 30-31, 58
Sisterhood, 72
Situational ethics, 209
Social adjustments of gay parents, 205
Social Darwinism, 6
Social functioning, effect of gayness on, 62-69
Social recognition, 54-55
Social relationships, 63-67
   with family members, 64-65, 74-75
   with friends, 65-66
   with people who do know, 66-67
   with people who do not know, 63-64
Social skills training, 83
Social time, 126
Sociological factor in psychosexual development, 29-31
Sociological perspective of gayness, 10-12
   appreciative approach in, 10-12
Sodomy laws, 23-24
Somatotype, 28
State intervention, child custody disputes involving, 202
Status differential relationships, 133-136
Stein, Gertrude, 55
Stereotype, belief in, 195
Stigma, advantage of, 193-194
Stimulative techniques in lesbian lovemaking, 104-105
   reluctance to engage in, 107-108
Student organizations, gay, 23
Students, gay, rights of, on college campus, 186-189
Supreme Court, authority of, 21
Syndrome
   androgen insensitivity, 29
   Klinefelter's, 28
   Turner's, 116
Syphilis, 116

T

Task Force on Gay Liberation of the American Library
    Association, 176
Teasing techniques, 102
Termination of lesbian relationships, 148-152
Therapists' attitudes toward gays, 18-19
Therapy; *see* Intervention
   sex, 103-104
Third World lesbians and gay men, 169-172
   Blacks as, 169-170
   generalities about, 169
   Mexican-Americans as, 170
Threesomes, 112
Time
   private, 126-127
   social and leisure, 126
*Tinker v. Des Moines Independent Community School
    District,* 186, 188, 189
Tomboy behavior, 30-31, 58
Transitional bisexuality, 38
Transsexualism, 32, 50
Transvestites, 50, 58-61
"True love, one and only," 148-149
Turner's syndrome, 28

U

Urination, 112
Urophilia, 112

V

Vaginal stimulation, 107
Vaginismus, 107
Victim, role of, 67
Violence, case study of, 75

W

Water sports, 112
Wilde, Oscar, 55
Woolf, Virginia, 55

Y

Youth, attitudes of gays about, 190-193

Z

Zoophilia, 112